Theoretical explorations in African religion

Monographs from the African Studies Centre, Leiden

Theoretical explorations in African religion

Edited by

Wim van Binsbergen and Matthew Schoffeleers

KPI

London, Boston, Melbourne and Henley

To the memory of Victor Turner

First published in 1985
by KPI Limited

Routledge & Kegan Paul plc
14 Leicester Square London WC2H 7PH, England

Routledge & Kegan Paul
9 Park Street, Boston, Mass. 02108, USA

Routledge & Kegan Paul
464 St Kilda Road, Melbourne,
Victoria 3004, Australia and

Routledge & Kegan Paul
Broadway House, Newtown Road,
Henley-on-Thames, Oxon RG9 1EN, England

Set in Times Roman by
Hope Services, Abingdon, Oxon
and printed in Great Britain by
Redwood Burn Ltd, Trowbridge, Wiltshire

© *Afrika-Studiecentrum 1985*

Library of Congress Cataloging in Publication Data

Theoretical explorations in African religion.
(Monographs from the African Studies Centre, Leiden)
Includes indexes.
Contents: Theoretical explorations in African
religion / Wim van Binsbergen and Matthew Schoffeleers —
Perspectives on divination in contemporary sub-Saharan
Africa / Renaat Devisch — Towards a semantic approach
to the principle of transformation / Wauthier de Mahieu
— [etc.]
1. Africa, Sub-Saharan — Religion — Addresses, essays,
lectures. I. Binsbergen, Wim M. J. van. II. Schoffeleers,
Matthew. III. Series.
BL2462.5.T48 1985   291'.0967   84-12194

British Library CIP data available

ISBN 0-7103-0049-2

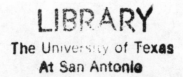

Contents

Notes on contributors   ix

1 Introduction: Theoretical explorations in African
  religion   1
  Wim van Binsbergen and Matthew Schoffeleers

2 Perspectives on divination in contemporary sub-Saharan
  Africa   50
  Renaat Devisch

3 Towards a semantic approach to the principle of
  transformation: An analysis of two myths concerning
  the origin of circumcision among the Komo of Zaire   84
  Wauthier de Mahieu

4 From waste-making to recycling: A plea for an eclectic
  use of models in the study of religious change   101
  André Droogers

5 Religious pluralism: An ethnographic approach   138
  Johannes Fabian

6 Oral history and the retrieval of the distant past: On the
  use of legendary chronicles as sources of historical
  information   164
  Matthew Schoffeleers

7 The historical interpretation of myth in the context of
  popular Islam   189
  Wim van Binsbergen

Contents

8 The consequences of literacy in African religion: The
  Kongo case   225
  John M. Janzen

9 The argument of images: From Zion to the Wilderness
  in African churches   253
  Richard P. Werbner

10 Religious studies and political economy: The Mwari
   cult and the peasant experience in Southern Rhodesia   287
   Terence O. Ranger

11 Dini ya Msambwa: Rural rebellion or counter-society?   322
   Robert Buijtenhuijs

12 Prophets of God or of history? Muslim messianic
   movements and anti-colonialism in Senegal   346
   Christian Coulon

Author index   367

Subject index   372

Illustrations

Figures

1.1 Relative positions of the contributors to this collection, along the dimensions 'material power versus symbolic syntax' and 'structural versus praxeological approach'   15
3.1 Transformational structure of the two Komo circumcision myths   93
6.1 Variations in the Mbona traditions   173
6.2 Social location of the various streams in the Mbona narratives   177
9.1 Harmony in imagery of Person and Space   259
9.2 Images of Person and Space in three religious movements in South Central Africa   271

Maps

6.1 Southern Malawi and the Lower Shire Valley   187
7.1 Selected shrines in Khrumiriya   201
7.2 Selected shrines in the hamlets of Sidi Mhammad and Mayziya   202

vii

Illustrations

Tables

5.1   Comparative pluralist scores for eight multinational
       sectors   144

7.1   Sequences of elements in the myth of Sidi Mhammad,
       as found in twenty variants   193

11.1   Cases of Dini ya Msambwa 'violence' (1943–55)   327

Cover illustration

Female spirit medium, Southern Malawi,
(photograph by Matthew Schoffeleers)

Notes on contributors

Wim M. J. van Binsbergen (b. 1947) is Head of the Department of Political
Science and History, African Studies Centre, Leiden. He is the author
of *Religious Change in Zambia* (1981), and co-editor of *Religious
Innovation in Modern African Society* (with R. Buijtenhuijs, 1976),
Migration and the Transformation of Modern African Society (with H.
A. Meilink, 1978), and *Oude Produktiewijzen en Binnendringend
Kapitalisme* (with P. L. Geschiere, 1982; English translation, *Old
Modes of Production and Capitalist Encroachment*, in press).

Robert Buijtenhuijs (b. 1936) is Senior Research Officer in the Department
of Political Science and History, African Studies Centre, Leiden. His
books include *Le Mouvement 'mau mau': Une révolte paysanne et anti-
coloniale en Afrique noire* (1971), *Mau Mau: Twenty years after* (1973),
Le Frolinat et les révoltes populaires du Tchad 1965–1976 (1978); he
has co-edited *Religious Innovation in Modern African Society* (with W.
van Binsbergen, 1976) and *Social Stratification and Class Formation*
(with P. L. Geschiere, 1978).

Christian Coulon (b. 1942) is a Researcher at the Centre Nationale de la
Recherche Scientifique. He is co-author (with J.-L. Balans and J.-M.
Gastellu) of *Autonomie locale et intégration nationale au Sénégal* (1975)
and author of *Le Marabout et le prince* (1981).

Renaat Devisch (b. 1944) is Senior Lecturer in Anthropology at the
Catholic University of Louvain. He is co-author of *Mort, deuil et
compensations mortuaires chez les Komo et les Yaka du Nord au Zaire*
(with W. de Mahieu, 1979).

André Droogers (b. 1941) is Professor of Religious Studies in the
Theological Faculty of the Lutheran Church of Brazil, Sao Paolo. He is
the author of *The Dangerous Journey: Symbolic Aspects of Boys'
Initiation among the Wagenia of Kisangani, Zaire (1980)*.

Johannes Fabian (b. 1937) is Professor of Anthropology at the University
of Amsterdam. He is the author of *Jamaa: A Charismatic Movement in
Katanga* (1971) and editor of *Beyond Charisma: Religious Movements
as Discourse* (1979).

John Marvin Janzen (b. 1937) is Professor of Anthropology at the

University of Kansas. He is the author of *The Quest for Therapy in Lower Zaire* (1978) and *Lemba (1650–1930): A Drum of Affliction in Africa and the New World* (in press); he has co-edited *An Anthology of Kongo Religion* (with W. MacGaffey, 1974).

Wauthier de Mahieu (b. 1933) is Senior lecturer in Anthropology at the Catholic University of Louvain. He is the author of *Structures et symboles* (1980), and *Qui a obstrué la cascade? Analyse semantique du rituel de la circoncision chez les Komo* (in press), and co-author of *Mort, deuil et compensation mortuaires chez les Komo et les Yaka du Nord au Zaire* (with R. Devisch, 1979).

Terence Osborn Ranger (b. 1929) is Professor of Modern History at the University of Manchester. His books include *Revolt in Southern Rhodesia 1896–1897* (1967), *The African Voice in Southern Rhodesia* (1970), *Dance and Society in Eastern Africa* (1975); he has co-edited *The Historical Study of African Religion* (with I. Kimambo, 1972).

Jan Mathys (Matthew) Schoffeleers (b. 1928) is Professor of Religious Anthropology at the Free University, Amsterdam. He is co-author (with Daniel Meijers) of *Religion, Nationalism and Economic Action* (1978), and editor of *Guardians of the Land: Essays on Central African Territorial Cults* (1979).

Richard P. Werbner (b. 1937) is Senior Lecturer in Social Anthropology at the University of Manchester, and Visiting Professor of Anthropology at the Hebrew University, Jerusalem. He is the editor of *Regional Cults* (1977) and of *Land Reform in the Making* (1982).

Chapter 1

Introduction: Theoretical explorations in African religion

Wim van Binsbergen and Matthew Schoffeleers

1 Overview

This collection of papers on theoretical and methodological perspectives in the study of African religion is the outcome of a conference which the editors were asked to convene on behalf of the African Studies Centre, Leiden, in December 1979.[1]

This introduction sets off with a brief description of the conference itself and the considerations which guided its organization. Following this, we discuss the papers in the present volume against the background of current debates in the field of African religious studies. While dealing with such rather divergent topics as a cross-cultural perspective on divination, the political significance of the Islamic revival in nineteenth-century Senegal, and the symbolic imagery of Southern African Christian churches – to mention but a few – the collection nevertheless displays a surprising convergence of theoretical problematics, as will be made clear in section 3. In section 4 we examine the specific arguments of the papers, adding our editorial comments. Throughout, we shall try to pinpoint some of the blind spots that we think can be discerned both in this volume and in other writings on African religion. These will be summarized in the conclusion in an attempt to define the limitations and the possible significance of the present collection.

2 The 1979 Leiden conference

For many years now the African Studies Centre at Leiden has

1

organized international conferences on topics that were considered vital to its research and publication programme. Since African religion has undoubtedly become one of those topics, as will be clear from the names of van Binsbergen, Buijtenhuijs, Daneel and Schoffeleers – all of whom have been associated with the centre over the past decade[2] – it seemed appropriate to make this the subject of one of these conferences.

The considerations that guided the convenors were the following.

Over the past fifteen years or so African religious studies have made considerable progress.[3] Before that time research was mainly limited to three topics: (a) local religious systems (ancestral cults, cults of affliction, regional cults, witchcraft and sorcery, magic, initiation, professional cults, royal cults) studied synchronically as aspects of a total social structure that was considered to be coterminous with an ethnic group, a nation, or a precolonial polity (cf. Smet, 1975); (b) the study of missionary and independent Christian churches in Africa (cf. Mitchell and Turner, 1966; Ofori, 1977; Wallis, 1967); (c) Islam in Africa, largely studies within the philological-historical tradition (cf. Willis, 1971; Zoghby, 1978). To this, a number of new interests had been added recently, by virtue of which the study of African religion became not only one of the most rapidly growing fields in African studies, but also a field where new insights in social, political and economic relations were being formulated which promised to be of importance also for the analysis of non-religious aspects of modern Africa.

One of these interests stemmed from the discovery that local religious systems have a history – and the subsequent exploration of that history, using new kinds of data such as oral tradition, language change, and patterns of ethnographic distribution (cf. Ranger and Kimambo, 1972). A necessary step towards such historical analysis is the production of regional syntheses of the available ethnographic materials.[4] Studies of Christianity and Islam had often acknowledged the relationships between these world religions and social, political and economic change in Africa. Now the study of the history of autochthonous African religions was also drawn into this orbit, as one began to explore the *transformation of historical African religious forms*. There was taking place, in this field, an intensive search for new conceptual and analytical frameworks within which these various innovatory religious phenomena could be grasped, and their non-religious referents systematically interpreted. In this context we thought not only of a number of recent approaches to religious change (by, for example, Horton, M. Wilson and van Binsbergen),[5] but also of the new concepts of the regional cult (cf. Werbner 1977), and the territorial cult (cf. Schoffeleers, 1979), as attempts to come to terms with African religious organization on a larger scale.

Not only was there a growth of insight into the dynamics of autochthonous African religion; in the established field of studies of Christianity in Africa, new analyses concentrated upon religious interactions, syncretisms and confrontations between various innovatory trends, both within each of the two world religions, and within traditional African religion.[6]

While these are trends towards greater historical depth, and towards contextual interpretation within the framework of a wider social, political and economic structure, other prominent researchers (such as Victor Turner and Mary Douglas)[7] have moved from their individual African field studies towards the formulation of broad, general principles concerning such topics as thought, language, meaning, symbolism and the social process in small groups. This development connects with the work of a number of American scholars including Fernandez, MacGaffey, Janzen, Fabian and Jules-Rosette.[8]

Behind us lay a fifteen-year period of eager and creative exploration. It was the aim of the conference to draw up a balance sheet, particularly with reference to the following points:

Is it possible to indicate, in recent work in this field, certain blind-spots, both descriptively and analytically?
Much recent work in this field has in common with all pioneering studies that its methods are defective and intuitive. What would remain of this work if strict methodological criticism were applied? Is it possible to develop more adequate methods? Is there really something like a uniquely African religion, the characteristics of which can be defined as more or less applicable throughout the continent?[9] Is it not impossible, for most of us, to study more than the mere surface of African religions (cf. Okot p'Bitek, 1970; Setiloane, 1979)? What would remain of African religious research if we were to adopt, in this field, the radical materialism advocated by such writers as Mafeje (1975) and Depelchin (1979)?

3

Finally, most recent studies have in common that their theory is implicit, little developed and often very eclectic. Would it be possible to formulate the underlying theoretical content explicitly, and to effect a confrontation of rival theoretical positions? Could we arrive at better theory? Should we? Like other sectors of African studies, the study of religion began to open itself to neo-marxist approaches.[10] What had the latter achieved so far in this field, and what was to be expected from them, especially with regard to various non-religious contexts which are relevant for the analysis of religious phenomena?

Briefly, at the conference we meant to evaluate recent religious research in Africa in order to arrive at greater methodological and theoretical precision and validity. For this purpose, primarily descriptive contributions were not considered appropriate, and papers were therefore solicited that would deal with attempts at synthesis, critical (including self-critical) reflections on earlier work, and explicit theoretical and methodological discussions of aspects of recent African religious studies. However, it was understood that these more general concerns could also be developed out of the discussion of specific case studies – provided that these would be analytical rather than descriptive, explicitly addressing themselves to a theoretical problematic.

The conference brought together close to forty participants, from Zaire, Zambia, South Africa, the Netherlands, Belgium, France, the United Kingdom, Sweden (Bengt Sundkler, the Nestor of African religious studies, attended the conference as guest of honour) and the USA. The participants belonged to such various disciplines as anthropology, history, political science and theology (particularly church history).

There were nineteen formal papers, duplicated and circulated in advance. These were supplemented by a number of oral presentations: the 'Welcoming Address' delivered by J. Voorhoeve (the chairman of the Board of the African Studies Centre), van Binsbergen's more thematic 'Opening Address', and a three-fold series of 'Concluding Remarks', by Ranger (Manchester), Schoffeleers and Sundkler – the latter in an inimitable style blending the African fieldworker and the minister of religion. The four days of the conference allowed for ample discussion of all papers, both by formal discussants and by the floor. One afternoon was devoted to a more informal panel discussion of the methodological, human and political-economic aspects of doing fieldwork on religion in contemporary Africa. R. Werbner (Manchester), W. de Mahieu (Louvain) and van Binsbergen delivered oral presentations on this occasion. This session enabled our African participants particularly to try and link, through their passionate and penetrating discussions, our perhaps rather esoteric approaches to African religion to the practical and political problems confronting Africa today. Due to the extensive non-academic support acknowledged in note 1, and to the participants' genuine desire to cross the cultural, disciplinary and paradigmatic boundaries that made for such a rich variety among them, the conference was an unqualified success.

The first day was devoted to problems of general theory and method. H. Turner (Aberdeen), A. Droogers (Amsterdam) and van Binsbergen discussed their particular solutions to the theoretical problems attending our study of African religion today, applying the framework of comparative religion, methodological eclecticism and neo-Marxism, in that order.[11] Then, M. Schoffeleers and J. Jansen (Kansas) dealt with such methodological problems as historical reconstruction and the impact of literacy.[12] J. Fernandez (Princeton) whose paper was presented *in absentia* by Janzen, applied himself directly to one of two major themes that, in a way unforeseen by the organizers, were to dominate the conference: the relation between contextualized, social-structural analyses, on the one hand, and non-contextualized, culture-specific, symbolic analyses, on the other.[13] Fernandez's emphasis on the religious images in African religion, that should not be swept away by 'image-less' analyses in terms of the social, economic and political context of African religion, formed a suitable transition to the papers by R. Devisch (Louvain), R. Bureau (Paris) and de Mahieu (Louvain), in which structuralist and phenomenological attempts to penetrate the symbolism of African religion were presented.[14] Ngokwey Ndolamb's (Kinshasa/Los Angeles) discussion of the dialectics of anti-sorcery movements swung rather in the contextualist direction, while Werbner's (Manchester) study of regional cults in Southern Africa formed an attempt at synthesis, dealing with both social-structural context and symbolic content.[15]

The social-structural approach was again to dominate the

conference's fourth day, when Ranger (Manchester), Buijtenhuijs (Leiden), J. P. Dozon (Paris) and J. de Wolf (Utrecht) discussed developments in African religion in terms of relations of production, class structures, class consciousness, and tensions and contradictions which these generate within individual societies.[16] With the exception of Ranger's, these papers referred to case studies of varieties of African Christianity, and thus introduced the second major theme emerging in the conference: the exchange between scientific observers of African religion past and present, on the one hand, and on the other hand theologians whose commitment to, and personal involvement in, the spread of Christianity in Africa naturally goes beyond academic interest. In this vein F. Verstraelen (Leiden), L. Pirouet (Cambridge) and Sundkler (Uppsala) presented papers on aspects of Christian history in Africa; A. Hastings's (Aberdeen) paper was available at the conference, but was in his absence only briefly introduced by Ranger.[17] In a way, the two emerging themes of the conference converged, in so far as the theologians' perspective could be seen as that of one particular category of insiders on the contemporary religious scene in Africa, inclined to absorb and rejoice in, rather than to take apart and contextualize, the images of African Christianity in its various independent and missionary forms.

It was clearly impossible to work the total written output of the conference into a single volume of the present series of Monographs from the African Studies Centre. When a selection had to be made, we felt that the theoretical and methodological papers, which explored the relation between symbolic structure and social structure as well as the limitations of the concept of structure itself, were more directly in line with the original aims of the conference. Plans to accommodate the theological papers in a separate collection have not yet borne fruit. Further selection of papers was necessary, since we insisted on including some additional papers that took their data from Islam in Africa (not represented at the conference), and papers that expanded the theoretical scope of the present collection into such topics as religious pluralism and religious responses to peasantization. All papers were substantially rewritten on the basis of both the conference discussions and our editorial comments which were partly informed by those discussions. In this respect the present collection greatly benefited from the concerted efforts at intellectual exchange and clarification by all involved in the conference, and we sincerely wish to acknowledge the great contribution made to it by the many colleagues who participated in the conference but whose papers do not appear here in print.

3 The present collection of papers

The papers brought together in this collection show great variety in the topics, approaches and parts of the African continent from which they draw their empirical data. Yet the collection has a distinct thematic unity, in that all papers may be seen as partial and converging contributions to a joint problematic. This is the development of a theoretical approach to African religion which would offer a synthesis along the following axes:

(a) semiotic analysis of interrelations between symbols versus social-structural analysis of the social, political and economic contexts within which these symbols are produced and reproduced; and
(b) structural analyses (of symbols and/or contexts) as under (a) versus more transactionalist approaches stressing the participants' ability to create, manipulate and innovate symbolic and social configurations, of varying degrees of permanence, in concrete settings (including such religious events as rituals, divining and healing seances, etc.).

A linguistic analogy may be illuminating here. Internal analyses of African belief systems, rituals, myths, could be regarded as syntaxes of religious symbols. Contextualized analyses of the way African religious symbols are related to the various non-religious aspects of the societies in which they occur, could then be regarded as syntaxes of social structure. Both types of syntaxes are actualized by participants whose more or less ephemeral cognitive and material transactions (being creative, manipulative, at times deviant) would display a tension *vis-à-vis* both symbolic and social structures, a tension not unsimilar to that between syntax and natural speech.

The problem of the merging of structural and transactional approaches in the study of religion has received relatively little discussion so far. The book entitled *Dialectic in Practical Religion*, edited by Leach in 1968, might be regarded as an early contribution to the debate. Within the field of African religious studies Victor Turner's *Drums of Affliction* (1968) is an attempt to combine both approaches in one masterly case study, whose method few of us could emulate for lack of data and, indeed, lack of genius. Recently, however, anthropology has undergone a shift towards approaches where participants are brought back in 'in the active voice' (the title of Mary Douglas's recent book which states this shift; Douglas, 1982). Where so much has been written, in African religious studies, on the structural side, time has come to render the notion of structure both more relative and more dynamic in the light of participants' concrete transactions in concrete situations that have religious relevance.

In the present collection, Fabian and Devisch address themselves specifically to this problem. Fabian's solution is a new 'ethnographic' approach, for which he offers detailed prescriptions. As in his other work (e.g. Fabian, 1979; 1981), he advocates an interpretive approach to African religion, exhorting the ethnographer, as it were, to collude with and to interpret African religion, rather than to adopt a detached attitude aiming at structural 'explanation'.[18] Devisch addresses the same problematic from the point of view of African divination. Here the solution, he argues, lies in what he calls a 'praxeological' approach, which focuses our attention on the diviner's capability to manipulate creatively his divinatory apparatus and symbolism so as to produce, in his audience, a sense of illumination, discovery, revelation. While Devisch's abstract treatment may leave some readers in doubt as to what 'praxeological' means in the context of divination, we have here in fact the closest possible analogy to a somewhat more familiar activity, viz. preaching (cf. Dassetto, 1980). In both cases

> meaning is constituted which by inventive manipulation shows itself relevant to the actual situation so as to achieve individual and collective goals or functions simultaneously. In this process the participants grow into the group of the concerned . . ., generating their concern. (Devisch, *infra*, p. 77)

A particularly pregnant illustration of this analogy may be found in

Fernandez's sensitive analysis of a sermon in the Bwiti cult of Gabon (Fernandez, 1966), but in a general sense it seems to hold true for every sermon which aims at explaining religious mysteries. Divination and preaching in many ways stand at the opposite pole from established ritual because of the role accorded to the diviner's or preacher's personal creativity. Instead of executing a fixed sequence of activities, both the diviner and the preacher are expected to explicate the inner meaning of things and they are given at least a certain amount of freedom to reveal new aspects or make conventional truths appear in a new light. It might therefore be fruitful in future to examine this analogy more closely and to explore in what sense African sermons may be viewed as a transformation[19] of the divinatory process. There is a structural similarity between these two forms of revelation just as there is one between African conceptions of the role of the diviner and that of the Christian minister (Kuper, 1979; Schoffeleers, in press). Students of Islam will recognize the same homiletic mechanisms to be at work there.

However, while Devisch and Fabian pose the problem and offer tentative strategies by which to build the transactional element into our researches on African religion, their arguments fall short of solving the problem; first because they do not attempt to bring the more permanent social-structural elements back in; second, because they hesitate to consider the role of the researcher himself. Devisch might have reflected on the similarities between the diviner's role, and that of the student of African religion. Are the intellectual operations which we perform upon the African religious data not a form of 'metadivination', seeking to reveal the inner meaning of the African phenomena and producing, in our academic audiences, a sense of illumination, etc.? Some African diviners are reported to look upon their handiwork as mainly technical and uninspired, while most scholars working on African traditional religion would pose as non-believers *vis-à-vis* that religion; what counts, in both roles, is not whether the specialist subscribes to the religious contents he is conveying, but whether he manages to weave a tale of sufficient cognitive subtlety and creative literary power to captivate his audience. In modern anthropology, Victor Turner's would be, again, the most obvious example of a scholarly stance in which such divinatory elements are unmistakable. Does this, perhaps, also mean that the validity

9

of the statements we produce as scholars of African religion is of an order comparable to the validity of an African diviner's statements?[20]

While from the praxeological point of view the researcher of African religion could be brought in towards the final stages of the empirical cycle (by the time he or she produces statements on African religion before an academic audience), Fabian's 'ethnographic' approach enables us, at least in principle, to understand this researcher at an initial stage: when, as a fieldworker, he or she is personally involved in the transactions that in concrete situations make up African religious events. Fabian has, however, not taken this opportunity to consider our role as fieldworkers. In his contribution, as in all others in this collection (with the exception of two short remarks in Drooger's paper), the fieldworker on African religion remains out of focus. Hundreds of scholars or would-be scholars have studied African religion through fieldwork. The fact that so few scholarly publications exist that take such fieldwork as their main topic (de Craemer (1976) and Jules-Rosette (1975) are, however, notable exceptions) may well indicate the extent to which our own epistemological, emotional and existential orientation as analysts comfortably escapes analysis.[21]

It is a major weakness of this collection as a whole that, while it clearly states the praxeological and the structure-centred analytical positions, it does not yet succeed in advancing a method that combines them in a balanced manner. As one of the present writers has argued elsewhere, this state of affairs has a particularly negative effect on comparative studies in African religion:

> The religious concepts and beliefs we are discussing . . . have a strong situational aspect. . . . They take shape, and alter, in concrete ritual actions mainly. . . . Such actions, and the religious notions which emanate through such actions, are therefore very specifically bound to concrete settings of time and place, to the relationships existing between the concrete people involved in a specific ritual situation, to the specific crises they go through, and to the creatively evolving symbolizing these people are engaged in. This means that it is already a very risky undertaking to make definite, comprehensive statements about the symbolic content of any one religious form, eg., ancestor worship, or the Bituma cult, among the contem-

poraₗy Nkoya religious forms with which my field-work has familiarized me. Even on the level of a single-tribe study, a generalized ethnographic account of a symbolic system is likely to produce artefacts of abstraction and systematization, which are far removed from actual, dynamic ritual practice. . . . *But at what hopeless level of extreme artificiality are we then operating if we attempt a regional and historical analysis of symbolic contents each of which is tied to the situational specificity of myriads of concrete social and ritual settings?* And finally, how justified are we at all to project our ethnographic knowledge of any contemporary symbolic system back into the past? (van Binsbergen, 1981: pp. 37–38; emphasis added)

It would appear as if only the development of metasyntaxes of ethnographic situations, capable of being generalized across societal, cultural and linguistic boundaries and thus amenable to cross-cultural application, could ultimately provide a solution on this point; but this would require, for each specific description of African ritual, finely grained data of a transactional nature (including the fieldworker's own reflexive analysis of the field responses generated in and by his or her presence). Classic African religious ethnography does not offer such data, and even in modern ethnography they are very scarce.

While the search for a solution to this dilemma has to continue, we should now turn to the second main problematic unifying this collection: the relation between two types of structural analysis, one that produces symbolic syntaxes versus one that produces social syntaxes.

The production of symbolic syntaxes has received a major impetus through the work of Lévi-Strauss and of French structuralism in general. In the last decade, under such names as 'cognitive anthropology', 'semiotics', 'symbolic anthropology', a whole new sub-discipline has emerged internationally. In the present volume, Droogers claims that this approach should have precedence over all others, while de Mahieu's contribution is an outstanding and original example of the sort of analyses which this approach seeks to produce. At the same time it is an extreme example, in that it refrains almost entirely from relating the symbolic syntax to a social syntax. In de Mahieu's argument the social, political and economic structure of Komo society (whose circumcision myth he analyses) remains out of scope.

Somewhat more common are symbolic studies which do try to contextualize symbolic syntaxes by explaining the nature and relations between major religious symbols at least partly in terms of social, political and economic structures. In the field of African religious studies, mention could be made of the work of Mary Douglas on the Lele, Elizabeth Colson on the Tonga, and much of Victor Turner's on the Ndembu.[22] In these studies the original inspiration of the seminal works of Durkheim and Mauss is strongly felt. At the other extreme of structural approach to symbolic data is the Marxist tradition, never really mute but much more vocal during the last two decades, which seeks to explain symbolic syntaxes primarily by reference to material conditions such as are defined in the political economy of the social formations in which symbolic forms emerge, mature, and are subsequently transformed or rendered obsolete, as the case may be.

These complementary approaches can only be brought together once the theory and method that define each are made explicit (e.g. by applying them to one well-analysed case), and are improved in the light of both internal and external criticism. Some of the papers in this collection do precisely this. Thus de Mahieu's paper is a statement of the present state of the art in the symbolic analysis of cosmological myth in Africa. Janzen's paper is a step forward in the internal, 'symbolic', not to say literary, analysis of the written texts whose production was prompted by the introduction of literacy in Africa. The papers by Buijtenhuijs and Coulon, on the other hand, can be read as exercises in the methodology of social contextualization – and its limitations.

However, confluence between these mainstreams of theory and method in the contemporary study of African religion cannot be brought about by merely widening and deepening the beds of the various streams. So what are the mechanisms through which this confluence is effected? And what are the implications of the confluence? Recently, this problem has taken great prominence in the work of a number of French authors, prominent among whom are Pierre Bourdieu and Marc Augé.[23] Taking the lead from Bourdieu, the problem at hand could be summarized, if not solved, in the following terms:

Symbolic power, a subordinate power, is a transformed – *i.e.* misrecognizable, transfigured, and legitimated – form of the other forms of power. A unified science of practices must supersede the choice between energy models and cybernetic models which make them relations of communication, *in order to describe the transformational laws which govern the transmutation of the different forms of capital into symbolic capital.* The crucial process to be studied is the work of dissimulation and transfiguration (in a word, euphemization) which makes it possible to transfigure relations of force by getting the violence they objectively contain misrecognized/recognized, so transforming them into a symbolic power, capable of producing effects without visible expenditure of energy. (Bourdieu, 1979: p. 83; emphasis added)

Whereas studies in terms of social, economic and political structures would cast light on the power relations between relevant groups and categories within a society (sexes, generations, kin groupings, classes, castes, ethnic groups, racial groups, etc.), syntaxes of symbols could be linked to such approaches once it is understood that the combinations and permutations of symbols, as studied in structuralist analyses, constitute a symbolic capital that, either in its own right or in specific relations with material capital, is manipulated in the interaction between individuals and groups. Bourdieu concentrates on the question of how material capital is transmuted into symbolic capital; in other words, how dominant classes make use of symbolic power to 'dissimulate' reality in the perception of the oppressed classes, and thus to buttress the former's position. But the alternative question is equally important: symbolic capital, once generated, can and often does lead on to material capital, and thus to the emergence of new relations between classes, ethnic groups or racial groups. Some of the contributions in this volume specifically deal with the process through which *symbolic power is mobilized from below*, by rural Africans in Kenya and Southern Africa (Buijtenhuijs, Werbner), or by Islamic leaders in nineteenth-century Senegal (Coulon), not as the expression of an already existing class relationship to be discussed in material political-economy terms, but as the precondition for the emergence of such class relations.

What are needed, therefore, are confluence theories that

combine analyses in terms of power (both symbolic and non-symbolic) with analyses in terms of symbolic syntaxes – in other words, communication. The distinction between both streams should not, however, be exaggerated: social, political and economic structures, and their development over time, are themselves also imbued with symbols of varying degrees of relative autonomy and interconnectedness. By no means should the relation between symbolic power and non-symbolic power be reduced to one between an allegedly epiphenomenal 'superstructure' and a material infrastructure, considered to be so fundamental that it automatically determines symbolizing processes (Godelier, 1975, 1978; van Binsbergen, 1981: pp. 52–4, 69–71). At the same time a second limitation of Bourdieu's view is not to be overlooked. His emphasis on symbolic and material power *structures* could, and should, be complemented by an exploration of the ways in which, *transactionally*, participants create and manipulate rather ephemeral symbolic and material power in concrete situations; Devisch's and Fabian's papers offer excellent examples of this.

To offer a fully fledged confluence approach is the ambition of Werbner's paper, whose attempt to read the 'argument of images' in the religious movements from Southern Central Africa blends symbolic syntax and social structure in a way that is highly stimulating – although we doubt whether this 'argument', as interpreted for us by Werbner's, could be developed into a generalized methodology that is less idiosyncratically Werbnerian.

The three papers to which we have not referred so far (by Ranger, Schoffeleers and van Binsbergen) deal with the relation between material and symbolic power in a historical perspective. Schoffeleers and van Binsbergen look at myths from Malawi and Tunisia respectively. Identifying the symbolic syntaxes that operate in these myths, the power relations that attended the myths' production in the first place, and subsequently their functioning in contemporary society, these authors manage to extract, from underneath layers of symbolism and manipulative distortion, the fragments of properly historical information that the myths contain. Ranger concentrates on the pronouncements through which the major Southern African regional cult (Mwari) reflects on changes in relations of production during the colonial period, and argues that these pronouncements were meant to maintain a viable peasantry in the face of threatening proletarianization; in passing, the cult's role in underpinning pre-capitalist modes of production (particularly the tributary mode) is indicated. These historical contributions, however, fail to address themselves to what seems to be the crucial historical question in the context of this book: why is it that history (as the intellectual product of local participants, and of outsider academic historians) should mediate between symbolic and material power? The papers tell us, convincingly, that this is what history does, but the underlying mechanisms escape explicit discussion.[24]

The various contributions to this collection could be regarded as situated at specific points in a Cartesian co-ordinate system comprising two axes. One axis is defined by the opposition between structural analysis and transactional or praxeological analysis. The other axis is defined by the opposition between analysis in terms of material power and analysis in terms of symbolic syntaxes, linked, as argued above, by symbols' capability of generating symbolic power. The specific positions of the various contributions could be tentatively represented as in Figure 1.1.

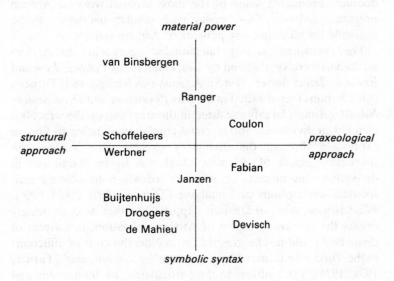

Figure 1.1 *Relative positions of the contributors to this collection, along the dimensions 'material power versus symbolic syntax' and 'structural versus praxeological approach'*

While the methodological and theoretical approaches offered in this book must be considered to be tentative and partial, they may not be hopelessly so. They may at least help us to formulate relevant questions. The history of science is there to suggest that this, and not the production of the 'right' answers, is the decisive step towards greater insight.

This said, let us now turn to a more detailed discussion of the individual papers.

4 Discussion of the individual arguments

Devisch

Devisch's encyclopedic paper contains a veritable *tour de force* of bibliographic compilation, critical evaluation and theoretical innovation in the field of African divination studies. This chapter owes much to the author's extensive field experience, and to the fact that divination studies have been undertaken for many decades, producing some of the most seminal work in African religious studies.[25] One would wish similar overviews to be available for all major components of African religion.

The prevailing, largely functionalist approaches to African divination were synthesized by Gluckman in his *Politics, Law and Ritual in Tribal Society* (1965). Against this background, Turner's contributions (republished in 1975 as *Revelation and Divination in Ndembu Ritual*) largely consisted in the emphasis on the structural element in divination: intrasocietal conflict was shown to find an expression through the divinatory process. For Turner, the revelatory aspect of Ndembu ritual was to be found *not* in divination, but in cults of affliction, of which he offered such splendid descriptions and analyses (Turner, 1957; 1962; 1968). What is new, now, in Devisch's approach is that he convincingly argues the revelatory aspect of African divination; this aspect of divination could not be grasped (as in Ndembu cults of affliction) in the Turnerian terms of '*anti-structure*' or '*communitas*' (Turner, 1974; 1975), yet it offers, to the participants, an illuminating and motivating perspective upon their social reality.

This discovery of the revelatory dimension in divination has considerable comparative significance, particularly in connection with the problem of prophetism in Africa. Implicit in Devisch's analysis is the point that, structurally, the African diviner may not be so totally different from the African prophet as we have always thought. Thus Devisch offers a possible mechanism for the transformation of diviner into prophet and vice versa. This transformation was first noted by Rigby (1975) for Buganda, but the latter author could not yet indicate the theoretical reasons and the underlying mechanisms that accounted for it.

Then, there is Devisch's emphasis on the performative, dramatical and generally aesthetic aspects of divination. Where so much attention has been paid to the cognitive and organizational sides of African religion, the time has come to develop an approach which enables us to appreciate the more implicit, momentaneous and ephemeral, partly non-verbal dynamic elements in African religious performances. It seems to be largely on this level that the power of religious symbols is effected, and that the emotive aspects of African religion (on which scholars have had so surprisingly little to say) are released. An aesthetic theory that pieces together our knowledge of African ritual interactions and performance with comparative material more habitually drawn into the orbit of aesthetic analysis (drama, poetry, rhetoric, music, dance, in Africa and elsewhere) might greatly enhance our insight into African religion, and would at the same time render more of a real-life feel to our scholarly discussions of the topic.[26] Devisch's argument clearly contains additional significant elements for the construction of such an aesthetic approach.

The third point we would make in connection with Devisch's paper refers to the well-documented potential of African divination (just like some cults of affliction, regional cults and the world religions) to cross ethnic, cultural and linguistic boundaries.[27] Especially in the increasingly polyethnic social situations of contemporary Africa, diviners are seen to cater for a clientele with whom they do not share basic tenets of culture, symbolism and social organization. Such crossing of social and cultural boundaries in divination by no means appears to be a recent phenomenon: on the African continent strangerhood seems rarely to have been incompatible with the diviner's role, and often it appears to be an asset. The praxeological approach, emphasizing symbolic manipulation and dramatic interaction between concrete participants in a specific setting, could be argued to transcend, in principle, whatever is culture-specific in divination. People's cognitions (and the symbolic and social-organizational structures underlying these) may separate them, yet the praxeological emphasis on their concrete interactions and transactions in the course of the seance enables us to see how those structural boundaries are crossed. Yet, beyond the specific concrete situation of the diviner's seance, it is a legitimate question to ask what precisely is being communicated between diviner and client when these two participants do not have full competence in each other's culture and when their communication is thwarted by the imperfect use of a lingua franca, or of a language of which only one of them is a native speaker. From the praxeological point of view, the answer would be that, for lack of a common symbolic language, diviner and client *create* one in the course of the session. But on what basis? Regionally distributed cultural traints, or the widespread idiom of world religions, can provide only part of such a basis. If one hesitates to invoke universal human traits which all individuals may have in common, the most obvious answer on this point would be in terms of the locally prevailing social structure. One could postulate that in the seance social, economic and political contradictions are being reflected upon. These contradictions (which partly stem from modes of production, power relations between generations, the sexes, classes and other major social groups) are brought to the fore in the disguise of symbolic oppositions contained in the divinatory apparatus, the diviner's manipulations, his pronounce-ments, etc., and receive a partial and temporary solution in the dramatic sequence of the seance. These contradictions might be sufficiently fundamental, and 'objective', so as not to be totally constrained by the communicable symbolic expressions of diviner and client on either side of the polyethnic and linguistic boundaries that separate these participants. In other words, whereas language and culture might create boundaries between diviner and client, on a deeper level these people would yet partake in a similar social context, share similar experiences, and communicate on that basis. If Devisch had extended his analysis into the social-structural domain, the validity of our speculations on this point might have been gauged somewhat more specifically. Now all we can say is that social structure remains to be brought into the praxeological approach as advocated by Devisch. The problem is particularly pressing with regard to Devisch's treatment of social innovation as mediated by divination. For why should divination, as if it were an immutable and uneffected basic datum, be the instrument *par excellence* to transmit and interpret social, economic and political change in the wider society, when the alternative is equally plausible: social-structural changes assaulting the very effectiveness of the divinatory model, depriving it of such legitimating and resolving power as Devisch now attributes to it?[28]

De Mahieu

If divination and preaching are to be seen as activities by which symbols are manipulated so as to generate meaning in relation to the flow of events, myths may be viewed as devices by which societies emphasize permanency. It has been this aspect which has particularly informed the Malinowskian (Malinowski, 1948) view of myths as legitimizing traditional positions and institutions, and there actually was not much more anthropology had to say on the subject till the advent of structuralism. Surprisingly enough, however, structuralism never came to occupy a place of prominence in Africanist anthropology; for apart from Luc de Heusch (1972) and Adam Kuper (1982) there seem to have been no major representatives of this approach. This may have been due partly to the long-lasting influence of a variety of functionalist approaches, and partly to their fairly rapid succession by a variety of neo-Marxist approaches. But whatever the case, semantic anthropology such as developed and as still developing in Africanist studies tends to be much more culture-specific than classic structuralism. De Mahieu's chapter on Komo circumcision myths in the present volume is a case in point, and it clearly brings out some of the advantages of such culture-specific analyses. Foremost among these is the possibility of accounting for the entire body of symbolic data contained in a mythical text and not just for part of it as is customary in the Lévi-Straussian tradition. In addition to this, the culture-specific approach may allow us to explore connections between seemingly unconnected texts revealing transformations of various kinds which otherwise would have remained hidden. The net result is that, at least in principle, we obtain a much clearer picture of the way such texts are woven into the total fabric of a culture.

With regard to de Mahieu's paper two points of wider significance could be made.

The first concerns the nature and scope of the concept of transformation. Following accepted structuralist approaches, which are firmly rooted in modern general linguistics (cf. Chomsky, 1965), de Mahieu uses the concept of transformation for a specific relation between two levels of the participants' reality: (a) an elaborate surface structure which is manifest in overt speech and action and which allows for direct inspection by outsider researchers; and (b) a simpler deep structure, which the participants are not consciously aware of and which is not open for direct empirical inspection by researchers, but which the latter can only try to reconstruct by their own intellectual efforts. The assumption is that systematic rules govern the process by which the deep structure is carried over, or projected, into the surface structure; in the structuralist idiom these rules are called 'transformations'. Since only the surface structure is open for investigation, the main problem of the structuralist approach (as well as its major methodological weakness) is how to argue the validity of statements defining transformation rules and deep structures. For surely, a multitude of possible rules, applied in a multitude of possible combinations to a multitude of possible deep structures, could be invoked to explain one and the same surface structure. Attempts over the last few decades to produce structuralist analyses for a great many cultural and artistic complexes from all over the world and from different historical periods have, however, led to the emergence of a basic structuralist methodology; e.g. one discovered a limited number of transformational principles (featuring such symbolic pairs as animate/inanimate, left/right, up/down, and their permutations and inversions) which seemed to apply to a very wide variety of settings. De Mahieu clearly draws on this comparative background with confidence, while enhancing the persuasiveness of his analysis by bringing to bear upon it his extensive knowledge of Komo culture and society. Still, the fundamental structuralist dilemma, as indicated here, remains. Thus, when de Mahieu invokes the tenets of structuralism to argue the necessity of transformation (pp. 85 f.), one cannot help wondering what would happen to his analysis if the structuralist dilemma would ultimately prove to be insoluble.

In passing we note that in the field of African religious studies the concept of transformation is also used in a non-structuralist sense, notably to denote sequences of configurational similarity, and systematic difference, in content, form or function (possibly to be explained by historical change) that connect two *surface* structures. Transformations such as we claimed above to exist between diviner, preacher and prophet are of this nature. Again, Werbner's analysis of the transformations between three concrete surface structures (religious movements in Southern Central Africa) on the whole follows this usage, despite the fact that the 'argument of images' he tries to reconstruct partly seems to develop at the level of some unspecified deep structure.

Our second observation concerns the necessity (to borrow de Mahieu's terminology) of contextualization. It was not de Mahieu's intention to explore the historical and social dimension of these texts, as he makes clear himself at one point of his analysis. Yet it would be an obvious next step to explore whether the two texts originated in different historical settings and whether they reflect social tensions in present-day Komo society. The point is, of course, that semantic analyses in terms of cultural categories have ultimately to be complemented by analyses in terms of broad historical movements and social contradictions. People's myths do not function at the metaphysical level alone. Why is it, for instance, that the Komo have *two* circumcision myths and not one? The author argues that this stems from some internal necessity – internal, that is, to the culture in question. But why does that same necessity apparently not operate in relation to other cultural features? And what about the possibility that the two myths came into existence at different periods in Komo history and/or that they are proper to different population segments, e.g. autochthones and invaders? In other words, could these myths not be part of the power struggle within that society, reflecting changing relations of production? We are not suggesting that this would destroy de Mahieu's analysis, which seems convincing enough as it stands, but it would certainly modify it to some extent.

Droogers

The similarity between, or at least complementarity of, African participants' religious cognitions and activities on the one hand, and our scholarly research and writing on these topics on the other, crops up in several places in Droogers's review of the merits and demerits of the classic approaches to religious change. Droogers argues that our theorizing should be eclectic and accumulative, instead of indulging in 'waste-making' of alternative approaches. He arrives at the conclusion that the semantic approach must be considered the most inclusive, since it provides room for both the informant and the researcher in their shared role of meaning-makers, and since it can be combined with other useful approaches.

One wonders if Droogers is not too generous on this point, for it would appear as if for the time being the combining potential allegedly inherent in the semantic approach has nowhere been explicitly realized. The semantic approach in so far as it has been developed or is being developed fills in the large space left open, particularly by functionalism and neo-Marxism, but it has as yet failed to make clear what relations exist between the material and the symbolling side of religion. More importantly, even, the semantic approach has still little to say about religious *change*, the very topic of Droogers's contribution. One can see this illustrated in the two specifically semantic contributions in this volume (Devisch and de Mahieu). Neither tells us much about the role of divination and myth in power relations and in the change of power relations. More precisely, neither makes clear how and in what sense their otherwise excellent analyses complement the functionalist or neo-Marxist views.

Second, while we wholeheartedly agree with Droogers that profound similarities exist between participants in African religion and ourselves, the researchers, one should not stretch the analogy too far. If students of African religion are like diviners, their clientele do not consist of participants in African religion, but of fellow-members of the North Atlantic society (and the extensions of that society, among intellectual elites in the Third World). Therefore, we may acknowledge the meaning-maker in the African participant, but we must at the same time realize that he makes meaning for a different audience. This calls to mind the severe criticism levelled by Okot p'Bitek (1971) against Western scholarship on African religion. While that criticism may seem fair (it has gone remarkably unchallenged over all these years), we may well wonder whether the nature of African religious studies allows us to produce anything but the very artefacts for which

Okot p'Bitek takes us to task (however, cf. Ogot, 1971); and even so, the result may have more value than Okot p'Bitek suggests.

Droogers's concern to save the heuristic potential of discarded theoretical approaches is praiseworthy (cf. van Binsbergen, 1981: pp. 68–9).[29] Yet, beyond a generalized eclecticism of 'let a thousand approaches to African religion bloom', one should develop a more qualified, hierarchical eclecticism, favouring some approaches over others, because they differ in illuminating power, or because rival approaches could be recast in terms of the favoured approach. This is in fact what Droogers himself does, when his own declared eclecticism yet leads him to favour the semantic approach.

Anyway, the historical development of science would seem to advocate a dynamic theoretical strategy. The state of the art in African religious studies today more or less unexpectedly imposed a converging problematic upon the contributors of this book. Each pursues a different approach, but the collection as a whole turns out to be far from eclectic. There is, also in this field, a historical accumulation of problems, tendencies, insights, which selectively informs the next step the discipline is to take. The point is not to preserve all leftovers for some unspecified future second use – they are bound to go stale; but purposely to select for the benefit of a new and more penetrating synthesis.

Fabian

Like Droogers, Fabian begins his paper with the image of the academic marketplace. Ever since Durkheim, anthropologists have preferred to think in terms of a single religious system in regard of the societies they studied. Although in many cases Christianity, either in its missionary or its independent forms or both, was very much part of the local scene, it was often carefully filtered out to arrive at or reconstruct so-called traditional forms of religion. Times have changed meanwhile, and even the most inveterate antiquarian in the anthropological profession has to admit to the inescapable reality of religious pluralism. But the blood creeps where it cannot flow, and equally inescapably Durkheim's ghost returned to the scene when pluralism was shown to be just another word for a unitarian system. Where the old missionaries had given their lives to explain that Christianity and traditional religion were irreconcilable entities – a creed to which many of the old anthropologists subscribed, even if they were themselves declared atheists – the younger generation of anthropologists and historians seems to delight in proving that the two are in reality one. Folk-Christianity and popular Islam have become the catchwords.[30]

Fabian rebels against this, but he goes further than that. He also objects to the classic approach to single religious systems as unitary constructs. That, he argues, is a distorted view which has come about by divorcing religion from the events in which it is always actualized. Taking his lead from sociolinguistics and more particularly the 'ethnography of speaking', Fabian argues that the quest for uniformity of dogma and conformity of behaviour is to be regarded as just one variety of religious expression and not its norm. Just as a speaker may switch from one language to another, or from one code or register to another, so it is with religious behaviour. As the sociolinguistic critics of structural linguistics rediscovered, speech can also be poetic, and the strictly referential sign-function of language is therefore also to be regarded as a special case and not as the rule. Fabian inveighs here against semiotic theories of meaning which at present occupy such a prominent place in the anthropology of religion – and of which, in this volume, de Mahieu and Droogers could be identified as exponents. Rather like Devisch he advocates a praxeological approach which frees religious behaviour from structural semiotics and which provides room for poetic invention and innovation. In fact, the manipulation of symbols in the lengthy verbal document that plays a pivotal part in Fabian's paper resembles divination – as does Fabian's treatment of this document.

One advantage of Fabian's approach is that it allows for the incorporation of history and the transactional element in religious behaviour, something one sorely misses in present semiotic studies. His ethnographic approach seems, moreover, at least in principle, to allow for the role of the fieldworker to be accommodated within our overall framework; even though, as remarked above, this potential is not realized in his contribution. But does his ethnographic approach also allow for the incorporation of the more permanent, structured, collective elements? The, latter may have been overemphasized in the study of religion, but they surely have not disappeared with the emergence of transactional approaches. It is certainly true that the ethnographic sequence to

24

some extent creates its own context (just as a work of fiction as a whole, presented as a sequence in time, provides an evolving context for each of its constituent elements); yet there is a wider social-structural context, which the participants in any specific religion do not themselves create, but take for granted and from which they derive most of the form and content of their actual exchanges; just as a reader needs knowledge of the world, and not just of the preceding pages of a novel, to grasp a particular passage in that novel. The 'ethnographic' approach advocated by Fabian does not seem to be particularly well equipped to explore this wider context and assess its religious significance, but it lays a timely stress on participants' freedom to manipulate and innovate that context in concrete situations.

Schoffeleers and van Binsbergen

With the next two papers we leave religious behaviour in a specific ethnographic setting as one situation where the confluence between symbolic and social-structural analysis could be effected, and we turn to another situation: the encoding of history in religious myths. As in all historical analysis, the problem of social-structural context operates on two levels here. On the one hand non-religious features in the past provide a structural context for past and present religious symbols, but on the other hand it is only through an analysis of the present-day social, political and economic structure that in any historical document (including mythical materials, typically collected in oral form) the grains of historical information can be winnowed from the chaff of participants' contemporary projections, legitimations, distortions, etc.

Addressing themselves to this problematic, the arguments of Schoffeleers and van Binsbergen complement each other in various ways.

Schoffeleers goes to great lengths to develop an interpretative method which, when applied to substantially different variants of the Mbona myth from Southern Malawi, produces historical information on that area which, when paired with ancient Portuguese documents (cf. Schoffeleers, 1978), makes these myths into an independent source of historical information. It has been customary in the past to base long-range historical reconstructions primarily on the oral recollections of ruling families, the reason being that it was these families that possessed the most extensive corpus of oral history. The result has been that many of the reconstructions appeared to be one-sided, representing the view of the aristocracy and little else besides. Most oral historians have recognized this danger meanwhile, and have therefore tried to draw their evidence from a broader base by concentrating not only on political history but also on economic and even on family history. Schoffeleers's paper points to another source for long-range historical reconstruction, which is available in many parts of Africa, and which has the advantage that it does not, or does not exclusively, base itself on the recollections of the aristocracy. We are referring here to the earth and fertility cults, which in many ways form a direct contrast to the royal cults because of their inclusivist character. They are cults that, in Turner's words (Turner, 1974: p. 185), emphasize common interests and values over those of specific social and political groups. The most obvious example of such a cult, or at least the best known nowadays, is the Mwari cult, which has its centre in Zimbabwe but whose influence reaches beyond that country into Botswana. But it is by no means the only one, as Mitchell showed as far back as 1961. In the collection of essays *Guardians of the Land* (Schoffeleers, 1979), a number of case studies are presented from Southern and South Central Africa which show convincingly the not inconsiderable historiographical potential of these cults. In the present volume, Schoffeleers makes the same point, presenting material from the Mbona cult in Malawi. His primary purpose in this paper, however, is not to engage in a detailed historical reconstruction, but to show in a more general way that the Mbona myths can be made to yield historical information. More particularly, he tries to show that this information is different from that obtained from the ruling houses in that it represents the folk view. While doing so, he makes a plea for a more careful consideration of evidence from religious sources, and he takes issue with structuralists such as de Heusch (1972) who deny the historiographical potential of mythical material.

Van Binsbergen's treatment of the myth of the Islamic saint Sidi Mhammad in North-Western Tunisia follows a different course. He argues that the variants of the myth he collected display no systematic and historically relevant variation. The myth is then subjected to cursory semantic and structuralist analysis (which shows that it contains themes that are standard in North African hagiography) and to a more elaborate social-structural analysis, which throws light on the relationship between territorial segments and saint worship. This relationship finds expression not only in pilgrimage and offerings, but also in geographical myths. The myths depict relations between saints and their alleged wanderings over the countryside in some mythical past – images which in a standardized way reflect the present alignment and recent migratory history of localized social groups. In order to pinpoint the unique, properly historical information contained in the myth of Sidi Mhammad, we have to identify to what extent the myth contains far from unique symbolic elements and references to social organization that follow a repetitive pattern. This requires very extensive knowledge of the local area's history over the last two centuries; and such knowledge has to derive from other oral-historical sources than the myth. When such information is brought to bear upon the myth, all the myth turns out to tell us, historically, is the specific direction of a migratory movement one small immigrant group (now no longer in control of the area nor of its shrines) made over a distance of a few kilometres in the beginning of the nineteenth century.

Thus while Schoffeleers manages to extract crucial historical information from a Malawian myth, van Binsbergen shows how the Tunisian myth he analyses contains only the most trivial bit of history. In this respect the myth of Sidi Mhammad is not so different from the medieval Christian legends which served to explain the origin of (mostly) minor pilgrimage centres in Europe – in contrast with the major centres (such as Rome, Compostella, Canterbury) whose origins are, through myths, linked to unique historical events (Turner and Turner, 1978). The slight historical content of the myth of Sidi Mhammad is concealed under so much semantic and social-structural material that the elaborate process of extracting that content seems scarcely worth our while – unless for two reasons. The extraction method itself, when read reversely, might come close to portraying the transformation process (in the non-structuralist sense) through which history is encoded in myth. And second, comparison between the Malawian and the Tunisian myth raises the question as to why it is that some types of myth are carriers of highly significant, traceable historical information, while others are mere trivial appendages of history (that is to say, of history as an outsider academic historian would describe it). Regrettably, the authors refrained from considering these essential questions in their arguments.

The presence, in the myth, of allusions to major social conflict which remain consciously interpretable for the participants appears to be a crucial variable in this connection. The myth of Mbona still carries a significant message concerning the relationship, in Southern Malawi, between secular and religious authority, and between the aristocracy and the commoners (whose hero Mbona is). Chieftainship and the territorial cult of Mbona are still viable institutions in the area, although both have, of course, undergone major changes since the inception of the Mbona cult some four centuries ago. The myth's message concerning the confrontation between major power blocs still carries relevance for the local people. The myth of Sidi Mhammad also reflects on some historical confrontation between social groups: notably, on the graduation of the immigrant 'Arfawiya group, from being co-residing dependants of the Ulad ben Sayyid group, to becoming equals of the latter, residing in their own acquired territory at some slight distance. While the myth of Sidi Mhammad initially constituted the 'Arfawiya's declaration of independence and of religious power (for it is they who erected and controlled the shrine of Sidi Mhammad), this message is now entirely lost on the present-day inhabitants of the valley of Sidi Mhammad: a newly immigrated group (the Zeghaydiya) eclipsed the 'Arfawiya, economically, politically and in terms of control over the shrines. The myth, and indeed the shrines, have taken on a new function, that of expressing the unity of the valley's population under the hegemony of the Zeghaydiya. The myth stresses local unity and dissimulates the local group's heterogeneous origins and immigrant status (which, if admitted, would jeopardize these groups' rights to local land and diminish their prestige); also genealogies, and the knowledge people have concerning past places of residence and migration, are incessantly manipulated so as to maintain the ahistorical illusion of common origins and non-divisiveness. Thus it appears to be variations in the contemporary social and political power structure which determine how past information on power relations is preserved in myth.

Janzen

Having thus explored some of the uses to which *oral* materials can be put in our research on African religion, Janzen's paper calls our attention to the consequences of literacy in African religion.

In Africa we have a great opportunity of examining the transition from spoken to written texts. This transition cannot fail but to have consequences for the form and content of African religion. Thus the introduction of the Bible and the Qur'an confronted African populations for the first time with canonic texts – that is to say, texts which are by definition unchangeable, but which allow individuals and groups to appropriate an interpretational monopoly, thereby providing an instrument for defining, allotting and controlling religious power in more or less formal religious organizations of considerable geographical scope.

On the other hand, Africans also began to produce their own written texts on a number of subjects, such as traditional cultural practices, history or their own interpretations of Christianity. If one is to analyse the impact of literacy on religion, so Janzen argues, one of the things to do is to analyse the literary forms, and in order to do this, one has to compare them with oral forms. Which oral forms are carried over into literature and to what extent? Second, one has to look for combinations of forms. Does literature provide opportunities for new combinations? Third, one has to consider the genesis of new forms. Janzen has identified such a new form in what he calls the 'ethnographic genre'.[31] This genre contains several coded expressive domains. Janzen identified six of these: (a) the spatial and temporal distribution of events, (b) exchange of gifts and prestations, (c) social structure, (d) ritual objects, and finally two verbal elements to complement the preceding non-verbal ones, (e) verbal categories of ritual action, and (f) the lyrical message.

These distinctions may foreshadow an emerging methodology with which we may be able to examine African religious texts in future. However, before we can do so confidently a number of questions will have to be considered more explicitly than Janzen does in his contribution. Thus, for instance, the systematic status of these six categories in the framework of some more elaborate theory of the production and change of religious images and forms remains unclear. As descriptive categories they may be useful for

the specific purpose of analysing the Lemba texts from lower
Zaire, but would they equally apply to other texts? How are we to
distinguish systematically between, for example, such closely
connected themes as 'exchange of gifts and prestations' and 'social
structure'? And what is the relation between the image of social
structure conjured up in the locally produced 'ethnographic' texts
(an image that is strongly theocratic, as if society wholly consists of
ritual roles and relationships), and the social-structural analysis
that an outsider analyst, primarily Janzen himself, would put
forward (cf. Janzen, 1978)?

Janzen's argument is comparable to Devisch's and de Mahieu's
in that he throws light upon aspects of symbolism without,
however, linking up with the social, political and economic
structures that surround, and that to a large extent prompt, the
production and functioning of the texts under analysis. Penetrating,
along the lines of Janzen's incipient method, into the internal
organization of these texts, we can now begin to explore the
sociological consequences of literacy for African religion. Does
literacy lead to changing modes of conceptualization, changing
patterns of ritual action, organization and control? And to what
extent are the analytical categories Janzen presents exclusive to
literacy? They might also apply, at least partly, to the content and
structure of African oral texts, and *a fortiori* to the oral texts
(sermons, pious stories, believers' testimonies, forms of oratory as
used at church council meetings, etc.) that feature in modern
African religion, as oral extensions of literacy.

Werbner

The struggle to arrive at a sophisticated joint treatment of both
symbolic and social structure finds a particularly balanced expression in Werbner's contribution. Problems of ethnic and cultural
pluralism, already referred to in connection with Devisch's and
Fabian's papers, provide a meaningful starting-point for the
analysis of transformations in religious movements in South
Central Africa. Thus Werbner organizes his argument around the
themes of strangerhood and estrangement. He performs his
analysis mainly with a view to explaining the different spatial or
locational imageries used in a number of Zimbabwean independent churches. His argument is that the spatial images used by

these various movements are systematically related to certain changes in the wider social field and that, moreover, they may be regarded as systematic transformations (rather in the non-structuralist sense defined above) of each other. In an earlier publication relative to West African cults Werbner had already argued, to use his own epigrammatic phrase, that 'religion and strangerhood transform together' (Werbner, 1979). In the Zimbabwean case (characterized not – as in the West African case – by the confrontation between a dominant white elite and a subjugated black population in the process of proletarianization) the argument is rather that religion and *estrangement* transform together. He argues his point in a complex manner by showing that the images themselves are in an argument with each other. And he furthermore shows that these images relate to such other dimensions of religious movements as consciousness, project and organization.

Although Werbner puts his argument quite convincingly, building upon and adding to the work of Horton, Fernandez, Eliade, Daneel and others, not every reader will be convinced by his use of terms like framed and unframed person (that is, set apart from or included among the rest of mankind), focused and non-focused space, or by the inferences he draws from their combinations. Thus focused space and framed person are both seen as representations of cosmos (order), and where the two are combined there is harmony. Where they are not combined, as in the Wilderness Church, there is disharmony. One wonders how to qualify another non-combination as in the mission churches. There, space is focused but the person is unframed. Should that also be disharmony? The problem is not so much any internal inconsistency of Werbner's argument, but the fact that the problems at hand are so complex, and our theories and methods still so inadequate, that an ambitious attempt like this could not very well be expected to be completed successfully at this stage, even when it can rest upon the author's profound knowledge of South Central African religion, and his extensive theoretical work in the field of regional cults.

Ranger, Buijtenhuijs and Coulon

Whereas Werbner tries to go all the way on his own, developing a somewhat idiosyncratic approach to symbolic and social structure in the field of Zimbabwean religion, the contributions which the remaining three papers have to make to the general theme of this book are more specific and easier to situate, since all three deal with well-defined aspects of sociopolitical structure building upon a well-defined body of recent literature in the field. Ranger reviews his data on the twentieth-century Mwari cult in Zimbabwe in the light of on-going discussions concerning this cult in itself (Ranger, 1967; 1979b; Werbner, 1977; Daneel, 1970a), more comprehensive approaches that have stressed the element of 'ecological concern' in Central African religion (Ranger, 1973; Schoffeleers, 1979), and finally the decline of that concern in the face of peasantization and proletarianization (van Binsbergen, 1981; Ranger, 1978). Buijtenhuijs assesses the extent to which the Dini ya Msambwa movement in Kenya could be regarded as a political protest movement (Wipper, 1977), or alternatively should be treated as an expression of class conflict or, again, as a 'counter-society' in terms of Baechler's theories (Baechler, 1970). Coulon discusses militant charismatic Islamic movements in Senegal at the time of the imposition of French colonial rule, and against the prevailing interpretation in terms of a primary anti-colonial resistance movement advocates a view that comes close to Buijtenhuijs's and Baechler's.

Ranger notes a number of prohibitions issued by the Mwari organization against the selling of agricultural produce by villagers, and against the purchase of European goods. Seeking to explain these prohibitions he first applies the idea of ecological concern: Mwari's admonitions might have to do with the husbanding and proper management of natural resources within an eco-system whose functioning could still be considered to be unaffected by the inroads of capitalism. However, one penetrates deeper into the power relations that underlie this 'ecological' concern (as represented by the claims of priests, chiefs, elders, in the domains of production and circulation, but also in the political and moral aspects of life) if one views the data in the light of an approach stressing the articulation of modes of production. Thus peasantization and proletarianization, as results of the articulation between the capitalist mode of production and pre-existing non-capitalist ones, might form the proper context in which to interpret the Mwari stance. Ranger argues that the prohibitions protect an internally complex 'communal' mode of production[32] and particularly the tributary mode inherent in the latter. The Mwari cult provides the ideological legitimation for chiefly tribute, and also by other means underwrites chiefly privileges. Thus the Mwari prohibitions serve to protect the non-capitalist modes of production against an encroaching capitalism. But which aspect of capitalist penetration? A more precise answer becomes possible when the evidence is put into a chronological sequence. The cult did not try to ward off the peasantization process: in the first decade of the twentieth century, when African peasants in Zimbabwe prospered, no prohibitions were issued from the shrines. Rather, the cult tried to keep the peasants from proletarianization, i.e. from a state where, divorced from their means of (rural) production, they would have become dependent upon a money income earned in the labour market. Curbing this process, the Mwari cult tries to keep the peasantry viable. Ranger argues thus that, like the Lumpa Church in van Binsbergen's (1981: chs 1, 8) analysis, the Mwari cult is one of the mechanisms by which people try to restore and maintain Central African peasant society.

This type of analysis convincingly argues the potential of class analysis for studies of African religion. While emphasis is here on peasants and proletarians, a different type of class analysis has long since been applied in this field: the role of the world religions in the formation of African elites constitutes a relatively well-studied topic.[33] It is therefore somewhat surprising that Buijtenhuijs in his discussion of Dini ya Msambwa wholly dismisses the idea of a class analysis of this religious movement. Adopting a narrow concept of class (in which poverty is emphasized, rather than a specific position within the system of relations of production), Buijtenhuijs argues that class *difference* cannot explain why certain people adopt a primarily religious response (such as Dini ya Msambwa), while others take to a political party: for all people involved in his analysis are poor and uneducated rural Africans. Buijtenhuijs certainly has a point here, but he overlooks other major analytical problems. Once we accept that people's experience as members of a class may and often does take on a religious expression, we have not only to explain the religious nature of that expression (a problem on which Buijtenhuijs seems to concentrate); we must also trace (like Ranger and perhaps also Werbner do in their contributions) the transformations between a class situation as defined in political-economy terms, and the form and content of its religious expression. It is the latter type of analysis in terms of class that Buijtenhuijs's study of Dini ya Msambwa fails to offer. The alternative he proposes for Wipper's reductionist analysis in terms of political protest (whose shortcomings Buijten-huijs exposes convincingly) is in terms of the concept of the 'counter-society', a response to rapid social change and anomie: under those conditions certain religious groups may renounce all power aspirations in the hostile wider society but instead retreat (in terms of organization but particularly of beliefs, moral codes, ritual) to 'a place to feel at home'. Political parties, on the other hand, would react first and foremost to political and economic oppression and aim at gaining political power.

Buijtenhuijs critically builds upon such academic theoreticians of African protest as Balandier (1963, 1971, 1976) and Ranger (1968). Coulon presents a thesis similar to Buijtenhuijs's, but his frame of reference is the attempts, by Senegalese *politicians*, to impose a particular interpretation (that of anti-colonial protest) upon Islamic charismatic movements in nineteenth-century Sene-gal.[34] Coulon argues convincingly that these movements were attempts on the part of the disprivileged, the poor and the landless, to reconstruct a new viable environment. Islamic ideas (e.g. the concept of the Islamic community, the concept of retreat – *hejira* – and the status accorded to Christians) stimulated the creation of a counter-society that was far more retreatist-Muslim in its outlook than it was anti-colonialist. Ultimately, this counter-society evolved into a hegemonic apparatus which today exercises control over a civil society that political society fails to organize, or does not want to organize. Thus Coulon's argument touches on a topic which has been prominent in African religious studies: the relation between religion and the state.[35]

The ideal-typical counter-society as sketched in Buijtenhuijs's paper will certainly ring a bell with some of us who have had first-hand experience with African religious movements, e.g. of the Zionist type. However, one may well hesitate to adopt Baechler's concept as long as its systematic theoretical status remains in the air, and its connections with more familiar concepts of proved analytical power (e.g. class, class conflict, transformation, contra-diction) are not made explicit. The superior analytical usefulness of the concept of counter-society remains to be established, particularly the distinction between counter-society and revolutionary protest movement remains shady. The ultimate test seems to lie in the historical outcome of either movement, which renders the argument circular. Application of the counter-society concept to the various religious movements as analysed in Werbner's paper; the Mwari prohibitions as discussed by Ranger; the familiar phenomenon of routinized, encapsulated rural Watchtower communities which, in present-day South Central Africa, form the cinders of the Watchtower effervescence of the 1920s and 1930s;[36] or to the Zambian Lumpa Church, would probably lead to the conclusion that Baechler's concept is incapable of accounting for the full range of religious responses. 'Re-contextualization' of counter-society analysis in terms of class and power seems required at this stage. Particularly, the transition, as described by Coulon, from counter-society to hegemonic apparatus that is intimately associated with the modern state in Senegal suggests that counter-societies retain more potential for subsequent growth, transformation, and accumulation of power than Buijtenhuijs's treatment (in terms of retirement to 'a place to feel at home') may suggest. More generally, the underlying theoretical question is: what happens to religious movements (be they counter-societies, messianic cults, witchcraft eradication campaigns, etc.) once the initial conditions that generated them disappear? How is their symbolic idiom carried over into an altered social, political and economic structure, and how is it transformed in the process?

However, Buijtenhuijs's and Coulon's contributions, which shrink from over-contextualizing African religious movements, both come from scholars with remarkable skill and experience in analysing political, social and economic structures. Their relativism *vis-à-vis* social-structural contextualization should therefore be taken seriously, even if it is clear that certain theoretical and methodological problems receive little explicit attention in their arguments.

5 Conclusion

In this introduction it has been argued that the present collection of papers has a contribution to make to African religious studies. The book is firmly situated in two of the several major debates that dominate the field today. However, it is proper to remind ourselves of the fact that vast portions of this field have remained out of view – some deliberately, others rather by accident or because of the systematic impact of a sociology of knowledge from which the production of scholarly views on African religion cannot escape any more than any other human intellectual activity. Let us briefly review some of these blind-spots as they are likely to suggest new steps to be taken, in empirical research, and in theorizing.

Students of African religion are relatively few in number, and they tend to work somewhat outside the mainstream of their disciplines – be these anthropology, sociology, history, political science, or theology. As scholars we have a vested interest in the persistence of our chosen subject. The emphasis on social, political and economic structure, as in this book, may well reflect the attempt, among our small and relatively close-knit academic community, to render our activities less esoteric and more immediately relevant in the eyes of colleagues working on class formation, economic history, or pastoral theology; and thus to safeguard the institutional and financial bases of our research activities. In this light it is significant that two questions about African religion have very rarely received explicit discussion: not only the question of *fieldwork* (which would painfully reflect on the validity and reliability of our data, and force us to consider our own conceptual and emotional projections onto African religion); but also that of *secularization* – which would remind us equally painfully of the possibility that our chosen subject, in contrast to the supernatural beings around which it revolves, may not live on for ever, while some Africans might take their religion less seriously than we do. Both problems are virtually ignored in the present volume, and that is nothing to congratulate ourselves on.

Contributors to this book range from agnostics (most of whom are first-generation), through actual adherents of world religions, to active Christian clerics. There is little to suggest that this book suffers from the biases of what Robin Horton (1975: pp.394f.) has called the 'devout opposition': scholars whose research on African religion is not free from the apologetic intention of furthering the world religion to which they themselves happen to adhere. Yet one wonders how different a book would have emerged if more of the contributors had been adherents of Islam, of autochthonous

African religions, of world religions hailing from South or East Asia, or had come from a long-established agnostic background (cf. Robins, 1973).

We decided to concentrate on the theory and methodology of African religious research, and to exclude that portion of the conference papers that had a more or less theological orientation. This meant that we could not touch here on a number of topics that have been prominent in the field for decades: world religions; the organization sociology of modern African religious bodies; the interrelations of these organizations (the problem of independency); the ideological and political relations between these religious organizations and African states. Each of these topics could have been chosen as a focus for the development of useful confluence approaches to symbolic and social structure. By accident and preference rather than for any systematic reasons other topics were chosen. However, much can be expected from further application of the tentative insights emerging from the present volume into these and a myriad other topics: e.g. power and terror in relation to African religion – a topic which also has to do with chieftainship and secret societies; marriage; morality; life crisis ceremonies; the emergence of national cultures in Africa; the ethnic embeddedness of world religions; the therapeutic effectiveness of African religion; African philosophy and Black theology; witchcraft and sorcery; and finally the problem of the unit of study, in the face of African religion's potential to buttress (as in ancestral and chiefly cults) but also to cross national, ethnic and class boundaries.

Finally, it has turned out that we have produced a volume whose contributors in at least two characteristics show significantly little overlap with the subjects of our researches: none of our contributors is African, and none is a woman. At the level of abstraction that is maintained in this collection, this state of affairs may not have led to dramatic distortions. Yet one may wonder whether the problematics pursued here would not have been taken a decisive step further if our African, and female, colleagues had joined in our efforts – drawing upon their own significant contributions to the subject, and exposing our limitations in the process. Let it suffice to say that this double blind-spot was not created intentionally, that we made efforts to avoid it, and accept responsibility for our failure to do so.

Few colleagues will perceive the limitations of this collection, both in scope and in depth, more keenly than we do as editors. Our contributors must not be offended at the extent to which we have taken them to task in the course of this introduction. We have expressed our doubts as to the possibility of a study of African religion that is more than a projection of the concerns of a North Atlantic intellectual subculture. The only way to alleviate that doubt is by honest, accumulative, painstaking intellectual debate; and to such debate we mean this book to contribute.

Notes

1 We are indebted to T. O. Ranger for his permission to incorporate in this introduction some of the ideas expressed in his closing address at the 1979 Leiden conference; to J. M. Nchabeleng for bibliographical research undertaken for this introductory chapter; to Mrs A. Kuyt, our fellow-member of the Organizing Committee, for attending to the logistics of the conference; to the secretarial staff of the African Studies Centre, the staff of the Eysingahuis Conference Hall, G. Grootenhuis (general secretary of the African Studies Centre), and J. Nijssen (bursar of the African Studies Centre) for services and moral support without which the 1979 conference and the present book would never have materialized; to Jocelyn Murray for her assistance in copy-editing; and to Ria van Hal for typing this introduction and several other chapters.

2 Martinus Daneel, Robert Buijtenhuijs and Wim van Binsbergen were (and with the exception of Daneel, still are) researchers at the African Studies Centre; Matthew Schoffeleers was a member of the board of the African Studies Centre until 1981. Cf. Daneel (1970a; 1970b; 1971; 1974), Buijtenhuijs (1971; 1973; 1978), van Binsbergen and Buijtenhuijs (1976), van Binsbergen (1980; 1981), Schoffeleers (1972; 1975; 1978; 1979), Schoffeleers and Linden (1972), Schoffeleers and van der Veer (1981).

3 For excellent surveys, cf. Ajayi and Ayandele (1974), Fernandez (1978).

4 E.g. de Craemer *et al.* (1976), MacGaffey (1972), Schoffeleers (1979), van Binsbergen (1981).

5 Cf. Horton (1971; 1975), Wilson (1971), van Binsbergen (1981).

6 Cf. Singleton (1977), Ilogu (1974), Bond *et al.* (1979), Linden (1974; 1977), Daneel (1971; 1974), Peel (1968), H. W. Turner (1979b).

7 Cf. V. W. Turner (1969; 1974), M. Douglas (1970; 1978; 1982).

8 Cf. Fernandez (1964; 1966; 1978), MacGaffey (1972; 1977a; 1977b), Janzen (1971; 1978), Janzen and MacGaffey (1974), Fabian (1971; 1979; 1981), Jules-Rosette (1975; 1978; 1979).

9 Cf. Mbiti (1969), Idowu (1973), Mulago (1977), and other African

researchers participating in the 1978 International Colloquium at Kinshasa – cf. Colloque International (n.d.).

10 Cf. Bonte (1975), Lebulu (1979), Lubeck (1980), Schoffeleers (1978), Bloch (1971), Godelier (1975), van Binsbergen (1981), Augé (1977; 1979), Terray (1978), Muller (1978).

11 H. W. Turner (1979a), van Binsbergen (1979), revised and expanded as chapter 1 of van Binsbergen (1981), Droogers (this volume, ch. 4).

12 Schoffeleers, Janzen, this volume, chs 6, 8.

13 Fernandez (1979).

14 Bureau (1979), Devisch, de Mahieu, this volume chs 2, 3.

15 Ngokwey (1979), Werbner (this volume, ch. 9).

16 Ranger (1979a), Dozon (1979), de Wolf (1979), Buijtenhuijs (this volume, ch. 11).

17 Verstraelen (1979), Pirouet (1979), Sundkler (1979), Hastings (1979a).

18 For similar views, cf. Vidal (1978), Ryan (1978).

19 For the concept of transformation, see pp. 20–1.

20 For similar views, cf. Jules-Rosette (1978), Bauer and Hinnant (1980).

21 Fabian's omission on this point may not be unrelated to the following peculiarity: he illustrates his 'ethnographic' approach with data that would not appear to be eminently 'ethnographic' to those of us who tend to associate the anthropological exercise primarily with participation and observation – i.e. with behaviour and interaction which involve more than words alone. Fabian's argument takes its cue from what is essentially a verbal document, in which people tell a stereotyped story featuring characters with allegorical names. How would the 'ethnographic' approach, and any fieldworker seeking to apply it, stand up to participants' ritual actions in real life?

22 Cf. Douglas (1954; 1963), Colson (1962; 1969), V. W. Turner (1957; 1967; 1968).

23 Cf. Augé (1975; 1977; 1979), Bourdieu (1977; 1979), Lacroix (1979), Muller (1978), Baré (1977), Terray (1978).

24 For an attempt to take up this point, cf. van Binsbergen (1981: ch. 1, especially pp. 54–65, 73–4).

25 E.g. Evans-Pritchard (1937), V. W. Turner (1975), Junod (1927).

26 Further elements for such an aesthetic approach could be gleaned from Biebuyck (1973), Zuesse (1978), Bloch (1974), Beattie (1977), V. W. Turner (1962; 1975).

27 Cf. Marwick (1950), Redmayne (1970), Devanges (1977), Leeson and Frankenberg (1977).

28 Beyond this at least two further problems could be fruitfully investigated: first, the basis and mechanisms of therapeutic power in African religions (cf. Piault (1975), Janzen (1978), Ademuwagun *et al.* (1979)). Second, what about the relation between mediumistic and shamanistic divination? The former type (in which the diviner is locally considered to be entered or possessed by an external, invisible revelatory agent) appears to be historically prevalent in Africa. Shamanistic divination (following an emic model according to which the diviner goes on a spiritual, visionary quest, from which he returns

with his revelations) is a rarer phenomenon in Africa. The shamanistic elements, however, as found in the biographies of a considerable number of twentieth-century religious innovators in, for example, South Central Africa (including John Maranke, Alice Lenshina, Mupumani, Chana, Simbinga; cf. van Binsbergen, 1981: p. 147 and *passim*, and sources mentioned there) would suggest that shamanistic divination is on the increase, particularly in a context of interaction between traditional African religion and Christianity. However, much more research is required on this point.

29 Or should we read Droogers's 'waste-making' metaphor of North Atlantic intellectual production as a critique of the hidden capitalist foundations of African religious studies? Should we, in line with such writers as Copans (1974; 1975), Asad (1973), Leclerc (1972), 'autocritically' denounce our intellectual efforts as an ideological response of late capitalism or neo-imperialism? The question is far from rhetorical, and in fact reflects a view which our African colleagues argued passionately at the 1979 conference.

30 Kuper (1979), Ranger (1982), Waardenburg (1979), Gellner (1981), van Binsbergen (1980).

31 Like Fabian, Janzen presents the reader with an idiosyncratic use of the familiar term 'ethnographic'. Fabian (cf. *infra*. pp. 145f.) means by this term a very specific stance on the part of researchers of African religion; he offers detailed prescriptions as to how this stance should be arrived at. By 'ethnographic genre' Janzen means simply locally produced texts which describe aspects of the local culture and society and which thus could be termed folk ethnographics.

32 The term 'communal mode of production' is somewhat unusual in the conceptual range available within present-day Marxist approaches (cf. Kahn and Llobera, 1980; van Binsbergen and Geschiere, in press). Within the social formation of Zimbabwe in the second half of the nineteenth century (cf. Beach, 1977), one would prefer to distinguish, more explicitly than Ranger does, between two articulated modes of production: a domestic mode at the level of local village communities, and a tributary mode revolving on surplus extraction from these communities for the benefit of chiefly courts.

33 The impact of world religions is a regular topic in the many studies of elite formation in Africa; among many works, we mention Ajayi (1965), Ayandele (1966) and some contributions in Fasholé-Luke *et al*. (1978). Besides Ranger's and van Binsbergen's work referred to in the text, references to the religious aspects of proletarianization and peasantization are relatively few, while theorizing in this field is still in an incipient stage; scattered material can be gleaned from Cohen (1980), van Onselen (1976: pp. 204–9), Lubeck (1975: pp. 180–200, 256–60; 1980), Sandbrook and Arn (1977: pp. 49–56, 64–66), Kiernan (1977). We are indebted to P. Konings for suggestions on this point.

34 There is a parallel here with Malawi, where the figure of John Chilembwe became a symbol in the hands of nationalist politicians, to be reassessed by academic historians stressing the non-political,

symbolic overtones in Chilembwe's message of the 'New Jerusalem';
cf. Shepperson and Price (1958), Linden and Linden (1971).
35 E.g. Fasholé-Luke *et al.* (1978), Hastings (1979b), Mazrui (1973),
Levtzion (1971), Cruise O'Brien (1975).
36 Cf. de Mahieu (1976), Cross (1970; 1977), Long (1968), Martin (1980).

References

Ademuwagun, Z. A., Ayode, J. A. A., Harrison, I. E., and Warren, D.
M. (eds) (1979), *African Therapeutic Systems*, Waldham: Crossroads
Press.
Ajayi, J. F. Ade (1965), *Christian Missions in Nigeria 1841–1891: The
Making of a new Elite*, London: Longmans, Green.
Ajayi, J. F. Ade, and Ayandele, E. A. (1974), 'Emerging Themes in
Nigerian and West African Religious History', *Journal of African
Studies*, 1, 1: pp. 1–39.
Asad, T. (ed.) (1973), *Anthropology and the Colonial Encounter*,
London: Ithaca Press.
Augé, M. (1975), *Théorie des pouvoirs et idéologie: étude de cas en Côte
d'Ivoire*, Paris: Hermann.
Augé, M. (1977), *Pouvoirs de vie, pouvoirs de mort: Introduction à une
anthropologie de la répression*, Paris: Flammarion.
Augé, M. (1979), *Symbole, fonction, histoire: Les interrogations de
l'anthropologie*, Paris: Hachette.
Ayandele, E. A. (1966), *The Missionary Impact on Modern Nigeria,
1842–1914*, London: Longmans.
Baechler, J. (1970), *Les Phénomènes révolutionnaires*, Paris: Presses
Universitaires de France.
Balandier, G. (1963), *Sociologie actuelle de l'Afrique noire*, Paris: Presses
Universitaires de France.
Balandier, G. (1971), *Sens et puissance: Les dynamismes sociales*, Paris:
Presses Universitaires de France.
Balandier, G. (1976), '*Les Mouvements d'innovation en Afrique noire*', in
H. C. Puech (ed.) *Histoire des religions*, vol. 3, *Encyclopédie de la
Pléiade*, Paris: Gallimard, pp. 1243–76.
Baré, J. F. (1977), *Pouvoir des vivants, language des morts: Idéologiques
sakalave*, Paris: Maspero.
Bauer, D. F., and Hinnant, J. (1980), 'Normal and Revolutionary
Divination: A Kuhnian Approach to African Traditional Thought', in
I. Karp and C. S. Bird (eds), *Explorations in African Systems of
Thought*, Bloomington: Indiana University Press, pp. 213–236.
Beach, D. (1977), 'The Shona Economy: Branches of Production', in R.
Palmer and N. Q. Parsons (eds), *The Roots of Rural Poverty in Central
and Southern Africa*, London: Heinemann, pp. 37–65.
Beattie, J. (1977), 'Spirit Mediumship as Theatre', *Royal Anthropological
Institute News*, 20: pp. 1–6.

Biebuyck, D. (1973), *Lega Culture: Art, Initiation, and Moral Philosophy among a Central African People*, Berkeley/Los Angeles: University of California Press.

Binsbergen, W. M. J. van (1979), 'Towards a Theory of Religious Change in Central Africa', paper read at the conference 'Recent African Religious Research: Towards an Evaluation', Leiden: African Studies Centre.

Binsbergen, W. M. J. van (1980), 'Popular and Formal Islam, and Supra-local Relations: The Highlands of North-Western Tunisia, 1800–1970', *Middle Eastern Studies*, 20: pp. 71–91.

Binsbergen, W. M. J. van (1981), *Religious Change in Zambia: Exploratory Studies*, London/Boston: Kegan Paul International.

Binsbergen, W. M. J. van, and Buijtenhuijs, R. (eds) (1976), *Religious Innovation in Modern African Society, African Perspectives 1976/2*, Leiden: African Studies Centre.

Binsbergen, W. M. J. van, and Geschiere, P. L. (eds) (in press), *Oude produktiewijzen en binnendringend kapitalisme: Anthropologische verkenningen in Afrika*, Amsterdam: Vrije Universiteit; English translation: *Old Modes of Production and Capitalist Encroachment*, London/Boston: Kegan Paul International (in press).

Bloch, M. (1971), *Placing the Dead: Tombs, Ancestral Villages and Kinship Organization in Madagascar*, London/New York: Seminar Press.

Bloch, M. (1974), 'Symbols, Song, Dance and Features of Articulation, or Is Religion an Extreme Form of Traditional Authority', *Archives européennes de sociologie*, **15**, 1: pp. 55–81.

Bond, G., Johnson, W., and Walker, S. S. (eds) (1979), *African Christianity: Patterns of Religious Continuity*, New York: Academic Press.

Bonte, P. (1975), 'Cattle for God: An Attempt at a Marxist Analysis of the Religion of East African Herdsmen', in Maduro (1975).

Bourdieu, P. (1977), *Outline of a Theory of Practice*, Cambridge: Cambridge University Press.

Bourdieu, P. (1979), 'Symbolic Power', *Critique of Anthropology*, **4**, 13–14: pp. 77–85.

Buijtenhuijs, R. (1971), *Le Mouvement 'Mau Mau': Une révolte paysanne et anti-coloniale en Afrique noire*, The Hague/Paris: Mouton.

Buijtenhuijs, R. (1973), *Mau Mau – Twenty years after: The Myth and the Survivors*, The Hague/Paris: Mouton.

Buijtenhuijs, R. (1978), *Le Frolinat et les révoltes populaires du Tchad 1965–1976*, The Hague/Paris: Mouton.

Bureau, R. (1979), 'An Interpretive Essay of an African Cult as Explained by the Hypotheses of René Girard', paper read at the conference 'Recent African Religious Research: Towards an Evaluation', Leiden: African Studies Centre.

Chomsky, N. (1965), *Aspects of the Theory of Syntax*, Cambridge, Mass.:Massachusetts Institute of Technology Press.

Cohen, R. (1980), 'Resistance and Hidden Forms of Consciousness among African Workers', *Review of African Political Economy*, 19: pp. 8–22.

Colloque International de Kinshasa (n.d.), *Religions africaines et christianisme: Colloque International de Kinshasa, 9–14 janvier 1978*, Kinshasa: Faculté de Théologie Catholique de Kinshasa.

Colson, E. (1962), *The Plateau Tonga of Northern Rhodesia*, Manchester: Manchester University Press.

Colson, E. (1969), 'Spirit Possession among the Tonga of Zambia', in J. Beattie and J. Middleton (eds), *Spirit Possession and Society in Africa*, London: Routledge and Kegan Paul, pp. 69–103.

Copans, J. (1974), *Critique et politiques de l'anthropologie*, Paris: Maspero.

Copans, J. (ed.) (1975), *Anthropologie et impérialisme*, Paris: Maspero.

Craemer, W. de, Vansina, J., and Fox, R. C. (1976) 'Religious Movements in Central Africa: A Theoretical Study', *Comparative Studies in Society and History*, **18**, 4: pp. 458–75.

Cross, S. (1970), 'A prophet not without honour: Jeremiah Gondwe', in C. H. Allen and R. W. Johnson (eds), *African Perspectives*, Cambridge: Cambridge University Press, pp. 171–84.

Cross, S. (1977), 'Social History and Millennial Movements: The Watchtower in South Central Africa', *Social Compass*, **24**, 1: pp. 83–95.

Cruise O'Brien, D. B. (1975), *Saints and Politicians: Essays on the Organization of a Senegalese Peasant Society*, Cambridge: Cambridge University Press.

Daneel, M. L. (1970a), *The God of the Matopos Hills*, The Hague/Paris: Mouton.

Daneel, M. L. (1970b), *Zionism and Faith-healing in Rhodesia*, The Hague/Paris: Mouton.

Daneel, M. L. (1971), *Old and New in Southern Shona Independent Churches, vol. I: Background and Rise of the Major Movements*, The Hague/Paris: Mouton.

Daneel, M. L. (1974), *Old and New in Shona Independent Churches, vol. II: Causative Factors and Recruitment Techniques*, The Hague/Paris: Mouton.

Dassetto, F. (1980), 'La Production homilétique catholique: L'Utilisation du judaïsme dans la liturgie', *Social Compass*, **27**, 4: 375–96.

Depelchin, J. (1979), 'Toward a reconstruction of pre-colonial Central African history', *Ufahamu*, 9: pp. 138–64.

Devanges, R. (1977), 'Croyance et vérification: Les pratiques magico-religieuses en milieu urbain africain', *Cahiers d'études africaines*, **17**, 2–3: pp. 299–305.

Diop, M. (1971), *Histoire des classes sociales dans l'Afrique de l'Ouest*, Paris: Maspero.

Douglas, M. (1954), 'The Lele of Kasai', in D. Forde (ed.), *African Worlds*, London: Oxford University Press, pp. 1–26.

Douglas, M. (1963), *The Lele of the Kasai*, London: Oxford University Press.

Douglas, M. (1970), *Natural Symbols*, London: Barrie & Jenkins.

Douglas, M. (1978), *Implicit Meanings*, London: Routledge & Kegan Paul.

Douglas, M. (1982), *In the Active Voice*, London: Routledge & Kegan Paul.

Dozon, J. -P. (1979), 'Remarques et variations autour de l'expression "politico-religieux"', paper read at the conference 'Recent African Religious Research: Towards an Evaluation', Leiden: African Studies Centre.

Evans-Pritchard, E. E. (1937), *Witchcraft, Oracles and Magic among the Azande*, Oxford: Clarendon Press.

Fabian, J. (1971), *Jamaa: A Charismatic Movement in Katanga*, Evanston, Ill.: Northwestern University Press.

Fabian, J. (1979), 'The Anthropology of Religious Movements: From Explanation to Interpretation', *Social Research*, **46**, 1: pp. 4–35.

Fabian, J. (1981), 'Six Theses Regarding the Anthropology of African Religious Movements', *Religion*, 11: pp. 109–26.

Fasholé-Luke, E. R., Gray, R., Hastings, A., and Tasie, G. (eds) (1978), *Christianity in Independent Africa*, London: Rex Collins.

Fernandez, J. W. (1964), 'African Religious Movements: Types and Dynamics', *Journal of Modern African Studies*, 2: pp. 531–49.

Fernandez, J. W. (1966), 'Unbelievably Subtle Words: Representation and Integration in the Sermons of an African Reformative Cult', *History of Religions*, **6**, 1: pp. 43–69.

Fernandez, J. W. (1978), 'African Religious Movements', *Annual Review of Anthropology*, 7: pp. 198–234.

Fernandez, J. W. (1979), 'Imageless Ideas in African Inquiry', paper read at the conference on 'Recent African Religious Research: Towards an Evaluation', Leiden: African Studies Centre.

Gellner, E. (1981), *Muslim Society*, Cambridge; Cambridge University Press.

Gluckman, M. (1965), *Politics, Law and Ritual in Tribal Society*, Oxford: Blackwell.

Godelier, M. (1975), 'Towards a Marxist Anthropology of Religion', *Dialectical Anthropology*, **1**, 1: pp. 81–5.

Godelier, M. (1978), 'Infrastructures, Societies, and History', *Current Anthropology*, **19**, 4: pp. 763–71.

Hastings, A. (1979a), 'A Discussion Relating to the Typology of New Religious Movements in Africa', paper read at the conference on 'Recent African Religious Research: Towards an Evaluation', Leiden: African Studies Centre.

Hastings, A. (1979b), *A History of African Christianity 1950–1975*, Cambridge: Cambridge University Press.

Heusch, L. de (1972), *Le Roi ivre ou l'origine de l'état*, Paris: Gallimard.

Heusch, L. de (1975), 'What shall We do with the Drunken King?', *Africa*, **45**, 4: pp. 363–72.

Horton, R. (1971), 'African Conversion', *Africa*, 41: pp. 85–108.

Horton, R. (1975), 'On the Rationality of Conversion', *Africa*, 45: pp. 219–35, 373–99.

Idowu, E. Bolaji (1973), *African Traditional Religion: A Definition*, London: Student Christian Mission Press.

Ilogu, E. C. O. (1974), *Christian Ethics in an African Background: A Study of the Interaction of Christianity and Ibo Culture*, New York/Enugu: NOK Publishers.

Janzen, J. M. (1971), 'Kongo Religious Renewal: Iconoclastic and Iconorthostic', *Canadian Journal of African Studies*, **5**, 2: pp. 135–44.

Janzen, J. M. (1978), *The Quest for Therapy in Lower Zaïre*, Berkeley: University of California Press.

Janzen, J. M., and MacGaffey, W. (1974), *An Anthology of Kongo Religion: Primary Texts from Lower Zaïre*, Lawrence: University of Kansas Publications in Anthropology, no. 5.

Jules-Rosette, B. (1975), *African Apostles*, Ithaca, NY: Cornell University Press.

Jules-Rosette, B. (1978), 'The Veil of Objectivity: Prophecy, Divination and Social Inquiry', *American Anthropologist*, **80**, 4: pp. 549–70.

Jules-Rosette, B. (ed.) (1979), *The New Religions of Africa*, Norwood, NJ: Ablex Publishing Corporation.

Junod, H. A. (1927), *The Life of a South African Tribe*, London: Macmillan.

Kahn, J. S., and Llobera, J. (eds) (1980), *The Anthropology of Pre-capitalist Societies*, London: Macmillan.

Kiernan, J. P. (1977), 'Poor and Puritan: An attempt to View Zionism as a Collective Response to Urban Poverty', *African Studies*, **36**, 1: pp. 31–41.

Kuper, A. (1979), 'The Magician and the Missionary', in P. L. van den Berghe (ed.), *The Liberal Dilemma in South Africa*, London: Croom Helm, pp. 77–96.

Kuper, A. (1982), *Wives for Cattle: Bridewealth and Marriage in Southern Africa*, London: Routledge & Kegan Paul.

Lacroix, B. (1979), 'The "Elementary Forms of Religious Life", as a Reflection on Power (Objet Pouvoir)', *Critique of Anthropology*, **4**, 13–14: pp. 87–104.

Leach, E. (ed.) (1968), *Dialectic in Practical Religion*, Cambridge: Cambridge University Press.

Lebulu, J. L. (1979), 'Religion as the Dominant Element of the Superstructure among the Pare of Tanzania', *Social Compass*, **26**, 4: pp. 417–59.

Leclerc, G. (1972), *Anthropologie et Colonialisme*, Paris: Fayard.

Leeson, J., and Frankenberg, R. (1977), 'The Patients of Traditional Doctors in Lusaka', *African Social Research*, 23: pp. 217–33.

Levtzion, N. (1971), 'Islam in West African Politics: Accommodation and Tension Between "Ulama" and the Political Authorities', *Cahiers d'études africaines*, **18**, 3: pp. 333–45.

Linden, I. (1974), *Catholics, Peasants and Chewa Resistance in Nyasaland*, London: Heinemann,

Linden, I. (1977), *Church and Revolution in Rwanda*, Manchester: Manchester University Press.

Linden, J., and Linden, I. (1971), 'John Chilembwe and the New

Jerusalem', *Journal of African History*, 12: pp. 629–51.

Long, N. (1968), *Social Change and the Individual*, Manchester: Manchester University Press.

Lubeck, P. M. (1975), 'Early Industrialization and Social Class Formation among Factory Workers in Kano, Nigeria', PhD thesis, Northwestern University, Evanston; Ann Arbor: Xerox University Microfilms.

Lubeck, P. M. (1980), 'Islamic Networks and Urban Capitalism: An Instance of Articulation from Northern Nigeria', paper read at the 23rd annual meeting, African Studies Association of the USA, Philadelphia.

MacGaffey, W. (1972), 'Comparative Analysis of Central African Religions', *Africa*, **42**, 1: pp. 21–31.

MacGaffey, W. (1977a), 'Fetishism Revisited: Kongo Nkisi in Sociological Perspective', *Africa*, **47**, 2: pp. 172–84.

MacGaffey, W. (1977b), 'Cultural Roots of Kongo Prophetism', *History of Religions*, 17: pp. 177–93.

Maduro, Otto (ed.) (1975), *Marxism and the Sociology of Religion*, special issue of *Social Compass*, **22**, 3/4, Louvain: Centre de Recherches Socio-Religieuses.

Mafeje, A. (1975), 'Religion, Class and Ideology in South Africa', in M. G. Whisson and M. West (eds), *Religion and Social Change in Southern Africa*, Cape Town/London: D. Philip/ R. Collings, pp. 164–84.

Mahieu, W. de (1976), 'Les Komo et le Kitawala', *Cahiers des religions africaines*, **10**, 19: pp. 51–66.

Malinowski, B. (1948), *Magic, Science and Religion*, Chicago: Free Press.

Martin, C. J. (1980), 'Millenarianism in Africa', *Critique of Anthropology*, **15**, 4: pp. 85–93.

Marwick, M. G. (1950), 'Another Anti-witchcraft Movement in East Central Africa', *Africa*, 20: pp. 100–12.

Mazrui, A. A. (1973), 'The Sacred and the Secular in East African Politics', *Cahiers d'études africaines*, **13**, 4: pp. 664–81.

Mbiti, J. (1969), *African Religion and Philosophy*, London: Heinemann.

Mitchell, J. C. (1961), 'Chidzere's Tree: A Note on a Shona Land Shrine and its Significance', *NADA (Native Affairs Department Annual)*, 38: pp. 28–35.

Mitchell, R. C., and Turner, H. W. (1966), *A Comprehensive Bibliography of Modern African Religious Movements*, Evanston, Ill.: Northwestern University Press.

Mulago, V. (1977), 'Eléments fondamentaux de la religion africaine', *Cahiers des religions africaines*, **11**, 21–22: pp. 43–63.

Muller, J.-C. (1978), 'Vers une anthropologie des pouvoirs/Towards an Anthropology of Powers', *Canadian Journal of African Studies*, **12**, 3: pp. 429–48.

Ngokwey Ndolamb (1979), 'Antisorcery Movements: Considerations for a Dialectical Orientation', paper read at the conference on 'Recent African Religious Research: Towards an Evaluation', Leiden: African Studies Centre.

Ofori, P. E. (1977), *Christianity in Tropical Africa: A Selective Annotated Bibliography*, Nendelsn: KTO.

Ogot, B. A. (1971), 'Intellectual Smugglers in Africa', *East African Journal*, 8: pp. 7–9.

Okot p'Bitek (1970), *African Religions in Western Scholarship*, Kampala: East African Literature Bureau.

Onselen, C. van (1976), *Chibaro: African Mine Labour in Southern Rhodesia 1900–1933*, London: Pluto Press.

Peel, J. D. Y. (1968), *Aladura*, London: Oxford University Press.

Piault, C. (ed.) (1975), *Propétisme et thérapeutique: Albert Atcho et la communauté de Bregbo*, Paris: Hermann.

Pirouet, M. L. (1979), 'Religion in Kenya: Indigenous or Immigrant?', paper read at the conference on 'Recent African Religious Research: Towards an Evaluation', Leiden: African Studies Centre.

Ranger, T. O. (1967), *Revolt in Southern Rhodesia, 1896–1897*, London: Heinemann.

Ranger, T. O. (1968), 'Connexions between "Primary Resistance Movements" and Modern Mass Nationalism in East and Central Africa', *Journal of African History*, 9: pp. 437–53, 631–41.

Ranger, T. O. (1973), 'Territorial Cults in the History of Central Africa', *Journal of African History*, 14: pp. 581–97.

Ranger, T. O. (1978), 'Growing from the Roots: Reflections on Peasant Research in Central and Southern Africa', *Journal of Southern African Studies*, 5: pp. 99–133.

Ranger, T. O. (1979a), 'Developments in the Historical Study of African Religion: Relations of Production and Religious Change in Central Africa', paper read at the conference on 'Recent African Religious Research: Towards an Evaluation', Leiden: African Studies Centre; in R. Willis (ed.), *Religion and Change in African Societies*, Edinburgh: Centre of African Studies, pp. 1–18.

Ranger, T. O. (1979b), 'Preface to the First Paperback Edition', in T. O. Ranger, *Revolt in Southern Rhodesia 1896–1897*, London: Heinemann, pp. ix–xviii.

Ranger, T. O. (1982), 'Varieties of Popular Christianity in a Zimbabwean District', paper read at the conference on 'Emerging Christianity in Modern Africa', Royal Anthropological Institute/St Catharine's, Windsor Park.

Ranger, T. O., and Kimambo, I. (eds) (1972), *The Historical Study of African Religion*, London: Heinemann.

Redmayne, A. (1970), 'Chikanga: An African Diviner with an International Reputation', in M. Douglas (ed.), *Witchcraft Confessions and Accusations*, London, etc.: Tavistock, pp. 103–28.

Rigby, P. (1975), 'Prophets, Diviners and Prophetism: The Recent History of Kiganda Religion', *Journal of Anthropological Research*, 31: pp. 116–48.

Robins, C. (1973), 'Secular Views of the Sacred: Western Approaches to African Religions', *African Religious Research*, **3**, 1: pp. 27–30.

Ryan, J. M. (1978), 'Ethnoscience and Problems of Method in the Social Scientific Study of Religion', *Sociological Analysis*, **39**, 3: pp. 241–9.

Sandbrook, R., and Arn, J. (1977), *The Labouring Poor and Urban Class Formation: The Case of Greater Accra*, Occasional Monograph Series, no. 12, Montreal: Centre for Developing-Area Studies, McGill University.

Schoffeleers, J. M. (1972), 'The History and Political Role of the M'bona Cult among the Mang'anja', in T. O. Ranger and I. Kimambo (eds), *The Historical Study of African Religion*, London: Heinemann, pp. 73–94.

Schoffeleers, J. M. (1975), 'The Interaction of the M'bona Cult and Christianity, 1859–1963', in T. O. Ranger and J. Weller (eds), *Themes in the Christian History of Central Africa*, London: Heinemann, pp. 14–29.

Schoffeleers, J. M. (1978), 'A Martyr Cult as a Reflection on Changes in Production: The Case of the Lower Shire Valley, 1590–1622 A.D.', in R. Buijtenhuijs and P. L. Geschiere (eds), *Social Stratification and Class Formation, African Perspectives 1978/2*, Leiden: African Studies Centre, pp. 19–33.

Schoffeleers, J. M. (ed.) (1979), *Guardians of the Land: Essays on Central African Territorial Cults*, Gwelo: Mambo Press.

Schoffeleers, J. M. (in press) 'Christ as the Medicine-man and the Medicine-man as Christ: A Tentative History of African Christological Thought', *Man and Life* (Calcutta).

Schoffeleers, J. M., and Linden, I. (1972), 'The Resistance of the Nyau Societies to The Roman Catholic Missions in Colonial Malawi', in T. O. Ranger and I. Kimambo (eds), *The Historical Study of African Religion*, London: Heinemann, pp. 252–73.

Schoffeleers, J. M., and Veer, P. van der (1981), 'Religious Anthropology', in P. Kloos and H. J. M. Claessen (eds), *Current Issues in Anthropology: The Netherlands*, Rotterdam: Anthropological Branch of the Netherlands Sociological and Anthropological Society, pp. 215–27.

Setiloane, G. M. (1979), 'Where are We in African Theology?', in K. Appiah-Kubi and S. Torres (eds), *African Theology en Route*, New York: Orbis Books, pp. 59–65.

Shepperson, G., and Price, T. (1958), *Independent African*, Edinburgh: Edinburgh University Press.

Singleton, M. (1977), 'Muslims, Missionaries and the Millenium in Upcountry Tanzania', *Cultures et développement*, **9**, 2: pp. 247–314.

Smet, A. J. (1975), 'Bibliographie sélective des religions traditionelles de l'Afrique noire', *Cahiers des religions africaines*, **9**, 17–18: pp. 181–253.

Sundkler, B. (1979), 'Patterns of Analysis for an Understanding of African Church History', paper read at the conference 'Recent African Religious Research: Towards an Evaluation', Leiden: African Studies Centre.

Terray, E. (1978), 'L'Idéologie et la contradiction: A propos des travaux de Marc Augé', *L'Homme*, **18**, 3–4: pp. 123–38.

Turner, H. W. (1979a), 'The Way Forward in the Religious Study of African Primal Religions', paper read at the conference on 'Recent

African Religious Research: Towards an Evaluation', Leiden: African Studies Centre; *Journal of Religion in Africa*, 12: pp. 1–15.

Turner, H. W. (1979b), *Religious Innovation in Africa: Collected Essays on New Religious Movements*, Boston, Mass.: G. K. Hall.

Turner, V. W. (1957), *Schism and Continuity in an African Society*, Manchester: Manchester University Press.

Turner, V. W. (1962), *Chihamba the White Spirit*, Manchester: Manchester University Press.

Turner, V. W. (1967), *The Forest of Symbols*, Ithaca, NY: Cornell University Press.

Turner, V. W. (1968), *The Drums of Affliction*, Oxford: Clarendon Press.

Turner, V. W. (1969), *The Ritual Process*, London: Routledge & Kegan Paul.

Turner, V. W. (1974), *Dramas, Fields and Metaphors*, Ithaca, NY: Cornell University Press.

Turner, V. W. (1975), *Revelation and Divination in Ndembu Ritual*, Ithaca, NY: Cornell University Press.

Turner, V. W., and Turner, E. (1978), *Image and Pilgrimage in Christian Culture*, Oxford: Blackwell.

Verstraelen, F. J. (1979), 'African Christianity in Mission Churches: Some Aspects of a Dialectic Process of Religious Innovation', paper read at the conference on 'Recent African Religious Research: Towards an Evaluation', Leiden: African Studies Centre.

Vidal, C. (1978), 'Les Anthropologues ne pensent pas tout seuls', *L'Homme*, **18**, 3–4: pp. 111–21.

Waardenburg, J. (1979), 'Official and Popular Religion as a Problem in Islamic Studies', in P. H. Vrijhof and J. Waardenburg (eds), *Official and Popular Religion*, The Hague/Paris: Mouton, pp. 340–86.

Walls, A. F. (1967), 'Bibliography of the Society for African Church History, I', *Journal of Religion in Africa*, **1**, 1: pp. 46–94.

Werbner, R. P. (ed.) (1977), *Regional Cults*, New York: Academic Press.

Werbner, R. P. (1979), '"Totemism" in History: The Ritual Passage of West African Strangers', *Man* (n.s.), 14: pp. 663–83.

Willis, J. R. (1971), 'The Historiography of Islam in Africa: The Last Decade (1960–1970)', *African Studies Review*, **14**, 3: pp. 403–24.

Wilson. M. (1971), *Religion and the Transformation of Society*, Cambridge: Cambridge University Press.

Wipper, A. (1977), *Rural Rebels: A Study of Two Protest Movements in Kenya*, Nairobi: Oxford University Press.

Wolf, J. J. de (1979), 'Class Analysis and Religion in Modern Africa', paper read at the conference on 'Recent African Religious Research: Towards an Evaluation', Leiden: African Studies Centre.

Zoghby, S. M. (1978), *Islam in Sub-Saharan Africa: A Partially Annotated Guide*, Washington DC: Library of Congress.

Zuesse, E. M. (1978), 'Action as a Way of Transcendence: The Religious Significance of the *Bwami* Cult of the Lega', *Journal of Religion in Africa*, **9**, 1: pp. 62–72.

Zuesse, E. M. (1979), *Ritual Cosmos: The Sanctification of Life in African Religions*, Athens: Ohio University Press/Swallow Press.

Chapter 2

Perspectives on divination in contemporary sub-Saharan Africa

Renaat Devisch

Introduction

Recent studies on institutionalized divination in sub-Saharan Africa approach divination as an almost psychotherapeutic institution for bringing into the open and releasing psychic and social tensions and conflictual feelings, and for reinforcing feelings of wellbeing and solidarity. It is also seen as a means for legitimating, restoring or manipulating the social order and cultural tradition. People look to divination to uncover the hidden, to gain insight into occurrences which go counter to the even tenor of life and to the normal sense of events, so as to enable remedial measures to be taken or to restore peace of mind. Such occurrences include dangers and needs outside technical control, disasters, exceptional losses, misfortune, mysterious illness and death, insoluble conflict . . . In using the term 'diviner', I refer equally to the male and the female diviner. I will not concern myself with the mechanism of manipulating divinatory items as, for example, in geomancy.

Divination is both a cultural and a social practice, but I will concentrate on it here mainly as a cultural practice. This concentration is integral to my aim. I seek to identify the characteristics specific to divination. They are more apparent in its cultural dimension than in its social role and social context.

I start by outlining the various forms of institutionalized divination. The subsequent analysis of the literature on divination shows that these studies reflect the main traditions within social and cultural anthropology and their presuppositions regarding science, society and culture. I select from the structural-functionalist, cognitive, semiotic and semantic approaches to the degree that they contribute to identifying the specific characteristics of divination and to the study of it as a social practice; this with a view to integrating these contributions at different levels in a praxeological study of divination. I have also drawn on personal fieldwork with the Yaka of Zaire.[1] Furthermore, it is apparent that the various practices and problems dealt with in divination have to do with the following dialectic relationships group versus the individual, perpetuation of the ancestral or ethnic tradition versus innovation, maintenance of the conventional and institutional versus change.

Some classifications of the institutionalized forms of divination

Although classifications and pre-established definitions may be useful for comparative sociological and historical investigation, they are of little help in identifying the specific characteristics of divination and the cultural and social dynamics evidenced therein. Moreover, the classifications that we have are defective in that they are based only on cognitive and communicative processes in divinatory practices, they overlap, they only inadequately translate the ethno-cultural characteristics. However, they do allow us to locate some ideal-typical characteristics of divinatory practices, and they enable us to bring out some of the systematic presuppositions underlying them and the monographs from which they draw.

Among others, the following authors have introduced forms of classification: Baumann (1975: pp. 630–5). Bourguignon (1968, 1973: pp. 3–35; 1976), Firth (1969), Zuesse (1975–6), de Heusch (1971: pp. 226–85) and Zahan (1970: pp. 129–43). These last two were the principal sources for Thomas and Luneau (1975: pp. 159–70; 1977: pp. 101–7). A large number of these investigations work from the outside, taking the phenomena at face value. They draw only from the literal meaning of the divinatory language and the clients' popular interpretations and do not take into account the essentially symbolic character of the divinatory practices and process. We can characterize them by saying they apply 'Western' criteria of rationality and objective knowledge. In so far as these practices satisfy these criteria they are typified as interpretative divination comparable to probabilistic inquiry. In so far as they fail to satisfy the criteria, they are typified as mediumistic in which the divinatory communication is thought to have an extra-human origin, exceeding ordinary ways of knowing and behaving.

Interpretative divination is taken to be a distinct type, the most developed of all because of its external form which is seen as sharing in the rational method of algebra, formal logic and statistics. In interpretative, deciphering divination, the diviner establishes the divinatory theme according to the scant information the clients offer of their needs, and, at another level, he encodes an interpretation or message. For this, he makes standardized use of divinatory vehicles. He might use any form of natural or artificial object chosen from among those having a particular function in daily life or in the world of symbols or myth, such as fowls, bones, teeth, nuts, shells, etc. These vehicles guide his intuition and clairvoyance. Manipulating the divinatory apparatus while applying a divinatory grid, he produces configurations. The diviner himself might then decode the configurations. This happens among the Mundang (cf. Adler and Zempléni, 1972) and Hadjeraï of Chad (cf. Vincent, 1966; 1971: pp. 89–98). In Ifa divination among the Yoruba the client is the interpreter (cf. Bascom, 1969), whereas the Sisala client in Northern Ghana is expected to examine the code-objects further by yes-or-no questions (cf. Mendonsa, 1976, 1978).

Forms of mediumistic divination do not allow for such clear-cut classifications since they are said to appeal to different extra-human agencies from among a wide range. These classifications often involve value judgments on the irrationality of the process and the exploitation of the clients' gullibility. At one extreme, mediumistic divination can be characterized as a form of knowing and communicating, performed through transformation in the diviner's consciousness, i.e. through the diviner's mediumistic involvement with tutelary ancestral shades, spirits or divine agencies. According to Bourguignon (1968) and de Heusch (1971: pp. 226–85), three types can be distinguished, those performed by a diviner in possession trance, in shamanistic trance or in trance. First, in the possession trance type of divination, which seems to be very common,[2] the diviner, while experiencing hallucination or visions, is considered to be acting out, in speech or behaviour, the message sent by the possessing spirit(s) to an audience. Second, in the shamanistic or visionary type of divination, the diviner, inducing some alteration in his sensory capacities, is considered to initiate some visionary contact with the spirit(s). Since the spirit does not speak directly, at the end either the individual tells of his visionary journey, or he imitates the actions of the spirit without himself being possessed. Shamanistic divination, which occurs very rarely in the traditional African religions (cf. de Heusch, 1971: pp. 273–6), seems to be the proliferating form in pluri-ethnic contexts, in many of the so-called independent churches, in new religions or in some peripheral purificatory movements. The puzzling question why there is this innovation goes beyond the purpose of my study. Third, in Bourguignon's terms, trance-like divination is considered to include forms of heightened awareness, although people do not always attribute sacredness to them. The outcome of these is interpreted by those concerned as reflecting an extra-human message. These forms are manifested by some specialists while diagnosing possessed or bewitched patients or in dreams as in high fever and in what Zuesse (1975–76: p. 163) calls insight or intuitive divination.

Besides these more extreme types of interpretative or mediumistic divination, there is the very wide range of mixed forms of oracular-interpretative divination. These are included as indication that they are to be counted on the same level as more complex institutions though the literature has treated them as esoteric, irrational, superstitious practices. In oracular-interpretative divination, mediumistic phenomena or oracular mediums intervene but they do not manifest themselves in the body of the diviner and they are decoded by a specialist using more standardized divinatory repertoire or procedures. First, there is the intuitive, experienced interrogation of the provoked movements of sacred objects or living beings, or of the forms or entrails of these beings. Second, there are the self-legitimating forms of guilt-divination or ordeal. Third, there are examinations where a mediumistic intervention is responsible for provoking the configurations of items in basket divination, the resistances in the divinatory apparatus (rubbing board, rubbing or pounding stick, detective horn, rattle, axe handle, gourd of medicines, etc.) or the reactions of the poisoned fowl, by way of response to the diviner's examination. The divinatory means are coerced by the diviner's yes-or-no questions into giving univocal information. Finally, I include in this category forms of indirect interrogation of spirits and of the recent deceased, and the interpretation by a professional of a special hunt, of omens or of dreams.

It will appear from the comparison of different approaches to divination that the external structural-functionalist and cognitive approaches evaluate these different types of divination according to the effectiveness of the impact of the communication and cognition processes on the social-cultural order, and especially on power relations. In contrast the internal semantic approaches consider the classification of divinatory practices of little relevance to the discovery of the dynamics in the creative dramaturgical performances of divinatory seances where clients, by some negotiation of meaning and messages, redefine themselves *vis-à-vis* each other and the context of their daily actions.

Diviner and divination: different approaches

The existing structural-functionalist (psychological and sociological), cognitive, semiotic and semantic interpretations of divinatory practices seem at first sight to be mutually exclusive. Roughly, divination is identified respectively as a kind of psychodrama; an instrument for control and social integration; a rational handling of the mysteries of life and a dramaturgical reinforcing of the basic social and cultural norms and values of the group; a performative creation of a significant reality in its own right, not seen primarily as functionally linked to a problem or a need. Looking more closely at the approaches with a view to integrating them, I try to discover which aspect of divination each approach is directed to, and how far each succeeds in respecting the specific and many-sided aspects of divination. Turner is included under more than one approach. Through the evolution in his writings, he realizes a kind of diffuse integration of different methods.

(Structural-)functionalist approaches

Important studies of divination, from the 1960s on, have applied various functionalistic and structural-functionalistic paradigms, either psychologizing the notions of function, meaning and communication or moralizing them. Turner, in his first period (1974), and members of the Ecole de Psychopathologie Africaine de Dakar (particularly Zempléni, 1966; 1975) borrowed from Freudian psychoanalysis. Members of the Manchester School appealed to thermodynamics and communication, exchange and decision-making theory. And only recently Marxist approaches to spirit mediumship in Africa, which are merely functionalist in application, are being developed (cf. Bonte, 1978; van Binsbergen, 1981).

In general, it appears that in the psychological approaches Western psychological categories and a Freudian paradigm strongly determine the selection and interpretation of data. Turner (1975b: pp. 213, 227) and other authors[3] hold that the social-cultural institution of divination can convert what appears as fearsome for the individual or the group so as to provide emotional reassurance. It seems to me that such an argument could only be validated by anthropological methods, particularly by the study of the symbolic practices in the divinatory process. This function of providing emotional reassurance cannot be validly deduced from the literal meaning of the consultors' declarations and of the oracles' contents which speak of emotional experiences. Turner claims that divinatory symbols in Ndembu actualize univocal meanings alone. But in spite of this assertion, we need to apply his concept of multidimensional symbols to the divinatory context. Turner rightly stresses the emotional resonance of the multireferential meanings and the fusing of sensory and ideational poles within the condensed symbols. He thus offers a valid, though as yet tentative, approach in anthropology to what can be considered the individual psychic level as distinct from the social-cultural, i.e. via an analysis of the way in which symbols articulate a relation between the psychic and the social-cultural dimension. Nevertheless, his anxiety-reassurance argument, in as far as he relates it to technological and scientific inadequacy (Turner, 1968: p. 46; 1975a: pp. 23–6; 1975b: pp. 213, 235), seems to be dependent on positivistic premises. This argument is rooted in a Western pragmatic and positivistic philosophy and comfort ideology which presupposes that mastery over a desacralized, 'thing-ified' environment is a compelling goal for all societies. Lévi-Strauss (especially 1962) and Sahlins (1976) question the universality of this assumption and ask whether the basic interest in some societies would not rather be semantic. Traditional divination cannot be said to be pre-scientific any more than any other authentic symbolic practice, nor can it be said to be contrary to a rational outlook: it is qualitatively different.

Zempléni (1966, 1975), Bohannan (1975: p. 153), Jackson (1978: pp. 128–30) and Retel-Laurentin (1974: p. 315) recognize in mediumistic divination a kind of psychodrama as well which, at the outcome, enables the patient to reassume social responsibility in a recovered identity. In the same way, as de Heusch argues (1971: p. 274), becoming a mediumistic diviner can be said to be therapeutic. This is the more persuasive in that many diviners begin their career during mental illness.

It is not my intention to question the therapeutic effect of divination and of becoming a diviner. But it should be noted that these approaches extrapolate the therapeutic effect by appealing to a structural correspondence, a functional consistency, or a relation of mutual reflection between two or more relevant elements in the social structure. These elements could take a large variety of forms:

(a) some types of social relations materialized in the diviner-client relationship such as that between members of the in-group versus the outsider, the ritual specialist versus the outsider, the kinsman versus the stranger, the superior versus the subordinate, etc.;
(b) social conflict or inequality brought to the fore in divination: diviners are recruited from the marginalized; political and social inferiority of women and their estrangement, especially in Islamic Africa; the irreconcilability of one's position as son and brother and as husband and parent;
(c) psychosomatic and psychic processes evidenced by the diviners: such as the need for certainty and confidence, anxiety, depression, hysteria, tendency to dissociation, paranoia, hallucination, symptoms such as apathy, sleeplessness, melancholy, digestive troubles and non-localized pains, etc.
(d) the divinatory process itself: engendering externalization, catharsis, displacement, transfer, sublimation and paranoiac hallucination.

Because the assertions regarding the correspondence between the first and last two levels, apart from those of Zempléni, are not based on clinical research, in the way that the Freudian paradigm is, they remain somewhat speculative extrapolations. And even limiting oneself to clinical research, the question remains (appositely put by Crapanzano, 1977: pp. 21–2) of the relevance of the Freudian paradigm and of clinical research to Africa.

Finally, it seems that there is reason to have reservations about approaches which do not base their models on an internal investigation and which are not formulated in terms of the co-ordinates and psychodynamics of the person in his ethnic and cultural context. These reservations are the better founded in so far as the approaches at face value continue to concentrate mainly on popular, reifying expressions of experiences and attitudes, failing to reach through to the underlying dynamics which become apparent in a semantic approach. In contrast to the psychological, the sociological structural-functionalist method seems to be more suitable to the study of divination in its social and cultural dimensions. But in so far as this method is pre-defined and applied from the outside, we will have reservations.

Sociological studies of the Manchester School do not consider divination itself but its contribution to the wider political processes and social order. A second group, in the tradition of Evans-Pritchard, studies the divinatory process itself as a decision-making, legitimation or consensus-offering procedure. Both of these groups focus on divination within a single tribal or lineage system. There is, finally, a totally different kind of sociological approach which looks for some kind of consonance between the type of social structure and the type of divination.

It is generally accepted that the earlier contributions on the lines of the Manchester School focus too exclusively on the conservative function of divination in sustaining or restoring the social order and ensuring conformity with traditional cultural patterns. It can nevertheless be valid to stress the carthartic function of divination (see, for example, Gluckman, 1971: pp. 229–35; Turner, 1975b: pp. 235, 241–2), or to focus on its obstetric or catalyst function in the process of segmentation (cf. Middleton, 1960: ch. IV). In this vein, favouring a symptomatology of social change, an exceptional increase of witchcraft accusations and demands for divination is interpreted as the symptom of a disjointed society, of a moral crisis brought about by intercultural contact, or by sudden industrialization or mechanization in rural areas.

In contrast to the classical long-term equilibrium and integration model, the contributors to *The Allocation of Responsibility* (ed. Gluckman, 1972a) have worked out a valid new approach from a transactional, communication and decision-making model. In this way they succeed in tracing the dynamic transformative function of the divinatory process in the wider multiple political processes of competition, factional alignment, altering or adjusting relationships, loyalties or rights in and between groups in traditional tribal contexts. The institution of divination, especially the semantic patterning of the divinatory message, is studied little in itself, but as being essentially an instrument of social analysis and politics, arbitration, redress, mobilization. Using the same methodology, Garbett (1969) shows how in the context of daily decision-making the spirit mediums are key figures in settling disputes among the Korekore of the Zambezi Valley. Adopting a transactional viewpoint, Harwood (1970: especially pp. 115–34) demonstrates, in relation to the Safwa of South-West Tanzania, that the diviner's interpretation of the social conflict assigned to a particular instance of disease or death reflects the transactional relationship between the parties to the dispute, and thus conditions an intervention regulated by the values and interests of this social relationship.

In line with Evans-Pritchard (1937: especially pp. 258–70), many have rightly concentrated on the way that divination generates a consensus of support for a decision which is not easily taken and simultaneously legitimizes it. As a result of divination, the individual who has offered the problem is able to do something, to take remedial measures in his particular situation, and others are able to co-operate with him since the diviner gives his interpretation in terms that the group collectively recognizes (cf. Jackson, 1978: p. 129; Werbner, 1973). Conversely, divination offers the individual the possibility of justifying for himself actions which would otherwise appear to him uncertain and problematic. Through divination, an individual ill becomes a social one. More generally, divination may offer legitimation and generate consensus for innovative decisions in many situations, not only in periods of crisis, precisely because it refers to an instance beyond normal human knowledge and perception. Turner (1968: p. 51) recognizes that divination has a coercive function within the micro-politics of Ndembu society, compensating for the lack of centralized political institutions. Gluckman (1972b: pp. 21ff., 32), Park (1967: pp. 233, 238, 249, 252) and Turner (1957: p. 124) have shown that the oracle's arbitration, because it is underwritten by beliefs in strong extra-social sanctions, can function as a procedural intervention in just those matters that lie outside the scope of formal juridical competence. Divination legitimizes innovation which would otherwise be rejected together with the innovators. Divination legitimizes decisions having important social repercussions which cannot be juridically enforced. Such a coercive function is possible only in so far as the divinatory institution is not subject to popular pressure. To guarantee an authoritative sentence that is to be binding in important matters, diviners are consulted who have been educated abroad in a prestigious tribe (cf. Redmayne, 1970) which is, for example, reputed to have powerful medicines, or diviners of reputation living far away. On the same lines, Colson (1966) shows how an alien diviner, whose behaviour is predictable, is used by the Tonga of Zambia to legitimate the outcome of a conflict between competing groups.

Divination as a self-sustaining decision-making practice, in the peri-urban community of Durban, has been studied by Fernandez (1967). For this study, he applied Goffman's dramaturgical approach to role performance. Any divinatory consultation dramatically deals with and tries to surmount the uncertainties within the human relationships: reflecting social dynamics, it almost naturally generates commitment to its outcome. Initially 'compounded of the uncertainties of their encounter' (ibid.: p. 12), diviner and client are 'anxious to maintain the situation so that the performance should not break down before its intended effects have been realised' (p. 14). Because the divinatory belief system and the dramatic procedure are shared by both diviner and consultors, divination consists in expressing within the idiom of the supernatural, and performing dramaturgically, the uncovering of a problematic situation, whose definition is suggested and simultaneously corroborated by the consultors' behaviour. Although very dynamic, contextual and subject-centred, Fernandez's approach at that time was lacking the insight in the metaphoric articulation process of debate and persuasion developed later (Fernandez, 1972: pp. 48ff.).

A third category includes studies focusing on some consonance between the social context and characteristics of the divinatory practices. These studies take as their starting-point the differences in social structure of various societies and seek to assess how they are reflected through corresponding differences in various features of divination.

There are first the studies which, from the sociology of knowledge, concentrate on the way the structure of a group is reflected in the structuring of its divination. Bohannan (1975) shows that Tiv divination – using four divining chains – is so structured as to allow all the parties to share equally in the investigation, thus protecting 'their non-authoritarian social organization and its way of taking decisions. Through it, and through the ritual that follows consultations, the community is "repaired"' (ibid.: p. 166).

Adler and Zempléni (1972) show that the composite aspect of Mundang society, which is composed of a heterogeneous population divided in indecisive political and religious hierarchies and according to a mixed clan and monarchic system, may explain why this society prefers 'to define itself and to reflect itself in a divinatory system lacking coercive power and able to describe and analyse in minute detail the elements and parts of a totality which is itself ill-defined' (ibid.: p. 70).

According to Bourdillon (1977), divination among the Shona of Zimbabwe is so much a part of everyday life that it is hardly institutionalized at all and the oracles reflect popular opinion. Conversely, 'if the oracles ignore public opinion, they are likely to be discredited' (ibid.: p. 125). This pressure is enhanced by the fact that Shona diviners live normal lives outside the ritual context, 'mingling socially with the community at large, and largely sharing the community's values' (ibid.: p. 137).

A second category of consonance studies includes those which clearly show the limits of the former studies in that they were restricted to a single tribal or lineage system and to divination as merely reflecting its social context. This category reveals the active role of divination in social and cultural change in a poly-ethnic context. More of such studies would be of interest if conducted along the line of Werbner's project (1977; 1980; and his contribution in this volume) on the study of regional cults.

Bourguignon (1973: pp. 30–3) and Rigby (1975), in his study of Ganda prophetic mediums, from a functionalist viewpoint concentrate on divination and mediumship as cultural practices.

Bourguignon contends that it is by bringing out, exploiting and overcoming ambiguity and crisis stemming from the clash with current values and beliefs that divination can lead to legitimate innovation. Charismatic and innovative persons succeed in situations where two value systems compete. They enjoy the prestige of oraculatory or prophetic mediumship which is self-legitimating. They bring out the ambiguity within the values and beliefs and overcome the ambiguity in their own mediumistic behaviour. This witnesses to a unified frame of reference and enacts traditional ideals. They can thus win acceptance of their own dissatisfaction with the existing patterns and compel the introduction of massive innovations. There is evidence of this in the African independent churches and other prophetic or revitalization movements, which may have a nationalist or even a pan-ethnic appeal. This occurs also in those African religions which have remained for the most part outside the Islamic and Christian tradition.[4] Rigby (1975: pp. 122, 128-9) shows in the case of Buganda, and it is true for other societies, that prophetic mediums belong to the same structural type as the diviners: the social contexts in which they operate differ.[5] They both pronounce judgment over the gap between norm and concrete events; the prophet deals with wider gaps and less individual matters than the traditional diviner does, or copes with new uncertainties encountered by a weakly organized society facing ecological disaster, apartheid, or change due to external impact and migration between town and country. In some cases, the prophet acts against the established order, and initiates both in himself and in others a process of moral regeneration. With social change, the same individual can change his role from that of diviner to that of prophet, later reverting to that of diviner.

As appears from Rigby's study, divination and mediumship have to be studied also as social practices. If it were less functionalist in its application, van Binsbergen's approach (1981: especially ch. II) to religious possession and mediumship in Zambia would inspire what I would call a macro-praxeological approach to the active role of the divinatory process in the shaping and transforming of social reality. I will consider this approach more fully at the end of this essay.

By way of general evaluation of these sociological structural-functionalist approaches, we can say that they succeed more than the psychological, and, as shall appear next, more than the cognitive, in situating divination in its dynamic function within the global sociopolitical life, and the attending belief and value system. The structural-functionalist starts by studying these cultural systems and sociopolitical organizations; he proceeds to concentrate on them, on the circumstance of divination, the policy of the consultors and of the diviner, and on the effects, so that the institution of divination is studied little in itself.

External, cognitive approaches

Where structural-functionalism pays particular attention to the instrumental role of divination in the functioning of the group, especially in the distribution and exercise of power, and to its expressive function, seeing it mainly as an instrument for restoring or consolidating social order, tradition and convention, the external cognitive approach considers rather the expressive and explanatory function of divination, seen as a conceptual system, a system of thought, a way of knowing. To a considerable extent these cognitive approaches share an organicistic view of society with structural-functionalists. Both presume that order, structure, regularity, safety, and especially its mental complements such as intelligibility are basic needs or aims of individual and group. Focusing on divination as a form of acquiring knowledge for establishing, controlling and predicting order, the cognitive approach offers the epistemological complement of the structural-functionalist interpretation of divination. Both approaches take the phenomena at their face value, considering mainly the literal meaning of the consultor's ideas on divination and of the matters dealt with in divination, and also the literal meaning of the context of oracles and divinatory oral tradition.

The positivistic, pragmatic theory of knowledge which inspires this approach, and the fact that it considers 'order' to be central, is taken as the standard. Stated simply, acquiring knowledge in a positive, scientific, objective way means retaining relevant data (whose value has been investigated by experience informed by cause–effect reasoning), and fitting these data into a whole. The elements of the whole and their interrelations are consistent with objective logic and should explain, or account for, and predict related data in a way that can be further controlled. According to this model of positive science, divination is then characterized as a procedure for gaining insight by comparing the data it is able to obtain with previously known data and fitting them into known forms of order, structure and regularity. Horton's cognitive theory on divination (1967: especially pp. 168–72) reflects very much this approach, and has been closely followed by Mendonsa (1978: pp. 42–50).

According to this approach, anything in a given culture outside order, conventional structure and classification, e.g. outside the normal course of events, is considered by the members as un-understandable, inscrutable, a threat to understanding and to certainty: therefore it demands such intervention as enables clarification. The following interpretations of divination as a way of acquiring knowledge first regard the need for divinatory consultation as a moralistic concern with social order or as a compulsion for deterministic classification. Second, evaluated according to positivistic scientific premises, the divinatory oracle is regarded as a non-rational way of investigating a moral domain or occult matters and of reinforcing the related beliefs. Third, I intend to show how the assumptions involved influence these interpretations, affecting their validity.

Turner, Bastide and Park, among others, recognize in the divinatory consultation a paradoxical search for deterministic order. The thought processes and mental attitudes displayed in divination have been clearly characterized by Turner in his recent introduction to the reissue of his earlier study on Ndembu divination. A neo-Saussurean influence is detectable in this introduction. 'Divination is a mode of analysis and a taxonomic system' and its exposure 'proceeds by a sequence of binary oppositions, moving stepwise from classes to elements' (Turner, 1975a: p. 15).

Many see divination as searching through a problem, showing that the general is present in the particular case.[6] Bastide (1968) writes of the mental attitude displayed in divination, or of its finality, and brings out the paradoxical character of the divinatory approach. In doing this, he echoes Lévi-Strauss's characterization of magical thought by its compulsory deterministic classification; Park (1967: p. 241) calls it the 'derandomizing function' of divination. On the one hand, divination has as its object the understanding of singular events and the particularities within the lives of individuals which are submitted for divination precisely because they are aleatory; on the other hand it tends to be a kind of omniscience as is apparent from its methodology: it treats these events according to a general logic designed to exclude chance from the course of events.

The characterization of the subject offered for divination and of its divinatory clarification reflects the models used by the authors, a moralizing hermeneutic, a positivistic and pragmatic philosophy.

Several authors, some of them working on the lines of the Manchester School, tend to psychologize or moralize, concentrating either on the function of the oracular consultation or on the meaning of the oracular statements and their clients' interpretations.

Applying a normative equilibrium model, the classical Manchester School focuses on the oracular consultation as one moment within a sociopolitical power game: divination particularly deals with problems involved in this power game, whose cause the oracle will locate in the present social interactions, their subjects' attitudes and the feelings underlying them. Since divination deals with present interests, those responsible for the various groups concerned are involved in public sessions. The divinatory clarification uses the moral language of the basic norms and values of social life. The clarification, in turn, may be dramatically worked out in rituals of affliction.

Turner in his earlier writings (1975b: especially p. 238) maintains that divination consists in throwing light on a concrete problem by using centuries-old wisdom enshrined in the general exegesis of the divinatory objects, which the diviner applies in his manipulation of these objects. This is an expression of the ethical code of the 'good man'. It is a crystallization of centuries of experience and insight into the unconscious impulses of man, his vices, his idiosyncrasies, the conflicts in his society, his needs in daily life and in periods of transition. The diviner uses the personal acuity and insight he has into the relations between individuals and local groups, and the information which he can provoke during the divinatory session in virtue of his sacral standing. He intuits the inner thoughts of his clients, and tries to apply this exegesis to the problem in hand (cf. Turner, 1975b: pp. 236–7; to compare with Evans-Pritchard, 1937: p. 170). For Turner, using the language of Western moral sensitivity, divination consists in uncovering the malicious and fraudulent, the disorderly, the conflictual, the excessively private, hidden in the feelings and in the relations between individuals, between the old and the young, between kin groups, between the living and the dead (Turner, 1975a: pp. 15ff.; 1975b: pp. 213–4, 232–2, 234–5).

Within this moralistic trend, there are studies which do not focus so much on the sociopolitical power game wherein the oracle is only one moment, but which focus rather on the content of the oracle as evidencing a moral concern. This view of the oracle is based on the literal content of the oracle and of the clients' interpretations. The oracle relates the un-understandable, troublesome or fearsome events in the present life of the clients literally to something past. If it is not a mythical past (cf. Fry, 1976: p. 117), or a 'timeless reality' as, for example, for Sisala divination (cf. Mendonsa, 1978: pp. 38–42), it concerns ritual neglect, transgressions and curses in a more recent social past for which the ancestors exact reparation (cf. Forde, 1964: p. 229; Shelton, 1965: pp. 1445–7). Turner (1975b: p. 209) and Zahan (1970: pp. 141–3) consider this retrospective characteristic as distinctive of African divination, in contrast to prophetic, augural mediumship. This concern with the past may indicate a traditionalist or even fatalist mentality. But appealing – as below – to a semantic approach to the symbolic meaning of these 'moralistic' oracular languages, I would contend, as Jackson (1978: p. 134) does, that divination is not so much concerned with uncovering and evaluating facts of the past, as with the present, by showing the continuity of meaning between the current problem and the meaning of analogous events in the past.

Other authors,[7] influenced by positivistic and pragmatic philosophy, contend that since there is no evidence of scientific rationality in divination, it is a pre-scientific way of knowing about matters as yet still beyond the knowledge and technology of these pre-scientific cultures, so that people are satisfied with irrational procedures, bridging gaps in their logic and empirical knowledge. In matters such as witchcraft or future undertakings, or in any matters where the client lacks the knowledge, the logic, the technology or the empirical means to understand or to come to any decision, divination compensates for his deficiencies.

Basing their opinions on the literal meaning of the oracular statements and popular sacralizing commentaries on these, and using the positivistic clear-cut distinction between the natural or empirical and the 'supernatural', some authors (listed in note 7) claim that divination has essentially to do with uncovering the occult. Holding that the belief in supernatural forces implies non-rational premises, it is a small step to label divination as a cognitive aberration. Most of the Ndembu diviners are said by Turner to be paranoid. Their accusations of witchcraft are 'mentifacts', mixing up reality and fantasy (Turner, 1975a: pp. 23, 56): they create witches and exploit the credibility of the people. Moreover, divination reinforces belief in the occult, precisely by associating fatal outcomes and happy twists with the realm of occult agents and forces, referred to by terms like magic, sorcery, possession, ancestral spirits, ancestral vengeance, natural spirits, or their ethno-cultural equivalent.

On the other hand, Evans-Pritchard (1937: pp. 69, 336–8) thinks he can attribute an authentic cognitive capacity to divination in spite of its irrational premises and mystical notions: the answers it offers form a closed, self-corroborating system. None the less it seems to Evans-Pritchard that the oracle is irrational in that it fails to conform to the laws of objective logic and avoids being invalidated by contrary statements of a second oracle or by the final outcome of the poison ordeal (ibid.: pp. 313–51). Evans-Pritchard is unhappy with the idea that the oracle owes its credibility not so much to objective logic but to cultural conditioning and social consensus, since as much credence is given to witch-doctors who are known to cheat as to oracle practitioners who do not (ibid., pp. 187–8, 322–8).

To decide whether or not these divinatory statements are rational and whether they are able to inspire credibility, we should examine whether the theory of knowledge and the ontological presuppositions underlying the anthropological interpretations are suitable for validly understanding the proper rationality of divination and of its authority. The presuppositions in the external cognitive approach favour a reductionist interpretation, staying at face value, unable to reach through to the symbolic articulation of meaning in the oracle, or to the specific credibility and authority of the divination. In defence of this evaluation, I refer here to the essentially symbolic nature of the divinatory process. I will work this out more fully in the following section.

Authors, drawing from popular beliefs in the occult, make reductionist truth judgments in so far as they fail to investigate beliefs in relation to actual human activity and consider them as metaphoric or metonymic symbolic ways of speaking of social, psychic or other puzzling experiences. According to Geertz (1975: p. 100), what is referred to in their belief in a spirit world, are the experiences at the boundaries of a people's analytic capacities, at the limits of their powers of endurance, and at the limits of their moral insights. It is even reductionist and irrelevant to require (in accord with a positivistic, scientific paradigm) of divination, or of other institutions forming part of an essentially symbolic world view, that they should produce statements which satisfy the canons of scientific consistency.

These external approaches to divination as a system of thought not only evaluate according to positivistic scientific premises, but also appeal to presuppositions proper to Western literate culture, implying its notions of matter, causality, time, human nature, person or self, other, relationship. Linked to this is the evolution-ist view of divination as a superstitious, backward, inferior way of knowing which will evolve towards a profane way of knowing, following processes, similar to those in Western history, of individualization, disenchantment, secularization, rationalization, etc., as necessary concomitants of urbanization and mechaniz-ation. Adducing evidence from his research in Buganda, Rigby (1975: pp. 122–6) questions this view.

The credibility and the authority of divination seem to be assured through a self-corroborative belief system (cf. Horton, 1967; Park, 1967), group dynamics and transactional effects (cf. Park, 1967), notwithstanding its so-called defective rationality.

Not all cognitive studies of divination are defective for not all of them evaluate divination according to the standards of positive science. We can include here some semiotic studies, more fully referred to in the next section. These approach the method underlying interpretative divination in its own right. They thus lead us to an internal approach, finally combining it, however, with an external one. The latter includes testing the degree of objectivity of the divination by measuring whether the manipu-lation, permutation and combination of the divinatory symbols, the yes-or-no questions and decoded messages, are in accord with statistical laws. Furthermore, it includes the notion that symbols displayed in this approach do not stand in their own right, but merely express another reality, an already constituted cultural and social order, its structures, classifications, regularities . . . To put it in another way, divination is still regarded as a product and instrument within a functional hierarchical relationship between 'social formation', 'social consciousness' and their cultural reflection.

Internal, semiotic and semantic approaches

Here I include the studies which bring the semiotic or symbolic patterning of thought or meaning into focus.[8] In these approaches, symbols are no longer seen merely as representations or as instruments of social reality, nor as a pre-scientific form of knowledge, but also as a reality in its own right. Those who see symbolic activity essentially as communication and exchange concentrate on the semiotic presentation in the oracle of social cultural ideas and principles, through the articulation of divinatory vehicles according to some inexorable cultural logic. But this semiotic configuration has significance only through its being referred to the daily context of the clients. Others focus on the performative production of a meaningful reality in trance and oracle, a reality which stands in its own right.

Several authors focus on the semiotic patterning of communication, exchange, and decision-making, particularly in interpretative divination and in the dramatic performance of the seance. From what has already been said about interpretative divination we recall only that the diviner establishes a divinatory theme following a standardized procedure and responding to the needs of his clients. He establishes this theme either by running through a divinatory repertoire or by bringing together the code elements or the divinatory vehicles in significant configurations. For Ndembu divination, Turner calls these divinatory symbols mnemonics (Turner, 1975b: pp. 219–28). They store memories or references to general dimensions of the particular culture, ultimately by some cosmological substitutions. Turner shows they are multidimensional and refer simultaneously to activities and goals of individuals and to aspects of culture and of the social groups and relations. At the end the oracular discourse or geomantic figure offers a message relating to the needs of the clients, to their past or present condition. Either the oracular message is univocal, as Vernant, Turner and Retel-Laurentin hold, or it is multivocal and applies to the existential condition in some analogous way, as Young shows, or makes a 'superabundance of understanding' possible (Werbner, 1973).

Vernant (1974: p. 17) describes very precisely a type of geo-mantic patterning of messages from a classic French structuralist viewpoint. Divination builds up a model of structural relations of homology and correspondence inscribed in a segment of space.

> To decipher these spatial configurations divination selects and isolates some objects to which it accords a value of symbolizing the microcosm: shells of tortoises, the viscera of sacrificed animals, figures traced haphazardly in the sand, areas delimited and orientated according to rule, visible parts of the sky, aspects of the face and of the body, combinations of dice, shells, cards. And, from this internal ordering of these objects or collections of objects, appearing as reflecting on a small scale the total cosmic order, it draws self-corroborative conclusions about events which are initially uncertain and wished for or feared by the consultors.

Turner (1975b: pp. 219–28) starts with a similar internal approach in his analysis of the multidimensional meaning of the divinatory symbols. The diviner produces configurations of the divinatory vehicles by his trance-like trembling. But Turner (1968: p. 44) contends that by their property of brittle segmentation, the divinatory vehicles actualize only a univocal meaning which is given by their place in the configuration. When he studies (1975b: p. 229–30) the way in which the diviner relates these configurations to the problem of his client (i.e. the operational meaning), his approach becomes a classic functionalist one: notwithstanding his reply to Horton's objection on this point (Turner, 1975a: pp. 18–21), he substantializes the divinatory symbols.

Applying medical etiology, Retel-Laurentin (1974) sees divination among the Nzakara in the Central African Republic as the clarification of the unknown by diagnosing the forces which are in danger of disturbing the normal flow of human life. As a doctor auscultates a sick person, the diviner examines his client's problem, basing his diagnosis on a series of yes-or-no questions, running through a repertoire of possible psychosocial situations and categories, of which he is the sole depositary. His art does not consist in deciphering signs, or interpreting more or less obscure messages. The diviner interrogates his divinatory tools using straightforward yes-or-no questions: rubbing sticks adhere or they do not, the powder sticks or it does not, the axe falls to one side or to the other; there is never a third answer. According to Retel-Laurentin, this divinatory logic conforms in its rigorous binarity with the Nzakara mentality which in every moment of their social life works with antinomies.

According to Young (1977), the Amhara of Ethiopia practise a form of medical divination based on astrological-numerological reckonings. The 'real order of things', against which misfortune and sickness can be located, is uncovered by *awdunigist* divination (commonly referred to as 'counting stars'). It consists in analogically linking categories of everyday events and agents with phenomenological domains of order: the regularity of stars, the Amharic system of syllabic writing, mathematical calculations and elemental oppositions. '*Awdunigist* divination is simultaneously a *metaphor* for communicating and connecting concepts of world order with notions of immanent power and an *expression* of this power': i.e. 'it shares the same or similar technical operations with the events and objects (i.e., therapies, prophylaxes, ensorcelling) that it divines', made tangible and concrete by the extraordinary powers embodied by the diviners (Young, 1977: p. 197).

Werbner (1973) analyses the kind of stylized rhetoric communication the Kalanga of Botswana use in their domestic divination and concentrates on the almost dramaturgical involvement of the clients in the seance. The diviner and his congregation develop a rhetoric, rich in metaphors, ellipses and other devices, referring at once explicitly and implicitly and on different levels to the past and present situations of the clients. In this way, diviner and clients collaborate to revise some interpretations (of chains of events, and of their actual, excluded or hypothetical outcomes), suggesting they imply an alternative, dominant message.

The internal semantic approach seems fitted to the study of the divinatory performative creation of drama, the autodialectical production of a self-contained reality in divination, in the trance and oracle. Before applying this approach to the study of trance and oracle among the Yaka of Zaire, I will first outline the method.

The descriptive semantic and internal approach as I see it involves certain basic assumptions regarding social-cultural reality. This view of social-cultural reality and the practice of semantic anthropology are interrelated. The semantic anthropologist tries to look at social-cultural reality as a form of happening, a 'living theatre' in the process of being generated, articulated. He focuses on how it 'works', not so much in the sense of its achieving something, but rather in the sense of how it works in itself, how social-cultural reality is always in the process of being brought about. For example, the ritual practice is no longer exclusively studied as communication, nor as a theatrical expression of a myth, nor as an expression of a tradition, nor as a reflection of social formation. More precisely, the object of this approach is to see how people are constantly bringing meaning from out of themselves – their bodies, their gestures, their actions, their social, spatial and historical contexts – by relating these significant phenomena to one another, and producing new relations to overcome tensions and contradictions in which they had enclosed themselves by previous ones. I follow this articulation process of meaning or of drama (in its etymological sense) from within. Its autodialectical production is seen as the actor. In a similar way, discourse can be followed from the angle of the argument built up, rather than from that of the speaker or listener. Or again, artistic creation can be viewed actively as forms, colours, rhythms, volumes interacting and embracing one another, rather than as the fulfilling of the project of the artist or his patron or the spectator.

As for the actual, internal semantic approach, three overlapping steps may be distinguished.

First, one concentrates by observation and comparison on the way in which a particular activity, such as a divinatory seance or the transition to divinership, is structured into a whole. An ideal type is constructed of the progressively revealed vocation of a candidate to divinership, of the growing recognition of this predestination, of the cultural patterning of the trance and the subsequent initiation of the diviner-to-be, and finally of the whole divinatory process leading to consultation, to the oracle and to its application. With this in view one focuses on the sensible, gestural, verbal, interactional, quasi-intentional significant elements, on what is done and said, and on the changing patterns of interactions between the participants.

Second, it is considered that any practice, such as ritual practice, gets its form from its combining significant elements selected from different semantic structures and classifications. All the different acts, objects and other phenomena are compared with analogous phenomena in oral tradition, in other rituals or in daily life. In other words, the component elements are distinguished. Through their references to other contexts, i.e. through their latent, lateral references, the conventional social-cultural structures and classifications of these elements of the rite are identified. One tries to delineate the various positions of the participants in the systems of kinship, hierarchy, sex and age categories, and so on. It is also important to see how the particular acts, objects, colours, ornaments, arrangements of space and time refer implicitly to the conventional classifications of female versus male attributes, of spatial, temporal or cosmological divisions, etc.

The third step consists in trying to find how a meaningful reality is brought about, i.e. in focusing on its dynamic, its quasi-intentionality. In order to identify how the ritual practice differs from a daily practice, that is to identify its specificity, it is studied *in se* as a species, not as the nth reproduction of a model. The unity and specific meaning of a ritual practice cannot be accounted for by the lateral references of the significant elements alone, that is by the contexts from which these elements are borrowed, or by the way they are structured and classified in their original, more conventional contexts. Nor can it be accounted for by an interpretation based only on its social significance, the ritual terminology, the informants' opinion, collective representations, or analogous rites and performances. This unity and specificity of meaning in a ritual practice is realized by the creative metaphoric transposition of meaning. I have analysed this generating process of a meaningful drama more fully than is possible here in another essay devoted to possession-trance of the diviner-to-be and the mediumistic oracle among the Northern Yaka of Zaire (Devisch, 1978a; 1978b).

The meaningful reality which takes shape metaphorically in the possession-trance of the Yaka diviner-to-be comes out by the transposition of the significance of the sensible phenomena of the cock which crows at dawn and the egg-laying chicken out of their conventional semantic context (of the classification of domestic animals, or of temporal divisions) and implanting them in the totally unusual context of trance. Thus in his trance, the Yaka diviner-to-be breaks down the conventional spatial and cosmological divisions. A chicken not only mediates between forest and village, heaven and earth, night and day, but the egg-laying chicken also gives sensible form to bipolar unity. In turn this metaphoric transposition of meaning in the subsequent initiation leads to metonymic substitutions of meaning concretizing the effect of the transposition. The diviner-to-be appears in the chicken symbolism as inverting the attributes of witches, or of anti-society and the 'forest'. By further exploiting cosmological and temporal significances of transition and mediation, the diviner-to-be appears as a social mediator and as the one who embodies the significance enclosed in the realm of day, *societas*, order, as opposed to the realm of night, the anti-world, chaos, social-cultural illness and death.

Roughly, the efficacy of the transposition of meaning in the trance, and in the subsequent initiation to divinership, consists in giving a new form to the social and ontological identity of the medium or diviner, i.e. a deep change takes place in the significance the medium has for himself and for the others. This change takes place by a sensible and dramatic symbolization of limit transcendence and of bipolar unity. The medium in trance breaks down the main semantic structures and classifications of the culture which are often actualized in dualist terms so that they give meaning to persons, to activities and to various kinds of phenomena in group life. By embodying these significant elements which are the means in which ontological, ethical and social divisions are expressed and evaluated and by surpassing them in this metaphoric performance, the diviner guarantees his ability to pass authoritative judgment in the oracle on any deviation from the existing patterns of social-cultural life.

The authority of the Yaka diviner's oracular interpretation of the existential problems of his clients is based on the metaphoric creation of drama in the possession-trance of the diviner-to-be. After an initial outline of the theme of the consultation, the oracle states the events leading up to the problem situation. It does so by connecting these events with others, and this very fact usually brings about the meaning of the problem situation. Concretely, the oracle orders the facts according to the axiological model, interlinking, for example, infringement – curse – illness – misfortune – death. The oracle connects the submitted illness, for example, with some recent infringement or abuse, or some quarrel involving the sick person, and also with an analogous situation in the history of the maternal line. This connecting of present and historical situations is metaphoric and reveals an important dimension of the meaning of the problem. This meaning is not brought out by substitution of past for present, but is brought out through the application of the axiological model, that is by referring to a common ground of meaning. There is reference to the only conditions under which social and cultural life is possible and to the potentiality of meaning which the diviner-to-be was actualizing during his trance and initiation. Finally, the oracle flows into an intervention which takes shape in such a way that the group and its cognitive and social structures are being symbolically redefined from within.

Since this internal semantic approach to divination has been defined in its application to a limited ethnic social-cultural context, there remains the very important question of the transcultural comparative applicability of this internal approach and of its understanding of divination.

The very complex problem of transcultural divination includes the question whether the diviner can work an oracle for clients of an ethnic background other than that from which the divinatory technique and etiology derive.[9] It also includes the question in what way different oracles can be meaningful for clients in an urban setting who for the same problem situation successively consult diviners of very different cultural backgrounds. Looked at from an internal, semantic viewpoint, this problem is not primarily one of expression, communication and comprehension. In other words, the relevance of divination has not to be approached primarily and fundamentally on the level of the patterning of communication. Thus our first question does not have to do with the extent to which clients and diviner share this patterning, nor to the extent to which this patterning of communication is received and understood. Divination is primarily doing rather than communicating, so that, on the one hand, attention has to be paid to the patterning and universality of signification, and, on the other hand, this patterning should be seen as an aspect of the creation of drama rich in cognitive, emotional, sensible, interactional, cosmological and historic significance, performed in a close and multidimensional interaction of all the participants, diviner and clients.

Drawing on my study of Yaka divination and comparing this with the studies of Adler and Zempléni (1972), Turner (1975a, b) and Roumeguère-Eberhardt (1968), it seems one might ask whether or not divination in its dimension of the performative production of drama is bringing about a very elementary kind of signification, using elementary structures and categories of symbolic patterning. In so far as these structures and categories are elementary, they are also likely to be underlying numerous cultural and social practices in the context of ethnic groups belonging to some 'general common cultural tradition'. In so far as the clients are dramatically involved in the oracle performed, e.g. by a diviner of another cultural background, they may be able to share actively in this patterning of signification. I have shown (Devisch, 1978a) how the possession-trance of the Yaka diviner-to-be (serving as a base for the performance of oracles) gives significant form to bipolar unity and to the transcending of the essentially ambivalent bipolar character of any form of classification and organization, or to the transcending of ambiguities, inconsistencies, oppositions in daily life. This metaphoric articulation process in trance and divination gives palpable form to the merging and conciliation of what may be defined as the one and the multiple, unity and duality or pluralism, the intensive and the extensive, the prior and the posterior, past and present, order and disorder, life and death, health and sickness, determinacy and indeterminacy, structure, its inadequacy and the transcending of it.[10] These elementary categories and structural principles do not have relevance for the Yaka only.

This performative generation of significance in ritual or in the oracle has the greater impact since it is generated in drama that is rich in cognitive, emotional, sensible, interactional, historic and cosmological significance; although to a lesser extent, this is also the case in divination by manipulation of a divinatory apparatus. Metaphoric transpositions bridge these various levels, bringing about a symbolic congruence between psychological, sensitive, social, cognitive and cosmological levels. Because of the metaphoric congruence, any articulation of meaning on one level implicates other levels and thus also the context of social identities (according to sex, age, matrimonial status, role, power . . .), and of actions and values. The dramatic expression of a context of social oppositions, or cognitive incompatibilities or inconsistencies, can take place through cosmological metaphors. Alternatives and mediations are brought into relation with these social or cognitive contexts. Rearrangement of the congruent cosmological terms can bring about a dialectical transformation of the social and cognitive contexts. Because the patterning of signification is internally transformative in such a way that it is objectified in the performative drama itself, it is capable of being seen by the participants as a transformation realized by themselves. The progressive, dramatic involvement of the clients weakens the maintenance of interactional activity between them which was constituted in conventional contexts of action and meaning outside the ritual. In the very effecting of transformations within the organization of their performance, these contexts of meaning and action may be transformed. The divinatory seance is dramatically built up by interaction, rhetoric, emotional manifestations, play, song, colours, even smell and smoke, organization of space, temporal co-ordinates, and the multireferential semiotics of the divinatory vehicles. The divinatory seance seems to consist of a dialectical alternation of phases so as to give form to the elementary paradoxes of multiplicity versus unity, disorder versus order, etc., so as to re-establish qualitative differentations, and to sensitize people to choose or to render order at other levels. Moments of bafflement in perception, complexity and non-signification in the configuration of divinatory items, of licence, emotional outbursts, ungrammatical speech, glossolalia, esoteric gestures (e.g. in possession-trance) may be alternated by moments of increasing configurational order in the divinatory items, articulated speech, more rational propositions, controlled and co-ordinated interaction, circumscribed ritual space.

In all that we have so far seen we have only begun to outline some ways of tackling the problem of transcultural divination. These include looking at the metaphoric bridging of semantic levels, looking at the ritual's transformational and dialectical relation with the realities in which it is emergent, amounting to the search for innovation. These could be refined very much by models offered by, for example, Babcock (1978), Kapferer (1977), Moore and Myerhoff (1977), Myerhoff (1975), Scheff (1979) and Turner (1969, 1974, 1977).

Towards a praxeological approach

The praxeological approach, although the most recently developed, seems to me the most promising. It integrates many of the more acceptable aspects of earlier approaches, offering one valid for studying a pluri-ethnic context of divination as a social and cultural practice, so that its presentation can serve as a conclusion to this study. It selects from these approaches according to the type and the aspect of the divinatory practice under attention. It unifies these approaches by following, from within, the way the divinatory practice gives dialectic form to social and cultural reality. It is a subject-centred approach, the subject being the diviner, or the supportive congregation and decision-making group constituting itself in the course of the divinatory process, or the institution of divination. In this way, this approach de-psychologizes the notion of comprehension and communication. Attention is focused on the aspect of purposeful articulation of meaning (the instrumental aspect), or more precisely on the praxis. The oracle or the diviner brings out what is problematic by giving it metaphoric form, through rhetoric or dramatic bridging of physiological, sensitive, cognitive, social, historical and cosmological domains. In this giving of a form, a meaning is constituted which by inventive manipulation shows itself relevant to the actual situation so as to achieve individual and collective goals or functions simultaneously. In this process the participants grow into the group of the concerned, committed to the quest, as Janzen (1978: e.g. pp. 130–1) sees it, to which the performance appears as self-legitimating, generating their concern (see, for example, Jackson, 1978: pp. 129f.). This performance can bring about insight, mastery of cognitive complexity, transition in the existential or social condition of the individual or of the group. It can bring about a change in the relations of power, mediation between the individual and the group, the old and the new, or can perform other dynamic functions.

This praxeological approach on a micro-scale manifestly needs to be complemented by a macro-scale praxeological study of the divinatory transformational relation to the wider social and cultural order. Special attention will need to be paid to the role that the symbolic manipulations of divination play in clarifying and drawing attention to the diverse overlapping domains of life, the different modes of production, the different principles of social organization and the contradiction between these, as well as the widening in scope and complexity of the social life of Africans that has occurred since the advent of capitalism and the modern state.

77

We will also need to ask how divination performs a generative and conciliating role in this macro-social and macro-cultural context.

Notes

1 My fieldwork, from January 1972 to October 1974, took place among the Northern Yaka in the Taanda settlement of thirteen villages, some 450 kilometres to the south-west of Kinshasa, in the Bandundu region of Zaïre. I gratefully acknowledge grants made available to me for this research in my capacity as 'Chercheur associé de l'I.R.S.A.C.' and 'Aspirant van het Belgisch Nationaal Fonds voor Wetenschappelijk Onderzoek'. I am especially grateful to Dr Wim van Binsbergen, Dr Wauthier de Mahieu, Dr Terence Ranger and Dr Richard Werbner for their constructive comments on an earlier draft.

2 For example, see Bascom (1969: p. 81), Crawford (1967: pp. 179–82), Forde (1964: pp. 230, 273), Fry (1976: pp. 27–8), Hammond-Tooke (1974: p. 348), Hauenstein (1976: pp. 474, 487, 496–8), Lienhardt (1961: pp. 68ff.), McLean and Solomon (1971: p. 25), Ngubane (1977: p;. 57, 102–3) and Vincent (1971: pp. 100ff.).

3 This kind of psychologizing and functionalist interpretation of divination is given by Beattie (1967: pp. 225, 230), Forde (1964: pp. 282–3), Fortes (1971: p. 254), Evans-Pritchard (1937: pp. 263–4), Park (1967: p. 234) and Retel-Laurentin (1974: p. 315).

4 See, for example, Fry (1976: pp. 47–53, 107–15), Peristiany (1975: p. 211) and Rigby (1975: p. 138).

5 See, for example, Crawford (1967: pp. 233–4, 278–81), Janzen (1978: p. 52), Jules-Rosette (1978: p. 559), MacGaffey (1970: p. 29), Peristiany (1975: p. 212) and Schoffeleers (1977: pp. 230ff.).

6 See, for example, Bascom (1969: pp. 68–9), Fortes (1971: p. 256), Jules-Rosette (1978: p. 557) and Lienhardt (1961: pp. 68–9).

7 See, for example, Beattie (1967: pp. 221–30), Gluckman (1972b: p. 21), Mendonsa (1978: p. 40), Shelton (1965: pp. 1444–9) and White (1948: pp. 94–5).

8 Adler and Zempléni (1972), Bascom (1969: pp. 26–59), Bohannan (1975), Evans-Pritchard (1937: pp. 286–94), Fortes (1971: pp. 261–7), Jackson (1978: pp. 125–9), Mendonsa (1978: pp. 37–42), Retel-Laurentin (1969: pp. 45–70; 1974), Shelton (1965), Turner (1975b), Vincent (1971: pp. 79–100) and Werbner (1973).

9 My information in this area is a-typical. I was able to take notes about some thirty seances led by a Pentecostal prophet of a neighbouring group who was passing through Northern Yaka land. His oracles, given in a lingua franca akin to *yiyaka*, were translated by a former traditional Yaka diviner in etiological terms and symbolic language of Yaka divination.

10 Fernandez's sophisticated approach (1977) to the *bwiti* cult among the Fang could offer a heuristic model to analyse how this primordial

experience, brought about by the metaphoric articulation process, is 'affirmed by extension into social experience, and social experiences revitalized by association with primary experience' (p. 127). In Turner's terms (1975a: pp. 31–3), it can be said that the divinatory metaphoric performance reaches the experience of unitary primitive flow, which is more a 'capacity' of mind, a potentiality of meaning, than a 'content', achieving thereby the merging of action and awareness.

References

Adler, A., and Zempléni, A. (1972), *Le Bâton de l'aveugle: Divination, maladie et pouvoir chez les Moundang du Tchad*, Paris: Hermann.
Babcock, B. (ed.) (1978), *The Reversible World*, Ithaca, NY: Cornell University Press.
Bascom, W. (1969), *Ifa Divination: Communication between God and Men in West Africa*, Bloomington: Indiana University Press.
Bastide, R. (1968), 'La Connaissance de l'événement', in *Perspectives de la sociologie contemporaine: Hommage à George Gurvitch*, Paris: Presses Universitaires de France, pp. 159–68.
Baumann, H. (1975), 'Die Sambesi-Angola-Provinz', in H. Baumann (ed.), *Die Völker Afrikas und Ihre Traditionellen Kulturen: Allgemeiner Teil und Südliches Afrika, Teil I*, Wiesbaden: Franz Steiner Verlag, pp. 513–648.
Beattie, John (1967), 'Divination in Bunyoro, Uganda' *Sociologus*, 14, 1964[1]: pp. 44–62; reprinted in Middleton (1967), pp. 211–31.
Beattie, John, and Lienhardt, R. (eds) (1975), *Studies in Social Anthropology*, Oxford: Clarendon Press.
Beattie, John and Middleton, John (eds) (1969), *Spirit Mediumship and Society in Africa*, London: Routledge & Kegan Paul.
Binsbergen, Wim M. J. van (1981), *Religious Change in Zambia: Exploratory Studies*, London: Kegan Paul International.
Bohannan, Paul (1975), 'Tiv divination', in Beattie and Lienhardt (1975), pp. 149–66.
Bonte, P. (1978), 'Aînés et prophètes: Religion et classes sociales chez les éleveurs d'Afrique de l'Est', in J. Maître (ed.), *L'Apport de la théorie et des méthodes marxistes à l'étude des religions*, Paris: Centre d'Etudes Sociologiques, pp. 53–78.
Bourdillon, M. (1977), 'Oracles and Politics in Ancient Israel', *Man* (n.s.), 12: pp. 124–40.
Bourguignon, E. (1968), 'Divination, transe et possession en Afrique transsaharienne', in Caquot and Leibovici (1968), pp. 331–58.
Bourguignon, E. (ed.) (1973), *Religion, Altered States of Consciousness and Social Change*, Columbus: Ohio State University Press.
Bourguignon, E. (1976), 'Spirit Possession Belief and Social Structure', in A. Bharati (ed.), *The Realm of the Extra-Human: Ideas and Actions*,

The Hague: Mouton, pp. 17–26.

Caquot, A., and Leibovici, M. (eds) (1968), *La Divination, II*, Paris: Presses Universitaires de France.

Colson, E. (1966), 'The Alien Diviner and Local Politics among the Tonga of Zambia', in M. Swartz, V. Turner and A. Tuden (eds), *Political Anthropology*, Chicago: Aldine, pp. 221–8.

Crapanzano, V. (1977), 'Introduction', in V. Crapanzano and V. Garrison (eds), *Case Studies in Spirit Possession*, New York: Wiley, pp. 1–40.

Crawford, J. (1967), *Witchcraft and Sorcery in Rhodesia*, London: Oxford University Press.

Devisch, R. (1978a), 'Towards a Semantic Study of Divination: Trance and Initiation of the Yaka Diviner as a Basis for his Authority', *Bijdragen, Tijdschrift voor Filosofie en Theologie*, 39: pp. 173–89.

Devisch, R. (1978b), 'Towards a Semantic Study of Divination: Authority in the Yaka Diviner's Oracle', *Bijdragen, Tijdschrift voor Filosofie en Theologie*, 39: pp. 270–88.

Douglas, Mary (ed.) (1970), *Witchcraft Confessions and Accusations*, London: Tavistock Publications, ASA Monograph no. 90.

Evans-Pritchard, E. (1937), *Witchcraft, Oracles and Magic among the Azande*, Oxford: Clarendon Press.

Fernandez, J. (1967), *Divinations, Confessions, Testimonies: Zulu Confrontation with the Social Superstructure*, Durban: Institute for Social Research, Occasional Paper no. 9.

Fernandez, J. (1972), 'Persuasions and Performances: Of the Beast in Every Body . . . and the Metaphors of Everyman', *Daedalus*, **101**, 1: pp. 39–60.

Fernandez, J. (1977), 'The Performance of Ritual Metaphor', in J. Sapir and J. Crocker (eds), *The Social Use of Metaphor*, Philadelphia: University of Pennsylvania Press, pp. 100–31.

Firth, R. (1969), 'Foreword', in Beattie and Middleton (1969), pp. ix–xxx.

Forde, D. (1964), *Yakö Studies*, London: Oxford University Press.

Fortes, M. (1971), 'Les Premisses religieuses et la technique logique des rites divinatoires', in J. Huxley (ed.), *Le Comportement rituel chez l'homme et l'animal*, Paris: Gallimard (translation from 1966[1]), pp. 249–68.

Fry, P. (1976), *Spirits of Protest: Spirit-Mediums and the Articulation of Consensus amongst the Zezuru of Southern Rhodesia*, Cambridge: Cambridge University Press.

Garbett, G. (1969), 'Spirit Mediums as Mediators in Valley Korekore Society', in Beattie and Middleton (1969), pp. 104–27.

Geertz, C. (1975), *The Interpretation of Cultures*, London: Hutchinson.

Gluckman, M. (1971), *Politics, Law and Ritual in Tribal Society*, Oxford: Blackwell.

Gluckman, M. (ed.) (1972a), *The Allocation of Responsibility*, Manchester: Manchester University Press.

Gluckman, M. (1972b), 'Moral Crises: Magical and Secular Solutions', in

Gluckman (1972a), pp. 1–50.

Hammond-Tooke, W. (1974), 'World-View II: A System of Action', in W. Hammond-Tooke (ed.), *The Bantu-Speaking Peoples of Southern Africa*, London: Routledge & Kegan Paul, pp. 344–63.

Harwood, A. (1970), *Witchcraft, Sorcery and Social Categories among the Safwa*, London: Oxford University Press for the International African Institute.

Hauenstein, A. (1976), 'Quelques formes de divination parmi les Wobé et les Guéré de Côte d'Ivoire', *Anthropos*, 71: pp. 473–507.

Heusch, L. de (1971), *Pourquoi l'epouser?*, Paris: Gallimard.

Horton, R. (1967), 'African Traditional Thought and Western Science', *Africa*, 37: pp. 50–71, 155–87.

Jackson, M. (1978), 'An Approach to Kuranko Divination', *Human Relations* (London), 31: pp. 117–38.

Janzen, John M. (1978), *The Quest for Therapy in Lower Zaïre*, Berkeley: University of California Press.

Jules-Rosette, B. (1978), 'The Veil of Objectivity: Prophecy, Divination, and Social Inquiry', *American Anthropologist*, 80: pp. 549–70.

Kapferer, B. (1977), 'First Class to Maradana: Secular Drama in Sinhalese Healing Rites', in Moore and Myerhoff (1977), pp. 91–123.

Lévi-Strauss, C. (1962), *La Pensée sauvage*, Paris, Plon

Lienhardt, G. (1961), *Divinity and Experience: The Religion of the Dinka*, Oxford: Clarendon Press.

MacGaffey, W. (1970), 'The Religious Commissions of the Bakongo', *Man* (n.s.), **5**, 1: pp. 27–38.

McLean, D., and Solomon, T. (1971), 'Divination among the Bena Lulua', *Journal of Religion in Africa*, 6: pp. 25–44.

Mendonsa, E. (1976), 'Characteristics of Sisala Diviners (Northern Ghana)', in A. Bharati (ed.), *The Realm of the Extra-Human: Agents and Audiences*, The Hague: Mouton, pp. 179–95.

Mendonsa, E. (1978), 'Etiology and Divination among the Sisala of Northern Ghana', *Journal of Religion in Africa*, 9: pp. 33–50.

Middleton, J. (1960), *Lugbara Religion: Ritual and Authority among an East African People*, London: Oxford University Press.

Middleton, J. (ed.) (1967), *Magic, Witchcraft and Curing*, New York: National History Press.

Moore, Sally, and Myerhoff, Barbara (eds) (1977), *Secular Ritual*, Assen: Van Gorcum.

Myerhoff, Barbara (1975), 'Organization and Ecstacy: Deliberate and Accidental Communitas among Huichol Indians and American Youth', in S. Moore and B. Myerhoff (eds), *Symbol and Politics in Communal Ideology*, Ithaca, NY: Cornell University Press, pp. 33–67.

Ngubane, H. (1977), *Body and Mind in Zulu Medicine: An Ethnography of Health and Disease in Nyuswa-Zulu Thought and Practice*, London: Academic Press.

Park, G. (1967), 'Divination and its Social Contexts', *Journal of the Royal Anthropological Institute*, 93, 1963[1]: pp. 195–209; reprinted in Middleton (1967), pp. 233–54.

Peristiany, J. (1975), 'The Ideal and the Actual: The Role of Prophets in the Pokot Political System', in Beattie and Lienhardt (1975), pp. 167–212.

Redmayne, A. (1970), 'Chikanga: An African Diviner with an International Reputation', in Douglas (1970), pp. 103–28.

Retel-Laurentin, A. (1969), *Oracles et ordalies chez les Nzakara*, Paris: Mouton.

Retel-Laurentin, A. (1974), 'La Force de la parole', in Vernant (1974), pp. 295–319.

Rigby, P. (1975), 'Prophets, Diviners, and Prophetism: The Recent History of Kiganda Religion', *Journal of Anthropological Research*, 31: pp. 116–48.

Roumeguère-Eberhardt, J. (1968), 'La Divination en Afrique Australe', in Caquot and Leibovici (1968), pp. 359–72.

Sahlins, M. (1976), *Culture and Practical Reason*, Chicago: University of Chicago Press.

Scheff, T. (1979), *Catharsis in Healing, Ritual and Drama*, Berkeley: University of California Press.

Schoffeleers, J. M. (1977), 'Cult Idioms and the Dialectics of a Region', in Werbner (1977), pp. 219–39.

Shelton, A. (1965), 'The Meaning and Method of Afa Divination among the Northern Nsukka Ibo', *American Anthropologist*, 67: pp. 1441–54.

Thomas, L., and Luneau, R. (1975), *La Terre africaine et ses religions*, Paris: Larousse.

Thomas, L., and Luneau, R. (1977), *Les Sages dépossédés*, Paris: Laffont.

Turner, Victor (1957), *Schism and Continuity in an African Society*, Manchester: Manchester University Press.

Turner, Victor (1968), *The Drums of Affliction: A Study of Religious Processes among the Ndembu*, Oxford: Clarendon Press.

Turner, Victor (1969), *The Ritual Process: Structure and Anti-Structure*, London: Routledge & Kegan Paul.

Turner, Victor (1974), *Dramas, Fields, and Metaphors*, Ithaca, NY: Cornell University Press.

Turner, Victor (1975a), 'Introduction', in Victor Turner, *Revelation and Divination in Ndembu Ritual*, Ithaca, NY: Cornell University Press, pp. 15–33.

Turner, Victor (1975b), 'Chihamba the White Spirit: A Ritual Drama of the Ndembu' (1962[1]); *Ndembu Divination: Its Symbolism and Techniques* (1961[1]), re-edited in Victor Turner, *Revelation and Divination in Ndembu Ritual*, Ithaca, NY: Cornell University Press.

Turner, Victor (1977), 'Variations on a Theme of Liminality', in Moore and Myerhoff (1977), pp. 36–52.

Vernant, J. (1974), 'Paroles et signes muets', in Vernant *et al.* (1974), pp. 9–25.

Vernant, J., *et al.* (1974), *Divination et rationalité*, Paris: Seuil.

Vincent, J. -F. (1966), 'Techniques divinatoires des Saba, Hadjeray du Tchad', *Journal de la Société des Africanistes*, 36: pp. 44–63.

Vincent, J. -F. (1971), 'Divination et possession chez les Mofu, Montagnards du Nord-Cameroun', *Journal de la Société des Africanistes*, 41: pp. 71–132.

Werbner, R. (1973), 'The Superabundance of Understanding: Kalanga Rhetoric and Domestic Divination', *American Anthropologist*, 75: pp. 1414–40.

Werbner, R. P. (ed.) (1977), *Regional Cults*, London: Academic Press.

Werbner, R. P. (1980), 'Totemism in History: The Ritual Passage of West African Strangers', *Man* (n.s.), 14: pp. 663–83.

White, C. (1948), 'Witchcraft, Divination and Magic among the Balovale Tribes', *Africa*, 18: pp. 81–104.

Young, A. (1977), 'Order, Analogy, and Efficacy in Ethiopian Medical Divination', *Culture, Medicine and Psychiatry* (Dordrecht), 1: pp. 183–99.

Zahan, D. (1970), *Religion, spiritualité et pensée africaines*, Paris: Payot.

Zempléni, A. (1966), 'La Dimension thérapeutique du culte des *Rab*: *Ndöp*, et *Samp*, rites de possession chez les Lebou et les Wolof', *Psychopathologie Africaine*, 2: pp. 295–439.

Zempléni, A. (1975), 'De la persécution à la culpabilité', in C. Piault (ed.), *Prophétisme et thérapeutique: Albert Atcho et la communauté de Bregbo*, Paris: Hermann, pp. 153–218.

Zuesse, E. (1975–6), 'Divination and Deity in African Religions', *History of Religions*, 15: pp. 158–82.

Chapter 3

Towards a semantic approach to the principle of transformation: An analysis of two myths concerning the origin of circumcision among the Komo of Zaire[1]

Wauthier de Mahieu

Introduction

A model of analysis employed by Lévi-Strauss in his *Mythologiques* will serve as our starting-point, since the approach that I am going to propose was suggested by certain orientations in that model. However, it is to distance myself from the latter that the title of this paper emphasizes the semantic dimension of my own approach.

Comparing in *Le Cru et le cuit* (1964: pp. 107–12) three myths on the origin of tobacco, Lévi-Strauss shows how the last, the Bororo version, constitutes a transformation of the two others, which come respectively from the Toba and the Tereno. True, the author himself does not use the term 'transformation'; he only qualifies the third myth as 'rigoureusement symétrique' in relation to the others (*op. cit.*: p. 112). But Sperber (1968: p. 203) and Badcock (1975: pp. 56–9), who compare the same myths to illustrate Lévi-Strauss's ideas and theory, do emphasize their transformational structure.

To start with, I shall indicate which features in Lévi-Strauss's thought and method I take exception to. If it is true that he has been profoundly influenced by structural linguistics, it is equally true, as Mounin (1970: pp. 200–1) has shown, that his major linguistic information dates from his contacts with Jacobson in the years 1943–4. The notion of transformation in linguistic theory, however, came to be developed only at a later stage by Harris (1957) and Chomsky (1957) in the context of transformational and generative grammar. This has for one of its consequences that, whenever Lévi-Strauss employs this term, he does not take into account the relations between deep structures and surface structures as, for instance, in the kind of analysis that Ardener develops in his more recent writings (Ardener, 1971a: especially pp. lxi–lxiii; 1971b; 1978), and as in the present paper.[2]

In addition to this, Lévi-Strauss also shares the view of the major transformationalists that transformations, of themselves, *do not generate meaning*. According to this viewpoint, transformations are of relevance only in so far as they allow the analyst to lay bare certain structural features. Thus, for instance, to limit ourselves to the field of myths, which is our principal concern here, transformations provide the objective criteria on the basis of which certain sequences are to be retained as mythemes, i.e. as coded elements that allow the message to be decoded, and other sequences have to be disregarded (Lévi-Strauss, 1958: pp. 233–4; see also Leach, 1976: pp. 25–7, who further systematizes Lévi-Strauss's ideas). The principle of transformation, on which Lévi-Strauss bases his analyses, is thus borrowed first and foremost from mathematical logic and the set theory (cf. Lévi-Strauss, 1966: p. 407; Marc-Lipiansky, 1973: p. 69). Besides this, he does not clearly distinguish between transformations, permutations and substitutions (Marc-Lipiansky, 1973: p. 72).

To the extent, then, that transformations do not generate meaning and therefore add nothing to the content of the message, but are rather to be seen as resulting from the logical possibilities offered by every system manifesting an internal coherence, in the Lévi-Straussian perspective they *are not necessary* (Sperber, 1968: pp. 201, 224).[3] However, this does not mean that, except for the way in which he sifts them out, they are arbitrary (Cohen, 1969: p. 349). This latter qualification, which is repeated time and again in Badcock's writings (1975: pp. 54–5), leads to confusion, as it contradicts the manner in which Lévi-Strauss himself conceives and defines structure (1958: p. 306). Having to follow *certain logical rules*, transformations in his line of thought seem to derive rather from the ludical properties of the mind. This causes

Sperber to wonder if, in that case, they might not be a characteristic of man rather than of myth (1968: p. 206).

These rules of logic impose themselves irrespective of differences between particular cultures; the transformations themselves are assumed to occur at the *transcultural* level and are studied as such by Lévi-Strauss. The analyst who works with such a perspective will thus have his attention drawn by readily-found transformations such as those – to take an example from the three myths mentioned – in which the mother is substituted for the husband, the son for the spouse, relations of consanguinity for those of marriage, plants for animals, matrilineality for patrilineality, etc. Moreover, these will have been grasped and translated by means of his *anthropo-logical categories*, that is to say by means of terms which, staying immediately at a universal level, might involve a false reproduction of the cultural reality because of the short-circuiting of it.

I do not think my criticism is exaggerated when I point out that the results of the analysis of Lévi-Strauss, which served as a model of reference, are on the whole rather meagre. True, they invite us to admire the mechanisms of the human mind, creator of myths. But when one sees how little they inform us about the cultures of the Toba, the Tereno and the Bororo, about the insertion of these three myths into their respective cultural contexts, and how many of their elements not only stay unexplained but do not even find their place in the alleged transformational structure, one comes to doubt the value of that method and wonders what most deserves our admiration: the so-called mechanisms of mythical thought or the feats of mind of the analyst (cf. Nathhorst, 1970: p. 71; Kronenfeld and Decker, 1979: p. 533). As Crick (1976: p. 52) points out, 'he only provides a grammar and not a meaning' (see also Strenski, 1974: pp. 581–3). Nevertheless, these results retain something provocative, and it is this challenge that I will attempt to take up.

This attempt will be articulated, as indicated in the title of this paper, around a double approach: transformational and semantic.

As regards the first, I do not pretend to apply the principles of transformational linguistics in their entire technicity. The linguists themselves have thought it necessary to put scholars in the humanities on their guard against a rather naïve application of their methods (cf. Mounin, 1975: pp. 12–13, 15–35; Ikegami, 1977; Gregersen, 1977). At the same time many anthropologists have pointed out that the same methods do not allow one to bring out all the meaning of social phenomena which their discipline researches (see, for example, Basso, 1976: pp. 116–6; Keesing, 1972; and 1979). I will simply proceed from the principle that the transformational dimension is an essential property of structures, if one considers these as dynamic entities; that is to say, as entities that, while being structured, are at the same time structuring (cf. Piaget, 1968: pp. 10–11). This structuring activity operates by transforming a deeper-lying structure into surface structures, the latter standing also in a transformational relation to one another.

Whereas transformation may thus be considered as a logical property of structures, their being put into operation is semantic. It seems to me that, rather than being the effect of a game of the mind – an assertion that easily derives from lack of serious investigation – the transformations become at once part of a system of meanings and remain at the service of this system. It is only this that gives them their true sense. Now, this system of meanings can only be discovered within the culture that carries it and is carried by it (cf. Heelas, 1977).[4] Let us now consider this concretely.

The Komo of N. E. Zaire

I have found among the Komo – a population of patrilineal hunters of the equatorial forests of North-East Zaire – two myths concerning the origin of circumcision. The first one is as follows:

Atóá-opho, a man of the *obusé* clan, had entered the forest with his bow and arrows to hunt monkeys. Having perceived an *osephe* monkey, he prepared to let an arrow fly, when, all of a sudden, his attention was attracted by the presence of a *bungú* squirrel hanging from a straight branch (*nkolo*) along which the monkey was walking. Curious to know what would happen, he restrained himself. At the moment the monkey reached the place under which the squirrel was hanging, *Atóá-opho* heard it utter a cry. He let an arrow fly and the monkey fell to the ground. A bite from the squirrel had circumcised it. Back at the village, *Atóá-opho* showed his fathers the animal. At first surprised, they decided the matter had to be tried on human beings. They called for a woman and excised her, but the ensuing haemorrhage caused her death. The elders then called a young man and circumcised him. On seeing the result they gave their approval by an 'aaa'. The young man was restored to health, and *Atóá-opho* was made *méná-gandjá*, holder of the circumcision rites.

The second myth tells us how *Boso*, a man of the legendary village *Obondoba*, had provoked by his sorcery the death of many people but refused to pay the sums of compensation that were demanded from him. Tired of having to pay each time on his behalf, his brothers bound him hands and feet, put him in a basket and threw him in the water. *Boso* sank until he hit against the roof of a hut in the village of his ancestors *bakéti*. Now this happened to be the hut of *Nkayá*, his paternal aunt, who hid him in her hut. As in those days circumcision was celebrated in the village of the ancestors, the aunt pierced a hole in the wall of the hut and advised her nephew to follow attentively the course of the rites. 'Have you seen everything clearly?' she asked him, when the festivities were over. 'Yes', he said. 'Well, go back to where you come from', she said, 'and organise everything as you have seen it done here. The money that it will raise will serve to pay your debts.' Thereupon she gave him a *yendji*, one of the sticks that are among the most secret elements of the circumcision ritual, and took him back to his wife's field where she made him sit on the trunk of a tree that was lying on the ground. A year had passed at *Obondoba* since *Boso*'s disappearance. His wife's head had been shaved, as a sign of ending the mourning, and she was permitted to resume her household activities. Going to her field, she found her husband sitting on the tree trunk. Startled, she ran and called her brothers-in-law. Arriving at the spot, the latter said to *Boso*: 'Because you have come back, we will not harm you.' They took him back to his house. *Boso* began immediately to prepare all he needed to celebrate the circumcision rites. (Here follows an enumeration of all the things needed in the ritual.) The rites were celebrated, and the elders found that everything was good.

At first sight there does not seem to be a close relationship between these two myths. One notices neither symmetry nor opposition, neither inversions nor transformations of the kind stated by Lévi-Strauss; and I am convinced that, if we had to be satisfied only with the anthropo-logical categories he uses as tools of analysis, we would not be able to say much about the connection between these myths.

There is, nevertheless, one striking contrasting detail. In the second myth, circumcision comes from under the water, while in the first it is discovered in the forest. Yet in itself, this detail does not teach us anything, as long as it is not situated in the larger context of the cosmological thought of the Komo. It is by thus situating it that we will begin, because it is from here on that the whole transformational perspective of the two myths will progressively open up.

It is important to note that, according to current conceptions of the Komo, it was the ancestors who revealed to human beings the several ritual complexes to which they can resort today, in order to help them solve their difficulties in life. Now, if the village is the only specifically human space, conquered at the expense of the forest, the extra-human space, to which the ancestors – as also the animals – belong, comprises everything that is not the village but that surrounds it: the firmament above, the forest round the village and the space under the earth, where water from the waterfalls is seen falling to the depths. Yet these different locales are qualified in different ways, and the ancestors – like animals – who are localized there are also differently qualified. The criterion or the model of representational order that is at the basis of this differentiation is the movement of water or of rain that, coming from heaven to earth, gives life to plants and to men and then loses itself under the ground. So the ancestors, too, who are considered as the origin of life and of wellbeing, are localized in the firmament. These ancestors, known personally and individually, are the immediate forebears of everyone. It was to allow those who had occupied on earth a social or ritual function of some importance to return to this representational locale that, in traditional times, after their death they were put high up on branches of trees in the forest.

On the other hand, the forgotten ancestors live in big villages under the waterfalls. They devote themselves to the celebration of rites. The rumbling of their drums can be heard in that of the cascade. In general, these ancestors are not interested in living beings: yet they often come back to earth under cover of night, in groups or alone, to harm them. I will not discuss here the forest which is ambiguous. Ancestors of the two kinds can be met there because this locale is the meeting point of the two spatial categories. (For more details, see de Mahieu, 1975; 1980: pp. 102–12).

These representations indicate the first stumbling-block that the transformational structure of the two myths will be called upon to face. If the personal ancestors of the sky are the only ones to be benevolent, one would expect them to reveal the rites to the human beings. Yet a revelation is made only during a celebration, and celebrations happen only where ancestors live in a community, i.e. under water.

The first myth answers the first expectation. The revelation, indeed, is made in the forest, but also high up, namely, on a branch, where those dead who were expected to become benevolent ancestors were hung. Furthermore, the revelation is made through a monkey. The animals of the forest, especially the monkeys, called *nyama k'égo*, 'quadrupeds of above', are often considered to be incarnations of the ancestors. Thus, it was the cynocephalus who, according to another myth, initiated *Abá-lambú* into the ritual of divination (*bumo*; cf. de Mahieu, 1973: p. 29). We will soon see what justifies the presence of the *osephe* monkey in this myth.

The second myth, on the contrary, conforms to the other dimension, according to which a rite is revealed only at the community celebrations in the villages situated under water. These celebrations are so peculiar to the ancestors situated there that a further distinction can be seen grafted onto the first. It is only as a non-ritualized operation that the circumcision is revealed to *Atóá-opho* in the first myth, whereas in the second *Boso* is initiated into its ritual form. Nevertheless, this specification – or more exactly, this first transformational solution of the aforementioned difficulty – raises another difficulty. How can the impersonal ancestors, localized under water and normally considered to be malevolent, reveal a rite to the living? The myth finds a roundabout way by having a personal and benevolent ancestor found under water, namely *Nkayá*, *Boso*'s paternal aunt, who will steal from the unknown ancestors the secret of their celebrations. The reverse is also true. Whereas *Nkayá* represents the personal element in a communitarian ancestral world, the *osephe* monkey introduces a dimension of community celebrations in the world of the personal ancestors. One of its epithets, indeed, is *méná-mutuanga*, 'the one who presides over the assembly of monkeys'. It is said that by his cry, *'tú-tú-tú'*, which is compared to the beating of the drum, he assembles around him the *mutuanga*, a regular assembly of monkeys of different species (cf. the myth quoted in de Mahieu, 1979: pp. 44–5).

There is, in this first group of representations, a final transformation which is very important because it will determine many others. Furthermore, one would risk passing it over if one were not acquainted with current Komo conceptions. If it is evident that, in the second myth, the revelation is made by the artifices of a woman, the *osephe* monkey, by which it is made in the first, has another epithet, *abá-baké/bási*, 'the father with the many wives' (de Mahieu, 1980: p. 42). He is, indeed, one of the principal symbols of masculinity which is thus associated with the forest, the earth and the world above, whereas femininity is associated with water and the world below. This association is confirmed by many representations exterior to the two myths (I will present some of them later), but also by certain representations that are found within them. So let us take them up from the beginning.

The name *Atóá-opho* means 'the one who pierces the leaves' and evokes the galago (*ésiá*) which, it is said, 'pierces the leaves' with his powerful penis. The animal refers thus to the act of deflowering and is itself a symbol of the *méná-gandjá*, the retainer of the circumcision ritual, who is forbidden to eat of it (de Mahieu, 1980: p. 44). Reduced to ashes, the galago's penis is put into incisions in the abdomen of men who have lost their sexual power. We will not pursue the historical and social elements that made *Atóá-opho* a man of the *obusé* clan, but will note that he leaves the village to go hunting in the forest, the social activity that most enhances a man's valour. The arrows with which he hunts are also a male sexual symbol as can be seen, for example, from the proverb *bánaogoba nsóa k'óngipho*, 'one does not use up one's arrows on *ongíphó* ants'. This serves as advice to a man to marry, or to take a second wife, rather than to run after all women. The *ongíphó* ants are a symbol of voracity (they are given the foreskin of the circumcised to devour) and of uselessness. It may thus be said that, by virtue of its association with the name *Atóá-opho*, and its meaning, the arrow represents the one who shoots it and goes in his name to fetch from above the model of circumcision. Indeed, whereas the spear is the instrument for hunting at ground level, the bow is only drawn upwards, while hunting monkeys and other animals living or nesting in trees.

The name *Boso* does not seem to have any special meaning, but *Obondoba*, from where the man originates, has one: it is the name of the legendary village of the uncircumcised. Now, in Komo society, the latter are part of the category of women (de Mahieu, 1980: p. 27). Furthermore, the antisocial practices of sorcery to which *Boso* devoted himself identify him still more with this category. Women being considered as inverted beings, in the culture of the Komo as in many others (cf. Rosaldo, 1974: pp. 31–8; Hoch-Smith and Spring, 1978: p. 21), it is especially to them that the representations link such practices, as also the beginning of sorcery, even though in principle anybody can be considered a sorcerer (de Mahieu, 1979: pp. 22–3, 27–9). The descent in a basket under water completes the identification. There is, indeed, a saying *koboko ńàotamba na djo*, 'virility does not walk along with a basket'. As an essential female implement, the basket, used here to carry *Boso* through the water, constitutes the perfect inversion of the ascending arrow, just as sorcery does for hunting.

After hunting, *Atóá-opho* comes back to the village and acquaints his fathers with the revelation while *Boso* is brought back by his aunt to the field of a woman – his wife – and is discovered by her. The principle of transposition of sexes is thus continued. Moreover, in many rites and in the representations of the Komo, the erect trunks of trees, called *kákálá* or *ntémá*, express or mediate contact with the ancestors, so that the fallen trunk upon which *Nkayá*, the paternal ancestor, makes *Boso* sit at the moment of his return to earth seems to mark the end of the contact with the ancestors and the taking up again of relations with human beings. Indeed, the same image comes back with a similar meaning in many other myths that give account, among the Komo, of the origin of a rite or of a clan.

An inversion of the opposition between the sexes marks the end of both myths. Where the female element predominates (i.e. in the second), circumcision is immediately applied to men, whereas in the other, with male predominance, it is first applied to a woman.

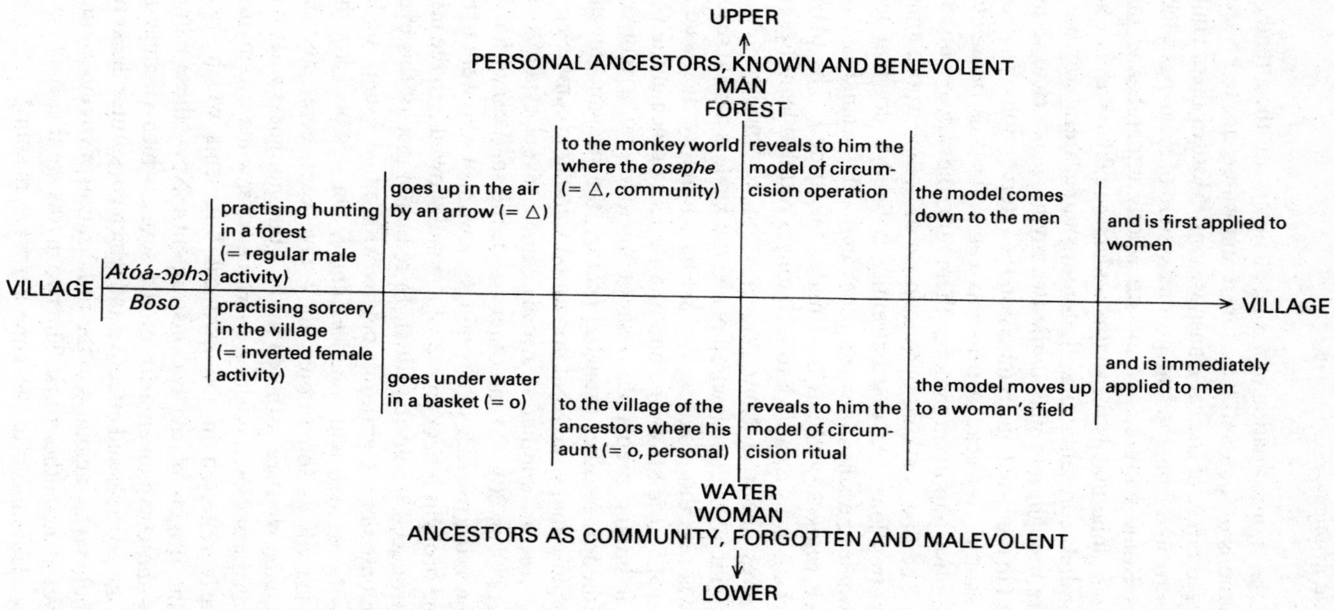

			PERSONAL ANCESTORS, KNOWN AND BENEVOLENT MAN FOREST		UPPER ↑ VILLAGE → VILLAGE
Atóá-ɔphɔ	practising hunting in a forest (= regular male activity)	goes up in the air by an arrow (= △)	to the monkey world where the *osephe* community (= △,)	reveals to him the model of circumcision operation	the model comes down to the men	and is first applied to women
Boso	practising sorcery in the village (= inverted female activity)	goes under water in a basket (= o)	to the village of the ancestors where his aunt (= o, personal)	reveals to him the model of circumcision ritual	the model moves up to a woman's field	and is immediately applied to men
			WATER WOMAN ANCESTORS AS COMMUNITY, FORGOTTEN AND MALEVOLENT LOWER ↓		

VILLAGE

Figure 3.1 *Transformational structure of the two Komo circumcision myths*

93

Neither the transformation of sexual elements nor the attendant transformations of high and low, forest and water, are to be seen as the simple effect of logical transpositions. Most of them could only be discovered from the background system of meanings which constitutes Komo culture, and all are wholly integrated in that system. This alone makes the myths understandable. This is what certain parallel representations, that nourish in a lateral way those which were brought into play in the two myths, make clear to us.

One sees in the ritual of circumcision the intervention of a whole series of esoteric musical instruments categorized as *bansémbé*. The two most important among them are the *kabíe* and the *mokumo*. The first is a kind of flute made of hollow wood, about 15 centimetres long. At one extremity is fixed a dry leaf that vibrates when one sings into the other end. The second is a big snail conch (*mokéké*) that is held under the armpit. The player makes it clang by using a stick to hit a longer rod that leans against it; he moves the rod from one position to another. As a representation of the circumcised penis, the *kabíe* is a male sexual symbol, whereas the *mokumo* represents femininity. It is said of the former that it fell from the end of a straight branch at the very moment a hunter prepared to shoot an arrow at a monkey. Distinguished from other branches (*ntábe*), the straight branches (*nkolo*) – those that stretch out horizontally and help climbers pass from one tree to another – are also male sexual symbols (de Mahieu, 1980: p. 20). On the other hand, the snail conch for the *mokumo* was discovered, so it is said, by a woman who went to the water. She brought it back to the village and showed it to the men. These introduced it into the ritual. In remembrance of this event every circumcision celebration begins with ritual fishing undertaken by the women and called *mangé*. On this occasion they bring to the village some object they have kept secret, and they make the men who are gathered in the ritual hut guess what it is.

The transformational position in which we saw the two myths is thus clearly reflected in the mythical fragments which try to explain the origins of the two instruments. Now, these express primarily the complementarity of the sexes, which circumcision has to make possible and effective and which constitutes the kernel of the whole set of meanings in the ritualization of circumcision, as I will develop in another work. The two myths are thus only one of the many elaborations of the same kernel of meaning.

I would like, by way of conclusion, to reflect on the modalities of this elaboration, as they proceed from this analysis and as opposed to the transformational principles of the structural way of thinking called to mind at the start.

Conclusion

As a rite of passage, circumcision certainly has a very specific function in Komo society. It assures transition from one age group to another, while maintaining between them a clear distinction. However, as has been pointed out, affirmations of this kind have a tautological character (cf. Abrahamson, 1978: pp. 39–40; Vizedom, 1976: p. 32). The fundamental meaning of circumcision for the Komo can only be understood relative to the manner in which they conceive themselves, their society and the world, and it is this meaning that is unfolded in the whole ritual and mythical elaboration of the operation itself.

This conception, at least in certain of its aspects, amounts to an all-pervading complementarity of sexes, the key to which is circumcision. This complementarity is transposed, in a metaphorical way, into other domains of the phenomeno-cultural reality, to the extent to which the latter lend themselves to such a transposition by presenting also a complementary structure, or at least by being experienced as presenting it. Such are, for instance, the cosmological domain, with its oppositions between upper and lower, earth/forest and water, the domain of the working tools, that of the musical instruments, etc. Some elements of these domains have been taken together and combined so as to form two myths that offer thus a transformational structure. By this it can clearly be seen that Eco's view of these relations is incorrect: we are not dealing here with single signifiers which in a continuous chain call upon each other in turn in order to give one another sign value, thus converting progressively the whole physical and cultural environment into a system of signs (Eco, 1973: pp. 57, 71; 1975: pp. 12–15; 1977: pp. 21–8). Instead, it is *some fundamental structures of meaning that project themselves* beyond themselves in all directions. The process called 'generative semantics' in transformational linguistics (Nique, 1974: pp. 160–8; Lyons, 1977: pp. 409–22), and extended to the anthropological domain by some authors (cf. Crick, 1976: p. 96; Ardener, 1971a; 1978), is thus rejoined but at a different level. At the same time it can be seen how these oppositional projections or transformations *are not a mere logic game capable of being expressed in anthropological categories*, but rather constitute a systematic occupation of the semantic space offered and carried by a culture and have thus to be rendered in terms of that culture.

As stated before, these metaphorizations, when occupying semantic space, need not always appear in the form of some clear-cut dualistic opposition (cf. Needham, 1973: pp. xxv–xxix). For instance, at the moment of their investiture, the holders of the circumcision ritual of the Komo are given a wooden necklace around which the tail of an *osephe* monkey is wound and on which hangs the skin of the *bungú* squirrel. This necklace recalls clearly the part of the myth according to which the monkey that walked along a branch was circumcised by a squirrel hidden under it, so that there is even doubt whether the shape of the necklace originated in the myth or the reverse. In a global system of meanings I think the answer is not so important. I only want to point out that the other myth does not have such a transposition at the level of garment attributes.

On the other hand, to the extent to which the entire system of meanings stays dynamic, the process of oppositional projection itself sometimes creates new problems or contradictions that need to be resolved as far as is possible. I have mentioned two of them. They concerned the double qualification of the ancestors: personal and benevolent when situated above; communitarian and malevolent when below. In each of these cases one of the qualifications militated in favour of the revelation of the ritual, while the other opposed it. With their semantic connotations the *osephe* monkey and the paternal aunt were destined, as we saw, to solve the contradiction. Nevertheless, a new difficulty is created by the culturally inverted position of the woman by whom the revelation was made, and the antisocial activities of sorcery in which Boso indulged. These elements risk throwing discredit on circumcision. It is by insisting on the fact that this revelation was made to a sorcerer so as to let him make reparation by redeeming his debts, that the second myth tries to absolve itself from these negative connotations.

Finally, if circumcision has a function within Komo society, the process of metaphorization that constitutes the significative elaboration of it could well have a function with regard to circumcision; at least, when we agree with Augé (1978) that function is 'in' meaning. Indeed, this metaphorization increases to cosmological dimensions both circumcision and the effective complementarity of the sexes to which it gives access. Through this it integrates circumcision into the conceptual universe of the Komo and, at the same time, unifies this universe. Thereby, this metaphorization with its transformational aspects not only *produces meaning*, but it is really a constituent part of the culture itself; and as far as a culture may be conceived of as a system of meanings (cf. Geertz, 1975: pp. 5, 89; Sahlins, 1976: p. x) it is also *fully necessary* at the level of culture – a necessity which is, of course, an internal one. Moreover, this same process implies an opening or a constant appeal to other domains of reality; and since the domain of significative references in which each of the two myths culminates is nothing but the extra-human world of the ancestors, the final meaning of this metaphorization could be to confer on circumcision its transcendent or religious dimension.

Notes

1 I would like to thank Matthew Schoffeleers for the insightful criticisms and suggestions he was willing to make on an earlier version of this paper.
2 Other tranformationalists, less anxious than Chomsky to maintain a distinction between syntactic and semantic analysis – in order that they may be able to answer the objection made to the latter that it is impossible to judge the accuracy of a transformed proposition without having recourse to its meaning (Mounin, 1968: pp. 120–1) – attribute a semantic dimension to deep structures. But for them, too, the transformations of these structures do not alter their meaning. This latter lies at their basis. That is why this orientation is called 'generative semantics' (Nique, 1974: pp. 160–9; Lyons, 1977: pp. 409–22).
3 Lévi-Strauss admits, however, that, from one culture to another, a transformation can entail an inversion of the message (1964: pp. 205, 207). Courtès (1973: pp. 103–22) shows exactly how the discovery of this fact can only result from a syntagmatic reading of the transformation, which completes its paradigmatic reading and allows the retrieval of divergences of a semantic order, that Lévi-Strauss has to take into account, in spite of his fundamental orientations.

4 Other authors have been interested in the analysis of myths under their transformational dimension. The principal contributions in this domain come first from Buchler and Selby who, ten years ago, showed how the epistemological principles that fed the analyses of Lévi-Strauss were just the same as those that lie at the basis of the Chomskyan generative grammar, in the sense that the variants of a myth are to be seen as different transformations of deep structures (Buchler and Selby, 1968: pp. 25, 28–39). Inspired by the 'connectivity analysis' borrowed from historical geography, Buchler and Selby searched for a stronger formalization for the study of transformations of myths passing from one cultural complex to another, but without giving attention to the reintegration of these myths in the cultural systems of meaning that carry them. Segal (1972) compares three myths that, rather than constituting structural transformations, are variants of a single topic. His semantic approach consists above all in drawing out the meaning of the varying dispositions of identical mythemes ('predicates') (cf. Segal, 1972: p. 217). Ikegami (1978) shows how the semantic structure proper to certain verbs helps to explain the transformations to which narratives have been submitted, but, like Buchler and Selby, he stays at the level of a formal analysis of abstract meanings. Yet the richest contribution, even if the theoretical side is not developed, and the one in which the author passes fully beyond the method of Lévi-Strauss, though he claims to follow him, is from Charachidzé (1979). Starting from the cosmology of the Georgians, he studies a transformation of the Promethean myth found among them. Nevertheless, the transformation itself is not situated at the level of Amirani's myth, the counterpart of that of Prometheus.

References

Abrahamson, M. (1978), *Functionalism*, Englewood Cliffs, NJ: Prentice-Hall.

Ardener, Edwin (1971a), introductory essay, in E. Ardener (ed.), *Social Anthropology and Language*, London: Tavistock (ASA Monograph 10), pp. ix–cii.

Ardener, Edwin (1971b), 'The New Anthropology and its Critics', *Man*, (n.s.), 6: pp. 449–67.

Ardener, Edwin (1978), 'Some Outstanding Problems in the Analysis of Events', in E. Schwimmer (ed.), *Yearbook of Symbolic Anthropology*, *I*, London: C. Hurst, pp. 103–21.

Augé, M. (1978), 'Vers un refus de l'alternative sens-fonction', *L'Homme*, **18**, 3–4: pp. 139–54.

Badcock, C. (1975), *Lévi-Strauss: Structuralism and Sociological Theory*, London: Hutchinson.

Basso, K. (1976), 'Wise Words of the Western Apache: Metaphor and Semantic Theory', in K. Basso and H. A. Selby (eds), *Meaning in*

Anthropology, Albuquerque: University of New Mexico Press, pp. 93–121.

Buchler, I. R., and Selby, H. A. (1968), *A Formal Study of Myth*, Austin: University of Texas Press.

Charachidzé, G. (1979), 'L'Aigle en clé d'eau: un exemple d'inversion conservante', in M. Izard and P. Smith (eds), *La Fonction symbolique: essais d'anthropologie*, Paris: Gallimard.

Chomsky, Noah (1957), *Syntactic Structures*, The Hague: Mouton.

Cohen, D. (1969), 'Theories of Myth', *Man* (n.s.), 4: pp. 337–59.

Courtès, J. (1973), *Lévi-Strauss et les contraintes de la pensée mythique*, Tours: Mame.

Crick, Malcolm (1976), *Explorations in Language and Meaning: Towards a Semantic Anthropology*, London: Malaby.

Ducrot, O., and Todorov, T. (1972), *Dictionnaire encyclopédique des sciences du language*, Paris: Seuil.

Ducrot, O.; Todorov, T.; Sperber, D.; Safouan, M.; Wahl, F. (1968), *Qu'est-ce que le structuralisme?*, Paris: Seuil.

Eco, U. (1973), 'Social Life as a Sign System', in D. Robey (ed.), *Structuralism*, Oxford: Clarendon Press, pp. 52–72.

Eco, U. (1975), 'Looking for a Logic of Culture', in T. Sebeok (ed.), *The Tell-Tale Sign*, Lisse: Peter de Ridder Press, pp. 9–17.

Eco, U. (1977), *A Theory of Semiotics*, London: Macmillan.

Geertz, Clifford (1975), *The Interpretation of Cultures*, London: Hutchinson, New York: Basic Books, 1973.

Gregersen, E. (1977), 'Linguistic Models in Anthropology', in W. McCormack and S. Wurm (eds), *Language and Thought: Anthropological Issues*, The Hague: Mouton.

Harris, Z. (1957), 'Co-occurrence and Transformation in Linguistic Structure', *Language*, 33: pp. 283–340.

Heelas, P. (1977), 'Intra-religious Explanations', *JASO*, 8: pp. 1–16.

Hoch-Smith, J., and Spring, A. (1978), 'Introduction', in J. Hoch-Smith and A. Spring (eds), *Women in Ritual and Symbolic Roles*, New York: Plenum Press, pp. 1–23.

Ikegami, Y. (1977), '"Meaning" for the Linguist and "Meaning" for the Anthropologist', in W. McCormack and S. Wurm (eds), *Language and Thought: Anthropological Issues*, The Hague: Mouton, pp. 69–85.

Ikegami, Y. (1978), 'A Linguistic Model for Narrative Analysis', in M. D. Loflin and J. Silverberg (eds), *Discourse and Inference in Cognitive Anthropology*, The Hague, Mouton, pp. 111–34.

Keesing, R. (1972), 'Paradigms Lost: The New Ethnography and the New Linguistics', *Southwestern Journal of Anthropology*, 28: pp. 299–332.

Keesing, R. (1979), 'Linguistic Knowledge and Cultural Knowledge: Some Doubts and Speculations', *American Anthropologist*, 81: pp. 14–36.

Kronenfeld, D., and Decker, H. (1979), 'Structuralism', in B. J. Siegel, A. R. Beals, and S. A. Tyler (eds), *Annual Review of Anthropology*, Palo Alto, Calif., pp. 503–41.

Leach, E. (1976), *Culture and Communication: The Logic by Which*

   Symbols are Connected, Cambridge: Cambridge University Press.
Lévi-Strauss, C. (1958), *Anthropologie structurale*, Paris: Plon.
Lévi-Strauss, C. (1964), *Le Cru et le cuit*, Paris: Plon.
Lévi-Strauss, C. (1966), *Du miel aux cendres*, Paris: Plon.
Lévi-Strauss, C. (1973), *Anthropologie structurale deux*, Paris: Plon.
Lyons, J. (1977), *Semantics*, Cambridge: Cambridge University Press.
Mahieu, W. de (1973), 'Het Komo Masker: Oorsprong en Functie',
   Africa-Tervuren, 19: pp. 29–32.
Mahieu, W. de (1975), 'Cosmologie et structuration de l'espace chez les
   Komo', *Africa*, **45**, 2: pp. 123–38; **45**, 3: pp. 236–57.
Mahieu, W. de, and Devisch, R. (1979), *Mort, deuil et compensations
   mortuaires chez les Komo et les Yaka du Nord au Zaïre*, Tervuren:
   Annales du MRAC, Sc. Hum. 96.
Mahieu, W. de (1980), *Structures et symboles: les structures sociales du
   groupe Komo dans leur élaboration symbolique*, London: International
   African Institute; and Leuven: University Press.
Marc-Lipiansky, M. (1973), *Le Structuralisme de Lévi-Strauss*, Paris:
   Payot.
Mounin, G. (1968), *Clefs pour la linguistique*, Paris: Seghers.
Mounin, G. (1970), *Introduction à la sémiologie*, Paris: Minuit.
Mounin, G. (1975), *Linguistique et philosophie*, Paris: Presses Universi-
   taires de France.
Nathhorst, B. (1970), *Formal or Structural Studies of Traditional Tales*,
   Stockholm: Kungl Boktryckeriet P.A. Norstedt & Söner.
Needham, Rodney (ed.) (1973), *Right and Left: Essays on Dual Symbolic
   Classification*, Chicago: University of Chicago Press.
Nique, C. (1974), *Initiation méthodique à la grammaire générative*, Paris:
   A. Colin.
Piaget, J. (1968), *Le Structuralisme*, Paris: Presses Universitaires de
   France.
Rosaldo, M. Zimbalist (1974), 'Women, Culture and Society: A Theoreti-
   cal Overview', in M. Zimbalist Rosaldo and L. Lamphere (eds),
   Women, Culture and Society, Palo Alto, Calif.: Stanford University
   Press, pp. 17–42.
Sahlins, Marshall (1976), *Culture and Practical Reason*, Chicago: Univer-
   sity of Chicago Press.
Segal, D. (1972), 'The Connection Between the Semantics and the Formal
   Structure of a Text', in P. Maranda (ed.), *Mythology*, Harmonds-
   worth, Middx: Penguin, pp. 215–49.
Sperber, D. (1968), 'Le Structuralisme en Anthropologie', in Ducrot *et al.*
   (1968), pp. 167–238.
Strenski, I. (1974), 'Falsifying Deep Structures', *Man* (n.s.), 9: pp.
   571–84.
Vizedom, M. (1976), *Rites and Relationships: Rites of Passage and
   Contemporary Anthropology*, London: Sage.

Chapter 4

From waste-making to recycling: A plea for an eclectic use of models in the study of religious change[1]

André Droogers

> I don't pretend at all that, because I think that way, I am entitled to conclude that mankind thinks that way too. But I believe that, for each scholar and each writer, the particular way he or she thinks and writes opens a new outlook on mankind. And the fact that I personally have this idiosyncrasy perhaps entitles me to point to something which is valid, while the way in which my colleagues think opens different outlooks, all of which are equally valid.
>
> Claude Lévi-Strauss (1978: p. 4)

Introduction

The call for a new approach to the study of religious change may be heard again and again (van Binsbergen, 1976: p. 203; van Binsbergen and Buijtenhuijs, 1976: p. 10; Welbourn in La Barre, 1971: p. 34). The purpose of this paper is to suggest that we should not regard models as mutually exclusive but as inclusive.[2] We must not, therefore, do away with the existing models too quickly. The new approach must be eclectic: recycling of models should take the place of the present waste-making.

In the first part of this article the notion of model will be discussed because of its relevance to the eclectic plea. In generating knowledge a model is selective. As models play a central role in the scientific process the insight gained through that process is partial. For eclectic purposes a meta-model, a model of models, is needed. The semantic model, depicting man as a meaning-maker, will serve as such a meta-model. This model will be shown to be a necessary complement to models which explain from utility, and also as logically prior to them (cf. Sahlins, 1976).

In the second part of the article specific approaches to the study of religious change in Africa – though not exclusively Africa – will be discussed in the light of the conclusions of the first part. The richness and complexity of the data will only be fully appreciated if more models are brought to the analysis.

Models

Definition and typology

It is very useful to explore the concept of model as this excursion will allow us to show what the various approaches to the study of religious change have in common *as models*.

The history of the concept of model is in itself an illustration of the complementarity of the work done by various scholars.[3] Initially, competing views were given on the definition, function and typology of models. Later on most of these ideas have been integrated into a more complex synthesis.

Several options were available. Thus a model has been seen as an intermediate station between reality and theory, or as a simplified version of a theory, or as an application of a theory. It has accordingly been considered as a *heuristic* instrument helping in provisionally formulating knowledge, or as a *didactic* instrument representing in a simple manner a complex theory while sharing its predictive quality, or as a *constructive* instrument used to manipulate, control and change reality on the basis of a theoretical view of that reality. Some have considered the model too crude an instrument and have therefore rejected its use in scientific work, others have reserved the term exclusively for the type of knowledge obtained through scientific work, while others have used the word 'model' as in both common-sense and scientific thinking.

Model has been seen as of the same nature as the reality which it represents, as when the changes in one religion are considered to be a model for the study of changes in another religion (Peel, 1973). On the other hand, models were said to differ in nature from the reality for which they stand, as when a social process is represented by a physical process. A third type is formed by abstract models, which are not taken from reality, but exist only in the mind of the researcher.

Caws offers an example of the synthesis I alluded to and it is useful to quote at length from his article as it is fundamental to the problems under discussion here:

> If we adopt the definition of *system* as a set of *entities* mutually interrelated and interdependent, themselves functioning to-gether as an entity at some higher level of organization, and of *structure* as a set of systematic *relations*, concrete if embodied in an actual system, abstract if merely specified but not so embodied, then the notion of a *model* can be defined as follows: an abstract structure is a model if it stands for a homologous concrete structure, a concrete structure is a model if it stands for a homologous concrete structure differently embodied. By 'stands for' I mean that the features of the model are substituted for features of the structure whose model it is, for purposes of presentation, or instruction, or explanation, or imaginative variation, or computation, or prediction. There need be no preferential direction of the relationship model/modelled: a theory according to one familiar view is a model of the aspects of the world with which it deals, in that we can work out the behavior of those aspects in theory without having to realize them in practice, in the confidence nevertheless that that is how it would happen in practice; but on the other hand, a perfectly concrete object (an orrery for example) can be a model for a theory, and so can another theory. To make the structural features of the model central reflects the fact that it stands for the relationships between the entities that constitute the system, rather than for the entities themselves. (Caws, 1974: p. 1)

A further echo from the history of the concept of model may be heard in Caws's distinction between representational and oper-ational models: 'The representational model corresponds to the way the individual thinks things are, the operational model to the way he practically responds or acts' (Caws, 1974: p. 3; cf. Bertels and Nauta, 1969: pp. 120–128). The individual in question is the anthropologist's informant. The anthropologist himself reports by means of *his* representational model for which Caws coins the term 'explanatory model' (Caws, 1974: p. 5) in order to distinguish common-sense views from scientific views.

In this approach both the anthropologist and his informant are seen as model-builders. In my view they are only able to build models because of the unique human capacity to create symbols, i.e. to see one thing as standing for another: 'The creation of meaning is the distinguishing and constituting quality of man . . . such that . . . relations among men, as well as between themselves and nature, are organized' (Sahlins, 1976: p. 102). While the positive sciences have objects of study, the social sciences may be said to have subjects of study. In establishing explanatory models the anthropologist takes his informants' representational and operational models into account.

Especially in the case of religious change, both scholars and informants are engaged in the process of understanding new phenomena through the creation of models. Both may then seek to make converts.[4] Both the scholars' and the informants' models make statements on the behaviour in time and space of men in relation to each other, to nature, and to a non-empirically verifiable reality of supernatural beings. Because our field of study is itself already full of model-builders, our work is more complex and it is virtually impossible to present things as they really are. 'In human studies objectivity is a type of disciplined intersubjectivity' (Crick, 1976: p. 167). Reality is always interpreted reality. Reality in the social sciences is twice interpreted reality. This should make us modest about the value of the models we produce.

Another insight given to us in the long quotation from Caws's article regards the relation between model and theory. They are shown not to be mutually exclusive but complementary notions, working on different levels, and having a different status. By using the notion of model the setting becomes the process of obtaining and transmitting knowledge. The notion of model takes us away from the established, abstract, sometimes static and petrified theory to the process of developing and amending scientific knowledge. For the purposes of this article, emphasis on the concept of model is inevitable. That concept will therefore be used even though sometimes it is meant as an alternative – perhaps with different functions – to theory. Not all models are theories, but all theories may be said to need models in order to be formulated or understood. If a theory becomes more than a model of an observable relationship, it takes the form of an *a priori* statement (Blok, 1976: pp. 50–1; cf. Bertels and Nauta, 1969: p. 159).

Caws's distinction between operational, representational and explanatory models offers a first typology of models. In fact, a double distinction is made: between informants' and anthropologists' models, between models of action and models of communication.[5]

A typology of models may also be based on the various functions models may have. As we saw, Caws mentions a number of these purposes: 'presentation, or instruction, or explanation, or imaginative variation, or computation, or prediction' (Caws, 1974: p. 1). One might add the functions of exploration and manipulation. In fact, this typology reflects the various stages of the process of scientific research. The representational model and the operational model have different functions (Bertels and Nauta, 1969: pp. 120–5). Representational models, whether developed by the informant or by the researcher, either serve heuristic purposes in the process of exploration, or reduce reality to describable proportions, or help to explain and predict. Operational models help to make reality manipulable.

Another distinction which will be of use for the purpose of this article is that between universal models valid for the whole of mankind, and specific models developed in the study of one or more cultures. The criterion is the pretension of validity claimed by the author of the model.

Following Sahlins (1976), a final distinction has to be made between models explaining from practical reasons or utilitarian interests, and models which explain from cultural reasons, acknowledging man's activity as a meaning-maker and the relative inner logic of the various symbolic systems which are the result of this activity (Crick, 1976: p. 3). The first type offers a statement on praxis or utility, the second on man's symbolling activity presupposed in that praxis or rational action (cf. Sahlins, 1976: pp. vii, 3, 54). In the first type of model symbols merely represent or reflect, in the second type symbols are used to classify and organize (Sahlins, 1976: p. 70). Thus classic functionalism, as an example of a utilitarian model, 'refuses to concede to any opacity in the cultural system, let alone attempt to understand its inherent logic. Whole areas of culture thus escape a functionalist explication, since th ey make no apparent practical sense' (Sahlins, 1976: p. 75). The option is between functional truth or meaningful content (Sahlins, 1976: p. 88).

Biased knowledge

Models involve substitution. A model stands for a homologous structure. A comparison is made. Comparison involves selection and reduction. A limited number of features is selected and serves as a guide in the comparison. Others are left out of consideration. Different people may select different features. If the model and the modelled are of the same nature and therefore categorically close, the criteria selected for the comparison seem to reduce – though not exclude – the risk of making irrelevant statements. If model and modelled differ in nature, this risk seems to be greater, as the number of possible models is incomparably larger. The use of the model seems less convincing and the presuppositions involved are far more hazardous. Besides, the more complex the reality under study is, the more risky the comparison through models will prove to be, as the selected characteristics then form only a minor portion of the available features.

Models, nevertheless, are often reified, and identified with reality. We then overlook the fact that a comparison is never total and complete. 'No map is ever equal to the world' (La Barre, 1971: p. 27). The most perfect map is identical to the landscape and therefore loses its utility (Bertels and Nauta, 1969: p. 147). An unlimited number of maps may be drawn.

Models, while opening up a certain part of reality, at the same time neglect those parts of reality that do not fit in. Comparisons never are on all fours. The strength of each model is therefore the complement of the others (Sahlins, 1976: p. 39). Models favour one-sidedness. We run the risk of being blind to those phenomena for which we have no eye-opening model. This is the price we have to pay for understanding.

Therefore, even models with pretensions of universal validity inevitably take only a part of the universal reality into account. In polemics between competing models the impression is often given that they are referring to the same reality. There is a fair chance that this is in fact not the case and that the competing models put different questions to different selections from reality. For this reason, too, it is important to know which area or society was studied when a certain model was developed. Our field is intercultural, so there is enough variation and there are enough translation problems between our culture and the one studied to produce more models and to keep us busy for several decades to come, especially if we ignore the eclectic plea. Then we will continue to create from the chaos of culturally divergent meanings our own new 'tunnel visions' (La Barre, 1971: p. 26). New schools and -isms will be founded, new maxims will be invented as a shorthand for these new -isms. The theoretical ships will continue to pass in the night (cf. Sahlins, 1976: p. 10).

A discussion between competing models is, furthermore, complicated by the fact that in advocating one's own model the danger of circular reasoning is present when it is forgotten that presuppositions determine the selection of features of the model. The model is considered to be of value just because reality – in fact, a part of reality – is shown to be homologous to the model. Subsequently the impression is given that the presuppositions are true because the model is matched by reality. What is presented as explanation is in fact only exploration (Homans, 1973: p. 54; Manyoni, 1977: pp. 601, 628). A man with blue glasses will maintain that the world is blue, another man with yellow glasses is convinced that the world is yellow, and they will never agree unless they are ready to take off their glasses, if only for a minute.

The difficult process of translating general theoretical questions into fieldwork questions should make one conscious of the distance between presuppositions and the reality under study. Models sometimes tend to be black-box models: it is only clear what is put into it – e.g. social or economic change – and what comes out – e.g. religious change – but what happens inside the black box is not clear.

In discussing the role of presuppositions attention must also be given to the idiosyncrasy of the author of a model. Often models tell us as much about the author as about the subject under study. Models may be self-portraits of the author and the society in which he lives. 'The anthropologist's "etic" is his own society's "emic"' (Sahlins, 1976: p. 75). In reviewing models on religion and religious change one sometimes wonders: whose world view is being discussed? In an implicit or sometimes even explicit way, the

academic, social, political or religious position of the author plays
a role in the substance of his theory.[6] We all cannot help but look
first and foremost for those facts we have been trained or even
conditioned to look for. 'Too often the "essence" of millenarianism has turned out to be the essence of the discipline from which
the observer has come' (Barkun, 1974: pp. 3, 4,). Non-scientific
factors influence our work. 'We, too, are influenced by jealousy,
lust, magical notions, status seeking, generosity, etc., even in our
most scientific moments' (Worsley, 1968: p. xxvi).

Within the scientific subculture, certain customs facilitate the
proclamation of absolute claims. The academic world seems to
give more prestige to builders of new theories than to patient
ethnographers. While there is a tendency to welcome cumulation
of ethnographic material, cumulation in the theoretical field is less
popular. Not infrequently, a new model is presented as being
exclusive and general.[7] Conditions which are at best only efficient
are presented as sufficient and final. The euphoric 'Entdeckungs-
freude', the joy once a new insight has been gained, tends to
provide scholars with blinkers. Consciously or unconsciously
following the example of the positive sciences, many model-
builders strive for universally applicable theories. Presuppositions
on supposedly universal biological, social and economic needs or
other general characterstics of man and society (cf. Sahlins, 1976:
pp. 77, 78) lead scholars to models with pretensions of universal
validity. As we shall see, these models cannot help but fail to
explain specific non-universal phenomena, proper to a local
culture.

A familiar way of presenting a new model is to start with a
devastating critique of the work of one's predecessors in the field.
Subsequently, a new road to salvation is presented to all readers
who feel lost and confused after this Last Judgment. Paradigm
lost, paradigm regained. The exploitation – and also the criticism –
of a single model may easily fill a scholar's life. Exceptions, even
only one, observed among the BongoBongo (Douglas, 1973: pp.
15, 16) are enough to refute other models totally. Often the
production of a new model reveals the blindness of its author to a
basic dualism in the options the social sciences are confronted
with. An exclusive model is often a glorification of one pole of an
opposition, starting with a critique of advocates of the other pole.
There may, for example, be a one-sided interest either in the

active individual or in an autonomous society, in continuity or in change, in order or in conflict, in external or in internal conditions, in genesis or in persistence (cf. Wallace, 1969b). Rarely is this dualism used as a source of inspiration for the dialectic integration of models. Yet it cannot be accidental. It seems that our culture, like so many others, is impregnated by dualism. It is our capital and we should work with it, whether we like it or not. Each redefinition of a model should therefore be complementary to most of the preceding definitions, instead of annihilating them.[8]

The more we create our own academic waste-making society, the more we shall have to look for a way to recycle the muddle of models we have left along the road. It would behove us to be more modest about the claims of our models. Much would be won if we became more conscious of the selective nature of our models. There is a great diversity within the religious field and within the African continent with its thousand or more ways of life, and with its variations between rural and urban areas (cf. Peel, 1973: pp. 341–4). The multivocality of meanings in this field necessitates an approach which is open to as many aspects as possible. The building of religious change in Africa has many entrances.

Eclectic use of models

In view of the fact that every model justifies itself ultimately by means of its own presuppositions and judges other models by its own criteria, a frame of reference for the objective comparison of models seems to be lacking. An eclectic use of models, however, is impossible without a meta-model above the existing models. Such a meta-model should be a model of models, summarizing the features all the available models have in common.

As was suggested above, the starting-point of such a meta-model might be found in the capacity which anthropologist and informant share, i.e. culture, the human capacity to create and recreate meaning in great variety. The diversity of cultures finds its parallel in the diversity of models. Because it encompasses both researcher and researched, this model of man as a meaning-maker is not just a model, standing in dualist opposition to or complementing another model, but it is a fundamental model, logically prior to any other model. Therefore this model cannot be compromised (Sahlins, 1976: p. 55). It is a meta-model.

In the preceding paragraphs an effort was made to show how models generate meaning. The observations we then made will help us to decide which aspects we will have to pay attention to if we want to make an eclectic use of models current in the study of religious change. The following questions may be asked when reviewing a model:

Which presuppositions determine the selection of features?
To which structure in society does the model give special attention, and which structures are neglected?
Is the frame of reference practical or cultural reason?
What place is given to informants' models?
Are the model and the modelled of the same or of a different nature?
Is the model about genesis or about persistence?
Does the model have a general or a specific origin and claim?
In which phase of the scientific process may the model be used and which function does it accordingly have?

In answering these questions it must be possible to discover the merits as well as the shortcomings of each model, and to show in which way these models are complementary.

Yet for our inquiry into the value of the various models, it is not enough to compare these models *as models*. The final question must be in how far these models open our eyes to the field we study. Are there areas which escape explanation? We touch here on the problem of the hermeneutic circle.[9] We should select our facts as a function of our models and expand our models as a function of our facts. This is no easy method to work with. We enter the field with our theoretical first chapter written in a provisional version, if only for the financing organization. When we return to our desks – or even before – we have to rewrite it. Again and again we must be open to amendments of our models when we confront them with the informants' representational and operational models and with our own observations. If we do not pay enough attention to our field, the study of African religions, we might as well rename our speciality. Having made our methodological options, 'let us proceed and see where they take us. Methodology should not be allowed to become an aim in itself' (van Binsbergen, 1981: p. 22).

Respect for our field of research urges us finally to deal with some misunderstandings which might be evoked by a purely methodological plea for an eclectic approach. Our data, even if they have been collected with more than one model in mind, may be of such a specific nature that the use of one model remains the best way to deal with the matter. This will especially be the case if the problem under study is narrowly limited and highly specific in that it deals with a part of social reality for which a certain model, partial as it is, has special relevance and interest. Eclecticism must not have as a consequence that specific problems are neglected.

Neither would it be wise to apply the eclectic approach so consistently that the development of new models or the amending of existing models is avoided. And consequently it goes without saying that eclecticism would fail if *all* models, just because they are models, were to be integrated in its approach. The comparison of models, in the frame of reference of a meta-model (also through the mutual criticism between models), is, on the contrary, a good occasion to find out what is useful and what is certainly not, for an understanding of the phenomena under study.

The eclectic approach in the study of religious change

Introductory remarks

The following discussion of the models which have been advanced for the study of religious change will be guided by the meta-model referred to in the preceding pages. In the context of this article it is impossible to do justice to the details of these models. Yet I trust that the meta-model will help us to summarize and compare these models, especially because it reveals the essential features of models.

A large part of the literature on religious change is devoted to religious movements. Institutionalized phenomena seem to be more suitable for observation. Besides, the political aspects these movements had – or were supposed to have – may have stimulated interest in them. The attention given to religious movements provides a link between the African situation and the other continents, as religious movements are not limited to Africa; neither, of course, is religious change.

111

The functionalist models[10]

The functionalist model focuses on society of which it has a holistic view. Society is seen as a system of interrelated parts. The relations between these parts are multiple, reciprocal and often causal. The system may be temporally out of balance, but it tends to an equilibrium. Consensus about values helps to keep the system intact. Conflict is abnormal and a deviation. If it occurs the system adapts itself in order to keep functioning. Changes occur, but not in an abrupt way. Change may be exogenous, a consequence of external influence. It may also be endogenous, through individual innovation, or through structural and functional differentiation of the system.

When this general model is applied to the study of religious change, it may take various forms. Most often the reasoning goes like this. Exogenous, i.e. Western influence causes disorder and stress. Religion helps society to adapt to the new situation. The moral order is restored or maintained via an appeal to old or new religious ideas. Whether traditional or new values are stressed, in either case they help to arrive at a new equilibrium. New values may be a mixture of traditional and imported values, or – rarely so – they may be purely imported, e.g. Christian values. Christianity thus may play a double role: trouble-maker and trouble-shooter. It is then part of the problem and part of the solution.

Sometimes the mechanism is said to have worked even before the colonial period, e.g. in the case of witch-finding movements (cf. M. Wilson, 1971: p. 43). M. Wilson's book *Religion and the Transformation of Society* (1971) offers an example of a functionalist model. Social change in colonial and post-independent Africa is a change in scale: both the number of interacting people and the closeness of their interaction are modified. This change in scale leads to more specialization and differentiation in the religious field. People have a greater choice, both outside and inside religion. Religion persists because it offers values which guide people in making choices. The bigger number of impersonal relations is reflected by a more impersonal view of causation. Though several traditional values continue to play an important role in the period of transition, ritual and the control of the environment become less magic and more symbolic. From her Christian point of view Wilson sees the change in scale as a positive phenomenon to which Christianity has contributed and in which it has a vocation to promote equality and tolerance. But a secular ideology, too, may have the function of offering values for the large-scale society. Pauw (1975) makes extensive use of Wilson's ideas in a study of religious change in Xhosa society.

Other variants of the functionalist model of religious change pay particular attention to the political function of religion, especially if religion takes the form of a religious movement. In these views religious movements as reactions to change are interpreted as nationalism in disguise, or as social protest, or as the ideological use of an invulnerable sacred institution or as political expression for want of democratic channels. Marx was a precursor of some of these interpretations when he wrote in 1844: '*Religious* suffering is at the same time an *expression* of real suffering and a *protest* against real suffering' (Tucker, 1978: p. 54; cf. Bastide, 1978: p. 1; Maduro, 1975a: p. 314). A movement may start as a purely religious movement, but in the course of time, under the impact of repression by the government, adopt political points of view.[11]

If the changes in society cause people to suffer heavily, religion may not only be used to create an island of consolation – either this- or other-worldly directed – in a sea of misery, but it may inspire the creation of an alternative, better society. Religion then helps to find not only new norms but also a new social structure. In that case, religion is not just an *expression* of anomy, but serves to find an effective *remedy*. In this variant of the model, a larger place is given to conflict and to the division of power in society. The consensus of values is mainly stressed in so far as it functions within the movement, instead of, as in the original model, in society as a whole. In recognizing the importance of conflict, this variant of the functionalist model is close to the Marxist model, as we will see.

In evaluating the variants of the functionalist model, the attention these models give to the effects religion may have in society may be positively valued. They have immensely stimulated research and provided the researcher with exploratory questions. The models may help to explain the place and moment of occurrence of religious movements. Every society needs a certain stability and order, otherwise people could not live in it. Once this is admitted, the role religion plays in these processes must be acknowledged. Especially if religion is important in the society in which the social changes occur, it may be understood that people use religious ideas in order to make sense of the changes they are confronted with. The social background of religion receives due attention.

But there are also important shortcomings and blind-spots. In fact, the social background is often the foreground. It is not religion which is explained, but the working of society. Even though it should be recognized that the religious and the social are mutually related, this does not necessarily lead to the conclusion that the religious is ultimately subservient to the social. 'One's explanation of society should not be mistaken for an explanation of religion, nor the sociological functions of religion for its basis and real nature' (Oosterwal in La Barre, 1971: p. 32).

One is reminded of the black box, because a detailed account of what is really happening when religion serves the social order is often lacking and the proof is only based on presuppositions about the functioning of society. Though M. Wilson, in some examples she gives, demonstrates the relation between social and religious change, 'change in scale' is just as often an indication of the time or the context in which religious changes occur. Jarvie (1963: p. 4), with respect to studies of cargo cults, spoke of the 'missing link' in the causal chain between unrest and cult. The direct relation between, on the one hand, the disorder and stress social change brings and, on the other hand, the religious reaction can frequently not be established on the basis of an examination of the ideas advanced by the participants in a movement. An exception is the case where an alternative society is promoted or created. But more often, especially in the purely religious movements, the political function does not show from the facts. In those cases the scholars give a show of ventriloquy with their supposed rational, but otherwise silent informants.[12]

The most important argument against the functionalist models, if they pretend to explain religion, is that they are not specific enough. This is the logical consequence of the application of a model with universal pretensions. Suprahuman society, with its universal needs, takes the place of the local human meaning-maker. The models hardly succeed in explaining why the reaction to social change takes a religious form, let alone why it takes the religious form it takes and no other. 'Why do we get cargo cults and not Mau Mau?' (Jarvie, 1963: p. 118). This flaw in the functionalist models is understandable because 'the nature of the effects cannot be read from the nature of the forces' (Sahlins, 1976: p. 206). The models are too rational and too utilitarian, thinking in means–ends relationships, and therefore they close their eyes to the non-utilitarian and irrational in religious change.

Similarly, because it emphasizes the religious contribution to cohesion, the functionalist approach fails to see that religious movements may also promote disintegration, and that, on the other hand, it is possible that movements occur without insta-bility.[13] Neither does it explain that often not the whole population takes part in a movement, or that, beside the masses under stress, elites may participate in a movement.

Barkun (1974) has shown how a failing functionalist model may be amended. As the eclectic approach refuses the outright rejection of a model, just because of its shortcomings, an effort to renovate a model must receive special interest. Therefore Barkun's contribution will be summarized here.

Barkun also raises the problem of the causal chain and suggests that social change, in itself, does not lead to stress.[14] If there is a relation between these phenomena, it is extremely complex and indirect. 'We wonder but are not told precisely what kind of stress must be involved, over how long a period of time, involving what proportion of the population. . . . How much is enough? How much relative deprivation is required to produce a particular effect?' (Barkun, 1974: pp. 39, 40). Stress may not even be a consequence of social change at all but may occur as a result of an adopted Western concept of stress (p. 47). Barkun, while maintaining that deprivation may play an important role, empha-sizes that other conditions must be prominent as well. In his opinion, for a religious reaction to occur,

> there must be multiple rather than single disasters; a body of
> ideas or doctrines of a millenarian cast must be readily
> available; a charismatic figure must be present to shape those
> doctrines in response to disaster; and the disaster area itself
> must be relatively homogeneous and insulated. (p. 6)

Barkun speaks of a disaster when it 'radically destroys or reshapes an individual's most highly valued human and physical surround-ings' (p. 6).

After these remarks on an amended functionalist model, I

115

conclude this paragraph by confronting the functionalist models with the general questions formulated above. These models start from the presupposition that society is a relatively stable system in which cohesion is brought about by value consensus. Religion is especially studied in its function of contributing to and legitimating the moral values. Consequently, in studying religious change the model focuses on the contribution religion makes to repair the social damage produced by social change. This means that the models study only one aspect of religion and are not primarily interested in the others. The functionalist models have something to say about the genesis of religious phenomena, but the persistence of religion is only explained from the stability of the social system, which in turn is presupposed.[15] The informants' symbolic system in principle only receives attention when it can be shown to satisfy, in a conscious and explicit way, social or political needs. Religion and religious change are not studied for man's role in them or for the internal logic of the symbolic system, but only for their social utility. The models claim universal validity. As a consequence specific local features receive no explanation. Despite the claim to a theoretical status, the value of the approach lies mainly in the exploratory phase of research, and then only in so far as the relation between religion and society is studied. The truth of functionalism as a theory depends too much on the acceptance of the, sometimes organicist, presuppositions. If order and cohesion are not as important as is presupposed, the value of the models diminishes accordingly.

In short, the functionalist approach is partial, because of its axiomatic presuppositions, because of its narrow focus on certain aspects of religious change only, and because of its restricted explanatory potential. Consequently, it needs to be complemented by other models.

The intellectualist model

Horton (1971; 1975), the author of this model of conversion, does not want to be considered a functionalist (1971: p. 93), and therefore a separate section will be devoted to his ideas. Yet, as we will see, he shares some opinions with the scholars under review in the preceding section. He criticizes functionalist – and certain symbolist – models of religion and religious change because they offer no answer to the question: 'Why *spiritual* beings?' (1971: p. 93). Like Barkun, though further removed from it, and in another way, he tries to amend the functionalist model. His objection is that it does not explain the religious dimension, a criticism I have formulated, too.

The intellectualist approach 'takes systems of traditional religious belief at their face value – i.e. as theoretical systems intended for the explanation, prediction, and control of space–time events' (Horton, 1971: p. 94). These events include the changes colonization and modernization have brought to Africa. Two types of religion are distinguished by Horton: religions in which explanation, prediction and control are combined with communion, and religions which are pure communion (1971: p. 96). According to Horton's 'thought experiment', as he terms it (1971: p. 102), within African traditional religions lesser spirits may be viewed as associated with the microcosm, while more important spirits and the supreme being may be seen as related to the macrocosm. When the macrocosm expands, e.g. through long-distance trade, or through state formation, or because of colonial rule, the adaptive potential present in the largely unelaborated concept of the supreme being is developed (1971: p. 102). The explanatory demands of the new situation are satisfied. When people go to live outside the microcosm the lesser spirits become less relevant.

'The obvious inference is that acceptance of Islam and Christianity is due as much to development of the traditional cosmology in response to *other* features of the modern situation as it is to the activities of the missionaries' (Horton, 1971: p. 103). 'Such a conclusion reduces Islam and Christianity to the role of catalysts – i.e. stimulators and accelerators of changes which were "in the air" anyway; triggers for reactions in which they do not always appear amongst the end-products' (1971: p. 104). The accent of Western Christianity on communion is not always adopted by the Africans, and Christianity is taken to be another way of explaining, predicting and controlling.

The merit of the model is that it has no universal pretension, but is specifically African and restricted to the problem of conversion. Besides, it seriously tries to give an answer to the question of why social change is accompanied by a religious change. Furthermore, it must be sympathetic to us, because it honours man's model-building capacities. At least a part of the traditional cosmology is integrated into the model which thus respects continuity (van Binsbergen, 1981: p. 28).

Yet there are also shortcomings. The model focuses, like the functionalist model, on the relationship between social change and religious change. Even more explicit than was the case with the functionalist model, the relation between society and religion is seen as a one-way street. The presupposition is that the religious reflects the social, and does not negate it (van Binsbergen, 1981: p. 40). Furthermore, Horton's model, too, has traits of a black box: social change is put into it, and religious change is the output, but it is not clear what happens in between (cf. van Binsbergen, 1981: p. 30). Another problem is where the frontier between microcosm and macrocosm is situated (van Binsbergen, 1981: p. 39) and when the transition from one to the other takes place.[16] How closed indeed were the microcosms?

A similar criticism may be put forward in connection with the two types of religion that are distinguished. Do explanation, prediction and control really play no role in Christianity, especially as brought by missionaries, i.e. by Christians who were least impressed by the scientific world view? Christianity and Islam, moreover, have been more than catalysts (cf. Pauw, 1975: pp. 337, 338), because they themselves have been changed while they brought about change (Droogers, 1980c; forthcoming). Catalysts, on the other hand, remain what they are. And, of course, in the process of conversion other factors, like material gain and the search for a new identity, may have played a role (Peel, 1973: p. 343). For suffering, so much stressed by the preceding models, there is no place in Horton's model. Without accepting that suffering explains religion, one might say that cognitive and material deprivation have contributed to the changes occurring in religion (Droogers, forthcoming). The Horton thesis limits itself to the utility of religion as a system of explanation, prediction and control. This is too narrow a version of man as a meaning-maker, and it does not exhaust the complexities of the symbolling activity. One suspects with van Binsbergen (1981: p. 40) that the symbolic systems are not as simple as a correspondence of microcosms and macrocosms with lesser and more important spirits might suggest.

Yet, in a sense, it is not fair to criticize Horton for what cannot be included in or deduced from his model. It is explicitly put forward as a partial model and as a thought experiment. Though Horton himself speaks of a theory, his model belongs more to the research phases preceding the formulation of a theory. Horton's thesis leads fieldworkers to important questions (cf. Ranger and Kimambo, 1972: pp. 15, 16).

In view of the general questions we put to models, it may be said that Horton's model is based on a presupposition about the correspondence between social and religious change. As a thought experiment it is not directly based on informants' models. Yet, through its emphasis on explanation, prediction and control, it rehabilitates the African in so far as he has been depicted as different from Western man. The frame of reference is utilitarian and the symbolic systems are not drawn in sufficiently. It explains the genesis of new religious ideas by reference to social change, but does not explain their persistence: a new phase of static cosmology seems to have been reached once the social change has found its religious translation.

To sum up, Horton's intellectualist model is even more partial than it already admits to being, and should be part of a series of complementary exploratory models.

The neo-Marxist models

Neo-Marxist models are less often used than functionalist models. They have amended the original contribution Marx made, selecting from it and transforming it in the light of other models and observations. The application of a model developed in Western nineteenth-century capitalist society, to non-Western situations, of course necessitates some amending. The way Marx looked upon religion was determined by his revolutionary point of view. Religion was not interesting in itself, but only received his attention in so far as he was confronted with religion as an obstacle on the way to a just society (Bühler, 1976: p. 323). This, too, implies a certain partiality in the model, and a need for amending. Bonte (1975: p. 395) speaks of 'the necessity of ridding historical materialism of all dogmatism and ethnocentrism, rather urgent tasks where the study of religion is concerned'.

Neo-Marxist models of religious change share with the classic

Marxist model the interest in the relation between religion and economy. The economic is seen as ultimately determinant. Yet it is recognized that non-economic social structures may play what is called a 'dominant' role. Paraphrasing Godelier (1973), Bonte (1975: p. 386n) writes: 'The constitution of an autonomous sphere of the economic . . . is proper to capitalist society. In other societies, kinship, political, and even religious relationships can simultaneously function as production relationships' (cf. Sahlins, 1976: p. 6). A social structure is dominant if it visibly organizes society.[17] Economic determinism is not regarded as contradictory to the dominant function of certain non-economic social structures as infrastructures. Thus, while economic determinism is maintained, it is recognized that, among other things, religion may play an important role. Bonte (1975: p. 391) even concludes from his East African research: '1) that it is impossible to reduce religion to a reflection of the material conditions of social life and the relationships of production; 2) that any transformation of these social relationships presupposes a prior transformation of the religious organization itself.' Religion may be more than an expression of the material reality, because it is capable of creating new relations of production (cf. van Binsbergen, 1981: p. 62). This implies that the classic Marxist distinction between suprastructure and infrastructure loses its sense when applied to a society in which the economic structure is not as dominant as in Western capitalist society.[18]

In Marxist and neo-Marxist models alike change, conflict and contradiction are normal phenomena. Consensus – a favourite topic of functionalists – is abnormal. Within a mode of production contradictions make for change. Here religion may serve to mask or retouch or overcome the contradictions. But especially in a society in which it dominates, religion may also play a role in generating changes in the mode of production (Bonte, 1975: p. 395; van Binsbergen, 1981: pp. 53, 62). Similarly, religious movements may either mask the contradictions, or stage a symbolic protest, or – rarely – transform society in reaction to contradictions, especially in situations where modes of production coexist or where there is a transition from one mode of production to another (Houtart, 1977: pp. 258, 259; cf. Maduro, 1975a: pp. 312–14). Religion is not only the opium of the people, it may also be a source of inspiration for the transformation of society.

Neo-Marxist studies on African religious change are not very numerous.[19] In summarizing, reviewing and amplifying his contributions to the neo-Marxist study of religious change, van Binsbergen (1981: pp. 42–74) offers perhaps the most advanced Marxist interpretation of religious change in Africa published so far. The fundamental presupposition of his approach is that 'The unit carrying a specific, distinct religious complex is . . . the mode of production – a unit defined by such primary determinants of experience as: *labour, production, reproduction, control, expropriation*' (p. 64). The concept of articulation plays a central role: 'modes of production can be said to be articulated ("linked") to one another if surpluses generated in one mode are expropriated so as to serve the reproduction of another, dominant mode' (p. 43). The notion of social formation is substituted for that of society because it allows for the recognition of diversity, change and contradiction inherent in modes of production and their articulation.

'The specific pattern a composite religious system takes at a given point in time and place, links up with the specific pattern of mutually articulated modes of production within the social formation' (van Binsbergen, 1981: p. 64). 'Links up' means that articulation is 'the crucial condition governing religious innovation' (p. 56). This may take various forms. First, there may be a one-to-one correspondence between a religious innovation and a mode of production, leading to acquiescence or even support. Second, the articulation process may be positively reflected but at the same time 'each constituent mode of production is now reflected, now negated' (p. 57), or one constituent mode of production may be explicitly rejected (p. 59). In the third type 'the total structure of articulation is negated which often leads to a positive confirmation of one *idealized* constituent mode of production' (p. 57).

In some cases a direct relationship between the religious innovation and the mode of production or the articulation process may be demonstrated, as in the case of chiefly cults, or that of the Lumpa movement's efforts to revive the domestic mode of production. But otherwise van Binsbergen admits that his 'emerging theory' (1981: p. 61) is in need of a symbolic theory of the exact relation between the religious and the economic aspect. Without such a theory the diversity of religious innovations within one articulation process cannot be accounted for (pp. 48, 54, 56, 63,

65). The new theory should integrate individual and structural factors (pp. 63, 64). As one of the sources of inspiration for the emerging theory, Sahlins (1976) is mentioned (van Binsbergen, 1981: p. 325, note 136). Room is left for a certain autonomy of the symbolic order *vis-à-vis* the relations of production (van Binsbergen, 1981: pp. 69–71).

In comparison with Horton's model, the distinction between microcosm and macrocosm has been replaced by that between modes of production. The expansion of the macrocosm has been identified as the articulation process. The more formidable spirits and God may be related to certain modes of production or to the articulation process itself. And religion is shown to be more than merely an expression of social change: it may take part in the formation of new relations of production. In these respects (van Binsbergen, 1981: pp. 61, 62) the modes-of-production approach amends and amplifies the Horton model.

The short discussion of van Binsbergen's 'emerging theory' has shown how fertile the eclectic debate between existing theories, including the elaboration and correction of one classic model, within the intellectual development of one author, can be. We have come a long way from the opium of the people or the criticism of religion. Historical materialism can, indeed, be rid of dogmatism. Yet, because of its central presupposition regarding economic determinism, the neo-Marxist model is still a limited model as it focuses on only one part of the religious field, viz. the relation between religion and economy. One consequence of his reductive presupposition on the central role of articulation is that van Binsbergen arrives at the conclusion that articulation does not explain everything and that therefore a symbolic theory is needed. In my opinion such a theory should not only discuss the exact relation between a symbolic system and the articulation process, but should be a more general theory, discussing the properties of symbolic systems as systems, the role often capricious and irrational individuals and their *condition humaine* play in developing them, and the relation of the symbolic system to the various aspects of society, including the economic.

The neo-Marxist model, for all its amendments, is partial because of its special interest in the universal role of the economic in religious change. It is a model about a continuous genesis, as change and contradiction receive so much attention that persistence, at least theoretically, is supposed not to exist. Again, we find the circular reasoning about presuppositions and results. The hypothesis about the importance of the economic aspect is almost from the start reified to a theory.[20] This model, too, is more exploratory than explanatory. Religion is largely explained from its utility in a mode of production or in the articulation process.

African models first

It has been suggested that one should abandon, at least provisionally, all models except those of the informants. Fabian (1979: p. 11) argues 'that overclassifying and overconceptualizing have been detrimental to the understanding of religious enthusiasms'. Fabian favours a method whereby the anthropologist immerses himself in the prophetical discourse and as it were continues it when he writes about it. This implies 'a notion of ethnography as *listening* and *speaking* (rather than observing) and an ideal of anthropology as *interpretative discourse*' (p. 27). Ethnography 'is based on communicative interaction with the people' (p. 10). 'Through prophetic discourse movements become accessible to meaningful interpretation. In fact, it is their discursive nature which makes it possible to give account of them – discursive and critical narratives, not just causal or structural reductions' (p. 11). 'We need a sharper and deepened historiographic consciousness as a prerequisite to theorizing about religious movements' (p. 20). We must develop a 'theoretical awareness of the views and preconceptions that determine historiography in our field' (p. 21). The core problem 'is the possibility of an interpretive discourse capable of transcending the kind of confining metaphors and rhetorical figures we found to be operative in much of the literature on movements' (p. 24). The emphasis on discourse should bring the question 'Why this religious form and not another?' closer to an answer. The focus should be on process and on emerging and changing meaning. This type of explicitly personal and emphatic research should produce other organizing concepts than those discussed so far. But first of all we should get as close to our informants' discourse as we can.[21]

A similar view is expressed by Fernandez (1978: p. 215) when he writes: 'our real enlightenment lies not in the application of imageless ideas exported from the West but in beginning with

African images and by careful method learning what they imply'. We should be more conscious of our own images. 'We learn most about the religious thoughts and religious intentions involved if, instead of imposing molar concepts and the vocabulary of macro-analysis, we stay close to those grounded images and by methodic micro-analysis proceed from them to what they imply' (p. 228).

Without coming to the same methodological conclusions as Fabian and Fernandez, de Craemer *et al.* (1976) also make a plea for giving more attention to the traditional African background of religious movements. In their view, 'these movements are an integral dimension of the cultures common to most parts of Zaire and to contiguous areas in Central Africa' (p. 458). Essentially, present-day movements are not different from those that occurred for centuries before the colonial period. Modern factors may play a role, but 'they do not explain why these movements have the shape and content they do' (p. 472).[22]

The African data are part and parcel of our field, and a methodological article needs the counterpoise of this reminder.[23] Fabian and Fernandez go further and, at least provisionally, prefer to immerse themselves in the field of African religious change, unhampered by methodological problems as discussed here.[24] But to me it seems inevitable that a description – and the fieldwork which precedes it – contains references to Western concepts and models, even if the author prefers to do without. For example the simple question 'What is to be called religious?' brings a host of presuppositions in its trail. A review of models may prove helpful if we want 'to look at our own images of understanding' (Fernandez, 1978: p. 219).

The semantic model

A semantic approach has, to begin with, the advantage of doing justice to the ambiguity just discussed. It may lead to very specific descriptions of symbolic systems and symbol-generating activity, thus giving insights from the inside. Yet it may also stress the common human nature of both researcher and researched, Westerner and African. It allows for the integration of universal and local aspects. It is a very minimal form of conceptualizing and almost by definition makes the researcher conscious of his own role as a meaning-maker.[25] This approach comes as close as possible to the informants' discourse *and* to accepting the criticism of Western models without, however, abandoning all models. Model-builders must be identified as scientific meaning-makers. Each selects from the spectrum of meanings the semantic field which he regards as central. The semantic model plays a double role. It may serve as a necessary complement to the models discussed so far, making up for their shortcomings. At the same time it offers a model of these models as it is presupposed in the activities of both anthropologist and informant. The semantic model regards both the contents and the form of the other models.

In order to make this clear we shall first pay attention to the presuppositions of the semantic model.[26] The human reality is seen as a world of meanings; 'meaning is the essential property of the cultural object, as symbolling is the specific faculty of man' (Sahlins, 1976: p. 22). This implies that social reality can only exist because man has attributed a special meaning to it. 'Social relations develop through and are maintained by symbols' (Cohen, 1969: p. 220); 'the social structure *is* a conceptual structure' (Crick, 1976: p. 6). Therefore meaning cannot be reduced to social structure, and *mutatis mutandis* religion – or religious change – cannot be explained exclusively from its role in society. 'Change begins with culture, not culture with change' (Sahlins, 1976: p. 22). The semantic model is therefore prior to the other models.

The human world of meanings is not arbitrary but structured. It may be shown to follow certain rules, to obey a code or grammar. Human praxis is the production of meaning in order to give structure to reality. Man's mental structure allows him to do so. It is from this structure that a culture derives its order and not from the function the culture has, e.g. in the struggle for life, or in the maintenance of social structure (Tennekes, 1979: p. 39).[27]

The process of creating meaning is a continuous one. The order which results is never absolute nor timeless. Man is able to say no, to think and act without consistency, to create exceptions and deviations. His symbolling capacity surpasses the practical functions it may fulfil. There is always a surplus of meaning. Therefore, not the symbol or the symbolic system or its internal logic but the process of generating meaning must be the primary unit of analysis.[28] The symbolic system is continually reproduced, re-created and renewed. It is not so much meaning as the meaning-maker which is the central subject in this approach.

This must not be understood to mean that reality depends for its existence on man's semantic activity. 'Meaning of course does not create the real and material forces, but so far as these are engaged by men meaning encompasses them and governs their specific, cultural influence' (Sahlins, 1976: p. 22). Moreover, the results of man's symbolling activities come to lead a life of their own. They are objectivated. But they may be internalized again through socialization: 'Society is a human product. Society is an objective reality. Man is a social product' (Berger and Luckmann, 1972: p. 79). There is a dialectic relation between man's meaning-making, its results, and the image he has of them. This means that symbols create order in reality, but may also reflect and be influenced by that order, whether it is social, or economic, or whatever. The regularity, however, must be looked for not in the empirical reality, just as grammar cannot be deduced directly from the way a language is used. It should be sought in the human concept of that reality, in the symbolling activity of man (Tennekes, 1979: pp. 38, 39). In the same way as a speaker of a language need not know the grammar of that language in order to speak it, man is not conscious of the whole code behind his semantic activity.

The semantic model is both complementary and superior to the other models we have been discussing, especially the functionalist and the neo-Marxist models. It has the merit of 'bringing man back in' (Homans, 1973). 'Relations between human beings are not like relations between things. They have a meaning; they pose the problem of understanding' (Bastide, 1978: p. 7). Some of the models we reviewed seemed to have no place for man, as was clear from their black box characteristics, a weak spot in the chain of reasoning from social or economic change to religious change. If religious meanings are explained from their effect on the social, economic or political level, their relative internal logic is neglected or not even taken into account. The properties of religious change cannot be deducted from the role religion plays on the secular level.

So the other models seem to start from the wrong end. The event and the act – social or economic change – are put at the beginning of the reasoning, and religious change – a change in meanings – is the result. However, no act or event exists without a concept, without a meaning given to it by man (Sahlins, 1976: pp.

21–3).[29] In Caws's terms: operational models presuppose representational models.

Thus social and economic change are not enough to account for religious change. Moreover, man must not only be brought back in for a better understanding of religious change. Models on social structure and social change, on modes of production and articulation, cannot do without a view on man. 'An "economic basis" is a symbolic scheme of practical activity' (Sahlins, 1976: p. 37). The conceptual scheme 'is the very *organization* of material production' (p. 56). The cause is mistaken for the effect if meaning is taken as the result of social structure or mode of production.[30]

The rehabilitation of man as a meaning-maker brings with it that all aspects of his life may be brought under study. The model is not restrictive in itself. One is not obliged, by a start from the wrong end, to focus only on, for example, the relation between the social and the religious, or the economic and the religious. Bühler (1976: p. 323) reminds us, for example, of the importance of 'le fait universel de la misère biologique et de l'incertitude face à l'origine et à l'avenir, fait universel . . . qui est préoccupation permanente de l'imagination sociale de la production du sens'. Religious change finally becomes a subject in itself, and not just for the role religion plays in social or economic change.[31] The study of religion can now go beyond the explanation from the needs of society or the reduction to a duplicate of the social structure (Crick, 1976: p. 6). Besides being complementary, the semantic model reveals itself as fundamental in two respects. First, it comprises the areas studied by the other models. Second, it encompasses the other models as models. It does not deny the importance of the structures on which these models focus, or their importance for religious life, but it only puts them in another, wider perspective. Moreover, it helps to recognize their relative value as models.

All this amounts to a different style of anthropology. According to Crick (1976: pp. 2, 3), one should even speak of a break, at least with the functionalist tradition, 'because semantic powers make human beings members of a self-defining species' (p. 3). Yet the break is not total, as this approach may integrate its predecessors. As it is not selective or restrictive in itself, the need for fieldwork makes itself even more felt (p. 126). Unfortunately, of the models mentioned in this article, the semantic model is the most recent, and has hardly been applied in research in the field. It seems that its approach is closest to that favoured by Fabian and Fernandez, even though Fabian (1979: pp. 26, 27) has expressed doubts about the value of the symbolic approach, of which, however, he describes only a special version, which emphasizes static and timeless aspects of symbol systems.

One suggestion, which might help to formulate research questions, is to apply some of the general questions we have put to each of the models under discussion, to the religious models of our informants. Here, too, it might be asked which presuppositions determine the selection of features regarded as essential. The plea made by Fernandez to look for African images might be translated into the question whether the model and the modelled are of the same or a different nature, e.g. what kind of symbols are used to represent the other reality of supernatural beings? Another question may refer to the special interest of the model in either genesis or persistence. It might also be a point of interest whether the model has a universal or specific origin and claim.

The fact that these questions may be asked means at the same time that they may also play a role in a comparison of competing or mutually integrating religious models – like, for example, African traditional religion and Christianity or Islam – just as they helped us to make a comparison of anthropological models and their possible integration. It may also be that in principle there is no difference between the amending of one model (as Barkun and van Binsbergen did) and the religious change effected within one African religious model under the inspiration of its contradictions, leading to a redefinition, with or without the impact of external circumstances. But these suggestions would form the start of another article and therefore will not be pursued here.

One obvious problem with the semantic approach is that, like the other models, it does not seem to explain the specific religious character of religious change. Yet if attention is given to the relative internal logic in symbolic systems and the uses to which they are put, it may be seen as inevitable that religious ideas enter the meaning-maker's activity in a process of change. This will especially be the case where religion is dominant, in the sense that it is the 'dominant locus of symbolic production' (Sahlins, 1976: p. 212). But this only changes the question to: Why can religion be dominant? The semantic approach may then refer to the fact that symbols, just because they stand for something which need not be there, almost suggest the possibility of another, invisible reality. Here again we are at the beginning of another article or book (e.g. van Baal, 1971).

It may be concluded that the semantic approach is the least selective model I have discussed. It even encompasses the other models. The primary place is given to the informants' models. Man is given a place in this model, more than was the case in the others. Religious change is removed from the practical frame of explanation. Justice is done to religion as a category *sui generis*, without, however, treating it in isolation. The model offers a felicitous combination of universal and specific aspects. As 'man is both a passive object and a causative subject of his culture, a *patiens* and an *agens*' (Droogers, 1980a: p. 345), both the meaning-maker and objectivated order, both genesis and persistence receive a place in the model. The model comes as close as possible to the modelled, also because it is a meta-model. For the same reason it occupies a central place in the series of models discussed here and in the scientific process.

Conclusion

The models reviewed are more important for their exploratory than for their explanatory value. It is still too early for real, fully fledged theories. For a certain time to come all studies in our field should carry the same subtitle as van Binsbergen's book (1981): *exploratory studies*. At the same time we should be more conscious of our presuppositions and of the role of models in our work. Models will, for the time being, mainly have heuristic functions, serving as eye-openers.

Our starting point must be man as a meaning-maker, and not the objectivated result of his semantic activity, even though we must acknowledge that man may be subject to the influence of his own product. We are *anthropo*logists. Man must be brought back in. We have always done so where we ourselves were concerned, and we would feel slighted if our work were to be reduced exclusively to social, political and economic changes in the world. Neither can we reduce the religious transformations we study to those same changes.

The central place of man as a semantic creature does not prevent us from studying the various aspects of religious change which had the selective interest of each of the models we discussed. On the contrary, these aspects can now be integrated, for their intrinsic quality as models, and for their interest in a specific area, into the meta-model of man as a meaning-maker. The semantic approach is not identical to a study of symbolic systems as such. Though it is important to rehabilitate the study of these systems and their internal logic, our main interest is with man and his capacity to generate meaning. This capacity is not only exemplified in symbolic systems, but also in man's social, economic and political activities. The application of the semantic model is therefore eclectic in nature.

This paper may also be summarized in one image, and Fernandez would be pleased to note that it is African. I would like us to become polygamists in the theoretical field. It is not good to have only one steady relationship, nor to have a series of short but intense love affairs with very attractive newcomers in the field. We should establish a more permanent relationship with a number of partners, even if we will never again be so much in love as we were and are with our first and primal partner who was intermediary in meeting the others, and who remains, dominating the others as a prototype and complementing them. Besides, we should remember that, at least from the point of view of the man, polygamy helps to reach optimal fertility. And that is, transposed to another level, what we want for our field of studies.

Notes

1 I am grateful to Peter Geschiere, Matthew Schoffeleers. H. G. Schulte Nordholt, Wim van Binsbergen and to my colleagues in the Institute for the Study of Religion (Free University, Amsterdam) for their comments on earlier drafts of this paper, to Maartje Bonda for secretarial help, and to Sheila Gogol and Tony Briggs for editorial advice.

2 This eclectic approach is certainly not new. Cf., for example, Bourdieu (1979: p. 78), Hoogvelt (1978), Jarvie (1963), La Barre (1971), Laeyendecker and van Steegeren (1978: p. 50), van den Berghe (1969), and Wallace (1969b).

3 The summary is based on Bertels and Nauta (1969: pp. 11–30) and Santema (1978: pp. 80–116).

4 Burridge (1969: p. 160), Fabian (1979: p. 9), Fernandez (1978: pp. 196–8), Jarvie (1963: p. 128), La Barre (1971: pp. 23, 27), van Binsbergen (1981: p. 36) and M. Wilson (1971: p. 5) make similar observations.

5 The latter distinction seems to be made on the same principle as that between practical reason and culture (Sahlins, 1976: pp. vii, viii, see below) or that between 'energy models which describe social relations as relations of force, and cybernetic models which make them relations of communication' (Bourdieu, 1979: p. 83). Religion has similarly been defined in a functional way by what it *does*, and in a substantial manner by what it *is* (Berger, 1967: pp. 175–8; Yinger, 1970: p. 4). Sahlins (1976: pp. 90, 91) associates 'cybernetic' with a systems approach 'displacing the property of "mind" from humanity to [in that example] the ecosystem' (p. 90) and he would therefore probably be critical of Bourdieu's terminology. It is striking how both Sahlins and Bourdieu strive to counterbalance a certain approach. While Sahlins criticizes 'practical reason' and Bourdieu is critical of the symbolic tradition, both, in their own manner, make a plea for an integration of models. Sahlins, though, retains the primacy of the cultural reason (e.g. Sahlins, 1976: p. 149), while Bourdieu gives a central place to the class struggle (Bourdieu, 1979: p. 80).

6 A few examples may be given here. Okot p'Bitek (1970) gives an African view on the biases of Western anthropologists writing on African religion. Horton (1975: p. 396) engages in a discussion with what he calls the 'Devout Opposition'. M. Wilson (1971: pp. 24, 101) states explicitly that she holds a Christian point of view and makes Christian value-judgments. Interest in religious change, especially when this change takes the form of religious movements, sometimes appears to be motivated only by an interest in the supposedly political aspects of these movements.

Social theory in general can be shown to be influenced by the society in which it was developed, either in confirmation or in criticism of that society. Functionalism in its orthodox form may fit a conservative political stance, as can, for example, be seen when its presuppositions are compared to those of the ideology of national security as current in present-day Latin American politics.

Sahlins (1976: pp. 95, 96), in criticizing utilitarian theories, writes:

> The general idea of social life here advanced is the particular behaviour of the parties in the marketplace. Now all culture is understood as the organized effect of individual businesslike economizing. Culture is Business on the scale of Society . . .. Social science elevates to a statement of theoretical principle what bourgeois society puts out as an operative ideology.

Marxism has, of course, its own political counterpart. O'Laughlin urges us to be conscious of the place of our scientific work in our own society: 'If we are to understand others, then we must understand ourselves in our social world – as researchers and teachers producing both science and ideology in the context of the advanced capitalist society' (O'Laughlin, 1975: p. 368).

7 Jarvie (1963: p. 1) makes a similar observation.

8 We may, of course, console ourselves with the fact that a new model may be presented as exclusive even if such a claim does not reflect its contents. While propagating one model, elements from the model at the other pole often are integrated, if only in the form of exceptions (Sahlins, 1976: p. 103). Van Binsbergen's collection of articles (1981) offers an example of a succession of various models following the author's intellectual development. Though the presentation of each new model implies a criticism of previously advanced models, every new model can be said to stand on the shoulders of the preceding one. Generally speaking, the book appears to be an example of the waste-making trend under criticism here, but fortunately there are also signs of a more eclectic approach and a consciousness (as expressed, for example, in the subtitle) that the models used do not offer a full explanation of the phenomena under study (see van Binsbergen, 1981: pp. 22, 23, 24, 29, 40, 48, 51, 54, 56, 58, 60, to mention only passages from the introductory essay of the collection).

9 If our models help us to open our eyes to the reality we study, how can we know that parts of reality escape our attention? Yet, on the other hand, our models cannot come about without reference to that reality; that which is modelled influences the selection of features for the model. We should therefore commute between the models and the field, and between alternative models.

10 For this paragraph I found valuable insights in van den Berghe (1969) and Tennekes (1979) who offer a critical review of functionalist models.

11 An example is Kimbanguism which currently has become relatively apolitical again; cf. Ustorf (1975).

12 See Fabian (1979: pp. 13, 14) for similar criticism.

13 Barkun (1974: pp. 36, 37, 63), de Beet and Thoden van Velzen (1977), Oosterwal in La Barre (1971: p. 32).

14 Paradoxically, social change in the face of disasters may also confer benefits:

> In the midst of disaster, its victims frequently experience moments of intense warmth, community, comradeship, and fellow feeling absent from their workaday lives. . . . Thus, curiously the disaster itself appears to prefigure the millenium, and the cultivation of ecstatic behavior becomes a mechanism for reproducing the disaster utopia experience. (Barkun, 1974: pp. 7, 8)

Instead of 'community' Barkun might have written 'communitas' and have referred to V. Turner (1969). In fact, more work could be done on the basis of what has been discovered about liminal situations. In the course of religious change, the inversion of hierarchy and authority is often accompanied by other inversions within the current symbolic system (cf. Droogers, 1980b).

15 Bastide (1978: p. 24), Dore (1973:, p. 66), Manyoni (1977: p. 615), Stern in La Barre (1971: p. 34), Zenner in La Barre (1971: p. 35).

16 This problem also pertains to M. Wilson's change-in-scale approach.

17 Houtart and Lemercinier (1977: p. 160; 1979: p. 408); cf. Sahlins (1976: p. 212).

18 Van Binsbergen (1981: pp. 48–54); cf. Sahlins (1976: pp. 20, 39).

19 Bonte (1975), Schoffeleers (1978), van Binsbergen (1981: chs 6, 7, 8).

20 The model, despite the distinction between determinant and dominant, is still too much under the impact of the Western experience where 'the relations of production constitute a classification reiterated throughout the entire cultural scheme' (Sahlins, 1976: pp. 212, 213).

21 The ultimate consequence of a total immersion in the field is the conversion to the religion under study (Jules-Rosette, 1975, and in a different way Martin, 1975). Continuing along this line, one might arrive at a position in which the scholar, who refused to develop his own models *of* the religion studied, sees it as a consequence of his work to offer a model *for* the participants in that religion (cf. Fabian, 1979: pp. 4, 5). Compare also the work done by Daneel among the independent churches of Zimbabwe, the role Martin plays in the theological education of the Kimbanguists, and Schoffeleers's relation with the present-day Mbona cult (personal communication).

22 Manyoni (1977), on the contrary, is not particularly happy with the special interest in the African background if this would mean that the study of African movements were to be separated from the study of similar movements elsewhere. His emphasis is on the fact that 'schismatic' movements, as he terms them, are a worldwide phenomenon. Therefore, one should look for a universal framework in order to find the reasons for the emergence and persistence of these movements. 'I suggest that the structure of African societies is itself a datum, not an independent variable, in schism; it is not, and cannot be a causal factor for a schism' (Manyoni, 1977: p. 603). African structural features only provide a channel for response to an exogenous impact.

23 Sometimes this welcome attention to traditional culture suffers from stereotyped ideas about the supposedly hyper-religious African (e.g. Rivière, 1977: p. 560 as a recent example; cf. Droogers, 1977: pp. 448–50 for more extended criticism).

24 From my own fieldwork experience I am familiar with their point of view (e.g. Droogers, 1980a: pp. 10, 12). The anthropologist lives between the poles of participation and observation. He may feel a strong sense of belonging at one time, and feel a stranger and an intruder at other moments. He may cherish the illusion of living in one world with the people he studies, and yet know that his roots are in another culture. This ambiguity should be reflected in his writings. It may take substantial artistic skill to do justice to the *empathic* side of the fieldwork experience, but even the most clumsy effort is better than a cool observational report.

25 'Semantic anthropology concerns the powers of human beings to construct meanings and is itself one manifestation of this capacity' (Crick, 1976: p. 169).

26 Berger and Luckmann (1972), Crick (1976), Harré and Secord (1976), Sahlins (1976), Tennekes (1979).

27 Yet we should view 'the human mental equipment as the instrument rather than as the determinant of culture' (Sahlins, 1976: p. 123). The structures of the mind 'compose a set of organizational possibilities' (ibid). 'Only the commonalities of structuring can be referred to the mind' (Sahlins, 1976: p. 122).

28 Devisch (1977: pp. 684, 705); cf. Fabian (1979: pp. 26, 27).

29 As Sahlins (1976: p. 21) puts it:

> circumstance itself does not engender form except as it is given significance and effect by the system in place. . . . such [human] action . . . takes its meaning as a projection of the cultural scheme which forms its specific context, and its effect by a relation of significance between this contingent reference and the existing order. An event becomes a symbolic relation.

30 O'Laughlin is an example: 'the central question is not the nature of knowing but the nature of human society. . . . It is not the intentionality of production that defines human activity, but rather its necessarily social character. To be human is to be social' (O'Laughlin, 1975: pp. 345, 346).

31 ' . . . the "real" content of new religious movements should not be located in some latent social or political programme' (J. Wilson, 1977: p. 150).

References

Baal, J. van (1971), *Symbols for Communication. An Introduction to the Anthropological Study of Religion*, Assen: Van Gorcum.

Barkun, Michael (1974), *Disaster and the Millenium*, New Haven, Conn., and London: Yale University Press.

Bastide, Roger (1978), *The African Religions of Brazil: Toward a Sociology of the Interpenetration of Civilizations*, Baltimore, Ma., and London: Johns Hopkins University Press

Beet, Chris de, and Thoden van Velzen, H. U. E. (1977), 'Bush Negro Prophetic Movements: Religions of Despair?', *Bijdragen tot de Taal-, Land- en Volkenkunde*, **133**, 1: pp. 100–35.

Berger, Peter L. (1967), *The Sacred Canopy; Elements of a Sociological Theory of Religion*, Garden City, New York: Doubleday.

Berger, Peter L., and Luckmann, Thomas (1972), *The Social Construction of Reality; A Treatise in the Sociology of Knowledge*, Harmondsworth, Middx.: Penguin.

Berghe, Pierre L. van den (1969), 'Dialectic and Functionalism: Toward a Theoretical Synthesis', in Wallace (1969a), pp. 202–13.

Bertels, Kees, and Nauta, Doede (1969), *Inleiding tot het modelbegrip*, Bussum: De Haan.

Binsbergen, Wim M. J. van (1976), 'Ritual, Class and Urban–Rural Relations: Elements for a Zambian Case Study', *Cultures et Développement*, **8**, 2: pp. 195–218.

Binsbergen, Wim M. J. van (1981), *Religious Change in Zambia: Exploratory Studies*, London and Boston: Kegan Paul International.

Binsbergen, W. M. J. van, and Buijtenhuijs, R. (1976), Introduction in W. M. J. van Binsbergen and R. Buijtenhuijs (eds) (1976), *Religious Innovation in Modern African Society*, *African Perspectives 1976/2*, Leiden: African Studies Centre, pp. 7–11.

Blok, Anton (1976), *Wittgenstein en Elias, Een methodische richtlijn voor de antropologie*, Amsterdam: Atheneum–Polak & Van Gennep

Bonte, Pierre (1975), 'Cattle for God: An Attempt at a Marxist Analysis of the Religion of East African Herdsmen', in Maduro (1975b), pp. 381–96.

Bourdieu, P. (1979), 'Symbolic Power', *Critique of Anthropology*, **4**, 13–14: pp. 77–85.

Bühler, Antoine (1976), 'Production de sens et légitimation sociale; Karl Marx et Max Weber', *Social Compass*, **23**, 4: 317–44.

Burridge, Kenelm (1969), *New Heaven New Earth. A study of Millenarian Activities*, Oxford: Blackwell.

Caws, Peter (1974), 'Operational, representational and explanatory models', *American Anthropologist*, **76**, 1: pp. 1–10.

Cohen, Abner (1969), 'Political Anthropology: The Analysis of the Symbolism of Power Relations', *Man*, 4: pp. 215–35.

Craemer, Willy de, Vansina, Jan, and Fox, Renée C. (1976), 'Religious Movements in Central Africa: A Theoretical Study', *Comparative Studies in Society and History*, **18**, 4: pp. 458–75.

Crick, Malcolm (1976), *Explorations in Language and Meaning: Towards a Semantic Anthropology*, London: Malaby.

Devisch, René (1977), 'Processes for the Articulation of Meaning and Ritual Healing among the Northern Yaka (Zaire)', *Anthropos*, **72**, 5/6: pp. 683–708.

Dore, R. P. (1973), 'Function and Cause', in Ryan (1973), pp. 65–81.

Douglas, Mary (1973), *Natural Symbols: Explorations in Cosmology*, New York: Vintage.

Droogers, André (1977), 'The Africanization of Christianity: An Anthropologist's View', *Missiology*, **5**, 4: pp. 443–56.

Droogers, André (1980a), *The Dangerous Journey: Symbolic Aspects of Boys' Initiation among the Wagenia of Kisangani, Zaire*, The Hague: Mouton for Afrika-Studiecentrum.

Droogers, André (1980b), 'Symbols of Marginality in the Biographies of Religious and Secular Innovators, a Comparative Study of the Lives of Jesus, Waldes, Booth, Kimbangu, Buddha, Mohammed and Marx', *Numen*, **27**, 2: pp. 105–21.

Droogers, André (1980c), 'An African Translation of the Christian Message: Changes in the Concepts of Spirit, Heart and God among the Wagenia of Kisangani, Zaire', in R. Schefold, J. W. Schoorl and J. Tennekes (eds), *Man, Meaning and History, Essays in Honour of H.*

G. Schulte Nordholt, *Verhandelingen van het Koninklijk Instituut voor Taal-, Land- en Volkenkunde* 89, The Hague: Martinus Nijhoff, pp. 300–31.

Droogers, André (forthcoming), 'Erosion and Sedimentation: The Changing Religion of the Wagenia of Kisangani, Zaire', in D. C. Mulder (ed.), *Secularization in Global Perspective*, Amsterdam: VU (Free University) Boekhandel/Uitgeverij.

Fabian, Johannes (1979), 'The Anthropology of Religious Movements: From Explanation to Interpretation', *Social Research*, **46**, 1: pp. 4–35.

Fernandez, James W. (1978), 'African Religious Movements', *Annual Review of Anthropology*, 7: pp. 195–234.

Godelier, M. (1973), *Horizons, trajets marxistes en anthropologie*, Paris: Maspero.

Harré, R., and Secord, P. F. (1976), *The Explanation of Social Behaviour*, Oxford: Blackwell.

Homans, George C. (1973), 'Bringing Men Back In', in Ryan (1973), pp. 50–64.

Hoogvelt, Ankie M. M. (1978), *The Sociology of Developing Societies*, 2nd edn, London: Macmillan.

Horton, Robin (1971), 'African Conversion', *Africa*, 41: pp. 85–108.

Horton, Robin (1975), 'On the Rationality of Conversion', *Africa*, 45: pp. 219–35, 373–99.

Houtart, François (1977), 'Mouvements religieux du Tiers Monde, Formes de protestation contre l'introduction des rapports sociaux capitalistes', *Civilisations*, **27**, 1/2: pp. 81–101; 3/4: pp. 245–60.

Houtart, François, and Lemercinier, Geneviève (1977), 'Religion et mode de production tributaire', *Social Compass*, **24**, 2/3: pp. 157–69.

Houtart, François, and Lemercinier, Geneviève (1979), 'Religion et mode de production lignager', *Social Compass* **26**, 4: pp. 403–16.

Jarvie, I. C. (1963), 'Theories of Cargo Cults: A Critical Analysis', *Oceania*, 34: pp. 1–31, 108–136.

Jules-Rosette, Benetta (1975), *African Apostles: Ritual and Conversion in the Church of John Maranke*, Ithaca, NY, and London: Cornell University Press.

La Barre, Weston (1971), 'Materials for a History of Studies of Crisis Cults: A Bibliographic Essay', *Current Anthropology*, **12**, 1: pp. 3–44.

Laeyendecker, L., and Steegeren, W. F. van (1978), *Strategieën van sociale verandering*, Amsterdam and Meppel: Boom.

Lévi-Strauss, Claude (1978), *Myth and Meaning*, London: Routledge & Kegan Paul.

Maduro, Otto (1975a), 'Analyse marxiste et sociologie des religions, en guise d'introduction', in Maduro (1975b), pp. 305–22.

Maduro, Otto (ed.) (1975b), 'Marxism and the Sociology of Religion', special issue of *Social Compass*, **22**, 3/4, Louvain: Centre de Recherches Socio-Religieuses.

Manyoni, Joseph R. (1977), 'Anthropology and the Study of Schism in Africa, A Re-examination of Some Anthropological Theories', *Cahiers d'études africaines*, **68**, 17,4: pp. 599–631.

Martin, Marie-Louise (1975), *Kimbangu: An African Prophet and His*

Church, Oxford: Blackwell.

Okot p'Bitek, n.d. (1970), *African Religions in Western Scholarship*, Kampala: East African Literature Bureau.

O'Laughlin, Bridget (1975), 'Marxist Approaches in Anthropology', *Annual Review of Anthropology*, 4: pp. 341–70.

Pauw, B. A. (1975), *Christianity and Xhosa Tradition: Belief and Ritual among Xhosa-speaking Christians*, Cape Town, London, New York: Oxford University Press.

Peel, J. D. Y. (1973), 'The Religious Transformation of Africa in a Weberian Perspective', in *C.I.S.R. 12th International Conference on Sociology of Religion*, The Hague, pp. 337–52.

Ranger, T. O., and Kimambo, I. N. (eds) (1972), *The Historical Study of African Religion with Special Reference to East and Central Africa*, London: Heinemann.

Rivière, Claude (1977), 'Religions africaines en mutation', *Cultures et développement*, **9**, 4: pp. 545–75.

Ryan, Alan (ed.) (1973), *The Philosophy of Social Explanation*, London: Oxford University Press.

Sahlins, Marshall (1976), *Culture and Practical Reason*, Chicago and London: University of Chicago Press.

Santema, J. H. (1978), *Modellen in de wetenschap en de toepassing ervan, Historische en systematische beschouwing vanuit christelijk-wijsgerig perspectief*. Delft: Delftse Universitaire Pers.

Schoffeleers, Matthew (1978), 'A Martyr Cult as a Reflection on Changes in Production: The Case of the Lower Shire Valley, 1590–1622 A.D.', in R. Buijtenhuijs and P. L. Geschiere (eds), *Social Stratification and Class Formation, African Perspectives 1978/2*, Leiden: African Studies Centre, pp. 19–33.

Tennekes, J. (1979), *Cultuur als experiment*, Amsterdam: Vrije Universiteit.

Tucker, Robert C. (ed.) (1978), *The Marx–Engels Reader*, 2nd edn, New York: Norton.

Turner, Victor W. (1969), *The Ritual Process: Structure and Anti-Structure*, London: Routledge & Kegan Paul.

Ustorf, Werner (1975), *Afrikanische Initiative: Das Aktive Leiden des Propheten Simon Kimbangu*, Bern and Frankfurt/M.: Lang & Lang.

Wallace, Walter L. (ed.) (1969a), *Sociological Theory: An Introduction*, London: Heinemann.

Wallace, Walter L. (1969b), 'Overview of Contemporary Sociological Theory', in Wallace (1969a), pp. 1–59.

Wilson, John (1977), 'Making Inferences about Religious Movements', *Religion*, **7**, 2: pp. 149–66.

Wilson, Monica (1971), *Religion and the Transformation of Society: A Study of Social Change in Africa*, Cambridge: Cambridge University Press.

Worsley, Peter (1968), *The Trumpet Shall Sound: A Study of 'Cargo' Cults in Melanesia*, 2nd edn, New York: Schocken Books.

Yinger, J. Milton (1970), *The Scientific Study of Religion*, London: Macmillan.

Chapter 5

Religious pluralism: An ethnographic approach[1]

Johannes Fabian

> Though it is very important for man as an individual that this religion should be true, that is not the case for society. Society has nothing to fear or hope from another life; what is most important for it is not that all citizens should profess the true religion but that they should profess religion . . . in the United States the sovereign authority is religious and consequently hypocrisy should be common.
>
> A. de Tocqueville (1969 [1835]: pp. 290f)

> Pluralism is never true, at most it is honest, expressing resignation with regard to the task of having to think about connections which are presupposed but not stated.
>
> C. F. von Weizsäcker (1977: p. 587)

I

The study of religious processes in Africa has not been immune to the boom-and-bust cycles on the market of theories. When independence and decolonization seemed to be on the upswing, 'change' was the perspective from which religious movements were commonly approached; dissent, innovation and differentiation were positively valued as signs of life. Now that even radicals among social scientists begin to resign themselves to analysing stagnant situations of neo-colonial dependency and imperialist domination, thought about religious diversity shows signs of returning to a liberal sort of law-and-order perspective called 'pluralism', reviving a concept which had much currency in an earlier period. *Pluralism*, it seems, is the capacity of political entities to accommodate a multitude of religious groups and institutions *and* the ability of individuals to follow more than one religious orientation at a time.

What are the prospects for revived 'pluralism'? The two epigrams with which I preface this paper do not create a mood of excitement and optimism and this reflects my own attitude. For many years I have studied a religious movement in a multi-ethnic, multilingual situation. I considered religion as one among several aspects of cultural differentiation, and as intricately involved in class and status differences. It also occurred to me early on in my research and writing about the Jamaa movement in Shaba (Zaire) that exaggerated expectations regarding the logical consistency and coherence of belief systems often lead to elegant but potentially misleading descriptions. True, had it not been for a bold Weberian-Parsonian approach in the beginning, subsequent revisions would not have brought the gain in knowledge which, I believe, they did. But I did not find pluralism to be a useful notion in this enterprise of deconstructing my initial theoretical bias (even though I used the term, very loosely, in my monograph; see Fabian, 1971: pp. 96–9).

In part, this theoretical aversion to pluralism is politically motivated. In the current jargon of politicians, journalists and, it seems, theologians – a realm of discourse which we must take seriously as at least one of the contexts in which we use the notion – pluralism has almost always (but, of course, not always consciously) the function to cover up for, distract attention from, elevate to a level of abstract inevitability, relations of unequal multiplicity. Opposition between dominating and dominated classes may thus be bent into 'ethnic pluralism', unresolved contradictions between power groups and interest groups become 'democratic pluralism', diversification in the culture industry, really a form of controlling and manipulating culture, is made to look innocent as 'cultural pluralism'. Finally, heretics, schismatics, sectarians, confessions and denominations, pagans, Jews and goyim are rendered innocuous by being declared 'plural' rather than the enemies of God, Truth, Humanity, or at least Unity.

We must consider the possibility that 'pluralism' is irretrievably compromised as a thoroughly ideological concept. It belongs to those figures of thought and speech which T. Adorno diagnosed as being afflicted with 'positive negativity': pluralism *negates* chauvinistic claims to dogmatic orthodoxy, value-hegemony or exclusive legitimacy, but it gratuitously *affirms* order and harmony from a point superior to unresolved strife between a multiplicity of groups, classes and nations. Pluralism, once again in Adorno's words, is a heart-warmer (*Herzenswärmer*, see Adorno, 1964: p. 29).

Whenever one finds a term which has currency in the language of politics and popular science one can, as a rule, trace it back to an earlier recondite existence in philosophical discourse and that of social science. I am not competent to do this adequately, nor do I have the space to attempt such a thing in this essay, but I should like to note a few observations of interest, limiting myself to three of the sources of what is now a river of pluralist talk.

First, one can point to philosophical origins in the (neo-)Kantian tradition. 'Pluralism' is here opposed to 'monism' and asserts the relative autonomy or irreducibility of human culture in general, and of different domains within culture. American culturalism and cultural relativism have acknowledged roots in that tradition. One should keep this in mind, especially if it is claimed that pluralism represents theoretical progress over good old relativism. An important connection between this philosophical trend and the social sciences was made through the influential work of Karl Mannheim on the sociology of knowledge and on ideology. For him, 'methodological pluralism' was a necessary corollary to the insight that different cultural objectivations constitute irreducible *Sinngebilde* (of which the now current 'provinces of meaning' might not be a bad translation; see Mannheim, 1964 [1918]: pp. 68, 77; [1921–2]: p. 101, note 7, where he gives acknowledgment to Rickert's *System der Philosophie*).

Mannheim is of special interest because he also illustrates, in his later work, how epistemic pluralism, carried to its logical extremes, leaves the analyst of plural points of view – of ideologies, for instance – without a position from which to derive generally valid insights. It was C. Geertz who, in an essay on 'Ideology as a Cultural System', noted the tendency of pluralist theory to cancel its own project. He offered a way out of 'Mannheim's paradox' by suggesting that an anthropological approach should shift the question away from objective validity to differences in 'stylistic strategies' (Geertz, 1973 [1964]: p. 230, see also p. 194). Now, he may have solved *a* paradox by adopting a pragmatic approach, but probably not that of Mannheim who suffered from what Geertz dismisses as a 'nervous concern with comparative epistemological or axiological status of the two forms of thought' (science and ideology in this instance) (p. 230). One can describe different thought systems as different ways to proceed ('strategies'), but is a thorough description of the procedures of meaning construction tantamount to critical evaluation? (One may ask the other way round: can the description of meaning be kept free of evaluative critique and, if not, what can we do about it?) The whole question of construing a scientific theory of multiple, conflicting, competing, or at least contrasting meaning systems hinges on the possibility (or impossibility) of eliminating the question of validity, or of at least subordinating validity to function, social control and political integration.[2]

To do just that is the 'solution' hinted at by my quotation from de Tocqueville. American political and social thought has taken the lead in considering 'pluralism under one law and constitution' an answer to the conflicting demands of secular and religious institutions and, more significantly, those of different religious groups. The literature here is too voluminous to be sampled, except for referring to two recent examples that directly regard our topic. One is the section titled 'Church and State: Limits of Religious Innovation Within the Social Order' in the volume edited by I. I. Zaretsky and M. P. Leone: *Religious Movements in Contemporary America* (1974). What I called the American solution is here documented with special attention to the position of 'marginal' religions. These essays are complemented by P. E. Hammond's article on 'Religious Pluralism and Durkheim's Integration Thesis' (1974) where he proposes an ingenious defence of both American religious pluralism and Durkheim's integrationalist theory of religion. Facing an apparent contradiction between the two, Hammond argues that, in the USA, religious pluralism *confirms* Durkheim's views because religious groups and creeds no longer perform the (religious) function of societal integration. The law now provides the common meaning system without which American society could not exist.

Whatever else is documented in these essays – and there are many points of interest that cannot be considered here, such as the suggestion that religious pluralism is a 'problem' mainly inasmuch

141

as different groups threaten *secular* American values (see Pfeffer, 1974: p. 26) – a perspective on the question of pluralism emerges which we will encounter later on: it is a view 'from above'; plurality constitutes a problem *vis-à-vis* a 'higher' instance which then provides the solution.

There is a third corpus of thought and writing about pluralism which confirms, even more than the epistemic and politico-juridical conceptions to which I have already alluded, that the notion should be traced back to social scientific attempts to 'explain' the unharmonious, often forceful 'integration' of diverse populations in imperial and colonial political entities from the Austro-Hungarian *Vielvölkerstaat* to South African apartheid. Here, too, American social scientists have been most concerned, as one finds out easily by consulting the literature about ethnicity. Interestingly enough, important elements of that theory have been imported, as it were, from anthropological and sociological thought about colonial societies outside the USA. There emerged between World War II and 1970, a regular school of pluralist social theory (at least there was an interest in proclaiming it a school, cf. van den Berghe, 1970: p. 17, note, with further bibliographical references), complete with classic texts (Furnivall, 1948; M. G. Smith, 1959–60), cross-cultural applications (e.g. van den Berghe, 1970), special adaptations to areas such as Africa (see L. Kuper and M. G. Smith, 1969), and a general 'framework for theory and research' (e.g. Schermerhorn, 1970).

Again, this is not the place for a balanced evaluation; I shall have to concentrate on a few points of critique. What I have said earlier about positive negativity applies to much of this writing. Pierre van den Berghe, for instance, a prominent and perhaps somewhat extreme theorist of pluralism, accomplishes major feats of intellectual and political obscurantism when he declares: 'Clearly, South Africa is one of the world's most pluralistic societies' (1970: p. 81). One would expect that the situation in South Africa, even as it was a decade ago, would have caused a sort of quantum leap in pluralist theory, an admission that the term 'pluralistic' can be stretched to a point where it loses any conceivable usefulness – where in a social theory that uses pluralism as a guiding concept even the most routine social scientific terms, such as 'society' itself, become equivocal and meaningless (can a concentration camp be analysed as a 'plural society'?). Nothing of that sort happens. Instead, pluralism saves its theoretical skin with a disarming *petitio principii*: 'Nevertheless, South Africa is integrated in some ways; otherwise one would not be able to speak of it as a society' (p. 82).

It is only fair to note that for many theoreticians pluralism was a critical reaction against functionalism and its bias towards integration, equilibrium and moral consensus. Especially in Africa and in the Caribbean, and especially after colonies had begun to be transformed into nation-states, sociologists and anthropologists faced societies which by no stretch of the imagination could be qualified as integrated, balanced systems. 'Pluralism' seemed to be the alternative. But did this critical movement bring about visions of relationships between these plural societies and between them and the Western world that would have changed the basic outlook of earlier approaches? To stay with Africa, M. Gluckmann, V. Turner and others introduced 'pluralistic' notions (rebellion, anti-structure) and to a certain extent succeeded in saving ethnography from the abstractions and platitudes of functionalism. However, if they brought dynamics and conflict to the fore, it was a social dynamic which, being cyclical and circular rather than cumulative and linear, was fundamentally different from change in advanced societies.

How very little pluralism theory changed in the basic outlook on the non-Western world can be seen if one compares older classifications and ranking of societies in terms of evolutionary stages, degrees of primitivity and similar indicators, such as backwardness or traditionalism, with scales constructed to measure degrees of new pluralism. Mentally comparing, for instance, Schermerhorn's 'comparative pluralist scores' (see Table 5.1) with ranking of societies in terms of simplicity, homogeneity and so forth, one finds that the sequence is more or less identical although the scales are based on opposite criteria.

Sub-Saharan Africa used to be at the bottom of the heap when comparisons were made in terms of evolutionary backwardness; it is still there, now that lack of integration is the criterion. One reason why opposite criteria can produce identical results is, of course, that they are applied to totally different units of comparison. On an evolutionary scale, 'society' had an abstract connotation of a social entity or grouping which could include anything between a band of pygmies and the United Kingdom; the pluralism scale

Table 5.1 *Comparative pluralist scores for 8 multinational sectors*

Sector	New pluralism score
1 Western European Nations and the derivative neo-European complex	2.0
2 Eastern Europe: the communist states	2.7
3 Iberian societies of the eastern and western hemispheres	2.3
4 Caribbean societies	2.6
5 Non-communist Asia and South-East Asia	4.6
6 Communist Asia	2.5
7 The Middle East and North Africa	3.3
8 Sub-Saharan Africa	6.1

Source: Schermerhorn (1970: p. 219).

refers to political entities (real and fictional) qualifying as nation-states. But that is not the only reason. *Any* global ordering or ranking of human societies is likely to produce hierarchical arrangements and taxonomies which place Western societies at the upper nodes or the apex. Such rankings are artefacts of a classificatory approach to human variation and difference whose results are predictable because they are ways of *imposing order from above* or, more accurately, from a point of view imagined to be located outside of, and at a distance from, the phenomena to be understood.

II

I am leading up to the argument that the fundamental problem with 'pluralism', of the politico-legal as well as of the comparative cross-cultural variety, is an epistemological one. What needs to be questioned is the exclusive validity of classificatory, hence hier-archical, treatments of difference and variation.

There would be no argument if alternatives could not be imagined. One must be able to point to ways of interpreting cultural and social pluralism which, with certain qualifications, can be said to *theorize from below*. I believe we can take a lead from recent trends in the study of language whose points of departure have been diversity, variation, multiplicity of codes and a host of related phenomena often summarily referred to as multilingualism. Certain approaches in this field have been classificatory and taxonomic and have produced explanations of linguistic diversity which are analogous to sociological 'pluralism'. There are others, though, which directly attack the dictatorship of taxonomy and the use of grammar as 'an instrument of hegemony' (Hymes, 1974b: p. 433). This is held against those linguists whose points of departure and return have been homogeneity, orderliness, uniformity and whatever else might be postulated as required for the systematic description of language. Analysts of religion in search of models for plurality and variation should, I believe, be interested in what sociolinguists have to say, especially those who conceive of their approach as an 'ethnography of speaking'.

Lest it be misunderstood, this recommendation needs a caveat. The 'ethnography of speaking' has itself been an effort to escape the methodological and theoretical dominance of 'pure linguistics'. To consider its implications for variety and plurality in other domains of culture is therefore not tantamount to exporting, once again, a ready-made method from linguistics. Sociolinguistics has inspired direct applications to religious, especially ritual, phenomena as communicative events. But beyond that it gives an impulse to a kind of theorizing about religion that could help to overcome a bias shared by Western believers and agnostic Durkheimian social scientists alike: a bias disposing us to take as the point of departure 'logically integrated systems of beliefs' shared by a 'church' (i.e. an institution), and to look down on everything else as deviant albeit occasionally creative. Few have done more for the preservation of religious hegemony than Durkheim.[3]

With these precautions in mind, I should like to propose the following catalogue of suggestions:[4]

1 Anthropologists should study religion 'ethnographically', i.e. in and through instances of action/interaction describable as (communicative) *events*. The point of this is that these events are not just to be taken as occasions producing 'data' or information; it is its event-character which distinguishes ethnography from other types of research.

2 Specifically, systems of beliefs (signs, symbols, myths, doctrines, etc.) and ritually organized sequences of acts or activities are to

be studied as they are actualized in (or mediated by) events which, as social events, occur in a physical setting, in real time, and in the presence of actors; they involve a choice of modes, channels, and codes of communication.

3 Events occurring under these conditions cannot adequately be understood either as mere 'enactment' of beliefs or as behavioural responses to some societal needs. Their relation to both the superstructure and the basis of a given society is dialectical in the sense that neither culture (religion) nor basic needs (economics, ecology) can ever be regarded as constants of explanation.

4 Being determined by, or composed of, a multitude of aspects, conditions and mediations, religious events are always historically situated, concrete and specific. Generalization about them must admit diversity, variation, even discontinuity and outright contradiction as 'normal' modes of religious action (they are not its 'modifications'). Thus, the quest for uniformity of dogma and conformity of behaviour is, if anything, *one variety* of religious expression, not its norm; it, too, is realized in concrete events constituting a certain praxis. Hence so-called uniform religions are not in principle distinct from so-called plural religions.

5 As there are no *a priori* reasons to consider a monolingual, standard speaker of a language an 'ideal speaker' (in the sense of being 'normal', uncomplicated, typical and so forth) we should reject the notion that a religious person (or a religious group) ought to enact one and the same belief system in order to qualify as normal or typical. Multilingual competences, phenomena described as diglossia, switching of languages, codes or registers[5] might provide models (based on analogy or homology) for religious pluralism as praxis.

6 Quite possibly, interesting perspectives on so-called religious syncretism may be opened up by the sociolinguistic study of 'vehicular languages' (pidgins, creoles, linguae francae). Here, too, the trend has been away from 'judging' isolated instances of such languages in terms of their (lacking) grammatical and lexical completeness, purity and logical organization, towards studying their practical functioning in communicative contexts and events. As a result, there is hardly any known vehicular language to which the status of a full language could be denied.[6]

7 Sociolinguistic critique of structural linguistics also discovered,

or rather rediscovered and revalued, the poetic nature of speech. As a result some have gone as far as declaring the strictly referential sign function of language a special case which cannot serve as a model for all other functions of language (see: Silverstein, 1976; Friedrich, 1980). Devaluating the referential function of language has consequences for semiotic theories of meaning which have at present such a prominent place in the anthropology of religion. Thus the crucial problem in the interpretation of meaning can no longer be that of matching expression and content, bounded provinces of meaning with distinct systems of symbols and then with distinct forms of behaviour. Such may in certain cases still be useful, but the main task of language-inspired theories would be to understand the *creation* of meaning, or of a meaningful praxis, in and through events of speech and communication. To free interpretations of religious behaviour from structural semiotics means that one must, even in ordinary communication, admit the important role of poetic invention, and in ordinary religious praxis the presence of innovation, hence of disorder.

I want to repeat that the significance of these hints, because they are scarcely more at this moment, does not lie in the (false) hope they offer of finding a ready-made, new theory of religion in the field of sociolinguistics.[7] Rather, the *kind* of critique which sociolinguists have formulated against taxonomic linguistics deserves to be taken up, especially as regards semiotic theories of religion. Cumulatively, the points listed above amount to a recommendation to steer the anthropological interpretation of religion – especially its 'cognitive' interpretation – in the direction of a theory of religious praxis (religious praxis being to religion what speaking is to language). Interpretations of religious 'plurality' are possible which are neither mere artefacts of a classificatory bias, nor expressions of scarcely concealed normative interests in rendering a situation manipulable by bringing diverse and often contradictory phenomena under one systemic hat. The problem of the *many* forms of religious consciousness, of competing beliefs and diverse expressions, is not resolved through more or less ingenious theories which save the rationality of religion by taking recourse to a plurality of systems, each perfectly logical in its own domain. Perhaps the pluralist approach is progress over forcible rationalization of religion which we owe to positivists, Durkheimians and latter-day functionalists (such as T. Parsons and, more recently, N. Luhmann; see Luhmann, 1977; Rappaport, 1979). But plural interpretations are not likely to further the aims of a liberating critique to which religion must be subject as much as science, politics, the arts and other cultural objectifications. Neither monopolistic nor free-market theories of culture and religion, being both tailored to the concerns of Western bourgeois science, are likely to produce challenging alternatives to those anthropological approaches which we now perceive as unsatisfactory.

III

Not everything I have discussed so far is just programmatic. Interpretations of communicative processes through which the specific identity of a religious praxis emerges (and which, therefore, produce diversity among religious expressions) have been given by anthropologists.[8] We can expect more and better ethnography of religion as theoretical insights from the ethnography of speaking begin to inform research designs and field methods.

In the remainder of this paper I will illustrate some of the principles and desiderata of an ethnographic approach. I will try to do this not just in general, but with special attention to 'pluralism'. It would be ironic if this appeal for a study of religion *qua* communication did not include a 'message from the people' in their own voice and language. I am going to present a text which, I believe, contains such a message. It originated as a tape recording during fieldwork on the Jamaa movement in Shaba (Zaire).[9] I shall assume that the Jamaa, a Catholic movement going back to the teachings of Placide Tempels (who is perhaps still better known as author of *Bantu Philosophy*), is by now notorious enough so that I need not describe it here in any detail.[10] Nevertheless, two observations might help to fill in the background to this particular text.

First, by the time the story was recorded, the movement had experienced serious conflict with the mission church over questions of doctrinal orthodoxy, moral conduct and hierarchical discipline. None of this had as yet resulted in a definitive break with the

Catholic Church, although some of the more far-sighted African leaders began to take such a possibility into account. Second, the situation was complicated by doctrinal and ritual diversification within the movement. These processes were little understood and hardly appreciated by the mission clergy. In many locations a sort of stable coexistence between groups considered orthodox and others perceived as heretical had been established. Dual or shifting membership was common so that a clear distinction between the groups proved impossible even by the best-informed priests. Outside observers, even those who were sympathetic to the Jamaa, saw this as a degeneration of an originally 'pure' impulse to revive the faith of nominal Catholics. Some spoke of 'syncretism', but that was little more than a euphemism for heresy. Most of the insiders, including the founder and some of his initiated confrères, had a different outlook. To them conflict, fission and more or less permanent separation were the necessary conditions under which unity (*umoja*), a key notion and value of Jamaa teaching, was to be pursued. These were the (dialectical) determinants of their praxis: unity was to be sought after, and created from, disunity, not imposed from above or achieved by expelling disturbing elements.

The recording of the text was preceded by several days of conversation in which *umoja* had a prominent place. The immediate occasion, however, was my probing into attitudes towards traditional lore and custom in which I used a previously recorded story as an example. After some consultation with elder members (in Kiluba) a man in his thirties, store clerk by occupation, offered (in Shaba Swahili) this tale of

Two people quarrelling about reason[11]

Jambo yetu bababa na bamama/ *jambo yetu baba/ bon*: sasa hapa tutaweza kujionyesha sawa vile namna tunaendelea na jamaa yetu/ ni vile: sawa mwingine jamaa: tuko tunakwenda: ao fasi tulitosha jamaa: shee bote tuyue asema: tulikuwa na ku mwanzo: tulipata hiyi mafundisho/ na tulizarikwa/

Greeting. All right, let us now show to ourselves how we progress in our Jamaa. It is the same with any other Jamaa: concerning the way we proceed, or the place from where we got the Jamaa – we all should know that in the beginning we received this instruction and were born. It's like it happens with

sawa vile watoto/ mutoto anatoka
ku nyumba ya baba yake: na mama
yake/ ni kwa saserdos/

kwa mufano/ tutatweza kuweka:
arisi moya/ kuko: wavijana mbili/
walibishiana/moya: anajileta kwa
jina yake asema: miye: niko: akili
moya/ alafu mwengine: anamwambia asema: hakuna muntu: iko
anatosha akili yee mwenyewe/ paka
unapata akili: ku muntu mwengine/
alafu ile mwenzake: anamwambia
asema: miye: niko akili ku wantu/
ni vile walibishiana/ alafu bubishi
bule: balitaka kwenda ku wantu
wakubwa wapate kuwanirosha:
kuwaweka mu njia/

walikwenda: kwa mfumu/ alafu ule
mwengine akili moya: aliwambia
wakubwa asema miye akili yangu
niko: paka mi moya/ nitaweza ku-
tosha kintu: paka mi moya/ alafu
ule kijana mwingine anasema:
miye sione muntu anatosha akili
yee mwenyewe/ mi naye: niko akili:
ku bantu/ ni vile mwee bakubwa
mupate kutuweka mu njia kwa hii
bubishi/

alafu wakubwa waliwambia asema:
mwikaleni watoto/ waliikala/

ule mfumu/ alimwambia bibi yake/
asema: upige chakula ya ao watoto:
mbili/ alikamata kuku: ya muntu
moya/ na tena anakamata na kuku
mwengine: ya muntu mwengine/
vile alipiga mabukari: mbili/ alafu
ile mabukari mbili alipiga: anakamata na kupiga: supu: na nyama:
anaweka paka mu sahani: moya/

children. As a child comes forth
from the house of his father and his
mother, so we came from the
priest.

As an example we can give an *arisi*:
There were two young people who
were quarrelling. One gave himself
a name and said: I am Reason-
alone. But the other one told him:
There is no one who makes his
reason [mind, intelligence] all by
himself; you get your reason from
someone else. So this other one
told him: I am Reason-from-
people. This is how they were
quarrelling. Finally, they decided
to go to the big people to get a
decision about their quarrel, so
that they might be put back on the
right path.

They went to the chief [diviner?].
Now Reason-alone told the elders:
My reason, that's me alone. I can
invent something all by myself.
The other young man said: I
haven't seen anyone yet who made
his reason all by himself. I am
Reason-from-people. It is about
this point that you, the elders,
should put us on the [right] path.

The big ones said: Stay here,
children, and they stayed.

The chief talked to his wife and
told her: Prepare a meal for the
two children. She took a chicken
for each of them and then she
cooked two *bukari*. But she put the
meat, the sauce, and the *bukari* all
into one bowl, the *bukari* on
top. She arranged it in such a way
that it looked as if there was only

tena bukari: anaweka yulu/ ana-
tengenesha/ inakuwa paka mu kintu:
moya/ anakamata tena sahani wa
mayi: anawekako/ anamwekea ule
kijana mwingine: ku nyumba yake/
anakamata tena bukari ingine: na
supu: na nyama: anaweka mu sahani ingine/ tena ne sahani ya
mayi/ anamwekea ule kijana mwingine: ku nyumba yake/

alafu: pa kuingia ku ile manyumba:
ule kijana: bale bijana mbili: bali-
ingia/ moya ule akili ku wantu
aliangaria asema: nitakulya namna
gani? sasa banaweka paka bukari
mutupu/ pasipo supu/ paka na mayi
ya kunawa na ya kunywa/ *bon*:
nitaweza kwenda kuuliza/ anakwen-
da kuuliza huyu mukubwa/ asema/
minaona paka bukari/ sione supu:
sione nyama/ paka mayi ya kunawa:
na mayi ya kunywa/

ule mukubwa anamwambia: ana-
muuliza asema: jina yako: uko
nani? anamwambia na kusema:
miye niko akili ku bantu/ *bon*/
anamwambia: *bon*: wee tutaweza
kuelezea/ wende ukakamate ile
mayi ya kunawa: unawe/ kiisha:
ukamate paka bukari ile: uweke
mu ile sahani ilikuwa mayi/ utaona
supu na nyama/ ni vile ule kijana
alikwenda kuonia ku nyumba yake
balimwekea chakula/ ananawa mu
ile sahani mulikuwa mayi: kiisha
anatosha ile bukari: anaweka mu
ile sahani ilikuwa mayi/ anaona
supu: na nyama/ anakula bukari:
anakula bukari: kiisha anashiba:
anakunywa na ile mayi ilikuwa mu
kopo/

one thing in the bowl. Then she
took a bowl with water and put it
on the side. And this she carried
into the hut of one of the young
people. Then she took another
bukai, sauce, and meat and put it
into another bowl, and also a bowl
with water. This she put into the
hut of the other young man.

Then the two young people came
back to their huts and entered.
One of them – the one called
Reason-from-people – looked [at
the food] and said: How am I going
to eat? They just gave us *bukari*
without any sauce, and just water
to drink and to wash with. All
right, I can go and ask about it. So
he went to ask an elder. He said: I
see only *bukari*, no sauce, no meat.
And only water to drink and to
wash with.

The elder asked him: What is your
name, who are you? he said: I am
Reason-from-people. He said: All
right, we can give you advice. Go
and take the water and wash. Then
take the *bukari* and put it into the
bowl in which the water was before
and you'll see the sauce and the
meat. So this young man went back
to his hut where they had put the
food to find out. He washed in the
bowl in which the water was, then
he took the *bukari* and put it into
this bowl, and he saw the sauce and
the meat. And he ate and ate of the
bukari till he had enough, then he
drank water from a cup.

ule mwengine iko anaongoya:
batakuwa kuleta tena supu na nya-
ma/ tena hataweza kuuliza hapana/
maneno akili yake: yee iko yee
moya/

kiisha banaona saa inapita/ wakubwa waliwatosha asema: watoto
mutokeni: tukakate mambo yenu/

bon/ walimutosha na ule kijana
asema: mi sikudie/ asema: maneno
gani hukukudia? maneno balini-
wekea paka bukari mutupu: pasipo
supu na nyama/

banamwambia ule kijana mwen-
zake/ asema: weye mwenyewe uta-
weza kumukatia mwenzake mambo
yake/ wende ukamuonyeshe sawa
vile tulikuonyesha wee/

bon/ walikwenda/ na ule kijana
mwengine/ ule kijana alinawa ku
mikono yake/ anakamata ile bukari:
anaweka mu sahani/ kiisha kuweka
ile bukari mu sahani: anaona supu
na nyama ndani ya sahani ingine/
alianza kula na ile bukari mwenyewe: anaisha/ paka yee mwen-
yewe/ ule kijana anabakia tena na
njala/

alafu wakubwa wanamuambia
asema: sasa unaona? unaona nini?
mambo yako: weye unanguka/ maneno wee ulisema: miye niko na
akili paka mi moya/ akili yangu
isitoke ku muntu: hata moya ha-
pana/

ni vile: sawa vile tulipata mafundisho yetu ya jamaa/ siye hatukutoshe
ya sawa vile ku ndoto: ao hatukutosha: namna gani? ao mu pori
hapana/ tulikuwa mbele na wasaser-

The other young man waited,
thinking: They are going to bring
the sauce and the meat. He did not
want to ask, because his reason was
from him alone.

Then they saw that the hour had
passed and the elders called them
out and said: Children come out, we
shall now decide your argument.

So they got this young man out,
but he said: I haven't eaten yet.
They said: Why not? Because they
gave me just *bukari*, without sauce
or meat.

Then they told the other young
man: You yourself can decide the
case of your friend. Go and show
him what we showed you.

So they went away. The other
young man, he washed his hands,
took the *bukari* and put it into the
water bowl. When he had done
so, he saw the sauce and the meat
in the other bowl. He began to eat
the *bukari* and finished it all by
himself. The other young man
stayed hungry.

The big people told him: Now you
see? What do you see? You were
defeated in your case because you
said: I am Reason-alone. My
reason does not come from any
other man.

This is how we received the teaching
of the Jamaa. We did not dream it
up, nor did we get it from the bush.
First, we had the priests, they
taught us all the matters of God as

dos/ wanatufundisha mambo ya Mungu yote/ sawa vile walijua: na sawa vile waliwatuma/ na kiisha wakiona namuna: shee tu mwenyewe tunaendelea na mifano yetu: walituasidia na kutupatia umoja wa shiye: kuungana nao: tukuwe kintu kimoya/ hiyi mambo ya jamaa: hatutoshe sisi wenyewe wakristu/ maneno mbele tulipata ubatizo: kwa saserdoes: kiisha: ndio tunapata kuendelea na mafundisho katika nkundi ya jamaa/ hatukutosha ku wankambo sawa vile ku nani? . . . ku . . . madawa: ao ku bintu ingine: ao ku kuteka hapana/ ni paka ku kwenzetu wasaserdos wajirudisha tena ungine asema tutaweza kuwasaidisha wantu: wapate kujua Mungu na kuendelea katika nkundi ya Mungu/ na wapate umoja na siye: na wao: si wote tukuwe wa muntu huyu moya/ tusiseme asema: ni shee mwenyewe tualitosha ile mambo: na tuko wapropheta hapana/ tulitosha hiyi akili: ni ku wantu: tulikuwa nao: sawa vile wakubwa/ ndio wale walituonyesha hiyi mambo/ yambo yetu bababa na bamama – *yambo yetu baba*/

they knew them and as it was their mission. When they saw examples of progress in us they helped us and we became united with them, as one thing. This is what the Jamaa is all about; we, the Christians did not make it up ourselves. Because first of all we received baptism from the priest, then it was given to us to progress in the teachings, in the group of the Jamaa. We did not get [the Jamaa] from our ancestors, as if it were a magic charm, nor did we steal it from somewhere. It comes from our own priests, who turned around and said: We will be able to help the people so that they may know God and make progress in the group of God. We and they should be united, and we all should be children of this one man. Let us not say that we ourselves brought forth these things and that we are prophets. Our understanding is Reason-from-people, from those to whom we looked as our leaders. They showed us these matters. Greeting.

Commentary

This is not the place to attempt a full reconstruction of context. I can refer to an earlier study about story-telling in the Jamaa in which most of the relevant aspects, such as generic status, rhetoric significance, and relation to traditional folklore are examined (Fabian, 1977). It should be noted, though, that this story appears to follow traditional models; it was not invented *ad hoc*.[12] Keeping in mind that we want to learn from the text something about the conception of religious diversity or plurality, I shall consider it under three headings: as a document, an event and a message.

Johannes Fabian

Document

There are reasons to insist that texts of this kind are documents, not 'data'. The difference lies more in the approach then in the nature of the information. 'Data' are pieces of information collected for the purpose of verifying, or at least illustrating, hypotheses. They are sought to confirm or disconfirm. Documents may also be used for that purpose but they have the property of not being used up, as it were, by analysis. Texts are resilient, quasi-independent 'monuments' of acts and words. Documents may be collected and classified (which is, in fact, all that happens to most of them) but they are not amenable to just any kind of ordering that satisfies the logic of extraneous schemes. This is why both quantitative and structural analysis must disregard the documentary character of texts; both must take the monument apart for their methods to work.

Of course, one may concentrate on certain documents rather than others with a purpose brought to the task, as I am doing here, trying to learn something about religious pluralism. Still, an interpretation of documents must be judged by its capacity to appreciate their proper life, their embeddedness in historical contexts and circumstances. Conformity to a canon of rules, methods and techniques cannot be the sole or even the primary criterion (although some such conformity will be inevitable, given the fact that interpretation produces a discourse which, like all kinds of discourse, follows certain conventions). Perhaps a way to put this would be to say that we must ask what an ethnographic document is a document 'of', rather than what it is a document 'for'. The answer to that elementary question ought to be that ethnographic texts are products of a communicative, in this case of a religious, praxis. Epistemologically it is important to insist on their being *products* of religious thought and action, not just representations. True, a text 'represents' a praxis. That function, however, is not adequately described if the text is only considered to be a sign or symbol (or a system of signs and symbols). Sign systems are by definition detachable from their referents and contexts; documents are not. To approach a text ethnographically, then, is to aim at the processes whereby it was produced.

To stress the processual nature of documentation is to say that anthropological interpretation, too, is part of that process by which a religious experience is 'expressed'. Oral, verbal expression is one stage; electronic recording, graphic transcription, translation into another language, and the interpretive discourse are further steps. In this approach, there is no essential difference, no radical cut between data and analysis. Many early ethnographers realized this (Boas, for example) when they cluttered their monographs with native texts.

Event

The story about the two young people and their quarrel is not only a document of a religious praxis in general. It connects us with a specific *event*: it was told on a certain date, in a certain place. The physical setting, the social occasion, the participants, the linguistic code, certain rhetoric conventions and numerous other determinants are known. These may be considered as 'components' of an event (in Dell Hymes's terms), not only to account for the *form* of behaviour but also to reconstruct the message, the *content* of that behaviour.

While it would be possible to give a thorough technical account of the components that made up the story-telling event under consideration (see, for example, Hymes, 1974), I will limit myself here to a summary of significant aspects.

The *situation* was, initially at least, set up by the ethnographer for the purpose of obtaining information about the use of traditional folklore by a religious movement of Christian inspiration. It was quickly redefined by the speaker and other persons present (and the fact that others were present was crucial, see Fabian, 1974: p. 256) as 'instruction' (*mafundisho*). Negatively, this expressed on the part of my interlocutors a refusal to treat a matter of importance in a question-and-answer format in which the researcher could have directed the course of the discussion. Positively, it conveyed to the exchange a communicative status higher than that of an incidental interview. To the Jamaa, *mafundisho* is (ritual) enactment of thoughts (*mawazo*), not just a vehicle of information.

The importance given to the situation indicated the importance of the *issue* which was, generally speaking, the identity of the movement. After all, I had come 'to find out about the Jamaa'.

The mere fact of an outsider asking questions about it puts identity into a problematic context. The speaker presumes that knowledge of dissent and conflict lies behind the researcher's inquiries. This, incidentally, was a constant throughout fieldwork, so that, from the point of view of the members, my study of the Jamaa was essentially a study of conflict while I, in the initial stages at least, had a thoroughly positive bias. I was trying to establish integration and cohesion. At any rate, it is clear that the researcher's presence as *audience* in a communicative exchange significantly determines the issue or content.

That is also the case of the physical *setting*. The recording took place in an up-country mission station, Kikondja, on Lake Kisale. While the group at Kikondja was rather marginal on other accounts (see Fabian, 1971: pp. 108–10), it was centrally placed with respect to the more virulent areas in the Kasai, in northern Shaba and in the cities to the south. From all directions, it received news of 'troubles', i.e. of conflict, schism, repression, including mass-excommunication. That the event took place at the mission and not in a private home only increased the apprehensiveness of the participants, as did the fact that, at the time of the recording, at least twelve different religious groups, denominations and cults were operating at Kikondja (not counting numerous traditional secret societies).

The event was also shaped by the choice of linguistic *code*, Shaba Swahili. It meant that two senior leaders of the group who were present but were not fluent in Swahili did not directly communicate with the ethnographer. It is difficult to say exactly what the consequences of this limitation were. There is little reason to assume that the difference in authority between senior leaders and junior speaker significantly changed the content of this 'instruction'. Specific semantic differences contingent on the chosen code may have been more important. It could be, for instance, that some of the key terms used in the story would have been more specific, more loaded with distinct cultural connotations, had the language been Kiluba. On the other hand, the choice that was made underscored the role of Swahili as a generalized medium of communication within a context of pronounced ethnic and cultural 'pluralism'. In Shaba, as in other parts of Zaire and of Africa in general, search for religious identity (through religious differentiation) is often being carried out through a linguistic medium which itself may be significantly shaped by these religious concerns.[13]

Message

Superficially, the message of the story appears to be quite simple. In a situation of conflict, tradition demands that the matter be brought to the authorities to be decided. Moral application: groups of the Jamaa in internal conflict should take their quarrels to the priests. On one level, that may indeed be its 'meaning', also for members of the Jamaa. The point is, however, that this story is not really located in that no-man's-land of abstract significance which is accessible to all and anyone. It is, as I hope to have shown, anchored in an event defined as teaching. It wants to convince, move, enlighten. The story is not just 'about' the problem of different views; it enacts the problem and gives a solution if only by practically and efficiently resolving the situation of disunity between researcher and researched. Both are drawn as participants in the event, into a discourse which, temporarily at least, unites them in one and the same process of communication and on the same level of reflection.

This, I take it, is a way to deal with pluralism without depending on a superior position outside or above 'systems' of meaning'. When the story recommends recourse to elders, chiefs, diviners (the semantic ambiguity here is itself part of the message) it does not ask for appeal to an extraneous hierarchy but to 'other people'. Even in traditional social organization, seniority marks primarily a position in lines of generation or filiation, and sometimes, by extension, positions in a hierarchy of power. Conversely, the elders insist that the litigants themselves can resolve their case and that the solution is not a matter of right or wrong but of 'asking'. And the reward is not just a favourable judgment but eating instead of going hungry.

Although its narrative form is that of an exemplary story or parable, the text is neither merely illustrative nor just entertaining. It is framed by introductory and concluding passages which lend to it the weight of doctrine.

There are elements pointing to an allegorical meaning which asks for esoteric knowledge available only to the initiated.[14] A gnostic streak in Jamaa thought may explain the significance of 'names'. Undoubtedly, it underlies the theme of *akili* (reason, intelligence, insight, knowledge in a transitive sense): trickery victorious is not the topic here (which it is in countless African stories), but life-giving knowledge, knowledge which connects with sources and origins (hence the references to beginnings and birth in the two framing paragraphs).

One may say, therefore, that this text declares the question of relationships between Jamaa and mission church, and between different Jamaa groups or factions, to be a matter of life (and death). In one sense, this radicalizes the issue of identity and difference to the point where superior distance from religious plurality cannot be kept. To these African believers it makes no sense to try and reconcile religious differences in a pluralistic manner. Life is one, so is religion, experienced as life (in Jamaa doctrine *uzima*, life, and *umoja*, unity, are interchangeable).

In another sense, this attitude makes possible extreme tolerance and adaptability. Life is realized less by order and discipline than by growth and strength. The Jamaa has had a long record of 'embracing' the authoritative claims and directives emanating from the church and its hierarchy without submitting to them. Authoritarian clergymen took this as a sign of shiftiness and dishonesty and not seldom as evidence for racially determined intellectual or moral inferiority. Anthropologists have no recourse to such 'explanations' but neither must they romanticize the people they study. I have argued elsewhere that the Jamaa may share the fate of countless forms of religious enthusiasm – routinization, internal exhaustion and eventual co-optation by the powers that be (Fabian, 1979c). Still, at the moment when the story event occurred, its message regarding religious pluralism was a true alternative to the conceptions we examined in the earlier parts of this paper. Diverse and conflicting religious expressions are not building blocks from which to erect schemes of law and order, they are food for thought and life.

IV

Pluralism – philosophical, juridico-political, sociological – is not a coherent theory, much less a methodology, for the study of diversity. At most it is a trend or style of thought derived from the

Kantian relativization of knowledge and its further application by Durkheim to religion and society. It is interesting, to say the least, to see anthropologists now considering religion a source of 'plurality' *in* a given society (that it serves to distinguish one society from another is seldom disputed). Perhaps this just reflects the fact that, as 'primitives' disappear under our hands, we are beginning to grant the peoples we study the kind of liberal eclecticism which has been the enlightened attitude towards religion among the Western bourgeoisie. Such liberal tolerance of diversity is certainly going to result in more interesting descriptions of religious behaviour compared to earlier evolutionist constructs and functionalist platitudes. But what makes that liberal stance possible (intellectually rather than ethically)? I have tried to show in the first two sections of this paper that 'pluralism' presupposes a ruler's or observer's position outside of, and above, the phenomena. Order under one law and constitution, order under one system of classification – these are the motives or implications of pluralist thought. When we push pluralist approaches to religious behaviour a step further, from the group or societal level to that of individual believers, we might be merely strengthening the grip that law-and-order theories have on our thought. Paradoxically, concern with 'pluralism' may have the effect of reinforcing rather than weakening the hegemonic attitude of the social sciences towards religion.

This was the reason why I proposed to consider pluralism 'from below', in such a way that the people we study are given a voice. I am glad to find that an African critic of the anthropological study of religious diversification comes to a similar conclusion:

> We are not likely to advance our investigation and understanding of religious movements if we continue to impose, upon empirical facts, categories and notions that are not germane to them and treat the observed phenomena as if they were explained by the labels attributed to them. . . .
>
> Sociologically fruitful analyses are more likely to emerge from an objective utilization of the subjective verbal, written, and published texts of a religious movement than from any theoretical assumptions about it. (Manyoni, 1977: p. 627)

There is, of course, a problem with what Manyoni calls 'objective utilization'. I hope to have given at least a suggestive example with an ethnographic interpretation of a Jamaa text.

Notes

1 The paper was written for a symposium on 'Plurality in Religion' at the International Union of Ethnological and Anthropological Sciences Intercongress, Amsterdam, April 1981. I want to thank the convener, M. Schoffeleers, for the invitation. Work on Jamaa texts, among them the story used in this paper, was supported by the Wenner-Gren Foundation for Anthropological Research, New York.

2 Geertz points to deeper connections between positivist (Comtean, Durkheimian) ways of dealing with religion and modern attempts to make scientific sense of plural, conflicting ideologies: 'We may wait as long for "the end of ideology" as the positivists have waited for the end of religion' (1973: p. 199).

3 Durkheim did this (e.g. in *The Elementary Forms of Religious Life*) by granting 'necessity' to categories derived from religion, claiming at the same time that this necessity could be empirically established. With that he pioneered a 'scientific study of religion' (characterized by an ability to reconcile religious faith with positivist scientism) and religious utilization of (social) science (a trait common to many modern religious movements).

4 Much of the following is inspired by Dell Hymes, especially by his essay 'Toward Ethnographies of Communication', originally published in 1964 and now available, together with other writings of his, in Hymes (1974a).

5 A handy introduction to these issues is provided by a reader edited by Giglioli (1972 and later printings).

6 But that demands important revisions of criteria by which language used to be measured. An interesting proposal, inspired, incidentally, by V. Turner and M. Douglas's writings on religion, was recently made by W. Washbaugh (1979). According to him we should abandon the notion of uniform language structure and consider degrees of structuredness, even 'anti-structure', as normal.

7 About this and other limitations of sociolinguistics, see my paper on 'Rule and Process: Thoughts on Ethnography as Communication' (Fabian, 1979a).

8 Some examples: Bateson (1974), Fabian (1974), Jules-Rosette (1975), Fitzgerald (1975); see also several essays in Fabian (1979b).

9 Taped at Kikondja, Shaba, on 16 December 1966 by the author. Fieldwork in Shaba was carried out between January 1966 and May 1967 and, as a side project, in 1972–4.

10 Numerous articles have appeared during the last twenty years and at least two monographs: de Craemer (1977) and Fabian (1971).

11 On standards of segmentation and transcription of texts in Shaba
Swahili see Fabian (1971: p. 228) (with revisions in later publications).
Two terms remain untranslated. *Bukari* (S. S. *ugali*) refers to the
staple which is the basis of every main meal. In Shaba it usually
consists of maize and cassava meal boiled in water. *Arisi* (S. S. *hadithi*)
means 'story' whereby a distinction between historical account and tale
is not made. Shorter *arisi* are often called *mifano*. The double meaning
of *mfumu*, chief or diviner-healer, was noted by Sacleux (1939: p.
547). Other items of interest for Swahili specialists must go without
comment on this paper.

12 There is a story in Doke's collection of Lamba folklore which revolves
around two brothers, 'Wisdom-is-being-told', the elder, and 'Wisdom-I-
have-it', the younger. But the plot is different, resembling that of
another Jamaa story (about the blacksmith and his son, see Fabian,
1969). Compared to the Jamaa versions, Doke's text looks mutilated
and fragmentary, which may reflect the conditions under which is was
recorded (see Doke, 1927: pp. 12f).

13 See on this topic the study by Bühlmann (1950), with further
references to the literature.

14 The 'name' of the litigants may be an esoteric formula. The proper
sequence of foods could be a reference to the stages of initiation and
that the chief's wife is involved may also have special significance; see
Fabian (1977) on allegoresis in Jamaa story-telling.

References

Adorno, Theodor W. (1964), *Jargon der Eigentlichkeit*, Frankfurt:
Suhrkamp.

Basso, Keith, H., and Selby, Henry A. (eds) (1976), *Meaning in
Anthropology*, Albuquerque: University of New Mexico Press.

Bateson, Mary Catherine (1974), 'Ritualization: A Study in Texture and
Texture Change', in Zaretsky and Leone (1974), pp. 150–65.

Bauman, Richard, and Sherzer, Joel (eds) (1974), *Explorations in the
Ethnography of Speaking*, London: Cambridge University Press.

Berghe, Pierre van den (1970), *Race and Ethnicity. Essays in Comparative
Sociology*, New York, Basic Books.

Bühlmann, Walbert (1950), *Die christliche Terminologie als missions-
methodisches Problem. Dargestellt am Swahili und anderen Bantu-
sprachen*, Schöneck-Beckenried: Ed. Neue Zeitschrift für Missions-
wissenschaft.

Craemer, Willy de (1977), *The Jamaa and the Church. A Bantu Catholic
Movement in Zaire*, Oxford: Clarendon Press.

Doke, C. M. (1927), *Lamba Folk-lore*, Memoir of the American Folklore Society, vol. 20, New York: G. E. Stechert.

Eister, Allen W. (ed.) (1974), *Changing Perspectives in the Scientific Study of Religion*, New York: Wiley.

Fabian, Johannes (1969), 'Charisma and Cultural Change: The Case of the Jamaa Movement in Katanga', *Comparative Studies in Society and History*, 11: pp. 155–73.

Fabian, Johannes (1971), *Jamaa. A Charismatic Movement in Katanga*, Evanston: Northwestern University Press.

Fabian, Johannes (1974), 'Genres in an Emerging Tradition: An Anthropological Approach to Religious Communication', in Eister (1974), pp. 249–72.

Fabian, Johannes (1977), 'Lore and Doctrine: Some Observations on Story-telling in the Jamaa Movement', *Cahiers d'études africaines*, 17: pp. 307–29.

Fabian, Johannes (1979a), 'Rule and Process: Thoughts on Ethnography as Communication', *Philosophy of the Social Sciences*, 9: pp. 1–26.

Fabian, Johannes (ed.) (1979b), *Beyond Charisma: Religious Movements as Discourse*. Spring issue of *Social Research*, 1979.

Fabian, Johannes (1979c), 'Text as Terror: Second Thoughts on Charisma', in Fabian (1979b), pp. 166–203.

Fitzgerald, Dale K. (1975), 'The Language of Ritual Events among the Ga of Southern Ghana', in Sanches and Blount (1975), pp. 205–34.

Friedrich, Paul (1980), 'Linguistic Relativity and the Order-to-chaos Continuum', in Macquet (1980), pp. 89–139.

Furnivall, J. S. (1948), *Colonial Policy and Practice*, Cambridge: Cambridge University Press.

Geertz, Clifford (1973), *The Interpretation of Cultures*, New York: Basic Books.

Giglioli, Pier Paolo (ed.) (1972), *Language and Social Context*, New York: Penguin.

Hammond, Phillip E. (1974), 'Religious Pluralism and Durkheim's Integration Thesis', in Eister (1974), pp. 115–42.

Hymes, Dell (1974a), *Foundations in Sociolinguistics. An Ethnographic Approach*, Philadelphia: University of Pennsylvania Press.

Hymes, Dell (1974b), 'Ways of Speaking', in Bauman and Sherzer (1974), pp. 433–41.

Jules-Rosette, Bennetta (1975), *African Apostles. Ritual and Conversion in the Church of John Maranke*, Ithaca, NY: Cornell University Press.

Kuper, Leo, and Smith M. G. (eds) (1969), *Pluralism in Africa*, Berkeley and Los Angeles: University of California Press.

Luhmann, Niklas (1977), *Funktion der Religion*, Frankfurt: Suhrkamp.

Macquet, Jacques (ed.) (1980), *On Linguistic Anthropology: Essays in Honor of Harry Hojer*, Malibu, Calif.: Undina Publications.

Mannheim, Karl (1964), *Wissenssoziologie. Eingeleitet und herausgegeben von Kurt H. Wolff*, Berlin: Luchterhand.

Manyoni, Joseph R. (1977), 'Anthropology and the Study of Schism in Africa. A Re-examination of Some Anthropological Theories', *Cahiers d'études africaines*, 68: p. 599–631.

• Pfeffer, Leo (1974), 'The Legitimation of Marginal Religions in the United

States', in Zaretsky and Leone (1974), pp. 9–26.

Rappaport, Roy (1979), *Ecology, Meaning and Religion*, Richmond, Calif.: North Atlantic Books.

Sacleux, C. (1939), *Dictionnaire Swahili–Français*, Paris: Institut d'Ethnologie.

Sanches, Mary, and Blount, Ben G. (eds) (1975), *Sociocultural Dimensions of Language Use*, New York: Academic Press.

Schermerhorn, R. A. (1970), *Comparative Ethnic Relations. A Framework for Theory and Research*, New York: Random House.

Silverstein, Michael (1976), 'Shifters, Linguistic Categories and Cultural Description', in Basso and Selby (1976), pp. 11–55.

Smith, M. G. (1959–60), 'Social and Cultural Pluralism', *Annals of the New York Academy of Science*, 83: pp. 763–77.

Tocqueville, Alexis de (1969), *Democracry in America*, Garden City, NY: Doubleday.

Washabaugh, William (1979), 'Linguistic Anti-structure', *Journal of Anthropological Research*, 35: pp. 30–46.

Weizsäcker, Carl Friedrich von (1977), *Der Garten des Menschlichen. Beiträge zur geschichtlichen Anthropologie*, Munich: Carl Hanser.

Zaretsky, Irving I., and Leone, Mark P. (eds) (1974), *Religious Movements in Contemporary America*, Princeton, NJ: Princeton University Press.

Chapter 6

Oral history and the retrieval of the distant past: On the use of legendary chronicles as sources of historical information

Matthew Schoffeleers

Some years ago, Luc de Heusch criticized Vansina and others for their somewhat overconfident use of legendary chronicles, such as those relating to the first Luba kings, as sources of historical information (de Heusch, 1972: pp. 15–18; 1975: pp. 363–7). If it were only overconfidence de Heusch was reacting to, there would be little cause for disagreement, for it is commonly recognized that Africanist historians have not always been sufficiently critical in their use of oral traditions, but de Heusch's criticism implied considerably more than that. Its tenor was, first, that these chronicles contained little or no historical information, since they were to be considered as no more than the transposition in pseudo-historical terms of a pre-existing body of myth (de Heusch, 1975: p. 364); and second, that the only valid approach would be to treat them as myths, that is, as statements about the cosmic order. Even seemingly historical events were in principle to be treated as cosmological metaphors (de Heusch, 1975: pp. 365–6).

It cannot be denied that de Heusch argued his case quite plausibly by pointing on the one hand to the striking similarities between the founding myths of a number of Central African kingdoms, and on the other hand to the parallels between these African myths and the chronicles relating to the first three kings of ancient Rome, which Dumézil (1948) had already shown to be essentially non-historical. But doubt creeps in when one begins to consider some of the implications of his approach. To begin with, it precludes any investigation of possible developments within the body of myth itself, which to all intents and purposes is presented as timeless. The myths are simply there. They are said to have already been in existence before the formation of the kingdoms in the fourteenth or the fifteenth century, and they apparently remained unaltered till the nineteenth century, when some of the kingdoms vanished and others were fundamentally transformed. The question which this poses is whether structuralism in this unmitigated form extends in another way the classic but erroneous view of a black continent which for countless generations remains unchanged, if not politically, then at least intellectually.

Second, de Heusch's approach to myths, with its assumption of a unitary world view in which a single text may contain in condensed form all the mythological thought of a people (de Heusch, 1975: p. 363), takes no account of the possibility that different sections of a single society may have entirely different views about the cosmic and social universe and the relations between the two. More concretely, it does not allow for a situation in which people express deep-seated social differences by means of different mythologies. Consequently, de Heusch makes no effort to look for counter-mythologies among the Luba and their neighbours, although they could in principle have existed among the numerous secret societies, to mention but one possibility. Throughout, however, his attention seems riveted on chiefs and kings as the central aspect of society, thereby perpetuating yet another perspective that in the meantime has come to be considered as lopsided and inadequate.

It is not the intention of this paper simply to turn the tables on de Heusch. For one thing, his questioning of the way ethno-historians sometimes treat mythical material is valid and to the point. For another, it is clear that structuralism has its uses for the historian also, as Willis (1980: p. 32) notes in his comment on Vansina's work. But the rapprochement in so far as it exists in the field of Africanist studies has remained one-sided, and the structuralists have still to come to the point where they acknowledge the relevance of the historical approach to their own work. It is with this issue that the present paper is centrally concerned.

In view of the criticisms just formulated, the ideal would have been to demonstrate that relevance by working from the same material that de Heusch uses, but since I cannot claim sufficient familiarity with the ethnography of the Luba and related peoples, the only alternative will be to use a body of myth with which I am personally acquainted and which is now being prepared for publication.[1] The myths in question, which belong to the Mang'anja people of South Malawi, purport to describe the foundation of an ancient earth cult whose patronal deity is called Mbona, and like the royal myths of Central Africa they exhibit a great deal of variation. The claims to be made in their connection are that it can be demonstrated (a) that they have their roots in different historical periods and that they can be made to yield a certain amount of information about those periods; (b) that, taken as a whole, they express a crucial development in Mang'anja thinking about the social order; and (c) that they represent a dual conception of that order.

If these various claims can be substantiated, the paper will have performed two tasks: it will have shown de Heusch's scepticism in regard of the historiographical potential of myths in principle to be unfounded, and it will have put his own structuralist assumptions under scrutiny. The cardinal question naturally is whether and to what extent substantiation will be possible. To answer that question, let me begin by acknowledging that historical reconstruction from mostly oral sources as in the present case is always a matter of circumstantial rather than direct evidence. In addition to this, such information as can be abstracted from them is, to use Willis's terminology (1976: p. 2), primarily of a qualitative kind, referring to social-evolutionary processes rather than discrete events. Given these provisos, however, it would seem that the Mbona material offers a suitable case against which to test de Heusch's central assumptions.

The argument will be developed in four parts. First, I shall provide a brief outline of this early period of Mang'anja history, which stretches from a hypothetical base-line in the fourteenth century to the first decades of the seventeenth century. Next, I shall introduce the various versions of the Mbona legend and show how and to what extent they seem to reflect that history. In the third part, I turn to the cosmological aspects of these legends, asking in what sense they represent different world views and what historical factors may have given rise to this differentiation. In the fourth and final part I return to de Heusch's assumptions to see how they stand up to these findings.

I

The Mang'anja are basically a society of hoe cultivators, who for the greater part live in the Lower Shire Valley of Malawi. Historically, culturally and linguistically they are related to the Chewa whose home area lies to the north and west of the valley, covering parts of Malawi, Mozambique and Zambia (Tew, 1950: pp. 30–50). Within the Chewa–Mang'anja complex, succession is matrilineal and marriage on the whole matrilocal. Politically, they are divided into a number of chiefdoms, which are internally ranked into a hierarchy based on a system of perpetual kinship.

Both the Chewa and Mang'anja have a dual tradition about their origins. On the one hand they maintain that their ancestors descended from the sky at a place known as Kaphiri-Ntiwa ('low flat-topped hill') on the border between Zambia and Malawi; on the other hand, however, they maintain that their forebears were immigrants from some country to the north (Ntara, 1973: pp. 1–16). Apart from this, they also hold that, instead of the dozen or so clan names that exist nowadays, originally there were only two clans, Phiri ('hill') and Banda ('plain'), both of which were exogamous (Ntara, 1973: p. 6). The generally accepted interpretation of these traditions among students of Chewa history is that they refer to the intermixture at some point in history of an autochthonous population, designated by the name Banda, with groups of immigrants, designated by the name Phiri, which came to form the nuclei of the later Chewa state systems (Hamilton, 1955; Marwick, 1963: p. 378). In line with similar situations elsewhere (Fortes, 1940: p. 258; Richards, 1959: p. 41; Turner, 1957: p. 4) this seems to have given rise to a dual structure in which ritual authority, particularly in respect of earth and fertility cults, was vested in the autochthonous section, while the immigrants came to hold secular power. In a general way, it can be said with Mitchell (1961: p. 33) that structures of this kind denote a form of interdependence between older and more recent population segments so that the stability and continuity of the social order depend on the combined exercise of their respective authorities.

This does not mean, however, that this state system necessarily covered the whole of the Chewa area, for as late as the early nineteenth century the Portuguese traveller A. C. P. Gamitto noted the existence of a stateless pocket in the eastern Chewa area

(Gamitto, 1960: pp. 66–7), and it is more than likely that similar pockets existed throughout much of the Chewa area until the advent of the Ngoni and in certain cases even until the beginning of the colonial period.[2] The overall picture which thus emerges is that of a collectivity of states whose centralizing and expansive tendencies were kept in check internally by institutions such as the earth cults and the village-based secret societies (Marwick, 1968; Rita-Ferreira, 1968; Schoffeleers, 1976), and externally by the persistence of interspersed stateless zones whose populations vigorously defended their independence (Gamitto, 1960: p. 67)

The main observation to be made at this point is that a similar system seems to have operated in the Mang'anja area till the closing decades of the sixteenth century, but that from then onwards a state system developed which was profoundly different from its Chewa counterparts. The cause of this was the rise to power of an aristocratic lineage, known as the Lundu dynasty, which was able to destroy or incapacitate virtually all the traditional sources of internal opposition and thereby establish a degree of centralization unparalleled in any of the neighbour states. This feat was in all probability performed with the help of an army of refugees from the south bank of the Zambezi who had been driven out by Portuguese military actions in the interior. We are fortunate to possess a certain amount of contemporary documentation allowing us to reconstruct an outline of the major events which took place in and around the Shire Valley between the late sixteenth century and the year 1622, when the Lundu section was temporarily defeated (Alpers, 1975: pp. 46–58; Bhila, 1977; Schoffeleers, 1978).

Within the valley itself the memory of this traumatic period is perpetuated in a number of ways. Thus, for instance, the area where the army in all probability had its base camp still bears the name of Tundu, its general, who has also gone down in folk belief as an evil spirit which causes destructive storms and locust plagues.[3] But the main repository of oral recollections pertaining to this period is the Mbona legends which form the subject of this paper.

II

In the course of my fieldwork I have collected more than twenty versions of the Mbona story. Although considerably varying in elaboration and content, they also possess a common sequential structure which in essence consists of three elements. First, Mbona is invariably portrayed as a male who had power over the rains and who for that or a related reason aroused the hostility of some rival. Second, all accounts tell us that he fled from his rival but that the latter managed to kill him in the end. Third, in all cases it is mentioned that after the killing a shrine was built to his name and that by this act the beneficial powers he had possessed during his lifetime were perpetuated. This basic structure constitutes the minimal dogma shared by all who have an interest in the cult.

Turning our attention to the variations in these stories, we find that these relate among other things to the location of Mbona's homeland, his ancestry and social personality, and the identity of his main antagonist. Other variations have to do with events said to have happened at the time of his flight, and yet others with the manner in which he was killed and the manner in which the cult came to be instituted. Taken together, however, these variations seem to fall into three distinct patterns, which appear in the texts in either pure or mixed form. In addition to this, each of these patterns shows close correspondences with successive periods in early Mang'anja history as contained in the oral traditions of the chiefdoms, thus establishing a broad parallel between their recollections of the political past and those of the cultic past. If we indicate these various patterns or streams in the cultic traditions as Mbona I, II and III, the following picture emerges.

Mbona I

In this stream Mbona is said to have been a Chipeta tribesman from the area of Kaphiri-Ntiwa, and the son of a rain-priest by the latter's junior wife. When Mbona was already a married man with several wives, a quarrel developed between him and his half-brother, the son of the priest's senior wife. Both managed to recruit a large following so that in the end the entire tribe was split in half. At this stage an arbitrator was called in who ordered that both parties undergo the poison ordeal. Some traditions have it that Mbona cheated by secretly taking an antidote which made him vomit; others hold that he objected to the ordeal, declaring it to be a human invention and therefore fallible. Whatever the case, the arbitration effort failed and Mbona decided to flee to the Shire Valley with some of his followers. He left behind imprints of his body as well as of his bow and spear on rocky surfaces along the route, and he even engraved the Chipeta tribal emblem on a boulder at the foot of the highest hill in the area. The local population welcomed him, since he brought them regular rains, something they had apparently never enjoyed before; but his sojourn among them was not to last, for when his enemies had found out where he was, they came down to kill him. After the killing they cut off his head which they then threw into a thicket, but local villagers buried the head and built a shrine over the place which then became a cult centre.

Mbona II

In these versions Mbona is portrayed as a member of the aristocratic Phiri clan and a maternal nephew of Kaphwiti, the reputed founder of the earliest state system on the north-western rim of the valley. Upon his marriage he was apprenticed to another uncle who held the position of the clan's official rain-maker. Once, at the time of a great drought, the uncle performed the rain-dance, but for the first time in his career without success. Explanations differ as to the reason why. Some traditions maintain that Mbona had applied sorcery against him. Others state that Mbona made his uncle powerless by accusing him of making improper overtures to the women assisting at the dance.[4] However this may be, Chief Kaphwiti, siding with his senior rain-maker, declared that Mbona had merited death, and the latter thereupon took to flight. On his way through the Shire Valley he managed time and again to elude his pursuers by repeatedly changing himself and his followers into a misty vapour, a clump of trees or a flock of guinea-fowl. In the end, however, overcome with fatigue, he was caught and killed. As in the first group of traditions, the head was severed from the body and a shrine built over it, thus marking the beginnings of the cult.

Mbona III

Here, Mbona's homeland is in the valley itself and he is now said to have been the maternal nephew of the first Lundu king. Normally, he would have been a candidate for succession to the kingship, but there were two obstacles. First, he was considered illegitimate, since his mother, whose name is mentioned as Tundu, had borne him out of wedlock. Second, although already an adolescent, he still behaved as a child, for contrary to accepted custom he continued to live in his mother's hut, whereas he should have been staying in a bachelor's hut like other youths. The king therefore despised him, but he did not know that his mother had conceived him by the power of *Mulungu*, the Supreme Being, and that he therefore was a son of God.

Once, at the time of a major drought, the king tried to perform the rain-dance as he was used to doing, but this time the dance was unsuccessful. Other members of the royal lineage took their turn, also without success. The public then urged the king to let Mbona try and, as was to be expected, the long awaited rains finally began to fall. An accident happened, however, for in the course of the performance a lightning bolt killed the king's young son. The king accepted this as an act of God, but his wife blamed Mbona and refused to sleep with her husband unless he promised to have him put out of the way. The king finally gave in and hired a band of assassins, but when the latter sneaked up to Mbona's hut, they found him and his mother already gone. Sensing the king's evil intentions, they had decided to flee southwards.

On the way Mbona performed a number of food miracles, such as creating a paddy field, to keep himself and his mother from starving. When they had come to the end of the range of hills which forms the western rim of the valley, the mother took leave of her son and was miraculously carried to the south bank of the Zambezi where she became a supernatural being in her own right with power over rain and drought. Upon her departure Mbona was caught by Lundu's men, but they failed to kill him until he told them that this could only be done in the valley below and by cutting his head with a blade of grass. This done, he died, but after the killing he revealed himself, amidst a raging storm, as a new spirit. He ordered the king to provide him with a woman who was

171

to be his wife at the shrine, and to co-operate with his people in making regular sacrifices to him. It was thus that the cult commenced.

It will be clear even from these brief summaries that each stream tells a very different story and that virtually the only elements that remain the same throughout are Mbona's name (but not his personality) and the three-phase plot structure. But it will be equally clear that some of the variations exhibit strikingly regular patterns. To begin with the most obvious example, Mbona's reputed homeland, moves as it were from north to south in an almost straight line (see Map 6.1): from Kaphiri-Ntiwa, which lies at a distance of over 300 kilometres from the shrine, to Kaphwiti's headquarters on the north-western rim of the valley, and finally to the king's capital within the valley itself. Concomitant with this, one notes that the society into which he is born becomes increasingly centralized, shifting from an apparently stateless system associated with the ethnic designation 'Chipeta', via a collectivity of small states represented by the name 'Kaphwiti', to a powerful kingdom.

Mbona's *de jure* status follows a similar upward curve as in each case he is a close relative and potential successor of the main office-holder. Yet at the same time we see that his *de facto* status follows a downward curve, for he is first portrayed as an adult with several wives, then as a young man with only one wife, and finally as someone who is socially still a child. In other words, the pattern is one of a steadily increasing power differential, Mbona becoming more and more powerless in comparison with his main antagonist. But that pattern is once again reversed in the final part of the story, when Mbona becomes a divine being, although in this case the variations are much less regular. Instead of the gradual changes, we find in fact an almost abrupt break between the first two streams and the third, a break which is already visible in the account of the killing. Thus, while in streams I and II Mbona seems to be at the mercy of his assassins, in stream III the latter are more or less at Mbona's mercy, since their weapons prove useless against him and he himself has to tell how to kill him. A similar break appears when we look at the founding of the cult, which in the first two streams is attributed to the initiative of human agents, while in the third stream it follows from a theophanic event in which Mbona himself takes the initiative by ordering the king to provide him with a wife and to co-operate with his people in the making of regular sacrifices. This distinction between graded and abrupt variations, which are graphically represented in Figure 6.1, forms a crucial element in our analysis and we shall return to it shortly.

		Mbona I	Mbona II	Mbona III
GRADED VARIATIONS	Homeland	Stateless	Chiefdom	Kingdom
	Adversary	Rain-priest or associate (half-brother)	Chief (uncle)	King (uncle)
	Mbona's social status	Adult with several wives	Young man with one wife	Child or child-like person
ABRUPT VARIATIONS	Manner of killing	With iron weapons		With grass
	Founding of cult	On initiative of local population		On Mbona's own initiative

Figure 6.1 *Variations in the Mbona traditions*

Before doing so, however, we need go into the possible historical content of these various streams, asking ourselves whether and to what extent they are to be regarded as reflections of factual history. I am committed to a view similar to Willis's in regard of the Fipa myths, which means that I see the Mbona narratives essentially as a cosmological discourse built upon a number of verbal nuclei that possess definable historical content. It is not possible and perhaps not even necessary to enter into much detail on this point, for I only need to show that there exist demonstrable correspondences between these narratives and certain historical events or processes known to us from other sources. This is easiest performed in the case of Mbona III, since the names Lundu and Tundu, which figure so prominently in that stream, also occur in Portuguese documents. Of course, Lundu is a perpetual royal title which has persisted into our own days and

which can therefore not be pinned down to just one historical
period, but Tundu is a proper name, which both in Mang'anja oral
history and Portuguese documentation is mentioned in only one
specific context, viz. the upheavals that took place in connection
with the rise of the Lundu kingdom just before and after AD 1600.
The fact that Tundu appears in the documentation as a redoubt-
able war leader and in the narratives of stream III as Mbona's
mother does not in any sense weaken the evidence. All it does is to
make clear that historical facts are transformed in myth in
conformity with the message that the myth conveys. I shall return
to this shortly, but it may be noted in passing that these two images
of Tundu are similar in that both may be seen as denoting a
generative principle. Thus, in so far as Tundu in the role of mother
is said to have brought forth Mbona as a person, Tundu in the role
of war leader may be thought of as having brought forth the cult
which, as I shall argue, underwent major ideational and organizational changes during that period.

Some of the names and titles in the other streams, too, appear to
possess historical content, an obvious case being the ethnic
designation 'Chipeta' and its association with a stateless system,
but I shall pass these by for brevity's sake to consider the set of
verbal nuclei represented by the various feats that Mbona is said to
have performed during his flight. It will be remembered that these
consisted respectively in a series of rock marks, metamorphoses
and food miracles. I must confess that these items were a source of
constant puzzlement to me, but the fact that each type of feat is so
consistently associated with a particular stream suggested quite
strongly that they contained information proper to that stream
only and not to another. In other words, the likelihood was that
the message would be of a historical nature. The solution which
finally offered itself was that the rock marks should be taken as
referring to the claims that the keepers of the oldest stream in the
Mbona narratives make with regard to the land, of which they
consider themselves the original owners. This, one might think, is
particularly clear where Mbona is said to have carved his tribal
(i.e. Chipeta) emblem in a rock. The accounts of Mbona's
metamorphoses in the second stream may possibly be taken as
referring to the pre-kingdom situation, when the valley population
oscillated between a stateless and a state-based organization.[5]
Finally, the food miracles of the kingdom stream almost certainly

refer to a condition of famine caused by a period of large-scale warfare and the presence of a considerable number of refugees in the valley.[6]

This, however, does not exhaust the historiographical potential of the various streams, for it appears that they can also be connected with specific aspects of the cult organization in such a way that they reveal something about the genesis of that organization. Since I have dealt with the latter extensively in a previous publication (Schoffeleers, 1977), I shall present only a brief outline at this point. The centre of the organization is the shrine itself which has the shape of a circular hut of normal proportions. This hut, which stands in a forest clearing, is guarded by half a dozen shrine keepers who keep the surroundings clean but who are not expected to carry out any repairs. Instead, the hut is rebuilt every five years or so, more or less synchronous with the minor drought cycle of the valley. Representatives from the various chiefdoms may come to the shrine at any time to make petitions on behalf of their area, but once a year, just before the rains, a sacrifice is offered on behalf of the entire cult region. In the past it was customary also for the king to provide Mbona with a woman, who would be known as his wife, and who would live at the shrine until old age or death. That custom has now ceased in that form despite repeated attempts to have it revived.[7] After the death of a spirit wife another would be installed, but often enough years went by before this was done. The usual procedure seems to have been to wait until a major drought occurred, which would mean that a new spirit wife was obtained from the king every twenty or twenty-five years on average.

This ritual cycle is paralleled by the organization of the cult which may be visualized as consisting of three concentric circles around the actual grounds of the shrine. The first of these circles covers the area within a radius of about three miles from the shrine grounds. Within this area reside the principals of the cult organization as well as the medium and a number of secondary officials. Of the two principals, one acts as the chief ritual officer and the other as the chief jural officer. Together, they are responsible for the day-to-day conduct of the cult, but their major responsibility is the annual sacrifice. The second circle is the administrative district of Nsanje, which in pre-colonial days existed in a different form.[8] The major personage here is a regional chief whose dynastic title is Tengani and whose main responsibility is the rebuilding of the shrine. The third circle covers the entire cult region which includes the Shire Valley and adjoining parts of Mozambique. The central personage here is the king, now paramount among the chiefs, who as we have seen customarily provided the spirit wife. His headquarters lies at a distance of about ninety kilometres from the shrine.

Looking now at the ritual cycle in conjunction with the organizational structure, we note that the former moves geographically outwards, involving the first circle every year, the second every five years and the third every twenty or twenty-five years. This, it should be repeated, does not mean that for the remainder of the time these outlying parts are not involved in the cult. They are, if only through the delegations that are intermittently sent by the individual chiefdoms, but their own specific role is defined in terms of the successive phases in the cycle.

The point to be made now is that there appears to be a close correspondence between the organizational structure and the ritual cycle on the one hand and the several streams in the Mbona narratives on the other. Thus, narratives of the Mbona I tradition are found only in the inner circle and more specifically among the family of the chief ritual officer and the group of his immediate associates. Narratives of the Mbona II tradition, on the other hand, are found both in the inner and middle circle. In the latter case they are kept by the Tengani family and associates; in the former case by some of the secondary shrine officials. Finally, Mbona III narratives are typical of the outer circle, where they are the specific property of the Lundu family, but they are also kept by the highest jural authority within the inner circle and by the population at large. Figure 6.2 provides a graphic illustration of these correspondences.

One can see from the pattern which emerges from Figure 6.2 that the crucial authority figure in each circle is of the same type as that in the successive streams, viz. a rain-priest, a chief and a king. How can this striking parallel be explained? It must be admitted from the outset that the various streams would appear to function as *post factum* charters, but in the light of everything that has been said so far one has to dismiss this as too simplistic. Certainly the narratives kept by the various officials do function as charters, but that does not necessarily mean that they are *post factum*

	Circle I	Circle II	Circle III
Mbona I	Chief ritual officer and associates		
Mbona II	Secondary officials	Regional chief and associates	
Mbona III	Chief jural officer and associates		King and associates
	Population at large		

Figure 6.2 *Social location of the various streams in the Mbona narratives*

inventions. As a matter of fact, the most obvious and at the same time also the most logical interpretation would be to view the different streams and the corresponding organizational circles as rooted in the same historical periods. This does not mean that they originated in more or less the same form that they have today, for that is contradicted by the evidence itself. Rather, what I wish to maintain is that each successive period after the initial establishment of the cult saw the formation of a new circle which influenced and to a certain extent transformed the core organization. Although the matter still requires further study, it does not seem unreasonable to accept the existence of a historical link between the secondary officials and the chiefdom phase, and between the chief jural officer and the kingdom phase. Both types of position may have merged at these points of history in consequence of secular rulers trying to obtain a certain degree of control over the core organization.

The inference to be drawn, then, both in relation to the narrative streams and the organizational circles, is that they are reflections of various stages in history in which the valley population had to seek accommodation with a succession of different power structures. In these accommodative processes their earth cult, like earth cults elsewhere, will have played a crucial role. The processes themselves seem to be graphically symbolized by Mbona's person who at first always forms part of the emerging power structure, but who by means of a series of stereotyped events, represented by the triad conflict–flight–murder, comes to be identified with the pre-existing community. The outcome in each case, then, is the emergence of a mediating figure which can be identified with both sides and thus becomes capable of symbolizing the resulting accommodation.

III

Having considered some of the links between the Mbona narratives and the political and cultic history of the Mang'anja, we may now discuss their relevance for the Mang'anja world view. The specific claims made at the beginning of this paper were (a) that we could infer from these narratives a crucial development in the Mang'anja world view, and (b) that the Mbona narratives represent not one but two contrasting world views, which are respectively those of the nobility and the commonalty. To substantiate these points, we may begin by distinguishing between the various imageries used to describe Mbona. The point which strikes one most in this connection is the mentioning of sorcery in the first two streams and the absence of this element in the third stream, and more especially the folk version of the third stream. In the first stream, as will be remembered, Mbona had to face the poison ordeal, which naturally implies that there had been an accusation of sorcery. In the second stream it is said that he used sorcery against his uncle, the rain-maker. Neither of these streams, however, is clear on this point for each has versions that depict Mbona as the perpetrator of sorcery but each also has versions which cast his opponent in that role.

The traditions of stream III, on the other hand, are of an entirely different kind. There Mbona is described in the imagery of a child or sometimes even of an infant, thus excluding the possibility of his using sorcery. If we compare the various narratives, we may observe that in the sorcery streams Mbona is not too different from his antagonists and that their roles are in principle even interchangeable, for either may be sorcerer or victim. Not so in the infancy stream, where the crucial point seems to be an absolute unevenness between the two parties, who stand to each other as adult and child. It seems to me that the core idea in each case, viz. 'more or less equal power' and 'decidedly unequal power', fits the political situation of the historical period which it purports to reflect. This requires little clarification as far as the pre-state situation is concerned, but even during the chiefdom period there existed, as we have seen, a system of checks and balances between the nobility and commonalty which could appositely be described in terms of sorcery. Most of the checks and balances, however, were destroyed during the early kingdom period with the use of extreme violence, and the resulting powerlessness of the commonalty apparently found its most apposite expression in the imagery of the defenceless and innocent child.

This having been said, let us look again at the accounts of the founding of the cult which, as will be remembered, was ascribed in the first two streams to the initiative of the local population and Mbona's followers and in the third stream to Mbona's own initiative. At first sight there seems to be no connection between this and the two imageries just referred to, but this may be misleading. Let us begin by considering the infancy stream. The logic which seems to underlie the plots of these stories appears to be that there are two kinds of reality, viz. that which is immediately perceptible and that which is hidden but which will reveal itself when it is vitally challenged. In the latter case, not only does it reveal itself, but it also establishes its superiority over the other type of reality. Thus Mbona, who at first appears as a child, defenceless against the king, in the end manifests himself as a powerful supernatural being, capable of forcing the king into submission. It is not difficult to see that the plot would be inconclusive and its message incomplete and ineffective without this final theophany, for without it we would never have known the true nature of the child. But what do these two realities refer to in sociopolitical terms?

In view of the widespread warfare at the time of the first Lundu kings (again, see Alpers, 1975: pp. 51–4, and Schoffeleers, 1978), an obvious suggestion would be that the contrast refers to the daily reality of oppression and violence as against the ideal of peace. The message which the stories of stream III thus seem to convey is that violence is self-defeating or, put differently, that peace in the end is stronger than violence. The king may seem all-powerful and the child totally defenceless, but when things have run their course the roles are reversed: it is the king who has become the weaker and the child who has become the stronger party. The reversal of roles, however, is not a simple inversion. The child does not kill the king; it inaugurates a new order in which the king's role, too, will be a peaceful one.

Historically speaking, what happened is that Lundu came to be defeated by a more powerful rival, but the dynasty remained in power until well into the nineteenth century. The political structure, however, was altered once and for all, and the power relations in the Lundu kingdom became quite different from those in the other Chewa polities, where secret societies, among other things, continued to provide a powerful instrument of opposition to the ruler. This was no longer the case in Lundu's kingdom, where these societies had been exterminated and where abuse of royal power was a much more realistic threat.[9]

It seems to me that the infancy stories and the 'two realities ideology' of which they are an expression would be functional in precisely this type of power structure. The reality of kingship cannot be and is not questioned, but is said to be kept in check by a higher order. The condition of extreme subjection in which the population finds itself is acknowledged at one level of consciousness but denied at another, and what at first sight seems unacceptable thus becomes acceptable.

The sorcery stories appear to be of an entirely different nature. They do not propound a doctrine but describe a conflict between two more or less equal parties. In line with this, the building of the shrine is not presented as the beginning of a new moral and political order. Mbona does not force the killers into submission. They just go back where they came from, and the two parties which confronted each other throughout the story remain separated even when the events have run their course. This continuing separation is not only the conclusion of the stories themselves, it is also, and in a sense much more forcefully, brought out by the existence of opposing traditions within these streams, viz. one which holds Mbona guilty of sorcery, and one which declares him innocent. This is the kind of reportage one expects when two sides vie for power without a victor clearly emerging.

At this point we may take up a question which needs to be answered, if only to round out the argument. It stems from the comparison I have made between the Mbona cult and the earth cults among the other Chewa-speaking groups, and more particularly from the assertion made at the beginning of this paper that the history of the Mbona cult in the pre-state and early state phases does not seem to have been very different from its companion cults. The question then becomes: why is it that these companion cults have no tradition of a martyr; or conversely, how does one explain the martyrdom theme in the oldest Mbona traditions? One might even go further and ask why they centre on a divinized human being and not on manifestations of the Supreme Being as the myths of the other Chewa cults do.

The answer, as I see it, is that the murder theme arose first in the kingdom period but that it worked its way backwards, so to speak, through the entire body of pre-existing mythology. This may have been made necessary by the fact that the murder episode had become the dominant legitimating theme of the cult in its new and untraditional form. Those among the cult officials whose rights were grounded in either of the two earlier cult forms could not but recast their traditions in this new mould, since the nature of the mythical discourse had become entirely changed. While doing so, however, they were careful to preserve the major verbal nuclei which contained both the charter to their office and the historical references on which that charter was based. For me, the main argument to support this theory is the observation that the murder episode fulfils no essential function in the first two streams. In other words, it could have been left out without in any way destroying the logic of the plot. The same cannot be said of the third stream where the murder of the child is necessary to bring out its true nature. Consequently, despite the presence of this common theme, the underlying philosophies remain contradictory. The myths of those in power defend that power, and the myths of the commonalty challenge and relativize it.

IV

Let me summarize what has been achieved so far.

1 I have been able, on the basis of internal textual criteria, to identify three streams in the Mbona narratives, each of which describes the power relation between Mbona and his adversary in a different way.

2 It has been argued, partly on the basis of direct archival evidence and partly on that of circumstantial evidence, that these streams to some extent reflect political processes which seem to have taken place between the fourteenth and the seventeenth centuries. The picture which thus emerged was one of a three-phase development represented respectively by a stateless organization, relatively centralized chiefdoms and a highly centralized kingdom.

3 It has also been shown that the three streams exhibit certain parallels with the cult organization as evidenced by the types of authority – priestly, chiefly and royal – that successively play a role in the rites, and by the keepers of the various traditions. These correspondences have been interpreted as deriving from the charter function that some of these traditions undeniably possess, but also as reflecting the historical development of the organization itself. More concretely, the suggestion was made that the various streams in the Mbona traditions and the different circles which can be perceived in the organization are both to be regarded as precipitates of the same historical events and processes.

4 Returning to the particularities of the narratives, it has also been noted that they contain continuous and discontinuous features, the former being exemplified by the gradual increase of power on the part of Mbona's main adversary and the corresponding decrease of power on the part of Mbona himself; the latter being exemplified by the imagery used to describe this power differential and by the accounts of Mbona's killing and the subsequent foundation of the cult. The discontinuity in so far as it was revealed was found to occur in the third group of narratives which suggested that the core message in these narratives was different from the core message in the other streams. That core message, then, seemed to refer (a) to an essential difference between political relations in the kingdom and pre-kingdom periods, and (b) to an essential difference in the religious reaction to these relations. As far as the nature of political relations is concerned, the opposition between the two situations was seen to be that between not too great inequality (the sorcery imagery) and total inequality (the infancy imagery), and as far as the religious reaction is concerned the opposition appeared to be between the view that religion replicates the

political power play, and the view that religion denies the validity of the power play.

5 The final observation was that the latter view developed during the early kingdom period among the commonalty in reaction to the aristocratic view which continued as the philosophy of those in power, thus establishing a dual world view which has persisted into our days.

Considering these various findings, we may, I think, claim with Willis (1976) that we have made a case for the validity of the historical approach in respect of a body of genesis myths in the sense that they may in principle be made to yield qualitative historical information. But we have also gone beyond Willis by arguing that it may even be possible in some cases to retrace the historical development of the myths themselves and thereby to reconstruct part of a people's intellectual history. Assuming that our exposé, despite the gaps that an exercise of this kind necessarily contains, is essentially plausible, two questions, or sets of questions, arise which respectively concern themselves with de Heusch's and Willis's approaches. In the case of de Heusch the question would be whether there exists a logical contradiction between the structuralist and historical approach, and in Willis's case the question would be whether or not Fipa oral traditions would allow for an analysis capable of bringing out possible developments within their mythology.

As far as de Heusch's structuralism is concerned my doubts, as stated earlier on, relate primarily to his assumption of a unitary ideology underlying the mythical constructs of a people or, as in his case, a congeries of peoples. One would think that the possibility of a unitary world view existing among a certain population at a certain stage of its political and cultural history cannot be reasonably denied, but the opposite possibility is not to be dismissed either. In fact, what I have tried to demonstrate is the existence of precisely such a situation among the Mang'anja, where the nobility and the commonalty from the seventeenth century onwards seem to have held very different views about the nature of social reality, differences which in our view resulted from historical events that led to an unusually sharp cleavage between rulers and subjects. My critique of structuralism is that it seems unable to say much about the political reality underlying the

183

conceptual contrasts it attempts to identify and interpret. Human reality means more than wrestling with intellectual problems. It includes also reacting against social inequality and political oppression, and it is these aspects which the structuralist approach leaves undiscussed or which it even obscures. The result in de Heusch's case is a relapse into two erroneous views of African society that scholars for two or three decades now have been trying to get rid of: first, the view that pre-colonial Africa was essentially static, if not economically and politically, then at least intellectually, for no other conclusion can be drawn from his treatment of myths; second, the view that chiefs and kings formed the hub of the African social and intellectual universe, thus moving other equally important roles and institutions out of view. It is not my intention to argue that structuralism is altogether useless. Rather, I would maintain that it has to be complemented and perhaps mitigated by the historical approach.

By way of conclusion I wish to make another general remark which applies more specifically to Willis's work but which also may have wider significance. It derives from the fact that the historical analysis of the mythical narratives in this paper has to an important extent been made possible by the coexistence in the Mang'anja case of two distinct bodies of oral history, one of which pertains to their traditional kingdom while the other pertains to the Mbona cult. Had it not been for the latter, it would have been impossible to arrive at the kind of insights with regard to the Mang'anja past that I think we have gained, for the simple reason that their political histories reflect little more than the views of the ruling families. If one is to get a glimpse of what happened to the commonalty, one has to turn to the Mbona traditions which in part at least reflect the views of the common folk. This, as I have shown in my introduction, is something one might expect, since earth cults, and more particularly earth cults that have regional significance, operate as institutions through which secular politics may at times be criticized or challenged. What strikes one in Willis's discussion of Fipa oral history is his almost exclusive reliance on traditions emanating from their political centres. It may be that the Fipa have no other bodies of oral history relating to the early phases of their society, but it may also be – although I must confess to total ignorance on this point – that alternative histories do exist but have remained unnoticed. Whatever the case may be, my contention is that our view of the Fipa past might have been considerably enriched and even altered had indigenous cult histories been available. That much, I think, may be concluded from the Mang'anja case, which at the very least suggests that it may be rewarding for oral historians to pay as much attention to religious history as they do to political and economic history.

Acknowledgments

The fieldwork on which this paper is based was carried out at various stages between 1966 and 1975 with financial aid from the Nuffield Foundation London, and the University of Malawi. I wish to express my gratitude to both these institutions and to Professor Terence Ranger, Dr Wim van Binsbergen, Dr Richard Werbner and Dr Jocelyn Murray for their useful comments.

Notes

1 The publication referred to will contain six major texts which are representative of the different streams discussed in this paper. Of these texts, one has already been published in Schoffeleers (1980).
2 The Chipeta appear to be the least studied among the Chewa-speaking groups. Tew (1950: p. 31) equates them with the Chewa proper without further comment, but Gamitto's testimony, cited in the body of this paper, suggests the existence of crucial differences between them in pre-colonial times. Although Gamitto visited only one Chipeta group during his travels, there are indications that his observations applied in equal measure to other Chipeta groups, the main indication being that all of them seem to have lived in the same physical environment, viz. grassy flatlands.
3 The reputed base camp, known to this day as Matundu ('land of Tundu's people'), is situated in the area of hills just south-west of the Mbona shrine. These hills are strategically well-positioned, offering an unimpaired view of the surrounding area as far as the Zambezi, and allowing for easy defence in case of an enemy attack.
4 The specification given in the texts is that the rain-maker sprinkled flour on their bodies, which in normal circumstances women do among themselves in certain ritual contexts. The precise meaning of this deviation from the norm is not altogether clear to me, but I suspect that it refers to a functional reversal, the rain-maker turning himself into a rain-withholder, which in Mang'anja terms is a form of sorcery. This would also explain why no rains fell on that occasion.

5 Students of Chewa history have hitherto routinely assumed that the pre-colonial Chewa states possessed something like well-defined contiguous boundaries. Gamitto's evidence, cited in the body of this paper, on the other hand suggests the existence of intermediate stateless zones. Although we know little as yet about the processes by which central government came to be extended over some of these areas, it does not seem unreasonable to suppose that there have been periods in which communities within these zones oscillated between a state based and a stateless organization. At any rate, it seems more than just coincidental that the accounts of Mbona's metamorphoses while fleeing from his enemies occur precisely in those traditions which recount the expansion of the earliest remembered state system into the valley.

6 A more extensive comment on the food situation in the valley during the early kingdom period may be found in Schoffeleers (1978).

7 The custom in recent times has been to select a suitable person from one of the villages in the neighbourhood of the shrine. Attempts to revive the institution in its ancient form have been made on various occasions till 1969, when they were finally given up.

8 Although the administrative district of Nsanje in its present form is a colonial creation, it functioned in a different form long before colonial days. At that time it consisted of a number of important headmanships, and the headmen acted as permanent representatives of the various chiefdoms at the shrine.

9 My reasons for assuming a wholesale extermination of mask societies in the early kingdom are set forth in Schoffeleers (1978: pp. 29–30).

References

Alpers, E. A. (1975), *Ivory and Slaves in East Central Africa*, London: Heinemann.

Bhila, H. H. K. (1977), 'The Kaphwiti-Lundu Complex in the Lower Shire Valley to 1800 A.D.: Myth and Reality', paper presented to the International Conference on Southern African History, Roma, Lesotho, August 1977.

Dumézil, Georges (1948), *Mitra-Varuna. Essai sur deux répresentations indo-européenes de la souveraineté*, Paris.

Fortes, Meyer (1940), 'The Political Systems of the Tallensi of the Northern Territories of the Gold Coast', in M. Fortes and E. E. Evans-Prichard (eds), *African Political Systems*, London: Oxford University Press for the International African Institute.

Gamitto, A. C. P. (1960), *King Kazembe*, Lisbon: Junta de Investigações do Ultramar, 2 vols.

Hamilton, R. A. (1955), 'Oral Tradition: Central Africa', in R. A. Hamilton (ed.), *History and Archaeology in Africa*, London: SOAS.

Heusch, Luc de (1972), *Le Roi ivre ou l'origine de l'État*, Paris: Gallimard.

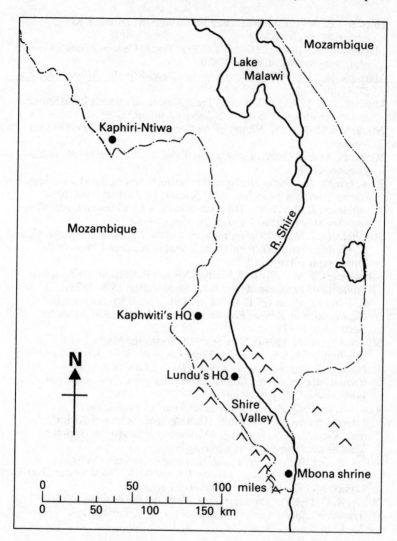

Map 6.1 *Southern Malawi and the Lower Shire Valley*

Heusch, Luc de (1975), 'What shall We do with the Drunken King?'
    Africa, **45**, 4: pp. 363–72.
Marwick, M. G. (1963), 'History and Tradition in Central Africa', *Journal
    of African History*, **4**, 3: pp. 375–90.
Marwick, M. G. (1968), 'Notes on Some Chewa Rituals', *African Studies*,
    27, 1: pp. 3–14.
Mitchell, J. C. (1961). 'Chidzere's Tree: A Note on a Shona Land Shrine
    and its Significance', *NADA* (Salisbury), 38: pp. 28–35.
Ntara, S. J. (1973), *The History of the Chewa*, Wiesbaden: Franz Steiner
    Verlag.
Richards, Audrey (1959), *Land, Labour and Diet in Northern Rhodesia*,
    London: OUP.
Rita-Ferreira, A. (1968), 'The Nyau Brotherhood Among the Mozambique
    Chewa', *South African Journal of Science*, 64 (January): pp. 20–4.
Schoffeleers, J. M. (1976), 'The Nyau Societies: Our Present Understand-
    ing', *Society of Malawi Journal*, **29**, 1: pp. 59–68.
Schoffeleers, J. M. (1977), 'Cult Idioms and the Dialectics of a Region', in
    R. Werbner (ed.), *Regional Cults*, London: Academic Press (ASA
    Monograph 16): pp. 219–39.
Schoffeleers, J. M. (1978), 'A Martyr Cult as a Reflection on Changes in
    Production: The Case of the Lower Shire Valley, 1590–1622 A.D.', in
    R. Buijtenhuijs and P. L. Geschiere (eds) *Social Stratification and
    Class Formation: African Perspectives 1978/2*, Leiden: African Studies
    Centre, pp. 19–33.
Schoffeleers, J. M. (1980), 'The Story of Mbona the Martyr', in R.
    Schefold, J. W. Schoorl and J. Tennekes (eds), *Man, Meaning and
    History: Essays in Honour of Prof. H. G. Schulte Nordholt*,
    *Verhandelingen van het Koninklijk Instituut voor Taal-, Land- en
    Volkenkunde*, 89, pp. 246–67.
Tew, Mary (1950), *Peoples of the Lake Nyasa Region*, London:
    International African Institute (Ethnographic Survey of Africa).
Turner, Victor (1957), *Schism and Continuity in an African Society*,
    Manchester: Manchester University Press.
Willis, R. G. (1976), *On Historical Reconstruction from Oral-Traditional
    Sources: A Structuralist Approach*, Evanston, Ill.: Northwestern Uni-
    versity. Melville Herskovits Memorial Lecture.
Willis, R. G. (1980), 'The Literalist Fallacy and the Problem of Oral
    Tradition', *Social Analysis* (Adelaide), **1**, 4, September 1980: pp.
    28–37.

Chapter 7

The historical interpretation of myth in the context of popular Islam

Wim van Binsbergen

1 Introduction[1]

The interpretation of myths, and the relative weight that should be attributed to mythical materials in historical reconstructions based, partly or wholly, on oral evidence, has been a bone of contention ever since Jan Vansina presented a comprehensive statement on methodology in this field (Vansina, 1965). In the domain of Central African history, which has been Vansina's main interest, this debate has been carried on by such scholars as Luc de Heusch (1972), Joseph Miller (1976), Roy Willis (1976) and Thomas Reefe (1977). Scholarly opinion has oscillated between the rather literalist early views of Vansina and the dismissively structuralist approach of de Heusch (which would read myths uniquely as timeless statements of dominant symbolic themes in a culture). As the body of available data expanded, and experience in the handling of such data accumulated, we have seen the emergence of more relativist approaches, best exemplified by Willis's work, which try to specify the conditions under which what aspects of what sorts of myth become amenable to what types of historical interpretation.[2]

Central Africa can be regarded in several aspects as the cradle of modern oral history and in my recent work on religious change in that region (1979 and 1981), I have had occasion to touch upon these problems. In the present article, however, I shall draw upon materials from North Africa collected during fieldwork in the Khrumiriya[3] highlands of North-Western Tunisia in 1968 and 1970.[4] The myth I shall focus upon is that of Sidi[5] Mhammad, a local saint venerated in the area where the foothills of the cool, forest-covered Khrumiriya mountains (which reach their summit near the town of 'Ain Draham, a colonial creation) give way to the luscious, wide-open plain of the Wad le-Kebir. This plain receives its name from a major river which stretches over fifteen kilometres, from its confluence with the Wad Ghenaka, northward to the age-old harbour-town of Tabarka. After presenting the myth[6] and briefly indicating the relatively ahistorical elements it has to offer to a cultural and structural analysis, within the simplifications enforced by an essay of limited length I shall build up a framework which opens out the historical content of this myth for analysis. This framework is informed, first, by an analysis of the social and religious organization of contemporary rural society in this region (such as it was at the end of the 1960s) and, second, by the historical evidence derived from other oral sources in the locality.

My argument will thus add a footnote to the religious anthropology and history of the Maghreb. But my main purpose is more general. I aim to show how the historical interpretation of myths should not be attempted in isolation, but against the background of much more comprehensive information about the past and present of a society and of a region. While in this way we may manage to decode a myth's historical message, it also becomes clear that the decoding procedure may be long, devious and uncertain. Finally, I shall demonstrate that, at least in the case of this one myth, the historical message may be carried over into a later period where the myth no longer can be claimed to sum up, in a detectable form, events that were of primary significance in the shaping of the political and social structures of that later period. The myth of Sidi Mhammad will turn out to be nothing like *the* key to the local past. Exciting as the process of interpreting the myth of Sidi Mhammad may prove to be, the conclusion will come as an anticlimax. The historical events encoded within the myth will turn out to be rather trivial and commonplace occurrences in nineteenth-century Khrumiri society.

This suggests that the great importance attached to the analysis of myth within the field of oral history may be somewhat exaggerated. Yet in many cases, particularly for the more distant past, and in the context of religious studies, a myth is all the evidence we have got. In such circumstances it would be a pity if we were forced to wholly fall back on the ahistorical structuralist alternative: and it is advisable for us to steer a middle course with the understanding that it would be dangerous to try to build historical reconstructions on mythical grounds alone.

2 The myth of Sidi Mhammad

The myth of Sidi Mhammad was known, in more or less elaborate form, to almost every adult inhabitant of my research area and adjacent localities. I managed to record as many as twenty variants of the myth. All agreed as to the basic narrative and only differed in the degree of detail that each informant spontaneously offered. On all occasions I recorded the myth as volunteered, without probing for more details. The variants could be aggregated so as to form one hypothetical and complete version. I am aware of the fact that this version is an analytical construct; yet the high rate of agreement and convergence between the variants seems to warrant such treatment. Table 7.1 summarizes which informants (numbered i–xx) presented which elements of the aggregate version. It is the public, consensual content of the myth that shall occupy us in the course of my argument, and not the specific minutiae of verbal activity as exemplified in the individual informants' presentations of the myth. I have not, therefore, attempted to relate systematically the differences (in length, precision, inclusion of certain elements and omission of others) to differences in sex, age, place of residence, descent group member-ship, etc., of the various informants. A more impressionistic inspection of these background variables, however, has convinced me that they had no significant effect on the distribution of variants. Variants of the myth that were recounted with third parties present did not differ significantly from those offered to me in private, and never gave rise to disagreement and critical discussion. This in itself suffices to place this myth, along with the other pious legends circulating in the region, in a class apart from other oral-historical statements in Khrumiriya. For (as we shall see, particularly in relation to evidence on genealogies, residential history, and histories of clans and lineage segments) oral-historical statements in contemporary Khrumiri society tend to be conten-tious, idiosyncratic, non-consensual and manipulative rather than collectively accumulated, shared historical images; and in this sense reflect the individual speaker's transitory position in a shifting network of interests and relationships.

The aggregate version, then, of the myth of Sidi Mhammad runs as follows (the elements, numbered 1–28, correspond to those in Table 7.1):

Sidi Mhammad (1) was a herdsman (2) employed by Sidi Slima (3) of Ulad ben Sayyid in the Khdayriya area (4). Sidi Mhammad took the cattle to graze in the immediate surroundings of what today are the hamlets of Sidi Mhammad, Mayziya, Tra'aya-sud and Tra'aya-bidh (5); various names of localities are specifically mentioned in this connection (6). There (implied or expressly: on the Hill-top[7] where later his main shrine would be located) he would sit down in order to sleep or to meditate (7). For that purpose he would take off some, or all , of his clothes (sometimes specified: his white burnous); towards the evening he would put these on again(8). The cattle he allowed to roam freely (9) in those parts (various names of localities are again specified in this connection) (10). Partridges came and alighted on his body (11), in order to pick away the lice (12). At dusk Sidi Mhammad would call the cattle to return to him (various ways are specified: he clapped his hands; he waved a flap of his burnous; or he made a to-and-fro movement with his walking-stick, which had a particularly large head) (13). The birds left him (14). He returned home (with all the cattle unhurt) (15). Sidi Slima became aware of this unusual way of herding (various ways are specified in which this information reached Sidi Slima: he is said to have followed his herdsman in the morning to watch secretly if the latter was doing a good job; or Sidi Slima's wife, or a passer-by, is said to have informed Sidi Slima of the strange ways of his herdsman) (16). (From his own reflection on this matter, or at the suggestion from others) Sidi Slima now understood that Sidi Mhammad was a saint (17), and notably: one greater than Sidi Slima himself (18). There were other signs to the same effect (e.g. Sidi Slima's wife noticed that Sidi Mhammad performed the Moslem's obligatory prayers before he went to sleep) (19). Therefore, when Sidi Mhammad returned home once again, he was treated with all signs of respect (his feet were washed, he was offered a choice meal – either by Sidi Slima or by the latter's wife but on his instigation)

Table 7.1 *Sequences of elements in the myth of Sīdī Mḥammad, as found in twenty variants*

	i	ii	iii	iv	v	vi	vii	viii	ix	x	xi	xii	xiii	xiv	xv	xvi	xvii	xviii	xix	xx
																				Informants
1	+	+	+	+	+	+	+	+	+	+	+	+	+	+	+	+	+	+	+	+
2	+			+	+	+	+	+	+	+	+	+	+	+	+	+	+	+	+	
3	+			+	+	+	+	+	+	+	+		+	+	+	+	+	+	+	
4	+				+			(+)			+						+			
5					(+)			+	+		+		+							
6				+	(+)			+	+	+	+		+	+	+				+	
7	+		+	+	+		+	+	+	+	+		+		+			+	+	+
8					+			(+)			+									
9	+				+			+	+	+			+					+		
10	+		+	+	+		+		+		+		+	+	+	+		+	+	+
11	+		+	+	+	+	+	+	+	+	+		+	+	+	+		+	+	+
12	+	+		+	+	+	+	+	+	+	+	+	+	+	+		+	+	+	+
13	+	+			+		+		+	+			+		+	+				
14					+						+									
15	+		+	+	+	+	+	+	+	+	+		+		+			+	+	
16					+				+								(+)	+		
17	+		+	+	+	+	+	+	+	+	+	+	+	+	+	+		+	+	
18	+			+	+	+	+	+		+			+		+	+		+	+	
19					+															
20					+			(+)			+		+			+	+			
21	+			+	+		+	+	+	+	+		+		+			+	+	+
22	+			+	+		+				+		+		+			+	+	
23	+			+	+	+		+			+		+				+	+	+	+
24	+			+	+	+		+		+	+		+		+	+		+	+	+
25														+		+				
26	+				+										+					
27	+			+	+				+	+	+		+		+			+		+
28				+	+				+	+	+		+	+	+	+	+	+	+	+

Note: the version as presented by, e.g., informant iii contained the elements 1, 7 and 11, in that order; further explanation in the text.

(20). Sidi Slima decided that the relationship of dependence between Sidi Mhammad and himself should be brought to an end (21). Sidi Mhammad settled on the Hill-top (22), which had been given to him (either by Sidi Slima or by some unspecified owner who may, or may not, have been Sidi Slima) (23) after Sidi Slima had urged him to name any gift that he might fancy (24). Good relationships, as between neighbours, continued to exist between Sidi Mhammad and Sidi Slima (25). Now everyone came to consider Sidi Mhammad as a saint (26). After his death he was buried on the Hill-top (27). And this was the origin of his present main shrine, called Sidi Mhammad le-Kebir (the Elder) (28).

3 The myth of Sidi Mhammad in the light of cultural and structuralist interpretations

It is perfectly possible to ignore any specific historical content in the myth of Sidi Mhammad; or to explain such content away as an accidental touch of *couleur locale* (allowing, moreover, for considerable free variation between the various narrators), of no consequence to the myth as a statement of cultural and symbolic structure. At least two lines of analysis are open then for such an ahistorical interpretation.

From the viewpoint of cultural analysis, the myth can be read as a particular combination of a number of hagiographic themes[8] which run through the Islamic cultures of North Africa and the Middle East, and which together serve to express the essence of sainthood as distinct from ordinary human existence. In these cultures the saint represents a distinct social category. He or she is characterized by an exceptionally close and harmonious relationship with God and with Nature; this enables the saint to circumvent the usual limitations of human toil and human social control, and instead to rely directly on divine grace (*baraka*). The saint reveals himself in various ways, ways which are often found in combination: through the ostentatious display of formal Islamic observance (in a cultural environment of popular Islam where very few people do perform the obligatory prayers, are sufficiently literate to have access to the Book, etc.); through wonder-working (*karamat*) and through the possession of material objects (such as stone cannon balls (*kurra*), or the white burnous) reserved for saints; and through a particular state of mind (*niya*) characterized by piety, humility and non-violence. Constituting a social category incomparable to that of non-saintly people, saints do not compete with ordinary human beings; on the other hand, the gradations of sainthood result in a saintly hierarchy, which defines some saints as being subservient to others, but which precludes relations of dependence between saints whose *baraka* is at the same level of excellence.

Considered in this light, the 'rags-to-riches' story of Sidi Mhammad is a restatement, cast in a local context, of what constitutes sainthood. Sidi Mhammad first appears as the essence of humility: a dependent herdsmen. His *niya* is further brought out by the fact that he keeps his saintly status a secret, and that he indulges in meditation or sleep unhindered by such social conventions as clothing and the behaviour expected from herdsmen. For herdsmen are supposed to remain alert in guarding the cattle entrusted to them against such accidents as may befall them on the steep and rocky forested slopes of Khrumiriya. The saintly herdsman's harmony with God and Nature is brought out by the fact that, even without the conventional attention, the cattle wander unhurt and return at the herdsman's first call, while partridges (like all birds, conventional messengers from Heaven) settle on his shoulders. The attempt on the part of a few informants to explain the partridges' presence rationally by referring to the poor herdsman's lice suggests that the divine symbolism of the bird has become lost on them. Anyway, as one would expect, Sidi Mhammad's sainthood could not remain a secret for long, and once detected, the relationship of dependence is supplanted by one of equality, via ceremonial actions and gifts through which Sidi Slima makes up for his original oversight. Incidentally, some variants also highlight the typical role of women in popular Islam as being more involved in, and familiar with, the supernatural aspects of life than men. In these variants it is Sidi Slima's wife who detects Sidi Mhammad's sainthood – thereby typifying the role of the wife as the mediatrix between her rural household and others, including the supernatural: it is the wife who processes food, cooks for visitors, visits saintly shrines and takes offerings there.

The second ahistorical line of approach to the myth would be that of symbolic anthropology or semiotics.[9] Despite much variation between individual authors and between schools, a consensus has developed over the past twenty years or so according to which a first step in the analysis of myth would be the application of fixed basic oppositions which, it has been argued, may be shown to underlie symbolic structures in a wide variety of cultures. Some of these oppositions are:

human	—	non-human
nature	—	culture
male	—	female
high	—	low (or, in general, vertical differentiation)
left	—	right (or, in general, horizontal differentiation)

Often, these oppositions turn out to be clad in oppositions between natural species (e.g. birds versus cattle) or types of natural environment (e.g. plain versus mountain). Through various logical operations (transformations) these oppositions are then shown to be connected to each other, and to form a deep structure revealing general features of human society and of the human mind.

Such a structuralist analysis of the myth of Sidi Mhammad would, I suppose, abstract even from the cultural model of the Islamic saint, and would instead stress the pairs of oppositions which are obvious in the story. In a somewhat diluted variant of the semiotic approach, the deep structure can then be related to fundamental formal aspects of the culture and the social structure in which it is found. Viewed in this light the myth contains much to please a structuralist's heart. In particular, the myth can be seen as a concentrated statement of vertical and horizontal oppositions, of which the 'rags-to-riches' theme (the movement from social *subordination* and vertical differentiation to horizontal *equality*) is only one aspect. Sidi Slima lives in the *plain*, whereas Sidi Mhammad takes the cattle into the *mountains*, and finally settles there as an independent pastoralist. While the cattle roam about in space (essentially *horizontally* – despite the mountain slopes), birds *descend* and *ascend*, and Sidi Mhammad remains *fixed in one place* as some sort of nodal point where the tensions between all these symbolic axes are resolved. While the saint transgresses the rules of *human Culture* through nakedness and socially unexpected behaviour as a herdsman (through which, in his *niya*, he reverts to a purer state of Nature under its human aspect), *non-human Nature* yet becomes domesticized under the effect of *Divine* Grace: wild birds fondly interact with the saint, and the cattle return unhurt. The rhythm of day and night should not be overlooked, either: from the point of view of his employer the saint is a herdsman during the day, only secretly to indulge in his sainthood through prayers at night; however, from the point of view of Nature, of God, and of the saint himself, it is during his day-time meditations and intercourse with the partridges that his sainthood is most clearly revealed. As a sort of transformational, vectorial solution to these and other binary oppositions (I only indicate the more obvious ones), the logic of the story almost inevitably leads on to a permanent geographical displacement of Sidi Mhammad from the plains, where his one-time employer dwells, to the mountains, where he now settles independently; from concealed sainthood expressed in interactions with non-human Nature, to an overt sainthood manifested in culturally patterned interaction with human beings (elements 26–8); and from a subordinate to an equal social position. That it should be a woman who, in some of the variants, forces this solution at crucial points is only logical, considering the symbolic ambiguities of women in Islamic rural cultures, along such axes as the opposition between Nature and Culture, subordination versus equality, and human society versus the supernatural.

It would not be difficult to relate this tentative and somewhat amateur structuralist reading of the myth of Sidi Mhammad to significant aspects of the social organization of the region. The Khrumiri mountain-dwellers are linked to the plain through economic ties (Tabarka has been a regional market for millennia), marital relations and pilgrimage (the Wad le-Kebir plain contains some major saints' shrines). In terms of supra-local relations, such as that between the plain (which for centuries has been economically and politically integrated in the international and intercontinental structures of the Mediterranean world) and the remote, somewhat inaccessible mountains (which, for example, in the nineteenth century defied beylical control and taxation), the myth of Sidi Mhammad could even be read as another restatement of the irony of the maghrebine local saint: as a stranger carrying elements of formal Islam into remote parts, he is soon encapsulated there so as to form, with his tomb, legend and *baraka*, a corner-stone of popular Islam, and a focal point for local, particularist social and ritual organization (cf. van Binsbergen, 1980). The horizontal/vertical deep structure of the myth reflects a symbolic accommodation of status differences, a dominant theme in the society of Khrumiriya and other parts of North Africa. In these societies we find on the one hand specific relations of interpersonal dependence (such as analysed by Favret, 1968), of which the institution of the stranger herdsman is but one example. On the other hand, the social process in these societies hinges on notions of honour and shame[10] which imply a potential equality between adults of the same sex. The myth of Sidi Mhammad and Sidi Slima can be read as a statement both of this contradiction and of its possible solution. It is perhaps significant that the act of quietly sitting on the Hill-top, at the intersection as it were of all these oppositions, conveys a suggestion of firm, legitimate individual ownership of land (*mulk*); and in this respect the herdsman's unusual behaviour (in which he denies being someone else's herdsman) anticipates the outcome of the story. Again, another major theme in Khrumiri society is, inevitably, the division of labour between the sexes in a context of reproduction and production; and a representation of this theme, the symbolic opposition between male and female, comes up in at least some of the variants.

In Khrumiriya saints only survive symbolically, as a cultural category explaining local shrines as places where saints living in the past have been buried. Unlike other parts of the Maghreb, contemporary Khrumiriya no longer has saints: the most recent actual encounter with a living saint as recorded in my oral-historical data took place in the 1910s. This might be all the more reason to consider the myth of Sidi Mhammad as a timeless symbolic statement for social-organizational or experiential referents, of whatever kind. The possibilities of relating the myth, and its deep structure, to the contemporary social organization in the region, without attributing any specific historical content to the myth, are many. Yet in the remainder of this paper I shall explore the limited sense in which the myth does convey a historical message.

4 Sidi Mhammad and Sidi Slima as contemporary shrines

The inhabitants of the region have good reason to be familiar with the myth of Sidi Mhammad. His shrine is still there. For anyone travelling from Tabarka to 'Ain Draham, the modest, square, white structure, with its domed roof (*qubba*) and horned ornaments on the four corners, can be seen across the Wad le-Kebir for about ten kilometres of the journey. In fact, the saint, and his shrine, have given their name to the entire valley south of the Wad Ghenaka, consequently called *hanshir* (patrimony of) Sidi Mhammad. In this valley, comprising the hamlets of Tra'aya-sud, Tra'aya-bidh, Sidi Mhammad, Mayziya, Raml al-'Atrus and Fidh al-Missay, three more shrines of the same saint can be found: another *qubba* right in the centre of the hamlet Sidi Mhammad; a hut-like structure (*kurbi*, consisting of a roof of arboreal material (branches, leaves, cork) on a foundation of large rocks laid out in the form of a rectangle) next to this *qubba*, and another *kurbi* between the hamlets of Sidi Mhammad and Mayziya. The *qubba* in the centre of the hamlet of the same name is called Sidi Mhammad al-Wilda (the Son) to distinguish it from the shrine on the Hill-top, designated le-Kebir (Elder). The collective celebrations during the massive festival (*zerda*), which is held twice a year in honour of Sidi Mhammad, take place almost entirely around the *qubba* of Sidi Mhammad al-Wilda. Sidi Mhammad le-Kebir's main function is that the valley's major cemetery is situated around this shrine. Hundreds of pilgrims (particularly women who, born within the valley, have married outside and who are under an obligation to visit the shrine) make the pilgrimage to Sidi Mhammad al-Wilda on the occasion of the *zerda* and throughout the year; however, on the same day, these pilgrims will also visit the adjacent *kurbi* as well as Sidi Mhammad le-Kebir (cf. van Binsbergen, in press). These three shrines are attended by a shrine keeper (*ukil*), who looks after the key to both *qubbas*, collects pilgrims' gifts, and performs a short ritual at all three shrines on Thursdays and Fridays. No such regular service exists for the *kurbi* half-way towards Mayziya, whose roof, however, is repaired twice a year by the inhabitants of that hamlet. The cemetery of Sidi Mhammad le-Kebir serves the hamlets of Sidi Mhammad and both Tra'ayas. Mayziya buries its dead at a separate cemetery, Sidi Rhuma. The hamlets of Fidh al-Missay and Raml al-'Atrus bury their dead near Sidi Bu-Qasbaya in Fidh al-Missay. This again is not the only local shrine of that name: in the western part of the hamlet of Sidi Mhammad, near a large farmhouse that during the colonial era (1881–1956) accommodated the only European presence in the valley, three more shrines bearing the name of Sidi Bu-Qasbaya can be found. The inhabitants of Fidh al-Missay and Raml al-'Atrus do participate in the festival at Sidi Mhammad al-Wilda; but they also have, on a much more modest scale, their own festival for Sidi Abdallah, represented by two *kurbis*, one in each hamlet.

Sidi Mhammad is clearly considered the major saint throughout the valley. In addition to the festivals, pilgrimages and burials near his shrine, all households regularly dedicate meals to him, to be consumed in his honour. The few people who can afford it irregularly sacrifice sheep, goats or a head of cattle for him. In everyday conversation, in the houses as well as the men's assembly grounds (which deliberately have been located so that the two *qubbas* can be seen from there), the name of Sidi Mhammad is frequently invoked to render force and credibility to a statement. And while a large number of saints and demons may be invoked in the course of the ecstatic dances in which over 20 per cent of the male population of the region specialize, the dancers (*fekirs*) in the valley of Sidi Mhammad tend to concentrate, in their song (*triq*), on that particular saint.

> My ancestor Mhammad,
> You who sleep under the fig-tree,
> Mhammad with the partridges,
> You who sleep under the hawthorn,
> Mhammad, assist me.

Nor is it only during the ecstatic dances that Sidi Mhammad is fondly called *djaddi*, 'my ancestor', 'my grandfather'. This is also what the women keep exclaiming in near-ecstasy, when they visit the shrines together, touch and kiss the walls and sacred objects inside, and dance near the tomb. This is how people in the valley choose to refer to their major saint. But so too are the scores of

Map 7.1 *Selected shrines in Khrumiriya*

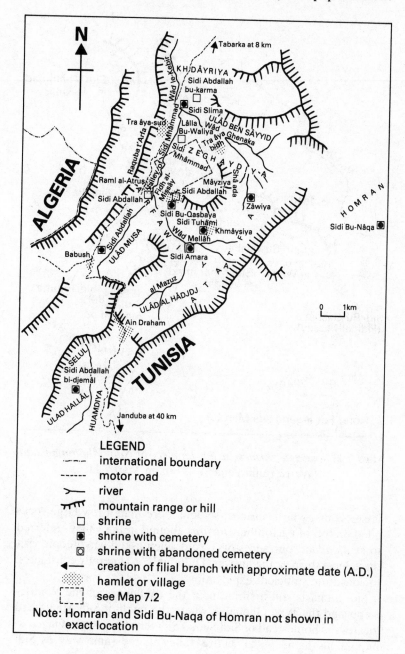

LEGEND
- ---·--- international boundary
- ------- motor road
- >—— river
- ⊤⊤⊤ mountain range or hill
- □ shrine
- ◉ shrine with cemetery
- ◎ shrine with abandoned cemetery
- ◀— creation of filial branch with approximate date (A.D.)
- ⠿ hamlet or village
- ⌐⌐⌐ see Map 7.2

Note: Homran and Sidi Bu-Naqa of Homran not shown in exact location

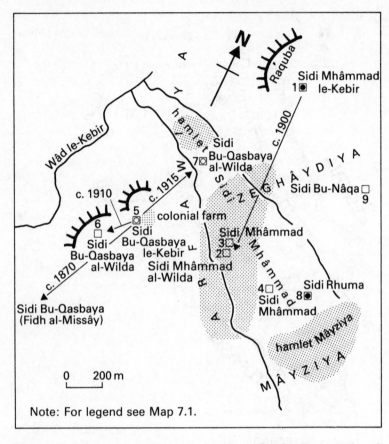

Map 7.2. *Selected shrines in the hamlets of Sidi Mhammad and Mayziya* (enlargement of box in Map 7.1)

lesser saints, whose shrines (seldom more than a few large rocks piled on top of each other: *mzara*) abound in the valley, referred to as *djdudna*: 'our ancestors'. And when asked why people visit these local shrines, the answer 'Djdudna!!' is generally considered to constitute sufficient explanation.

Sidi Slima is still a shrine near the confluence of the Wad le-Kebir and the Wad Ghenaka, where the myth of Sidi Mhammad locates the homestead of Sidi Slima. Sidi Slima has not managed to impose his name on an entire valley in the same way as Sidi

Mhammad has. Instead, the wider area (a chiefdom)[11] is called Khdayriya, and the place immediately around Sida Slima is known as Ulad ben Sayyid; the latter is a clan name which is traditionally associated with the Drid tribe. Segments of the tribe can also be found scattered in other parts of Tunisia, including elsewhere in Khrumiriya, as we shall see below (cf. Souyris-Rolland, 1949: p. 135; Bel, 1938: pp. 378ff.; Miedema, 1967: p. 19; Cuisenier, 1962; Hartong, 1968; and van Binsbergen, 1970: pp. 93f.).

The shrine of Sidi Slima is of a somewhat unusual shape, but is rather reminiscent of the rectangular structures of large rocks that form the foundation for *kurbi* shrines. It consists of a shallow pit surrounded by a rectangular wall (about 7 × 7 m) built from large rocks each about 40 cm in all dimensions. An ancient olive-tree stands at the edge of the pit. Behind the tree, at the other side of the pit, a less heavily constructed inner wall about 80 cm high, connects two opposite sides of the outer wall. There is a suggestion that it is a Roman ruin.[12] The bottom of the pit is covered with hundreds of clay candle-sticks (*mosba*), clay saucers on which incense can be burned (*tassa*), and paper wrappings containing incense – the usual pious gifts that also abound in all the other shrines in the region. The edges of the pit are fringed with myrtle shrubs, a vegetation typically found in Khrumiri cemeteries. For like Sidi Mhammad le-Kebir, the shrine of Sidi Slima is surrounded by a vast cemetery.

No other shrines bearing the name of Sidi Slima seem to exist locally, and certainly no festival is held for this saint. Instead, the people of Ulad ben Sayyid have two festivals annually for Sidi Abdallah bu-Karma ('with the fig-tree'), whose shrine is located less than a kilometre from Sidi Slima.

5 Aspects of the contemporary social and ritual organization of the region

The *hanshir* Sidi Mhammad is one of four valleys which the French colonial government in the 1880s united to form one chiefdom, 'Atatfa. The other valleys are al-Mellah, al-Mazuz and Shaada. The population of these valleys belongs to a number of different clans and lineage segments. The nature of these social groupings is much too complex for justice to be done to the subject within the scope of this article. I must limit myself to the following summary (see van Binsbergen, 1970 and 1971a for fuller accounts).

Every Khrumiri places himself or herself in a genealogy based on patrilineal descent. These genealogies usually have a depth of four or five generations, and the participants regard them as repositories of the literal historical truth. In the Khrumiri view, contemporary rural society is still governed by a structure of segmentary patrilineages, which is supposed to regulate rights to land, male residence, the nature and intensity of interpersonal ties, and the relations between people and saints. Residential units which are clearly visible in the landscape (from the level of the individual household, via such higher-level clusters as compounds, neighbourhoods, and hamlets, up to the valley and chiefdom level) are supposed to correspond with lineage segments at various levels as defined by the generations in the lineage genealogy. In the participants' folk theory, therefore, all inhabitants of a valley, and all the residential units at various levels, could be fitted into one large genealogy. Since patrilineal descent uniquely and ideally defines membership of local residential groups and rights to local land, people who at a given moment in time happen to live at a particular spot are under strong ideological pressure to justify their presence there in terms of patrilineal descent from the local apical ancestor. At the ideological level the migration of individuals and groups, and the acquisition of rights to land by means other than filial inheritance, are not recognized. Yet, of course, the various patrilineal descent lines that are locally represented (I do not call them lineages to avoid confusion with the particpants' ideologically distorted view of social groupings) do not, on the level of some analytical, objective historical truth, converge towards one and the same historical ancestor. Most local descent lines have only immigrated into the valley which they are occupying now in the course of the nineteenth and twentieth centuries; and most have acquired land rights not through filial inheritance but by other much less prestigious means: by matrilateral inheritance, gift, patronage, purchase, violent conquest, collusion with the colonial authorities, and theft. While there is no reason to assume that genealogical manipulation is a recent feature in Khrumiriya, the insistence on ideologically acceptable rights to local land appears to reflect, partly, the dramatic increase in population pressure on the land since the beginning of the colonial period.

This increase is due to a number of related factors: a five-fold numerical increase of the population in less than a century (the valley now supports 60 inhabitants per square kilometre); the alienation of land for the purpose of state exploitation of cork forests and for the benefit of a few colonist farmers; the politically inspired state alienation of pious-endowment land (*habus*) attached to shrines and religious brotherhoods; and the concentration of land in the hands of the chiefly family, which I shall discuss in more detail in section 7.

At any rate, the existing ideological pressure forces people constantly to revise their genealogies so as to bring these into line with the actual residential situation in the valley, and with the existing social relationships between the inhabitants. It may be attractive for a recent immigrant to trace descent to an undisputed local ancestor: but he will only be allowed to do so if his presence is appreciated by those already firmly established in the valley. Alternatively, negative social and political relationships are inevitably expressed in terms of recent immigration: anyone will try to dispute his enemy's right to local residence, and to participation in the local community. There are other reasons why genealogies are not complete or true reflections of historical reality. When genealogies serve such a clear purpose defined by the pattern of relationships that prevails here and now, there is no point in burdening one's genealogies with whole series of collateral relatives who have left the valley long ago and who no longer take part in local affairs. As a result, genealogies mainly hark back to those past occupants of a valley who have living descendants there – unless an informant is strategically placed, e.g. as the youngest of an otherwise extinct generation who has personal recollections of the emigrants. Finally, genealogies are constantly revised so as to reflect the relative numerical, political and economic strength of contemporary kin groups who are presented as the descendants of particular ancestors in the genealogy. So, as the relative importance of various clusters of agnates waxes and wanes on the contemporary scene, the genealogical relationship said to have existed between their ancestors is revised accordingly. Segments descending from two brothers (or less closely related segments that once were equals and allies and for that reason were considered to be 'as brothers') may assume a genealogical relationship of father and son, or even grandfather and grandson, if their subsequent fortunes at the local scene take a substantially different course.

Since genealogies are so manifestly the outcome of shifting contemporary relations and are only subject to discussion and alteration at abnormal moments, during open conflict *or* when an anthropologist comes along with intrusive questions, the manipulation of genealogies by individuals produces genealogical fictions which seldom dovetail neatly. No two informants, not even full brothers, produce exactly the same genealogy of their own line of descent, or of that of their neighbours. And no genealogy taken down in the field can be said to be historically correct in all its detail.

In order to serve such ideological purposes the revision of genealogies has to be covert and, in fact, largely subconscious. The situation recorded for the West African Tiv (Bohannan, 1952), of lineage segments publicly revising their genealogies so as to bring them into line with their altered social relationships, is unthinkable in Khrumiriya. The revision process works at incredible speed. It is common for a line of descent that has immigrated into a hamlet as recently as thirty or forty years ago to find itself firmly attached to the locally dominant genealogy, provided interpersonal relationships within the hamlet are harmonious.

Yet there will always be cases of immigrants whose arrival has been too recent to be included in genealogies in this fashion; or there will be ties too distant to be encompassed within a single master genealogy of the sort which the participants themselves consider historically correct. The main device by which Khrumiri genealogies overcome this difficulty is by attaching one or more mythical ancestors to the head of each allegedly historical lineage chart. These ancestors are said to have lived in some unspecified past and, as founders of clans, allow people to claim common descent without having to invent specific and connecting descent lines. The clan name becomes a sort of surname which people adopt (and sometimes alter) without having to overhaul all the more recent elements in their genealogical knowledge. Clan names, and therefore mythical ancestors or clan founders, turn out to be attached to particular areas, for the most part irrespective of the specific genealogical position of the people to which each clan name is attached.

Thus summarized and greatly simplified, the social organization of contemporary Khrumiriya can be said to rest upon three interconnected principles:

(a) *A structure of shallow segmentary patrilineages*, which are continuously redefined in the process of migration and fission. In so far as it serves as an organizing principle in the Khrumiri understanding of their own society, this ideology provides us with an explanation for the genealogical manipulations and the distorted perceptions of local residential history which are so widespread in this area. Therefore, this organizational principle also allows for the detailed reconstruction of actual historical events (i.e. actual residential movements of people in the past), provided we have a sufficient quantity of distorted material at our disposal to inspect and assess the many possible permutations. Genealogies are the most readily available, and the least specialized form of oral-historical evidence in this region. On the basis of some 200 genealogies collected in the late 1960s among inhabitants of the valley and adjacent valleys, supplemented by statements regarding the places of residence of all the individuals concerned and by more comprehensive traditions concerning migratory movements and the attendant social and political repercussions and disputes,[13] I was in fact able to reconstruct, more or less to my own satisfaction, the residential and migratory history of the people in the valley of Sidi Mhammad since *c.* 1800.

(b) *A structure of residential units*, units which are clearly identifiable on the ground and which, beginning with individual households, combine in a segmentary, pyramidal fashion to form compounds, neighbourhoods, hamlets, valleys and chiefdoms. The everyday social process that determines the economic, social and political structures in contemporary Khrumiri life mainly takes place within these residential units. At all levels (except that of the individual households) they are heterogeneous as far as unilineal descent is concerned. For although these residential units are named after lineage segments and are considered to be founded by ancestors belonging to a comprehensive fictive patrilineage encompassing an entire valley, in fact most compounds, and all neighbourhoods and hamlets, comprise more than one patrilineal descent line. The social relationships that inform the continuous manipulation of genealogical ties so as to bring them into line with the participants' patrilineal ideology are mainly acted out within these residential units. Moreover, the contemporary local ritual

207

structures can be adequately described and explained in terms of these residential structures. From the most inconspicuous *mzara* concealed somewhere behind a cactus hedge to the *qubbas* that are the focus of massive festivals, the patterns of collective and individual pilgrimages, offerings and sacrifices, dedication of meals, and burials within any valley are *entirely* determined by the fact that each shrine is attached to a residential unit at one level or another (cf. van Binsbergen, in press). Thus Sidi Mhammad le-Kebir serves as a characteristic attribute of the residential unit encompassing the total valley of Sidi Mhammad. The *kurbi* half-way towards Mayziya, however, may share the name of Sidi Mhammad, but it is only a characteristic attribute of one hamlet, that of Mayziya, and does not feature in the ritual activities of the inhabitants of other hamlets in the valley. The same applies to Sidi Abdallah at Fidh al-Missay. Likewise, at the residential levels below the hamlet level there are a considerable number of *mzaras* whose names I have not mentioned here but which serve as the characteristic attributes of these lower-level units, and thus as foci for (typically lesser) dedications and offerings, and small-scale collective pilgrimages exclusive to the members of one compound or neighbourhood. In the collective pilgrimages which entire hamlets direct to a major shrine such as Sidi Mhammad le-Kebir, the impact of these lower-level units becomes eminently visible, when from the various households women (under the supervision of one elderly woman from their midst who is referred to as the *kebira*) team up to form a group of pilgrims representing their compound; then various compound groups join into one neighbourhood group as they proceed; until the various neighbourhood groups under their respective *kebiras* team up into one massive procession on their way to the shrine. On their return home the same process can be observed in the reverse order. It is in the contemporary ritual structures that the social organization of Khrumiri society becomes most manifest. *Shrines are the symbols of residential units which pose as kin groups and desperately revise their genealogies in order to conceal the fact that they are not kin.* This is in fact the underlying meaning of the participants' characterization of the saints as *djdudna*. But in order to perform this function it seems imperative that the local saints should never themselves figure in the genealogies. They are primarily attached to residential units. If, through the inclusion of local saints in their genealogies, patrilineages were allowed to lay exclusive claims by birth-right to these saints, the integrative symbolic function which the saints now provide for the residential units as a whole would be jeopardized.[14]

(c) *A structure of localized clans* which loosely categorizes the population and which is so flexible that it facilitates the transformation of lineage segments into residential units, and permits the latter to pose as lineage segments.

With these summary insights into the contemporary social organization of the region set against the background provided by a painstaking reconstruction of the settlement history of the valley of Sidi Mhammad since *c.* 1800, we may now return to the myth of Sidi Mhammad and see if it can be shown to contain some specific historical information in addition to the cultural and symbolic messages explored in section 3. We know that shrines and saints serve as symbolic foci for the collective identities and activities of contemporary residential units. They are more than likely to have done so in the past. If, in the past, the valley of Sidi Mhammad turns out to have been the scene of continuous migration, and if the existing residential units have therefore been subject to continuous alterations in their composition, the shrines and saints that characterized and symbolized those units are likely to have been distributed and redistributed as a reflection of these social processes of fission and fusion. The myth of Sidi Mhammad speaks of the geographical displacement of a saint, and of his attaining independence *vis-à-vis* another saint. Would it be too far-fetched to read into this myth the record of an actual migration of a social group that has taken the saint Sidi Mhammad as its focus, its characteristic attribute, and its symbol? And would it be possible, on the basis of the information available on the area, to pinpoint this social group? To answer these questions, we shall now look at other myths which present relations between saints and explore the historical background of these myths.

6 Saintly myths and the history of shrines in Khrumiriya

Though the myth of Sidi Mhammad and Sidi Slima may be the best-known myth in the region, it is by no means the only myth featuring saints.

One common type of myth seeks to explain the presence, within one valley or two adjacent valleys, of the shrines of several saints not having the same name. Although dead and invisible, the saints are more or less considered to be dwelling in the area, and when all ordinary human beings inhabiting the sâme valley should ideally fit into one genealogy, participants are inclined to apply the same model to saints. So the presence of lesser shrines within a valley is often explained in terms of the saints associated with these shrines being junior relatives of the valley's main saint (the one with the most elaborate festival). The myth usually takes the extremely simple form:

Sidi X was the younger brother/sister/son/etc. of Sidi Y.

It is important to stress that this myth forms a kind of productive model, in which any minor saint can be substituted *ad libitum*; in other words it is a model which informants are prepared to invoke as a standard explanation even if they cannot give any more specific, colourful details concerning the relationship between the saints involved.

There is another folk explanation of the relationship between saints which is even more significant because it introduces a non-kin connection which suggests that strangers or immigrants have been incorporated: it runs thus:

Sidi X was the friend/servant/herdsman of Sidi Y.

The myth of Sidi Mhammad and Sidi Slima clearly forms an elaborate version of this type of myth. But also of Sidi Tuhami, of the hamlet of Khmaysiya in the valley of al-Mellah, it is said that he was the servant of Sidi 'Amara, that valley's main saint. Likewise, Lalla Bu-Waliya, a female saint associated with a *mzara* in Tra 'aya-sud, is said to be the servant of Sidi Mhammad.

Sidi Mhammad and Sidi Slima ultimately became friends and neighbours. Two saints who, according to a local myth, have always been friends were Sidi 'Abdallah and Sidi Bu-Naqa.

So inseparable were they that after their death their servant Hallal put the former on a male camel and the latter on a female camel (*naqa*), to travel to a place where he could bury them. Wherever the animals stopped Hallal would start to dig graves, but the animals would always get up and continue their journey before the graves were ready. People living in those parts would

turn the unfinished graves into shrines, either for Sidi 'Abdallah
or for Sidi Bu-Naqa. Finally the camel stopped among the
Huamdiya clan in the Selul chiefdom south of 'Ain Draham.
Here Sidi 'Abdallah was buried. The female camel stopped in
the chiefdom of Homran, where Bu-Naqa was buried.

This myth explains to the participants' satisfaction the occurrence
of a number of shrines having the same name throughout
Khrumiriya. We have already encountered Sidi 'Abdallah in Ulad
ben Sayyid, Fidh al-Missay and Raml al-'Atrus. To this is now
added one in Selul, while a fifth exists in Ulad Musa, in the valley
of Babush. All these places are connected by ancient footpaths,
along which pilgrims, traders and local people going to the
regional markets must have travelled for many centuries. In
addition to the major Sidi Bu-Naqa shrine in Homran there is a
minor *mzara* of that name east of Tra 'aya-bidh, and others are
likely to exist a few kilometres further to the east. Incidentally,
Hallal was never raised to sainthood, but instead became the
mythical ancestor of the Ulad Hallal at Huamdiya, another
example of the implicit rule that saints do not appear in
genealogies.

There is also a less ornate topographical myth to explain shrines
having the same name. This myth lacks specific references such as
those to the servant Hallal and to the animals, and constitutes
rather a productive model similar to the one discussed above. It
takes the following form:

> Sidi Z travelled through the countryside. Wherever he sat down
> or slept, people created a shrine for him. Therefore today we
> find shrines for him at A, B, C, D, etc.

That this is in fact a productive model which people apply to any
actual case of a number of shrines having the same name,
irrespective of more specific mythical or historical knowledge, is
clear from the fact that I have heard this myth applied not only to
the multiple shrines of Sidi Mhammad and Sidi Bu-Qasbaya, but
also to those of Sidi 'Abdallah!

Finally, there is a local explanation for a number of shrines
having the same name, which on the one hand forms a productive
model and may be applied, just like the preceding explanation, to
all cases with which an informant is confronted, but which on the

211

other hand turns out to have very solid foundations in living memory. When people emigrate from one area and settle in the next, they cannot take with them the shrine that is the main characteristic attribute of the residential unit they are leaving behind. In many cases they will join an existing residential unit where they will be received as dependents, clients, herdsmen, etc. In those cases they will not be in a position to erect their own shrines, and instead will try to ingratiate themselves with their hosts, and with the latter's saints, by directing ritual activities to the shrines in their new place of residence. When, however, they move to a relatively unoccupied area, or when they emigrate to an area not as dependents but as purchasers of land or even as violent invaders, then they will insist on erecting there a branch of the shrine of their area of origin – as a sign of their identity, as a focus for the new residential unit they are in the process of establishing, and *particularly as a symbol of their recently won independence* vis-à-vis *the residential unit they have left behind*. From the original shrine they take a few relics: the bones of the saint if these in fact can be found there, or else a *mosba* or *tassa*. Around these, the new shrine structure is erected. The new shrine receives the same name as the original shrine; when both are in the same valley, the latter is distinguished by the addition 'al-Wilda', the son.

There is ample oral-historical evidence that several of the shrines having the same name in the valley of Sidi Mhammad have been created in this fashion during the course of the nineteenth and the early twentieth centuries. In those cases informants could mention the names of the historical people who actually created these branches, and could indicate some of the surrounding circumstances. This might seem paradoxical in the light of my previous statement that in Khrumiri society migration (the precondition for the creation of filial branches of shrines) was not cognitively recognized. However, in the course of oral-historical fieldwork one builds up, with some informants at least, a level of trust that allows one to penetrate beyond their formal normative image of their own society. Particularly if one's informants are unusually intelligent and belong to generations otherwise extinct, and if the researcher can feed into his interviews bits of information that indicate that he has already advanced some way towards a more objective truth, and if, finally, one can play off such tensions and rivalries between residential units and lineage segments as exist in this highly competitive society, then, glimpses of the objective truth concerning events in the last century may yet be revealed. Much depends also on finding the proper operational translations for a research question. For instance, informants would not have a clear picture of the succession of cemeteries in the valley of Sidi Mhammad. But they would know where, ever since *c*. 1900, specific people have been buried; and thus the history of cemeteries (and the attendant shrines) could be gleaned from shifts in lists of individual burials.

It became fairly well established that of the three shrines named Sidi Bu-Qasbaya in the hamlet of Sidi Mhammad, two have been created in the early twentieth century, after a European colonist built his farmhouse on the original shrine and cemetery of that saint. The Sidi Bu-Qasbaya shrine in Fidh al-Missay already had been created in *c*. 1870 as a filial branch of that same shrine. Likewise, Sidi 'Abdallah in Raml al-'Atrus was created around 1850 upon relics taken from the shrine of that name in Fidh al-Missay. Similar processes were recorded for some of the minor shrines in and around the hamlet of Sidi Mhammad. The most significant case, however, for the interpretation of the myth of Sidi Mhammad was the creation of Sidi Mhammad al-Wilda on the basis of relics taken from Sidi Mhammad le-Kebir. This event took place around 1900, when two of my informants were small boys and witnessed this activity. Both of these shrines were then *kurbis*; their transformation into *qubbas* was only effected in the late 1910s by a European contractor under contract to a local chief.

This solid piece of evidence suddenly transports the shrine of Sidi Mhammad al-Wilda, and its associated saint, from the obscurities of antiquity into the more sharply delineated world of recent events. It strengthens our hope of penetrating the history of the original shrine of Sidi Mhammad le-Kebir, and of understanding its relationship with the figure of Sidi Slima.[15]

7 The history of Sidi Mhammad

Sidi Mhammad al-Wilda was erected on a flat stretch of land between the cemeteries of Sidi Rhuma and Sidi Bu-Qasbaya following the migration of the shrine-keepers and their associates to the area one kilometre south of Sidi Mhammad le-Kebir. This migration followed a dramatic and violent conflict that took place at the festival of Sidi Mhammad. For, before the migration of the shrine-keepers, the original shrine of this saint was not a place of death, but the site of one of the most famous *zerdas* (saint's festivals) in Khrumiriya. On such occasions not only did the inhabitants of the local residential unit, and the out-married women who were under obligation to return annually to their shrine, forgather at the ritual centre, but they were also joined by pilgrims from the surrounding valleys; and even when interaction between the Khrumiri groups was characterized by violence and feud, such pilgrims were assured of safe-conduct by virtue of the sanctions attached to the supernatural powers of the saint himself. At the same time the *zerdas* were (and they still remain) the principal occasions when the local population revealed their strength, their alliances and the splendour of their saint and shrine. The ensuing sense of competition has been known to raise tempers, not only in the past but also in recent years.

During the *zerda* of Sidi Mhammad, *c.* 1900, a male pilgrim from Ulad ben Sayyid insulted the local men by making sexual allusions concerning their wives and daughters. As a result, he was put to death. This bloodshed triggered further violence and disrupted social relations in the hamlet of Tra'aya, near the shrine, to such an extent that the hamlet split in two parts, 'Bidh' (White) and 'Sud' (Black), and a part of the original population migrated to what is now the hamlet of Sidi Mhammad. This event by no means forms the explanation of the myth of Sidi Mhammad; but it indicates the existence of long-standing tensions between the groups living around the shrines of Sidi Mhammad and Sidi Slima, and the role which the shrines and their festivals have played in enhancing these tensions and bringing them to a critical point.

But who were the people who were in control of the shrine of Sidi Mhammad around 1900, and who, by the creation of Sidi Mhammad al-Wilda, established the conditions under which the present hamlet of Sidi Mhammad could emerge, thrive, and become the site of a major *zerda*, whereas Sidi Mhammad le-Kebir declined and became a mere cemetery?

It is an indication of the great changes that have taken place in the valley of Sidi Mhammad, and in the chiefdom of 'Atatfa as a whole, that the contemporary situation does not even suggest, at least on the surface, what I now take to be the correct answer.

Sidi Mhammad today is a hamlet dominated by the Zeghaydi clan. The Zeghaydiya ultimately trace their descent to the mythical ancestor Zaghdud, who is claimed to hail from the holy city of Kairwan, in Eastern Tunisia. One of the major constituent lines of descent within this clan has supplied all the chiefs of 'Atatfa since the office was created in the 1880s (with only a short interruption immediately after Tunisia became independent). Moreover, the confederation of clans which gave its name to the 'Atatfa chiefdom was created in the 1870s by another member of that same line of descent. Today the most wealthy people in the valley of Sidi Mhammad, and indeed in the chiefdom as a whole, belong to this chiefly family. Most of the land in the valley of Sidi Mhammad belongs to people of the Zeghaydi clan, and particularly to the chiefly family. However, the expansion of the Zeghaydiya is relatively recent; it depended largely on their association with the French colonial power, and on their ability to convert this association into lasting economic power and influence through land ownership, education, and office in independent Tunisia (where members of this chiefly family are holding posts in local government, unemployment relief work, etc.).

The Zeghaydiya present a totally different picture from the other main clan in the chiefdom, the 'Arfawiya. This clan, an offshoot of the Drid tribe, traces its origin to the mythical ancestor 'Arfa. From times past, they have been associated with the religious brotherhood of the Shabbiya, and with tax collection. Contrary to the Zeghaydiya, the 'Arfawiya have a specific clan myth which centres upon the head of a partridge that is said (by the cook who had eaten it) to have been burned in the cooking-fire. The 'Arfawiya settled in the valleys of Sidi Mhammad and al-Mellah around 1800. In 1870 they created in the latter valley a lodge (*zawiya*) for the Qadiriya brotherhood which later was moved to the valley of Shaada. Members of the 'Arfawi clan still control this lodge, the only one of its kind in the region of 'Ain Draham. Moreover, the 'Arfawiya are considered to be strongly represented among the lodge membership, and to be more expert than other groups in the ecstatic dancing that is the brotherhood's main ritual in Khrumiriya. Throughout the chiefdom, the 'Arfawiya command considerable religious prestige (further enhanced by their claims to a purer Arab descent than most Khrumiris, by their predilection for horses, etc.); but their economic and political power is, these days, hardly comparable to that of the Zeghaydiya.

The Zeghaydiya and the 'Arfawiya are by no means the only clans in the chiefdom of 'Atatfa. Yet these two clans, whose interactions have constituted the main political and religious developments in the chiefdom for the past hundred years, have been so prominent that they have imposed a moiety-like structure upon all the valleys in the chiefdom except the southern part of al-Mellah. Most people would claim identity as either 'Arfawi or Zeghaydi – even those who belong to older descent lines that traditionally link up with mythical ancestors other than 'Arfa or Zaghdud. Their own mythical ancestors (such as Bu-Maza, Bu-Tara, Rshab, Bu-Dabus) are then treated as descendants of either of the founders of the two dominant clans; for instance, the Tra'ay and Mayzi clans in the valley of Sidi Mhammad today largely pretend to be members of the Zeghaydi clan.

At present one finds members of both the Zeghaydi and 'Arfawi clans residing in the valley of Sidi Mhammad, but the saint Sidi Mhammad is strongly associated in the popular mind with the Zeghaydi clan. Within this valley the 'Arfawiya are now exclusively associated with the western part of the hamlet of Sidi Mhammad, and with Fidh al-Missay and Raml al-'Atrus; and here they are associated not with the saint Sidi Mhammad but with Sidi Bu-Qasbaya and Sidi 'Abdallah. Even, since at present the 'Arfawi clan is most prominent in the valley of al-Mellah, whose major shrine is Sidi 'Amara, it is suggested that the main saintly patronage of the 'Arfawiya who reside in the valley of Sidi Mhammad should lie with Sidi Amara rather than with the saint Sidi Mhammad.[16] The people of the Zeghaydi clan, on the other hand, live closest to the four shrines of Sidi Mhammad; and the wealthy, powerful Zeghaydiya in the hamlet of Sidi Mhammad, including members of the chiefly family, have a major say in the organization of the *zerda*. For the past forty years, the keepers of the shrine have been Zeghaydiya, close relatives or clients of the chiefs. The present-day *fekirs* specializing in the ecstatic dance for Sidi Mhammad largely have the same relationship *vis-à-vis* the chiefly family.

Yet the ecstatic dance, and the Qadiri brotherhood within which it is loosely incorporated, is primarily an 'Arfawi affair. What is more, Sidi Mhammad was originally an 'Arfawi shrine!

In fact, the present Zeghaydi control over the shrines and the cult of Sidi Mhammad dates back only to the 1920s. In half a century the Zeghaydiya, and especially the chiefly family, went through a dramatic expansion in the valley of Sidi Mhammad, both numerically and in terms of wealth, political power and ritual control. Their latterday kinship-based control over the shrine-keepers and the local *fekirs* has been the outcome of a concerted effort on the part of the Zeghaydi chiefs to break the ritual power of the 'Arfawiya, and to legitimate their own political and economic power by whatever symbolic support the ritual sphere had to offer. It was through the influence of a Zeghaydi chief that the original festival function of Sidi Mhammad le-Kebir was transferred to Sidi Mhammad al-Wilda. That chief would person-ally supervise the collective *zerda* rituals around al-Wilda, which at that time still included the preparation and consumption of a huge meal for hundreds of pilgrims. Again, it was he who converted the site of Sidi Mhammad le-Kebir into a cemetery; he even had himself buried directly in front of the entrance to the shrine of Sidi Mhammad le-Kebir. By these means he drastically altered the ritual organization of the valley. Before that time the 'Arfawiya would be buried at the 'Arfawi cemetery of Sidi Bu-Qasbaya, while the Zeghaydiya would be allowed to bury their dead at the Mayzi cemetery of Sidi Rhuma. The creation of the cemetery of Sidi Mhammad le-Kebir ended Zeghaydi dependence on the Mayzi cemetery; it also sealed the defeat of the 'Arfawiya by the Zeghaydiya (for burial at Sidi Bu-Qasbaya would be discontinued and henceforth all the Arfawiya within the hamlet of Sidi Mhammad would bury their dead at the Zeghaydi cemetery). However, the Zeghaydi chief could only do this after wrenching cultic control from the hands of the original 'Arfawi shrine-keepers, whose line of descent had created the original shrine of Sidi Mhammad le-Kebir, who had administered the *kurbi* on the Hill-top until the bloodshed desecrated the *zerda* there, who had (as a cultic expression of the emigration from Tra'aya of both the 'Arfawi and Zeghaydi households) then created the shrine of Sidi Mhammad al-Wilda, and who had continued to administer that shrine and the original one for another twenty years or so until the Zeghaydiya took over. The change-over is clearly marked in the succession list of shrine-keepers of Sidi Mhammad: after a number of close agnates of a 'Arfawi line of descent which succeeded each other according to a perfect patrilineal adelphic pattern from the

1870s onwards, in the 1920s suddenly non-'Arfawi keepers crop up, all of whom have close relations with the chiefly family. This indicates that the 'Arfawi keepers lost control over the cult and were economically and numerically brought to virtual annihilation within the valley, as the Zeghaydi chiefly family utilized their collusion with the colonial authorities to acquire rights over pious-endowment land that belonged to the shrine of Sidi Mhammad. The creation and expansion of the colonist's farm in the western part of the hamlet of Sidi Mhammad, and the decline, therefore, of the shrine of Sidi Bu-Qasbaya, furthered the downfall of the 'Arfawiya in the valley – a process that reached its culmination in the 1950s when the chiefly family obtained ownership of this farm as well.

The dominant Zeghaydi group, therefore, have a strong interest in denying the original 'Arfawi connection with the shrine of Sidi Mhammad. They laid a dense smoke-screen of historical distortion around what I now take to be the objective historical facts. And significantly, all informants, and, for a long time, I myself, found it difficult to step out of the illusion that the present-day associations between local groups and shrines (shrines that gave the impression of having been there for ever) should be projected wholesale into the distant past.

8 Conclusion: The history of Sidi Mhammad and Sidi Slima

We are now finally ready to glean the historical message from the myth of Sidi Mhammad and Sidi Slima. At this point let me remind the reader of the anti-climax which I have already anticipated in my introduction.

As my painstaking reconstructions of the residential history of the valley of Sidi Mhammad during this century and the last bear out, a number of distinct groups from the 'Arfawi clan settled along the Wad le-Kebir around 1800 in what today are the hamlets of Fidh al-Missay, the western part of Sidi Mhammad, Raml al-'Atrus, and both Tra'ayas. They hailed from the area around Sidi 'Abdallah in Selul, and along with their awareness of belonging to the Drid tribe they brought with them the 'Arfawi myth of origin featuring the burned partridge. So closely associated is the 'Arfawi clan with the valley of Sidi Mhammad that the mountain slope west of the Wad le-Kebir facing the hamlet of Sidi Mhammad is still called Raquba t' 'Arfa, after their clan founder. Many informants make specific reference to this place name in their version of the myth of Sidi Mhammad and Sidi Slima (elements 6 and 10).

One of these immigrant 'Arfawi lines of descent was that of the original pre-Zeghaydi shrine-keepers of Sidi Mhammad. In contrast with their fellow-clansmen, they were pacifists. On various occasions during the turbulent nineteenth century, they would intervene in the battles which the militant and expanding 'Arfawiya fought with earlier inhabitants of the region; carrying the flags of their shrine, the shrine-keepers would come to the battlefield and exhort the parties to end hostilities. Among all the lines of descent in the region, these shrine-keepers come closest to the type of pacificist saintly lineages which Ernest Gellner (1969)[17] describes for the High Atlas, some 1,500 kilometres to the west.

The prominence of the partridge in the myth of Sidi Mhammad and in the ecstatic song associated with him; the fact that, unlike the other clans in the area, the self-perceptions of the 'Arfawi immigrants supported their identification with the Ulad ben Sayyid on the basis of common affiliation with the Drid tribe; and the occurrence of shrines for Sidi 'Abdallah both among these 'Arfawi groups in the valley of Sidi Mhammad, and among the Ulad ben Sayyid – all these items of evidence lead to the conclusion that the myth of Sidi Mhammad and Sidi Slima symbolically embalms the historical interactions that occurred between the 'Arfawiya of Tra'aya and their close neighbours, the Ulad ben Sayyid of Khdayriya, during the first half of the nineteenth century. Their common association with the Drid tribe enabled the immigrant 'Arfawiya to find hospitality and patronage among the Ulad ben Sayyid living around the shrine of Sidi Slima. It is most likely that the early 'Arfawi immigrants in the Tra'aya area received not only land to the south of the Wad Ghenaka to settle on, but also the right to bury their dead in the cemetery of Sidi Slima. However, as the immigrant group expanded, they asserted their own distinct identity *vis-à-vis* their hosts, and created their own shrine. Partly because of its strategic location in the ecology of the region and partly because of the backing which the guardian lineage received from their non-pacifist clansmen, within a few decades this shrine became one of the major shrines of Khrumiriya, worthy of a myth that is known throughout the region. This transformation of the 'Arfawi/Ulad ben Sayyid relations from one of dependence to one of equality took place in the first half of the nineteenth century, and the shrine of Sidi Mhammad le-Kebir must have been built by about 1850, that is, by the time the eldest remembered 'Arfawi guardian of that shrine was born. The bones which, half a century later, my informants saw dug up and transferred to another site to create the shrine of Sidi Mhammad al-Wilda, must have been those of a man, very likely called Mhammad, who lived and died in Tra'aya in the first half of the last century.[18] True to type, he does not occur in the genealogies of the guardians' line of descent. Nor would he ever have sat on the Hill-top as a herdsman of Sidi Slima, who by that time must have long since rested at the cemetery that bears his name. It is likely that the partridges that alighted on Sidi Mhammad's shoulders flew out of the 'Arfawi clan myth rather than from Heaven. And the 'Arfawi connection itself has been all but concealed in the course of half a century of Zeghaydi expansion. It is my contention that the devious 'mountain paths' of my historical reconstruction have brought the myth of Sidi Mhammad and Sidi Slima into the 'plain' of history, in the sense in which 'history' is commonly understood by scholars today.

Notes

1 I am indebted to the following persons and institutions: D. Jongmans, Hasnawi ben Tahar, H. van Rijn, J. Boissevain, A. Hartong, J. van der Klei, M. Creyghton, A. Huitzing, C. Beeker, P. van Dijk, E. Gellner, K. Brown, M. Schoffeleers, the people of 'Atatfa, the University of Amsterdam, the African Studies Centre (Leiden), the Musée des Arts et Traditions Populaires (Tunis), the Free University (Amsterdam) and those mentioned in note 13, for various important contributions to my research and to the present argument. Moreover, I am grateful to Michael Roberts for editorial suggestions, and to A. van Wijngaarden, Ursula Cornish and Anne Monten, who typed successive drafts of this paper. An earlier version appeared in *Social Analysis* (Adelaide, South Australia), 4, September 1980; pp. 51–73.
2 For a recent application of this debate to religious history, see Schoffeleers' contribution to the present volume.
3 The rendering of place names poses a particular problem in scholarly writing dealing with the former French Maghreb. Distorted and unsystematic transliterations of the Arabic names appear on maps and

in the literature. For instance, the French called the highlands of North-Western Tunisia 'La Kroumirie'. The name derives from a local saint, Sidi Bu-Khmirra. I could not bring myself to retain the colonial place name, and instead invented the fake arabization of 'Khrumiriya'. Another problem relating to place names in this article is that, for profound structural reasons which will become clear in the course of my argument, the same name may apply to a locality (valley, hamlet), a residential unit, a kin group, a saint and a shrine. The awkward repetitions in the text resulting from this could not be avoided. The other Arabic words used in this article are all rendered in the singular, with plurals loosely indicated by -s. The simple transliteration system that has been adopted after Gibb and Kramers (1974) inevitably obscures many orthographic and phonetic distinctions.

4 Cf. van Binsbergen (1970; 1971a). A combined English version of these studies is currently being prepared (van Binsbergen, forthcoming). In this work one important omission of the present paper will be put right: the fact that the oral evidence of which I make use is not explicitly identified with names of informants, etc. I am grateful to the Free University, Amsterdam, for enabling me to revisit the area briefly in 1979.

5 *Sidi* ('Lord', 'Saint') is the conventional epithet for saints' names in the Islamic world.

6 The distinction between myth and hagiographic legend is ignored in this study.

7 In Arabic: *Raquba* – a place commanding a wide view, hence a protruding hill-top overlooking a valley, the abrupt end of a mountain ridge, and the open-air, windswept men's assembly grounds which are found in every Khrumiri neighbourhood.

8 From the vast literature, I mention: Brunel (1926), Demeerseman (1964), Dermenghem (1954), Eickelman (1976), Geertz (1968), Gellner (1969), Marçais and Guiga (1925), Montet (1909), Wester-marck (1926).

9 Cf. Lévi-Strauss (1958; 1964; 1966; 1973) and Leach (1967; 1976). For reflections on this approach, and an overview of the recent literature, see de Mahieu's contribution to the present volume.

10 Cf. Bourdieu, 1965; Davis, 1977: pp. 89–101; Jongmans, 1968; Blok, 1979; and references cited in these works.

11 Although the petty administrator created by the colonial government was called by the title of honour *shaykh*, which is also the term used for religious leaders and for saints, I shall designate this secular office by the terms used elsewhere in Africa: chief, chieftaincy and chiefdom.

12 A suggestion corroborated by the ordnance map for the area: Institut Géographique National, Carte topographique 1:50,000 (*La Calle*, Paris, n.d. probably early 1960s).

13 Part of this material was collected by P. Ernsting, P. Geschiere, C. Holzappel, G. von Liebenstein, P. Tamsma (deceased), and myself, in the course of a collective project under supervision of K. W. van der

Veen in March/April 1968. I am grateful to these colleagues for their permission to use this material. Earlier accounts of genealogical and oral-historical research in the chiefdom of 'Atatfa include that by Hartong (1968), while I also gleaned some information from Beeker's (1967) preparatory study for a housing project (which never materialized) in the hamlet of Sidi Mhammad.

14 On the other hand, when a clan founder who figures in a genealogy has some association with sainthood (e.g. in the clan of Ulad al-Hadjdj – 'Descendants of the Pilgrim' – in the valley of al-Mazuz), he has no shrine locally and is never the subject of a cult.

15 The details which informants could supply with regard to the history of Sidi Mhammad le-Kebir and Sidi Mhammad al-Wilda contrast sharply with the absolute lack of specific historical information concerning the two remaining *kurbis* of the same saint: the one adjacent to Sidi Mhammad al-Wilda, and the one half-way to the hamlet of Mayziya. Mechanical application of either of the two productive models for shrines having the same name led some informants to suggest that Sidi Mhammad might have rested at the sites of these *kurbis* in the course of his wanderings through the region. But in general the informants were remarkably taciturn on the subject. Elsewhere, I offer a reconstruction of the history of these two *kurbis*, suggesting that they were originally named after a totally different saint who was associated with a clan that had prevailed in the area before the immigration of the shrine-keepers and their associates from Tra'aya (van Binsbergen, 1971a: pp. 281ff.).

16 Yet the fact that Sidi 'Amara is not called Sidi 'Abdallah, and my reconstruction of the valley's residential history, suggest that Sidi 'Amara was not originally an 'Arfawi shrine, but one created by pre-'Arfawi members of the Mayzi clan, to whom the 'Arfawiya had come as client immigrants.

17 Cf. van Binsbergen (1971b).

18 Why has not the shrine of Sidi Mhammad le-Kebir been called Sidi 'Abdallah like the other shrines established by the 'Arfawiya? The fig-tree in the ecstatic song of Sidi Mhammad cannot be found on the Hill-top today, and although there are traditions of it having been destroyed by lightning at the beginning of this century, it is most likely a vestige of Sidi 'Abdallah bu-Karma, in Ulad ben Sayyid. The shrine of Sidi Mhammad might originally have been dedicated to Sidi 'Abdallah, only to be renamed after Sidi Mhammad once the Tra'aya 'Arfawiya had produced from within their midst a saintly man of the name of Mhammad.

References

Beeker, M. C. (1967), 'Mozaiek van het Wonen', University of Amsterdam, Drs. Soc. Sc. dissertation.

Bel, A. (1938), *La Religion musulmane en Berberie*, vol. I, Paris: Paul Geuthner.

Binsbergen, W. M. J. van (1970), Verwantschap en Territorialiteit in de Sociale Structuur van het Bergland van Noord-West Tunisië, University of Amsterdam, Drs. Soc. Sc. dissertation.

Binsbergen, W. M. J. van (1971a), 'Religie en samemleving: een studie over het bergland van Noord-West Tunesië', University of Amsterdam, Drs. Soc. Sc. dissertation.

Binsbergen, W. M. J. van (1971b), 'Ernest Gellner: Saints of the Atlas', *Cahiers des arts et traditions populaires*, 4: pp. 203–11.

Binsbergen, W. M. J. van (1979), 'Explorations in the History and Sociology of Territorial Cults in Zambia', in J. M. Schoffeleers (ed), *Guardians of the Land. Essays on Central African Territorial Cults*, Gwelo: Mambo Press, pp. 47–88.

Binsbergen, W. M. J. van (1980), 'Popular and Formal Islam, and Supralocal Relations: The Highlands of North-Western Tunisia, 1800–1970', *Middle Eastern Studies*, 16: pp. 71–91.

Binsbergen, W. M. J. van (1981), *Religious Change in Zambia: Exploratory Studies*, London and Boston: Kegan Paul International.

Binsbergen, W. M. J. van (in press), 'The Cult of Saints in Northwestern Tunisia: An Analysis of Contemporary Pilgrimage Structures', in E. Gellner and E. Wolf (eds), *Religions of the Mediterranean*, Berlin: De Gruyter.

Binsbergen, W. M. J. van (forthcoming), *Shrines and Ecstasy in the Social Structure of North-Western Tunisia*.

Blok, A. (1979), 'Rams and Billy-goats: Breaking the Mediterranean Code of Honour', paper read at the conference on 'Religion and Religious Movements in the Mediterranean Area', Amsterdam: University of Amsterdam and Free University.

Bohannan, L. (1952), 'A Genealogical Charter', *Africa*, 22: pp. 301–15.

Bourdieu, P. (1965), 'The Sentiment of Honour in Kabyle Society', in J. Peristiany (ed.), *Honour and Shame*, London: Weidenfeld & Nicolson, pp. 191–242.

Brunel, R. (1926), *Essai sur la confrérie religieuse des 'Aîssâoûa au Maroc*, Paris.

Cuisenier, J. (1962), 'Endogamie et exogamie dans le mariage arabe', *L'Homme*, 2: pp. 80–105.

Davis, J. (1977), *People of the Mediterranean*, London: Routledge & Kegan Paul.

Demeerseman, A. (1964), 'Le Culte des saints en Kroumirie', *Institut des Belles Lettres Arabes*, 27: pp. 119–63.

Dermenghem, E. (1954), *Le Culte des saints dans l'Islam magrebin*, Paris: Gallimard.

Eickelman, D. (1976), *Moroccan Islam*, Austin and London: University of Texas Press.

Favret, J. (1968), 'Relations de dépendance et manipulation de la violence en Kabylie', *L'Homme*, 8: pp. 18–44.

Geertz, C. (1968), *Islam Observed*, New Haven and London: Yale University Press.

Gellner, E. (1969), *Saints of the Atlas*, London: Weidenfeld & Nicolson.

Gibb, H. A. R., and Kramers, J. H. (eds) (1974), *Shorter Encyclopaedia of Islam*, Leiden: E. J. Brill.

Hartong, A. M. (1968), 'De Geschiedenis van het Sjeikaat Atatfa op Basis van de Orale Traditie', Catholic University of Nijmegen, Drs. Soc. Sc. dissertation.

Heusch, Luc de (1972), *Le Roi ivre ou l'origine de l'état*, Paris: Gallimard.

Jongmans, D. (1968), 'Meziaa en Horma', *Kroniek van Afrika*, 3: pp. 1–34.

Leach, E. (ed.) (1967), *The Anthropological Study of Myth and Totemism*, London: Tavistock.

Leach, E. (1976), *Culture and Communication*, Cambridge: Cambridge University Press.

Lévi-Strauss, C. (1958), *Anthropologie structurale*, Paris: Plon.

Lévi-Strauss, C. (1964), *Le Cru et le cuit*, Paris: Plon.

Lévi-Strauss, C. (1966), *Du miel aux cendres*, Paris: Plon.

Lévi-Strauss, C. (1973), *Anthropologie structurale deux*, Paris: Plon.

Marçais, W., and Guiga, A. (1925), *Textes arabes de Takroûna*, Paris: Éditions Ernest Leroux.

Miedema, A. W. F. (1967), 'Verslag Leeronderzoek Tunesië', University of Amsterdam, Antropologisch-Sociologisch Centrum, typescript.

Miller, J. C. (1976), *Kings and Kinsmen*, Oxford: Clarendon Press.

Miller, J. C. (ed.) (1980), *The African Past Speaks*, Folkestone: Dawson.

Montet, E. (1909), *Le Culte des saints musulmans dans l'Afrique du Nord*, Geneva: Librairie Georg & Cie.

Reefe, T. Q. (1977), 'Tensions of Genesis and the Lunda Diaspora', *History in Africa*, 4: pp. 183–206.

Souyris-Rolland, M. (1949), 'Histoire traditionelle de la Kroumirie', *Institut des Belles Lettres Arabes*, 12: pp. 127–65.

Vansina, Jan (1965), *Oral Tradition*, London: Routledge & Kegan Paul.

Westermarck, E. (1926), *Ritual and Belief in Morocco*, vols. I and II, London: Macmillan.

Willis, Roy (1976), *On Historical Reconstruction from Oral-Traditional Sources: A Structuralist Approach*, Evanston, Ill.: Northwestern University. Twelfth Melville Herskovits Memorial Lecture.

Chapter 8

The consequences of literacy in African religion: The Kongo case

John M. Janzen

Introduction

Although sub-Saharan Africa has been involved with European languages and literacy for over a century, and has seen numerous 'national literatures' arise in these languages (Gérard, 1972), and although Christian literature has been introduced in many African languages in connection with biblical translations (Hastings, 1979), relatively little scholarship has been conducted on the consequences of literacy, *per se*, in African religion.[1] This essay proposes such a project for the Kongo tradition of coastal Zaire, Angola and Congo, and puts forward methodologies for the analysis of the articulation of oral and written language use in Kongo religion. The essay will examine genre uses in the oral and written phases of Kongo religion, and will then study at closer range two examples of early Kongo writing on religion. The first is part of an account by African teachers of North Kongo's major historic healing cult, Lemba, written in the 1900–20 era on commission by missionary–linguist Karl Laman as part of a vast corpus of writing about a way of life that was rapidly disappearing (Janzen, 1972). The second is a much briefer text, written in 1921 by the personal secretaries of the Kongo prophet Kimbangu, describing the remarkable beginning of one of the major independent churches of Black Africa (Nfinangani and Nzungu in Raymaekers, 1971). These two very different texts have, as we shall see later, similar structures for the portrayal of religious phenomena.

The implications of literacy for religion are, of course, part of the overall set of transformations that literacy unleashes upon an entire culture, as is apparent in the great civilizations of Mesopotamia, China, India, Greece and Central America, where writing emerged indigenously. It is necessary, in these important classic cases of the transition to literacy, suggest Jack Goody and Ian Watt (1968: pp. 34–6), to distinguish between those settings which have witnessed ideographic writing and those which have witnessed phonetic writing. In the former, which include the majority of early cases, the extreme complexity of writing in hieroglyphs and specialized symbols, requiring years to master, gave rise to 'restricted literacy' in a society controlled by a priestly elite, used in the maintenance and extension of authority over others. By contrast, the phonetic alphabet, introduced first in ancient Greece, permitted relatively easy learning by whoever was exposed to it. This, rather than some mysterious Greek genius, gave rise to relatively widespread education and to Greek democracy, argue Goody and Watt (1968: pp. 40–3).

In societies which have undergone the transition to literacy in recent centuries, as in many African settings, it is possible to distinguish forces leading to restricted or generalized access – whether it be the type of script or another factor such as economics – and to note the particular areas of life in which literacy has had a transforming impact – such as religion, commerce, science or something else. In the study of literacy in religion the issue of control and function of text looms large.

Control of text often makes itself manifest in the process known as 'canonization', which is the final stage of the elimination of diversity and variation in written accounts of an important religious event or experience, according to Juha Pentikäinen in a recent study of the transition to literacy in religion (1979: pp. 38–42). Not only is access to text controlled in this process, but orthodoxy is established within narrow confines where previously there may have been diversity. Although the emergence in a religious tradition of a canonic text – an official scripture – is not the only consequence of literacy upon religion, it is often an important end-point against which to evaluate the uses of writing.

In African religion, the major canonic texts have been the Qur'an and the Bible, sacred scriptures of the two main religions of *the Book*, with their own unique impact. As Jack Goody argues, religions of the Book – notably Christianity and Islam – emphasize the 'true interpretation' of things and the condemnation of heresies (Goody, 1968: pp. 2–3). They are exclusive religions to which one is 'converted', in contrast to eclectic shrines and cults of pre-Christian or pre-Islamic and non-literate religion. Literate religions are less tolerant of change, once their fixed point of reference has been determined to be a sacred text. Although they are less flexible, they are more universalistic, covering a larger societal scope; therefore they are also more 'ethical'. Congregations of worshippers extend beyond the clan, tribe or nation and are quasi-kin groups with their own primary allegiances. Finally, literate religions are individualizing and salvationistic, emphasizing the individual path of righteousness in a complex social order. To what extent have all these characteristics of religion of the Book pervaded Africa, where, to be sure, apologists of Christianity and Islam have been the principal proponents of literacy as well?

It would be a mistake to believe that the foregoing features of book religion had been mechanistically transmitted to African societies. For one thing, there has been selective use of the Bible and the Qur'an, corresponding to priorities in pre-established world views with unique notions of time and space, of power, and of human relationships and forces in nature. Furthermore, African history has given Africans the distinctive experience of slavery, colonialism and recent liberation through which to understand the scriptures of two world religions. And the African use of language, with its own distinctive and powerful genres such as the proverb, the call and response style, and other skilful oratorical techniques, continues to offer original forms for the interpretation of experience. Also, of great importance to the African use of literacy in religious experience is the production of new texts in the form of songs, vision-messages, prophetic declarations, a growing set of creeds, and distinctive contemporary religious institutions. The Africanization of Islam and Christianity, and the continuing changes in indigenous forms of African religion, suggest that one cannot assume the fixed nature of the introduced canons. Finally, it is apparent that the acquisition of literacy in African religion has not, *ipso facto*, led to the end of oral uses of language in religious experience and expression.

Ironically, the scholarship of religion and language has taken a renewed look at oral tradition right at a time when Africanists are becoming increasingly aware of the presence of written texts in African religion. Scholars of historical religion look at the relationship of the oral uses of language in religion to the production of written texts in an effort to understand fragments of ancient scripts. Contemporary scholars wish to understand the relationship of living cult practices to book religion. Eric Havelock, in his *Prologue to Greek Literacy*, offers part of the rationale for the renewed emphasis on oral language uses in the study of literacy. The introduction of a phonetic alphabet in ancient Greece offered

> not literacy, but a permanently engraved and complete record of the ways of non-literacy. Because of its phonetic superiority, it provided an instrument in which for the first time the full complexities of an oral tradition could be adequately revealed, for in theory any linguistic noise could now be automatically recognized in the transcription. (Havelock, 1971: pp. 14–15)

Accordingly, in the present essay the transition to literacy, and its early products, will be examined in the light of on-going oral uses of language. Analytic methods will be offered to interpret religious text composition in the Kongo tradition of coastal Equatorial Africa.

A brief background to modern Kongo literacy

The origins of modern Kongo literacy – excluding literacy of the sixteenth and eighteenth centuries, which died out[2] – may be traced to the late nineteenth century and the introduction by Protestant missionaries of Bible translations, schools and, in 1892, the first KiKongo newspaper. The early community of graduates from the Protestant mission schools, who had in two years learned to read and write by phonetic methods, received the rudiments of the Christian faith and been baptized, took up posts across the Lower Congo as teachers. Many subscribed to the *Minsamu mia Yenge* (Peace News) printed at the Swedish mission, or to comparable later journals, and contributed to it with their correspondence, reports of their work, and hymns and other inspirational writings (Janzen and MacGaffey, 1974: pp. 107–17). By the turn of the last century these new literati may have numbered around a thousand.[3]

Expansion of the uses of print in subsequent years included

further parochial bulletins of the missions (including Catholic missions), instructional booklets, hymnals and the complete KiKongo Bible (by 1905). With the end of the Congo Free State's erratic presence and the establishment of the Belgian Congo in 1908, bureaucratic uses of print in the form of identity cards, tax-books, government instructions and laws, offered an increasing number of models for written language uses. However, the active use of print by Africans in KiKongo continued to be that in the missions, churches and schools, primarily among the catechist-teachers.

Many of the catechists had come from the marginal classes of Kongo society; Christianity afforded them an active association, in the missions, with the new prevailing social order. Literacy was perceived to be the means of access to the authority and power of the missionary priests, pastors and doctors, through access to their printed word and especially their Bible. However, when after a generation of literacy it became apparent that this access to power was in some ways restricted, disillusionment set in. The KiKongo newspaper *Minsamu mia Yenge* reveals that as early as the 1890s questions began to be raised about salary differences between Africans and Europeans, about Africans' rights to further education (beyond two or three years) and about the possibility of pursuing advanced study in professions such as medicine. Frustration over the double standard of early colonialism, in general, despite excellent primary instruction in the mission schools, led to the circulation of rumours about the 'true Bible' that had been withheld from Africans; the one available to them lacked the power of the Holy Spirit.

This frame of mind among the Protestant catechists appears to have contributed directly to the outbreak in 1921 of the prophet movement which Simon Kimbangu, an unemployed, self-appointed catechist has come to personify. This movement, which actually consisted of a wide range of prophetic personages, offered a perceptible way around the obstacles to power in the new society, in the form of direct access to the Holy Spirit.[4]

Kimbangu and the other prophets were quickly imprisoned or exiled by the colonial government, forcing the movement under-ground for the next several decades. Deprived of public communi-cations, the Kongo prophetic tradition was forced to seek alternative means of keeping in touch with a fragmented, scattered following. After World War II, as colonial harassment relented somewhat, earlier writings began to be printed in the form of tracts for the faithful, diaries, collections of prophetic pronouncements, codes of conduct, and above all manifestations of visions, usually in the form of 'songs of heaven' or 'songs of the spirit' (*minkung'a mia mpeve*).

Concurrently with the mission-sponsored KiKongo publications and the prophet movement's various ups and downs, KiKongo writing also produced a host of materials of a cultural revivalist nature: collections of folktales and proverbs, dictionaries and grammars, and ethnographies and histories, by African writers and others. In recent decades the novel has made its appearance, often in French-language but Kongo culture-oriented settings; numerous journals and magazines of both a religious and cultural nature have appeared. It is fair to compare this KiKongo–European literary tradition to a number of other 'African literatures' such as Xhosa-English, Sotho-English, Zulu-English (Gérard, 1971).[5]

Literacy and genre: source criticism

One important approach in the research of emerging literacy in a tradition such as Kongo is the identification of oral genres which have been carried into writing. This is essentially the approach taken by Mbelolo ya Mpiku in his pioneering 'Introduction à la littérature KiKongo' (1972). In a specialized study of literacy and religion emphasis must be placed on religious genres.

Perhaps the first oral genre in KiKongo to be carried into writing was the already mentioned song or hymn (*nkung'a*), an expressive form in which European Christianity and Kongo culture had obvious congruence. Mbelolo notes that the first collection of hymns composed in part by Kongo catechists, the 1889 *Minkung'a mia Yenge* (Hymns of Joy), portrayed features of numerous nkung'a sub-genres, including: praise poetry (*nkung'a masika*), used to celebrate exploits of heroes, ancestors or living persons of note, and thanksgiving songs (*nkung'a matondo*) to honour a benefactor; also included, to a lesser degree, were traces of the palaver song (*nkung'a mambu*) used in public debate, the lamentation song (*nkung'a maniongo*), the funerary song (*nkung'a kidila*), the dance song (*nkung'a makinu*) and the lullaby (*nkung'a ndezi*) (Mbelolo, 1972: pp. 124–6). The object of praise, gratitude, challenge and overall attention had been shifted from heroes, ancestors and the living to Christ or God, as composers worked through their Christian experience in the Kongo cultural idiom.

Other oral genres adapted to mission-related writings included the folktale (*nsamu, kimpa*), the fable and the proverb (*ngana*). A favourite device of the early Kongo catechists, no doubt encouraged by their mentors, was the moralizing folktale, which would take a classical story and tell it unchanged but attach at the end a 'moral' with explicitly Christian didactic intent. At other times the folktale or fable was revised so as to make it Christian in form and outcome. Numerous anthologies of folktale, fable and proverb were published by the missions, some achieving widespread fame. As the concern for cultural survival grew, publications such as those by Bahelele (1953; 1964), although published by missions, sought to convey the oral tradition as accurately as did explicitly scholarly studies of folktales such as that by Struyf (1936).

An intriguing oral genre which appeared early in Kongo writing was the dream or dream-vision (*ndozi*), a common device in Kongo culture to legitimate any message or set of composite truths. Mbelolo notes that the first publication of dreams in the *Minsamu mia Yenge* in 1894 stimulated further Christianized dream or vision interpretations, some, such as John Bunyan's *Pilgrim's Progress* with its visionary land, drawn from European literature (Mbelolo, 1972: p. 129) and serialized in the KiKongo journal with great success. The dream-vision, like the dream-song, would become a vehicle for the prophet movement several decades later to keep the faithful in touch with one another and with the master vision. One well-known Kongo prophet composed a massive diary while in labour camp in the 1930s, consisting of lengthy visions about the state of the world and Africa. It is still being edited by his followers.

Genres of oral literature which were excluded from early Kongo writing are as noteworthy as those which were included. Riddles, according to Mbelolo (1972: p. 124), were not common. Although praise poem forms were used in hymns, praise names were rarely seen in the Christian literature setting. The historical or genealogical reconstruction (*kinkulu*), although attempted by missionary writers to relate Kongo origins to Biblical origins (DeMunck, 1956; Stenström and Palmaer, 1961), was used by Kongo writers only in the prophetic groups where the *kinkulu* served to legitimate the prophet's calling by tracing it back to Kimbangu and Jesus (Nkindu, 1974). Prayers were, of course, used in early Kongo Christianity, with the word for it (*nsambulu*) being taken from the palm wine (*nsambu*) libation and the ancestral prayer; however, there is little use of prayer in print.

The incorporation of oral genres into early mission-sponsored writing in Kongo culture may be generally characterized by its disarticulation. That is, oral genres appear in print as if pieces had been cut out of a fabric, severing them from their related ritual and social meanings, and inserted somewhat arbitrarily onto a new fabric, that of the Christian way of life. Conspicuously absent from the borrowed oral genres of this early Kongo writing are the more composite forms of expression such as those used in the consecration of medicines, the inauguration of chiefship and the initiation to collective cults. Of course, some of the composite oral genres reported from elsewhere in Bantu-speaking zones of Africa, such as dynastic poetry, codices, royal genealogies, and epics, if they had ever existed in Kongo, were either on the decline or had long ago been given up because of the absence of an appropriate social setting.[6] A few of the Kongo hero cycles, such as that of the trickster, have been published (van Wing and Schöller, 1940) and have been reintroduced, via literacy, to popular consciousness, but without the close links with rituals they appear to have had earlier (Janzen, 1982).

The composition of consecrated medicines (*min'kisi*) afforded early Kongo writers with perhaps their clearest model of inter-linked genres – song, dance, genealogy, rules, prayers, visions, rituals – but a model missionaries sharply criticized. When songs and dream-visions were printed in the *Minsamu mia Yenge*, they were portrayed as Christian and individualized manifestations of spirit. However, seen from the perspective of Kongo cultural structure, these two forms of expression are the first stages of an integrated construction of either medicine, chiefship or any other innovation. A full manifestation of this process would lead to anchoring the dream-idea in ancestral or spiritual hierarchies with some type of *kinkulu*-genealogy to give it a legitimate identity; to the elaboration of a ritual technique, be it medicinal, symbolic or political; songs (*min'kunga*) and dances to awaken the powers; and rules (*min'siku*) to bind the society, or sub-group, together around and in respect of the new vision. It is in the prophetic writing, beginning in 1921, that these various genres are first integrated. In some instances, such as that mentioned above, the prophet writes his own 'inspired' narrative, including glossolalia; at other times, such as that which will be examined in the next section, the prophet's words *and* actions are recorded by a scribe (see Janzen and MacGaffey, 1974: p. 20).

It would be misleading, at this stage of the analysis of Kongo religious writing, to conclude that the review of oral genres transposed to written form explained everything about the transition to literacy. First of all, definitions of genre are not agreed upon by the scholarly community, but vary from attempts to create a universally applicable set of terms (von Sydow, 1948; Bascom, 1965) to emphasis upon the uniqueness of particular traditions, or even of individuals within those traditions. To explain manifestations of literacy only in terms of antecedent oral genres is to miss the subtle manner in which form, function and context may have changed in the transition. In other words, both formal and contextual consequences of literacy must be examined.

A definition of the genre, in language use, must be found which permits some flexibility of use, and some shifting in context, rather than an exclusive adherence to such restricted forms as 'folktale', 'proverb', 'fable' and the like. Juha Pentikäinen, in his valuable paper mentioned above (1979: pp. 42–5), has emphasized the importance of defining genre in terms of the consistent use of a combination of the following criteria: content, form, style, structure, function, frequency of use, distribution, origin, age and context of use. He also has emphasized the importance of noting the relationship between various genres at all phases of the transition from, or the interaction between, oral and literate language use. Thus, in the case under consideration, the isolated use of 'songs' or 'dreams' would not be the same as their use in a combined, 'consecrated' setting. In religious genres and contexts, notes Pentikäinen, function is extremely important in determining the religiosity of a text, i.e. the extent to which it is believed in and is relied on to convey or legitimize values within a tradition. It is also important to take note of the control or sanction to which a given genre is subjected, such as the examination of dreams for their 'Christian' context, or of healing acts for their 'orthodoxy' within the Kimbanguist context (Pentikäinen, 1979: pp. 42–5).

233

Some of these requirements of scholarship are satisfied in the Kongo case by noting the relationship of the particular genres – song, folktale, proverb – to the two major functional modes of communication existing in this society: (a) public advocacy speaking (*kinzonzi*, the art of oration, debate, judging, from *zonza*, to speak), and (b) the magical manipulation of language (*kinganga*, from the *nganga*'s art) or esoteric symbols (Janzen and MacGaffey, 1974: pp. 5–10). Public speaking often takes the form of a debate between two parties in arranging a marriage, conflict resolution or other settings in which one group or individual confronts another. The orator's art (*kinzonzi*) is laced with the use of call and response phrases, persuasion songs, the judicious use of proverbs, and dances. Adoption of the *kinzonzi* format permitted one Kongo writer, Vingadio (Vingadio *et al.*, 1928), to assemble a variety of particular genres in one work; not a direct carry-over of the public debate format, but a pleasing and popular format for the printed word none the less. The art of the magician (*kinganga*), in its spoken form, is accompanied by the ability to weave a clever verbal fabric of analogy between verbal categories, natural objects and social processes so as to give ritual and therapeutic settings an intense affective charge. Carried over to print the imperatives of this language function are perhaps less successful, resulting in textual 'mumbo-jumbo', unless, as in the case of the prophet's diary using glossolalia, the function of the text is clarified through more discursive writing. In the prophetic text to be introduced in the next section, the prophet's scribe offers explanatory comments for precisely this reason.

In putting together our *Anthology of Kongo Religion* MacGaffey and I sought to come to grips with the foregoing problems of genre definition and function by outlining a number of functionally derived language categories which we hoped would account for both oral and written examples of text. These we identified as (1) *monologue*, referring to such forms as prayer or language uses in which one speaker or writer addresses an audience; (2) *dialogue*, referring to public debate, a correspondence or some other instance in which two parties actively address one another; (3) *apology*, referring to the defence of a corporate community or group *vis-à-vis* its adversaries or antagonists, or efforts to persuade interlocutors as in lineage genealogies, conversion reports or sermons. A final category we identified as (4) *ethnography*, referring to a rather new use of language, especially in writing, to describe and interpret an experience, event or history for another party removed in time and space (Janzen and MacGaffey, 1974: pp. 4–5). The *Anthology* presented sixteen oral and thirty-six written 'primary' texts from Kongo religion around themes such as cosmology, uses and abuses of power, personal religious experiences, common rituals, and texts derived from corporate groups such as lineages, healing cults, mission churches and independent prophet churches.

Although the 'ethnographic' genre of writing was created as a somewhat residual category, it is now apparent that it requires more careful analysis precisely because it displays genuinely new functions of language use. First, it often describes and compares cultural usages and viewpoints, thereby showing a greater degree of detachment from the subject matter on the part of the writer. It contains many of the features Goody and Watt (1968: pp. 46–9) attribute to *historia* in ancient Greece: the comparison of the past with the present, and the effort to criticize alternative and contradictory variants of myth, creed and event. The early Kongo catechists manifested exactly such reactions to customs in their teaching posts which differed markedly from those of their home communities. Kimbangu's scribes note carefully the reasons why the prophet is critical of other 'false' prophets who come to Kimbangu for a blessing. While perception of contradiction and variance is certainly not limited to literate society, it is in the widened scale of society offered by written communication, over space and time, that disjunctures become more apparent and can be more readily entertained. Much recent writing in Kongo consists of interpretations of cultural characteristics such as witchcraft, the role of ancestors, the benefits of Western versus African solutions to problems, issues which suggest the detached evaluation of alternative ways of life and thought. Second, this 'ethnographic' genre of writing is distinct in the way it synthesizes all the other genres, as well as borrowings and inventions. Even where it appears formally to adopt a particular oral genre, its function and probably its context are different. We will see in the two texts studied in the next section how broad are the formal ranges of such 'ethnographic' texts, and how their functions can vary: from recording for posterity something believed to be dying out, to interpreting an unprecedented prophetic appearance to perhaps sceptical readers.

Two texts in the 'ethnographic' genre

The two texts used here to illustrate the ethnographic genre of Kongo writing shall be called respectively the 'Lemba Notebooks' and the 'Appearance of the Prophet'. The authors of the former are Kwamba, Konda, Lunungu and Babutidi, all mission catechists who, for Karl Laman, contributed to the massive 23,000-page corpus in response to a questionnaire on Kongo life. The 'Lemba Notebooks' are a small fragment of the responses to the request for a description of consecrated medicines (*min'kisi*). Kwamba's account has been published in the *Anthology* (Janzen and MacGaffey, 1974: pp. 97–102); it, and the accounts of the other writers, as well as other evidence, has been used in a major volume on Lemba (Janzen, 1982). These Lemba texts, at their least, are routine replies to Laman's questions; at their best, they are marvellous, free-ranging, open-ended accounts of local history, descriptions of healing cults, autobiographical notes, genealogies of chiefship, legends, songs and more.

'Appearance of the Prophet' was written by Nfinangani and Nzungu, Simon Kimbangu's two scribes who, in May 1921, during his public ministry and prior to his arrest in August, observed and recorded his work. Their journal was seized by colonial officials in June and filed in the colonial archives, possibly after Kimbangu's conviction, where it was discovered by Paul Raymaekers, who published it in French translation (Raymaekers, 1971). I have not seen the original KiKongo; however, many kongoisms in the French text permit an approximate identification of original phrasing. The construction of scenes and the various points of view taken by the narrator reveal much about the context and function of the text.

The approach taken here in comparing 'Lemba Notebooks' and 'Appearance of the Prophet' follows largely from recent work on Kongo therapy (Janzen, 1978), healing cults such as Lemba in particular (Janzen, 1979b; 1982; Janzen and MacGaffey, 1974), and on Kongo prophetic religion, Kimbanguism in particular

(Janzen, 1979a). I wish to ask these questions of the two texts: How do they describe, and select, events? How do they interpret them? How is religion, or its constituent features, defined? And, how is language used? In sum, is there here a basis for a common portrayal of Kongo religion in written language? Both texts were produced for others. Laman wished to understand Kongo religion so as to translate the Bible more effectively. Kimbangu, we may surmise, wished to record his ministry for the faithful, and to give evidence to others of the power of the Holy Spirit in him.

In answer to the first query, we may note that both the 'Lemba Notebooks' and the 'Appearance of the Prophet' select and generalize in their depiction of, on the one hand, an intricate ceremony requiring many days to prepare and perform, and on the other, the life and work of an adult individual. The 'Lemba Notebooks' give the impression, on first reading, of being largely descriptive, of relating events 'as they happened'. Detail after detail about ritual actions, about ritual objects, and about the setting are given. Closer examination indicates that the 'events' being related are usually not specific historic events – e.g. the Lemba seance of such and such a place in a given year – but rather normative accounts of what we may presume are institutionalized events. And even within these reconstructed normative event accounts of Lemba rituals there is selectiveness. Thus, for example, in Kwamba's (1974: p. 100) account, a song that is sung 'all night' is only seven lines long. It is not clear whether it was repeated all night, or whether we are given the first verse. The basis of selective reconstruction apparently is the author's judgement of representativeness. In another example Kwamba (1974: p. 100) describes the payment of part of the initiation as follows: 'the debtor [profaner] pays the chief speaker a person or ten pigs and to the Lemba Father a secret pig. . . ' The sum due is indicated in two possible denominations, the one a slave, the other its equivalent in pigs. Was this one particular initiation? It is unlikely, suggesting a degree of institutional reconstruction by the author.

The more skilled authors of the 'Lemba Notebooks', as of the catechists' notebooks in general, avoid the tedious recitation of names, items, acts and places, interspersing their normative reconstructions of rites and institutions with interpretations about the significance of an event. Thus in the case of the foregoing payment, Kwamba (1974: p. 100) suggests why the payment must be made: 'so that the Lemba statue will see and respond correctly'. In another part of the initiation rite, a similar account is given, of the use of colour and its significance (p. 101): 'then [the Lemba priest] takes *nkula* and *ndimba* [red] and rubs it around his eyes and in lines along his arms so that the respect of the priesthood will be made manifest in him'. And, with regard to the climactic patrifilial exchange of wives between Lemba son (neophyte) and Lemba father (initiator), the following description and interpretation is given (p. 101):

> the priests say to the Lemba child: 'when we return to the village, you shall lie with the priestess wife of your Lemba father and he shall lie with your wife. In doing this your eyes will be opened to ways of exacting money from the profaners and the transgressors of the laws of Lemba which give the priest his power.'

Not all details are given this kind of interpretation, of course. Few of the song texts, of which there are many, are given any exegesis. The following verse shows an enigmatic song phrase of this kind (p. 98):

> What Lemba gives,
> Lemba takes away;
> What the sun gives,
> The sun takes away.

Presumably this reference to Lemba giving and taking, with metaphoric allusion to the sun, has to do with the force behind sickness and cure. In my book on Lemba (Janzen, 1982) I have examined these songs at length and shall not consider them further here.

The various statements – songs, accounts of ritual actions, interpretations – suggest that these 'ethnographic' texts are internally differentiated into levels, serving various communicative audiences and needs. The songs may be taken to represent the conscious, although often enigmatic, formulations of the Lemba priesthood. The ritual actions similarly are statements made in regard to particular normative settings. The authors' interpretive comments are for the benefit of the reader; they are the aspect of speech and act which I take to be especially original in writing. Thus, when another writer, Konda, strives to explain the entire institution of Lemba to Laman, he uses this formulation (Note-book 119): 'Lemba is a sacred medicine of the ancestors; it mediates between village and cemetery'. The first is a statement that would be comprehensible to any adult in Kongo society. The second, however, is an additional phrase, a second-order explan-ation of an explanation. This type of clarifying statement would not be impossible in Kongo oral culture, but it would be unneces-sary, especially within a ritual setting such as Lemba. Writing in this context bridges the cognitive and social gulf between the internal consciousness of an esoteric cult setting and another consciousness removed from it. The process consists in clarifying the context of internal, esoteric actions and words, and of giving the entire institution signification for an outsider, at least someone removed from the immediate events at hand. This is similar to Lévi-Strauss's view of myth which may stand on its own internal structural terms, but may likewise be derived from, or associated with, social institutions. Thus, for him (Lévi-Strauss, 1971: p. 603) myth moves through 'empirical and transcendental deductions', shifting for clarity or appeal to physical referents, geographical and astronomical realms on the one hand, and to imaginary and fantasizing entities or abstract generalities on the other.

'Appearance of the Prophet' contains many comparable passages of ranked levels: descriptive statement interspersed with mythic, esoteric internal meaning on the one hand, and external, inter-pretive statements on the other. Early in his prophetic career, Kimbangu twice tried to raise a child from the dead, and again a third time tried and failed – the number three is itself significant in Kongo cosmological terms, indicating interaction with the realm of spirits and the dead. Having failed, he asked the child's parents the following (Raymaekers, 1971: p. 29):

> 'Are you sad about your child?'
> 'I am not sad.' [said the mother] '. . .I asked the father, too;
> 'I am sad about my child.' [said the father] Thus because of the
> mother, my strength disappeared. I told them to leave. They
> went to bury the child alone because God forbade me from
> going to the cemetery, for they had refused to believe in God's
> power. I returned to the village.

At one level there is the conversation with the parents about their mood, and their journey to the cemetery. Kimbangu's own rationale for action as it were inverts the rationale of the parents; they bury their child in the cemetery of their families, without faith; he strives for a faith that reverses the customary order of the living and the dead. In another, more successful action, recorded in a third-person voice by the secretary, the following is noted (p. 32):

> The prophet said, 'What do you want?'
> He replied, 'I would see.'
> The prophet spat on the ground, made mud, and rubbed it on
> his eyes, telling him to go wash himself. He saw and glorified
> God for what had happened to him.

This time the religious meaning of the event is derived from the recipient of a healing act.

The pattern of action followed by rationale or explanation is most evident in a series of encounters between the prophet and his antagonists: first, a group of 'false' prophets, in one place a Baptist missionary, and in another a Belgian administrator, Morel, who has come to investigate the prophet. Called to come to the administrator's tent for interrogation, Kimbangu confronts the administrator with prayer (a reading of Psalm 3), after which (pp. 42–3)

> the power of the Holy Spirit made itself manifest in him and he
> cried with a loud voice: 'I call Jehovah with my voice!' He
> raised his eyes to heaven and spoke in a new language: 'Tek
> tektel tek.' His aides also raised their eyes to heaven and spoke
> in this celestial language.
>   The reason for these glances to heaven and these words is
> that God had promised Simon Kimbangu that whenever your
> enemies arrive, it is not you who will speak, but I will send the
> Prince of angels Gabriel to be your defendant. Thus God did
> not fail in his promise when the Whiteman arrived.

This is perhaps the first transcription in Kongo writing of vision-speech (glossolalia). Small wonder that the explanation is much longer than the passage in the celestial tongue. The interpretation given to this heavenly speech before the administrator is that Kimbangu is addressing 'the world' from the mystical realm, which is ironically also known in Kongo religion as 'the white' (from *mpemba*, clay or chalk, realm of ancestors and spirits, the beyond).[7] Thus the structure of the message in this written text is very similar to that of the 'Lemba Notebooks' in terms of the emphasis on society's purification and the power of the beyond pervading certain privileged ones.

Decoding ethnographic text

Written texts, in contrast to oral ones, have a life of their own beyond the immediate function which produced them; they are potentially available to whoever discovers them, and for a variety of purposes.[8] The two early Kongo texts discussed above, the 'Lemba Notebooks' and the 'Appearance of the Prophet', were shaped by a combination of the writers' (and commissioners') intentions and the immediate context which they were describing: the historic Lemba initiations and Kimbangu's ministry in 1921. Neither text has an unbroken record of active use and popularity leading into some sort of official status. In fact, both, after their initial use, ended up in archives where they collected dust for decades. It is difficult to speak of the 'consequences of literacy' with reference to texts which are tucked away in archives. Nevertheless, these texts are part of a larger process of written communication in Kongo culture and religion which is having profound effects on the way Kongo people see their lives and express beliefs.

The 'Lemba Notebooks', and other parts of the Laman corpus of catechists' writings, were used to prepare a dictionary, an ethnographic monograph series, a grammar, and a series of cultural tools which, with the whole generation of early ethnographies, formulated in print a reflexive image of a culture, one that was received back in that culture as a veritable canon, to be joined by indigenous writers interested later on in cultural revival. Similarly, the 'Appearance of the Prophet', although confiscated, was the first of a series of prophet writings, written by the prophet or dictated to a secretary, which continue to be produced, as songs, pamphlets, decrees, as well as lengthy sustained accounts of visions. Wherever the prophet has a following, these writings become important messages, permitting a corporate body to exist over space and time on a scale not possible before writing. Where the prophet has died, leaving an organization behind with leaders in charge of it, these writings become potentially sacred scriptures. The scope of this work does not permit a fuller discussion of these cases; a few have been alluded to in the *Anthology of Kongo Religion* (Janzen and MacGaffey, 1974: p. 27). The point that is significant for present purposes is that out of the variety of studies of historic culture, and the revealed words of visions, come materials which, as time goes by, are likely to be scrutinized, manipulated, controlled, edited, printed and distributed as canons of their respective areas of life: 'custom' on the one hand, as Kongo or African culture really was, and 'divine' or 'ancestral' truth as received by a given prophet, on the other. What Kimbanguist church authorities will do with the 'Appearance of the Prophet' is not known at this point.

Apart from the consequences of literacy in a society, or within a religious or cultural community, is the question of a detached scholarly analysis of the content of texts such as those considered here. Even where writing about religious experiences or rituals has been controlled by the direct descendants of prophets, or where the copying of texts is the pastime of dedicated scribes, scholarship focuses on the content and structure of the text. Having in the previous section examined the structure of 'levels' within our two Kongo texts, it is appropriate to suggest briefly how their content might be examined. This issue is pursued in the light of the conclusion reached earlier that traditional oral genres had dissolved in written texts and that a new approach to form, content, context and the like was needed. What follows is the elaboration of a method of textual analysis developed with the 'Lemba Notebooks' (Janzen, 1982), and applied here to both texts comparatively.

The illustrations in the previous section suggest that these ethnographic texts are structured at several levels of description and interpretation. The examples selected reveal that the texts also articulate a number of coded domains of expression, such as economic transactions, social role sets pertaining to marriage, kinship and authority, spatial and temporal ordering, ritual colour, medicines and others. Pertinent writings on the analysis of such codes of cultural expression are found in studies of language use and ritual, among others. Sometimes a distinction is drawn between verbal and non-verbal communication, or between the 'said and the unsaid' (Tyler, 1978), or between multiple channels, each with its own code (Leach, 1966; Bateson, 1972). The reason for multiple channel communication, or 'ritualization', is explained in terms of a combination of the desire for heightened affect (Sperber, 1974) and the need to overcome, cope with, or actually create ambiguity or conflict and contradiction in a communication. The result, whether in text (verbal), or in context (non-verbal) communication, or in a written account of both, represents what Fernandez (1972, 1977) has called the pluralization of 'quality spaces' or expressive domains which interact, juxtapose and coalesce to form interlaced metaphors of considerable power. Both denotative statements as propositions or acts, and connotative 'echoes' across to other statements within the same or another domain, create 'dominant metaphors' which focus an event in a single meaning (Barthes, 1964; 1967; Armstrong, 1971), or on the tensions, contradictions and creativity of movements between several strands of meaning (Fernandez, 1977). The analytic method proposed here identifies such expressive domains and their codes within the ethnographic text. The Kongo texts cannot be said to contain a fixed number of such coded expressive domains; but some domains clearly stand out and it is possible to begin with those. In the Lemba study (Janzen, 1982, Part II) I have analysed the 'Lemba Notebooks' and supporting ethnography, history and material culture in terms of regional variants; expressive domains such as those which follow permit the organization and content analysis of disparate evidence.[9]

The first coded domain evident in the texts is the *spatial and temporal distribution of events*, evidence of an active principle contrasting the visible world of the here and now with the invisible world of ancestors, spirits and the beyond. In the texts, as in many rituals, these opposed realms are represented by village and cemetery, village and river, above ground and beneath the ground. In Lemba initiations, a closely choreographed rhythm of events contrasts, then mediates, the two space-fields. In the prophet's text the contrast is more situational. Visits to Kimbangu's mother by a missionary to whom is attributed the prophet's 'annunciation' and blessing, scenes from the prophet's childhood in which he disappears in a subterranean 'hole', or where he is plagued by runny bowels, as well as later in his ministry where he confronts his antagonists and trembles ecstatically, all clearly indicate this structuring of space–time by the narrator so as to convey the image of the sacred power governing the prophet's life. The code of this domain is the selective opposition of events, spaces, persons and powers into 'the world' (*va nza*) and 'the beyond' (*mpemba*).

A second coded domain, particularly in the Lemba texts, is the *exchange of gifts and presentations*, integrating the ceremonial economy with the wider pre-colonial and colonial economy. The Lemba texts describe an elaborate pattern of exchange: pigs, chickens, wine, various other foods, medicine, gestures, are portrayed as being collected by Lemba priests and redistributed to the profane, so as to create the reciprocation of material goods with symbols of authority of the newly inaugurated priest. At the beginning of prophet's text, the writers note exchanges of food and drink for the blessing of the prophet-child. Also, the woman who at one point lends the prophet a *kinsakulu*-tomato, a form of purgative medicine, becomes his chosen bride. But there the conventional exchanges end. The domain is henceforth found only in a negative sense or in a rejection of the mode altogether. Kimbangu finds himself robbed of his earnings in Kinshasa where he runs away to escape his calling. After accepting his calling, the only allusion to material exchanges is his outright rejection of payments for his healing acts. This corresponds to the culture-wide contrast between the magician-healer who charges fees for his skills, and the prophet who receives his gifts directly from God and therefore may not ask for remuneration. It is as if he had altogether transcended the domain of material exchange.

Parallel to the pattern of exchange is the *social structure*, which may be considered a third coded domain. In the Lemba texts, clear relationships are demonstrated between the major *dramatis personae*: the neophyte, his wife (wives), the personnel of the Lemba order and the community supporting the neophyte couple, especially the patrifilial children (dependants and political supporters) of the new priest. The texts spell out prohibitions and prescriptions in the relationships between Lemba and non-Lemba members of society, as well as the social ideology behind Lemba. In the prophet's diary there is a similar elaboration of the new society of the prophet, his followers, his apostles, the mass clientele, all of which are set off in opposition to his detractors and opponents, including 'false prophets', selected missionaries and colonial officials. In Lemba and the prophet movement there exist clearly coded demarcations between the community of the pure and the impure, a line conceptualized in terms of the ideology of the 'world' and 'the beyond' (*mpemba*). Codices which were implicit or verbally articulated in pre-literate society, are often found in print in independent churches, print permitting wider dissemination and control.

The coded domain of *ritual objects*, most often concentrated in sacred medicines (*min'kisi*) and related songs, dances and paraphernalia, figures prominently, although contrastingly, in the two texts. In 'Lemba Notebooks' the reader may trace the progressive composition of the portable shrine, plant by plant, symbol by symbol, incantation by incantation, until the composite object stands as a representation of the universe of spiritual powers, of the Lemba hierarchy, ancestors and various segments of the community, resolving the new priestly couple's affliction and providing them with a new grasp of their role. It is the new priest's memento, to be used in healing others. The prophet's text lacks this systematic composition of Kongo medicinal symbols. However, such symbols as there are conspicuously point to the presence of a power posture. On several occasions the *binsikulu* fruit is used in a purge ordeal, indicative of the aspiration for greater purity and spiritual receptivity amongst the prophet's followers. In another incident the prophet is asked by the husband of a woman he has just healed whether he has any 'plants' – a euphemism for a *n'kisi* cure – for his wife. The prophet replies that nothing of the sort is necessary, for she has received 'more than that'. This transcendence beyond conventional codes of healing reflects both the momentous changes of the hour requiring a radical solution to serious troubles, and the Kongo perception of the difference between the magician-healer (*nganga*) and the prophet (*ngunza*), on the one hand, and between the chief (*mfumu*) and the prophet, on the other (MacGaffey, 1970). Just as the prophet rejects material medicines in favour of his 'greater' spiritual power (he emits a tic-like cough before each healing act, indicative, perhaps, of the surge of spirit (*mpeve*, air) rushing through him), so he also transcends chiefship. In another passage, Kimbangu treats a sufferer of an illness associated with the leopardskin chiefship, recommending that he follow the prophet to be cured. The code of Kongo ritual and medicine dictates the terms for the integration of powers and materials so as to realize an ultimate unity of harmonies and purities in the universe. If there is no appropriate material embodiment for these powers, medicines and chiefly roles of authority must be dismantled so that a new harmony and purity may be achieved. It may be that this is where newly revealed and transcribed text enters into the prophet's purview as a new embodiment of power.

The foregoing coded domains are non-verbal and their presence in the events being described must be inferred through analysis of behaviours and symbols. The following two domains are verbal, and may reflect those aspects of written text that are more self-conscious, intentional. The first I call *verbal categories of ritual action*; the second, the *lyrical message*.

Both the Lemba and the prophetic texts spell out through labels the major process of ritual action, as if they wish to offer a theological or dramaturgic typology to the reader, for use in comparisons and interpretations of the action. Thus the Lemba texts portray the course of the neophyte through his inauguration. He has been polluted (desecrated, had objects thrown upon him by others, been sinned against), and must be purified (sucked clean, bathed, cleansed, redeemed); through the observance of prohibitions (laws, rules) and sacred fear he will gain power (force or strength, judgment, prestige, mystical access and cunning). Although the KiKongo original of the prophet's diary is not available, the translation conveys similar concepts. The prophet and his helpers must be pure and open in order to be imbued with spiritual force. It is possible to trace the path, sketched by the author, of the prophet's blessing which gave him the right, indeed the obligation, to demand the allegiance of others who came to him to be helped. These descriptive texts about Kongo ritual are immensely helpful in understanding structural nuances in it. Furthermore, they are more explicit about these nuances than, for example, native exegetes often are because they are themselves etching out the definition of the event, not merely responding to questions.

The lyrical domain consists mainly of songs performed as messages between actors in the events described, although it may also include references to, or selections from, legends, origin myths or creeds. It is here that one may place chunks of oral genres lifted out of an event or context and copied into an ethnographic text. In the 'Lemba Notebooks' there are many songs to demonstrate the consciously conveyed messages between major actors in the inaugural/healing rites: between Lemba father and Lemba son, from the priests' chorus to the people gathered during a large public dance, from one segment of priests to another in an esoteric session, from the Lemba wives to the neophyte at the consecration of his household, and from the neophyte's patrifilial children to their father during the final distribution of gifts, and his receipt of his medicine-shrine. There is no room to go into these songs here; but it is possible with them to understand their metaphoric and metonymic construction that 'moves' the neophyte through his course: from sickness to health, from novice to master priest, from possession by the afflicting spirit to mastery of that spirit's forces, and the like. All these lyrics are 'drummed up' with *ngoma*, *nkonzi* or *nkonko*, giving, in text, a glimpse of the power of the entire oral-ritual genre of the 'drum of affliction'. But, of course, the dance and drum rhythms, the cathartic releases of energy, and the intensity of an oral perform-ance are not present; these must be put in with interpretive words. In the prophet's text the lyrical is present in healing actions and in the confrontations with antagonists. At these moments the writer has recorded bits of conversation, poignant excerpts in particular which suggest selective reconstruction. Also recorded are the prophet's ecstatic trembling and his outbursts of glossolalia, and the hymn singing with which the faithful break out afterwards. The prophet's secretaries also frequently anchor a particularly poignant demonstration of the prophet's gift with an appropriate scripture reference. The lyrical domain's code is thus articulated by one or several systems of legitimation, whether this be spirits, patron ancestors and God, or the Christian trinity through scriptures, hymns and the African prophet.

Conclusions

What then are the consequences of literacy in African, more particularly Kongo, religion? This study has shown them to be both formal, within the structure and content of the text, and contextual or functional, within the framework of the text's origin and progressive utilization for a variety of ends. The genre of oral tradition may be picked up and put in print; seemingly songs lend themselves most widely to this end, as Zulu, Xhosa, Kongo and other religious literatures indicate. However, the use of print in religion, to record and interpret significant events and experiences, often represents unprecedented textual forms resembling early Greek *historia*, or non-academic ethnographies. Without wishing to create a neologism, but in need of a term to describe this new form, I have used 'ethnographic genre' to characterize it. In this new genre, prophets' secretaries record their masters' visions, encounters and miraculous deeds; disciples and ordinary lay people may record their encounters with the spirit world or with prophetic or priestly figures. And thus a potential religious literature is born.

But such written records do not become significant because they collect dust in drawers and archives. It is their secondary use as continuing evidence of a treasured experience or believed event, after primary evidence has disappeared through the prophet's death, or simply changing times, which calls forth the possibility of canonization: that is, the analysis, categorization, editing and selecting of these textual accounts by recognized authorities who establish their legitimacy. Examples from here and there suggest that many African religious traditions – regional Islamic communities, independent Christian churches, nationalizing mission churches, and renewed historic traditions of African religion – are involved in one or another stage in this transition to literacy.

The consequences of such a transition are far-reaching. Literacy, as such, permits a greater degree of uniformity in a religious order; it certainly permits the existence of such an order on a larger social scale; it permits the renewal of cultural and spiritual traditions to occur with reference to the past-in-the-present; it permits a greater participation in the central ideas of a religious order. Where canonization has occurred, and a 'scripture' has emerged, this broad participation is controlled and sometimes restricted. In the great majority of language traditions, such control has existed from the outside in the form of official Bible translations.

The implications for scholarship of these consequences of literacy, both the formal and the contextual, are significant. Religious scholarship has begun to have a renewed interest in the ritual contexts which gave rise to religious texts. The early stages of canonization are of tremendous importance to the understanding of a scripture. African materials, such as those which have been reviewed here, should be of great use in such study, for in many instances the ritual settings, the individuals involved or those who knew them, and the oral traditions from which they sprang, are still alive. The role of the scholar is surely that of identifying representative texts, of developing analytical tools for their analysis, and of observing the context within which they are produced and perpetuated.

Notes

1 Recent works on African religion such as Jules-Rosette's (1979) *New Religions of Africa* and Hastings's (1979) *History of African Christianity 1950–1975*, important as they may be, hardly mention the issue.

2 Evidence of this earlier literacy includes correspondence between Kongo and Portuguese kings; a KiKongo–Latin–Spanish dictionary based on instructions given by Kongo abbot Emmanuel Roboredo to new missionaries, recorded by the Capucin Georges de Gheel in 1651 (van Wing and Penders, 1928); a catechism in KiKongo by Mathieu Cardozo published in 1624; and a grammar of the KiKongo language published in 1659 by Hyacinthe Brusciotto de Ventralla (Söderberg and Widman, 1978: p. 9).

3 This figure is based on an estimate midway between Mbelolo's statement in his 'Introduction à la littérature KiKongo' (1972: p. 122) that printing runs of *Minsamu* were 2,000 at a time he does not indicate, and the figure of 400 subscribers mentioned in an 1894 issue of the journal, two years after its beginning. In addition to Mbelolo's history of this early period of Kongo literacy, see also Söderberg and Widman's (1978: pp. 9–13) 'Aperçu général de la littérature kongo' and Janzen and MacGaffey's (1974: pp. 1–27) 'Literacy and Truth'.

4 Early events and circumstances of this movement had been extensively – although not exhaustively – studied and continue to stimulate interest. Still valuable is E. Andersson's (1958) *Messianic Popular Movements in the Lower Congo*, giving mainly missionary accounts. For a detailed reconstruction of events based on a more recent coverage of eyewitness accounts in the literature, see Cecilia Irvine's (1974) 'The Birth of the Kimbanguist Movement in the Bas-Zaire, 1921'. For a theological interpretation of Kimbanguism's origins which is close to the preferred public image of the church's contemporary leaders, see Marie-Louise Martin's (1976) *Kimbangu: An African Prophet and his Church*. For an account of Kongo prophetism within the perspective of Kongo religious history, see Janzen and MacGaffey's (1974) *Anthology of Kongo Religion*.

5 Of special interest in this connection are the examples of Ntsikana's early nineteenth-century Xhosa hymn-writing and accounts of his life by his disciples (Gérard, 1971: pp. 24–9), and Isaiah Shembe's Zulu

hymns, as well as the collection and codification of testimonies of his miracles by his successors (Gérard, 1971: pp. 184f.).

6 On genres of Bantu oral tradition, see the following: for the Cameroons, Alexandre (1972); for eastern Zaire forest areas, Biebuyck and Mateene (1969), Biebuyck (1970); for the interlacustrine areas, Vansina (1965).

7 Fukiau's *Nza-Kongo/La cosmogonie Kongo* (1969) remains the best treatment of this key opposition in Kongo art, religion and ritual.

8 In the words of another author writing about language and culture generally, 'Once written, a text assumes an independent existence and acquires meanings of its own quite apart from those intended by its author'(Tyler, 1978: p. 378).

9 This set of 'coded expressive domains' is similar, in analytic aim, to that developed by Fabian to analyse numerous oral transcriptions and one written version of the Jamaa instructions (*mafundisho*) (1971: pp. 160–3).

References

Alexandre, Pierre (1972), 'De l'oralité à l'écriture', lecture to Department of Anthropology, McGill University, Montreal.

Andersson, E. (1958), *Messianic Popular Movements in the Lower Congo*, Uppsala: Almqvist & Wiksell (Studia Ethnographica Upsaliensia XIV).

Armstrong, R. P. (1971), *The Affecting Presence*, Urbana: Illinois University Press.

Bahelele, J. (1953), *Bingana bia Nsi a Kongo*, Matadi: L'Imprimerie de la Svenska Missionsforbundet.

Bahelele, J. (1964), *Kinzonzi ye Ntekolo andi Makundu*, Matadi: Église Évangélique de Manianga et Matadi.

Barthes, R. (1964), 'Éléments de Semiologie', *Communications*, 4: pp. 91–135.

Barthes, R. (1967), *Systèmes de la Mode*, Paris: Plon.

Bascom, W. (1965), 'The Forms of Folklore: Prose Narratives', *Journal of American Folklore*, 78.

Bateson, G. (1972), 'Redundancy and Coding', in his *Steps to an Ecology of Mind*, New York: Ballantine Books, pp. 411–25.

Biebuyck, D. (1970), *Anthologie de la littérature orale nyanga*, Brussels: Académie Royale des Sciences.

Biebuyck, D., and Mateene, K. (1969), *The Mwindo Epic*, Berkeley and Los Angeles: University of California Press.

DeMunck, J. (1956), *Kinkulu kia Nsi eto*, Tumba: Imprimerie Mission Catholique.

Fabian, J. (1971), *Jamaa, A Charismatic Movement in Katanga*, Evanston: Northwestern University Press.

Fabian, J. (1979), 'Man and Woman in the Teachings of the Jamaa Movement', in Jules-Rosette (1979), pp. 169–84.

Fernandez, J. (1972), 'Persuasions and Performances: Of the Beast in Every Body . . . and the Metaphors of Everyman', *Daedalus*, **101**, 1: pp. 39–60.

Fernandez, J. (1977), 'The Performance of Ritual Metaphors', in Sapir and Crocker (1977), pp. 100–31.

Fukiau kia Bunseki (1969), *Nza-Kongo/La cosmogonie Kongo*, Kinshasa: Office Nationale de la Recherche et du Développement.

Gérard, A. (1971), 'Black Africa', *Review of National Literatures*, **II**, 2.

Gérard, A. (1972), *Four African Literatures*, Berkeley and Los Angeles: University of California Press.

Goody, J. (ed.) (1968), *Literacy in Traditional Societies*, Cambridge: Cambridge University Press.

Goody, J. and Watt, I. (1968), 'The Consequences of Literacy', in Goody (1968), pp. 27–68.

Hastings, A. (1979), *A History of African Christianity 1950–1975*, Cambridge: Cambridge University Press.

Havelock, E. (1971), *Prologue to Greek Literacy*, Cincinnati: Cincinnati University Press.

Honko, L. (ed.) (1979), *Science of Religion: Studies in Methodology*, The Hague: Mouton.

Irvine, C. (1974), 'The Birth of the Kimbanguist Movement in the Bas-Zaire, 1921', *Journal of Religion in Africa*, **6**, 1: pp. 23–76.

Janzen, J. (1972), 'Laman's Kongo Ethnography: Observations on Sources, Methodology, and Theory', *Africa*, **42**, 4: pp. 316–28.

Janzen, J. (1978), *The Quest for Therapy in Lower Zaire*, Berkeley and Los Angeles: University of California Press.

Janzen, J. (1979a), 'Deep Thought: Structure and Intention in Kongo Prophetism: 1910–1921', *Social Research*, **46**, 1: pp. 106–39.

Janzen, J. (1979b), 'Ideologies and Institutions in the Precolonial History of Equatorial African Therapeutic Systems', *Social Science and Medicine*, **14**, 1B.

Janzen, J. (1982), *Lemba 1650–1930: A Drum of Affliction in Africa and the New World*, New York: Garland Publishers.

Janzen, John M., and MacGaffey, Wyatt (1974), *An Anthology of Kongo Religion*, Lawrence: University of Kansas Publications in Anthropology no. 5.

Jules-Rosette, B. (ed.) (1979), *The New Religions of Africa*, Norwood, NJ: Ablex Publishing Corporation.

Konda, J. (n.d., *c.* 1915), *Notebook 119*, Lidingö: Laman Collection, SMF Archives.

Kwamba, E. (1974), 'Initiation to Lemba', in Janzen and MacGaffey (1974), pp. 97–102.

Leach, E. (1966), 'A Discussion on Ritualization of Behavior in Animals and Man', *Philosophical Transactions of the Royal Society of London*, Series B, **251**, 771: pp. 403–8.

Lévi-Strauss, C. (1971), *L'Homme nu: Mythologiques IV*, Paris: Plon.

MacGaffey, W. (1970), 'The Religious Commissions of the BaKongo',
   Man (n.s.), **5**, 1: pp. 27–38.
Martin, Marie-Louise (1976), *Kimbangu: An African Prophet and his
   Church*, Grand Rapids: W. B. Eerdmans Publishing Co.
Mbelolo ya Mpiku (1972), 'Introduction à la littérature KiKongo',
   Research in African Literatures, **3**, 2: pp. 117–61.
Minkunga mia Yenge (1887), Mukimbungu.
Minsamu mia Yenge (1892–), Kibunzi & Matadi.
Nkindu, G. (1974), 'The Heritage of Kimbangu', in Janzen and
   MacGaffey (1974), pp. 148–53.
Pentikäinen, J. (1979), 'Taxonomy and Source Criticism of Oral Tradition',
   in Honko (1979): pp. 35–52.
Raymaekers, P. (1971), 'Histoire de Simon Kimbangu. Prophète, d'après
   les écrivains Nfinangani et Nzungu' (1921), Kinshasa: BOPR, Univer-
   sité de Kinshasa; *Archives de Sociologie des Religions* (Paris), **16**, 1:
   pp. 15–42.
Sapir, D., and Crocker, J. (eds) (1977), *The Social Use of Metaphor*,
   Philadelphia: University of Pennsylvania Press.
Söderberg, B., and Widman, R. (1978), *Publications en kikongo:
   Bibliographie relative aux contributions suédoises entre 1885 et 1970*,
   Uppsala: L'Institut Scandinave d'Études Africaines; Stockholm: Le
   Musée Ethnographique de l'État Suédois.
Sperber, D. (1974), *Rethinking Symbolism*, Cambridge: Cambridge
   University Press.
Stenström, O., and Palmaer, G. (1961), *Mavanga ma Nzambi mu Kongo*,
   Matadi: Église Évangélique de Manianga et Matadi.
Struyf, I. (1936), *Les Bakongo dans leurs légendes*, Brussels: Institut
   Royale Coloniale Belge.
Sydow, C. von (1948), *Selected Papers on Folklore*, Copenhagen:
   Rosenkilde & Bagger.
Tyler, S. (ed.) (1978), *The Said and the Unsaid*, New York: Academic
   Press.
Vansina, J. (1965), *Oral Tradition*, Chicago: Aldine.
Vingadio, T., *et al.* (1928), *Nsweswe Ansusu Ampembe ye ngana zankaka*,
   Kimpese: EPI.
Wing, J. van, and Penders, C. (1928), *Le plus ancien dictionnaire bantou:
   Vocabularium P. Georgii Gelensis, Capucini, 1652*, Louvain:
   Imprimerie J. Kuyk-Otto.
Wing, J. van, and Schöller, C. (1940), *Legendes des Bakongo orientaux*,
   Brussels: Bulens.

Chapter 9

The argument of images: From Zion to the Wilderness in African churches

Richard P. Werbner

The dynamic interplay of reality and imagination

In meeting the challenge of radical change, the religious imagination often creates and recreates alternative images of space and
place, of movement and passage in this world and the next.[1] Even
the most familiar locational imagery, such as that of the body or
the home, is then given a new significance. A whole series of cults
and churches may arise, each with its own specific imagery, but
often as variations on the same basic elements and themes.
According to a widely accepted explanation, such religious
innovation is a way of restoring order. In other words, it is a kind
of redressive mechanism; through it, people adjust to a changed
social environment, and they find some consonance between
otherwise contradictory experiences.

Following Horton (1967), Fernandez suggests that in response
to a change in the scale of social life 'images of adaptive
conversion' make it possible for people to negotiate 'the disorder
present in expanding social relationships' (1978: p. 224). According to this view, the religious imagination invents or rediscovers
images of an overarching order in the world, while striving to
counteract the felt disorder and contradictions in experience. The
implication is that the religious imagination uses solely the kind of
locational imagery which is somehow consonant in itself, and in
harmony with the changed social environment. Order is not
imposed on experience arbitrarily, but through imaginative forms
that are iconic or correspond directly with some external, social
reality. The comparison Fernandez draws is between the play of

253

imagination in folktales and the 'argument of images' in religious movements:

> In religious movements, however, we discover imagination struggling with more challenging displacements in which the outer has become a greater reality than the inner . . . a more attractive reality. We miss the heart of such religious thought if we neglect the fact that this decentering and the acute sense of peripherality it produces is imaginatively negotiated in primary images of body and household, field and forest life . . . . (1978: p. 229)

There is a danger in this view, when it comes to studying the phenomena of religious pluralism. The 'argument of images' may be turned into something of a monologue, leaving aside the locational imagery of dissent and non-conformity. By this I mean the imagery through which people direct themselves and others, for the sake of spiritual regeneration, to remake their environment, rather than merely adjusting to it. I have in mind the imagery which, as I explain later, I would call disharmonic, with a view to its semantic structure. Using disharmonic imagery, people may resist and reject the state; they may break away from one mode of production to seek another; they may abandon some existing economic or social niche in order to go about gaining a new one. What the people perceive as disorder, as something negative, is not here converted by the religious imagination into order or something positive. Instead, the disorder is recognized, even embraced for what it is, in images of pervasive dislocation: God's chosen people are wanderers in the wilderness (on the negative in religious imagination cf. Fabian, 1979: p. 170f.).

As an illustration, the image of the Wilderness Church is illuminating. It conveys what are the phenomena that constitute the locational image of a religious movement; and it also prepares the way for my main account of the contrasting imagery generated by three Zionist or Apostolic churches in Zimbabwe. The disharmonic image of the Wilderness Church focuses on indefinite space instead of either permanently or temporarily defined place. God's chosen people are in exile. They are migrating towards the Promised Land, and wherever a congregation meets, it is the Wilderness. Bereft of any enclosure, the usual space for ritual is not marked apart in any way, and it is boundless: the space for ritual must be in the open. God has no earth-bound house of substance, no material building temporarily or permanently set aside for ritual, instead the house of God is personified. It is one of the biblical houses, the house of Ham, and thus the house of all Africans, indeed all blacks. Similarly, the temple is the church leader, or another person or persons specially dedicated to God. Moreover, there is a passing vessel (such as an ark for the sea or, later and more radically, certain virgins as sisters of the church) to carry God's chosen people, the pure who are to be rescued from among the exiled mankind, when the day comes for the great destruction of the powerful of the present sinful world.[2]

The use of sacraments is rejected; and while baptism in Jordan (i.e. in a flowing river) is essential for salvation, only the church founder has the power to baptize. Thus, the spatially transformative ritual uses external lustration of the person only, without internal transformation through communion. Some local congregations in the countryside have their own places of ascension, but there will be no height for regular, church-wide pilgrimage, no single place of ascension for the chosen people as a whole, until the founder's death and the reforming of the church's image. This image is in an argument of images with others belonging to other churches, including one image that focuses on the eternal place for the kingdom of God on earth, the New Jerusalem, and another that focuses on the ephemeral places of humankind on earth, the tabernacles of the Pentecost. My main aim in this chapter is to interpret that argument while developing a conceptual framework which enables us to explain it comparatively.

The social field, strangerhood and estrangement

If we are to get much further in studying the argument of images where there is a plurality of cults and religious movements, certain steps are essential. Let me put these somewhat abstractly, by way of introduction, and then attempt to pursue them more concretely through a comparison of cults and churches in West and Southern Africa.

First comes the problem of conceptualizing the social environment as changing, and as subject to change through the impact of the locational imagery. The metaphors we ourselves use to

255

interpret this interplay may impoverish the locational imagery of the people we study, as well as imposing a simplistic social determinism. A critical example is the metaphor of increasing 'scale' which is so widespread in the literature on religious conversion and African churches. Its use has weakened our understanding of the nexus between locational imagery and the changing social environment. My point is not simply that 'increasing scale' lumps together quite disparate transformations, or that it imposes too neat an evolutionary bias on history (cf. Kuper, 1979). Even more fundamentally, 'increasing scale' diverts attention away from changes in the structural placement of part-societies, their variable centre–periphery relations, their evolving encapsulation within wider social fields. Yet these are the very changes in which, and for which, locational imagery so often matters the most. Hence, such changes require explicit conceptualization and analysis no less than the imagery itself.

Second, we need to show how the imagery informs and is informed by certain culturally perceived predicaments and contradictions in experience. Displacement, or the cultural perception of a decentring of reality, is the broad predicament which Fernandez illuminates (Fernandez, 1978; 1979). But this remains too broad for systematic comparison, and we need to see various alternative predicaments in terms of problematic conditions of personhood, conditions which bring into question the cultural definition of the person *vis-à-vis* significant others.

To explore the systematic comparison, I focus in this chapter on alternative predicaments that relate to movement in space, especially labour migration, and that fall within the polar contrast between strangerhood and estrangement. As developed by Skinner, the distinction between 'stranger' and 'estranger' conceptualizes the relative capacity of outsiders to convert their hosts into aliens in their own land and community. Skinner's concern is the colonial or post-colonial impact of different kinds of outsiders. On the one hand, there are the strangers who are able to remain as immigrants near their hosts yet somehow detached from them, without being able to dominate them. On the other hand are the estrangers who, as conquerors and colonizers, have the power to dominate; they act as if they can determine who their hosts are and can treat the indigenous people as aliens on their own soil. Thus Europeans as estrangers 'alienated the lands, resources, persons and even psyches of the indigenous populations, who eventually became subordinated to the interests of their conquerors' (Skinner, 1979: p. 282; cf. also Skinner, 1974: p. 145).

As put by Skinner, the contrast seems to exaggerate alienation as total and inflates the capacity of colonizers actually to determine the condition of the estranged, rather than affecting their perceptions. Without that implication, but with an emphasis on the problematic relation between us and ourselves as mediated by dominant others, the concept of estrangement in contrast to strangerhood is illuminating (for a helpful formulation of stranger and estranger relationships, see also Levine, 1979). For my purposes, it is especially useful, because it enables me to relate religious movements to the movement of labour migrants – as strangers, away from home, and as estranged home-comers, on their return. Moreover, as will be shown, an important reason for distinguishing between the predicaments of stranger and estranged systematically is that this helps in answering a key question: which of the predicaments have an emphasis on the microcosm in their associated imagery, which emphasize the macrocosm, and why? For the sake of clarity, I must explain further at this point that my notion of predicament allows for the possibility that the same individuals may know different predicaments – for example, predicaments of strangerhood and estrangement as well – and that they may express their consciousness of each separately, in distinct religious movements or cults. The notion does not necessarily imply a single predicament as being the exclusive one for a whole society or even for a single individual.

The semantic structure of the imagery

Third, the much neglected semantic context of the imagery needs to be explored. The temptation has been to turn directly to a relation with the social environment – i.e. the social field – and to ask how religious images correspond with or negate conditions in the social field. Or put in Marxist terms, the question that easily takes priority at the expense of semantic analysis is: how are the religious forms related (in the way of either simple correspondence, dialectical correspondence or negative dialectical compensation) to articulated modes of production (cf. van Binsbergen, 1981: p. 57)? What this approach misses is the fact that it is on the semantic structure, the inner logic and relative coherence of the image that its force depends, *qua* image. Hence a semantic analysis is essential. In no way does this imply adopting an approach that divorces the forms and images from the socio-cultural configurations out of which they arise.

For a start in a semantic analysis, we have to identify whole patterns of imagery and their basic semantic elements: i.e. the semantic elements that recur in one guise or another, either in a series of successive images belonging, for example, to earlier and later churches, or in a set of images which are in contrast with each other as contemporaries. The underlying problem is a familiar one: to appreciate historical transformation – the changing pattern of imagery in a series – while accounting for contemporary dynamics – the patterns of permutation in contrastive sets. Only thus – by doing both – can we begin to say what makes a particular image forceful for consciousness of one kind or another.

Part of the basis for comprehending the semantics of locational imagery is already well established in the richly insightful studies by Eliade. Writing about the imagery which 'archaic man' uses for the world around him, Eliade discerns what he considers to be two modalities, with the imagery belonging in one modality or the other: Chaos and Cosmos (cf. especially Eliade, 1974: pp. 9f. and passim). Chaos refers to the part of the world that is perceived according to an exemplary model of the undifferentiated, formless, ephemeral condition; an example is the flux of the wilderness or unknown seas. By contrast, the rest of the world takes on the reality of being Cosmos, the differentiated, the eternal, and all that is organized by forms and norms. A corresponding example is the sacred city, built after a celestial model, with its temple at the centre of the world. Eliade's insight advances our discussion, if we take into account the simple fact that a single locational image may encompass both Chaos and Cosmos. Indeed, its very significance may arise from the tension in the imagery between Chaos and Cosmos, as I show later when discussing the disharmonic imagery of the Wilderness Church. Hence, it is the *polar aspects* of an image, not its modality, that we need to consider in the light of Eliade's insight. Moreover, freed from the notion of 'archaic man', the general relevance of the insight must be stressed, lest we seem to be distancing it from ourselves, with regard to a spirituality or mentality that is pre-modern, not shared by us.

In my view the systematics of locational imagery can be better appreciated if we compare the structuring of the perceptions of Chaos or Cosmos in the images of a set or series. The comparison has to be made with regard to the general terms which are fundamental, and which serve as the co-ordinates of the imagery as a whole. Chaos and Cosmos are a co-ordinate's polar aspects or, one might say, relative values. Given the nature of locational imagery, I take such co-ordinates to be simply: 'Person' and 'Space' or 'Space/Time', which is a shorthand for space *and* time-expressed-as-space (for a discussion of such 'spaced time' see Sharron, 1981. In Figure 9.1 is shown the structural variation in the semantic harmony of imagery, according to whether the imagery has 'Person' and 'Space' with like values (the harmonic image) or unlike values (the disharmonic image).[3] Chaos is indicated by the negative value ($-$), and Cosmos by the positive ($+$). Four structures are shown; and because my discussion is limited by the criterion of relevance to the polyethnic churches, and thus to a concern only with the two structures in the upper half of the diagram, a caution is in order, for which I refer the reader to n. 4, p. 283 below.[4]

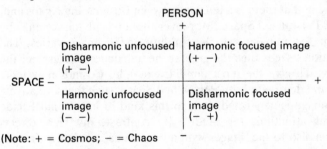

PERSON
+

	Disharmonic unfocused image (+ $-$)	Harmonic focused image (+ $-$)	
SPACE $-$			+
	Harmonic unfocused image ($-$ $-$)	Disharmonic focused image ($-$ +)	

(Note: + = Cosmos; $-$ = Chaos

$-$

Figure 9.1 *Harmony in imagery of Person and Space*

To illustrate briefly, in advance of my main account, I refer to the image of the Wilderness Church, described above. In this image, relative to certain others, Space is unfocused and has the aspect of Chaos as indefinite boundlessness, ever in flux. Person, however, is framed and has the aspect of Cosmos, as organized by forms and norms, in that the pure person is well set apart from the impure by baptism and other rites and rules of purity or purification.[5] In other words, this is a disharmonic image, relative to certain others, for it is constituted by a tension balancing Chaos as the aspect of one co-ordinate, Space, and Cosmos as the aspect of the other, Person.

The question must be asked: can Eliade's insight contribute to the kind of semantic analysis that is needed? It might be thought, for various reasons, that Eliade's approach runs counter to our project, which is to view cults within socio-cultural configurations in history, and that we are being misled into viewing the image as a discrete entity, somehow given significance by its internal aspects, in a void. What has happened to the *argument* of images, to the persuasive discourse generating and regenerating alternatives under conditions of religious pluralism? In response to this challenge, I attempt, later in this chapter, to examine the nexus between the changing social field, harmonic or disharmonic semantic structures, and the varieties of consciousness which the images project.

For the sake of clarity, however, let me stress a further major difference between Eliade's approach and mine. Eliade views the image as static, despite his concern with cyclical time, largely because he fixes attention on one kind of image almost exclusively. But my view, taking in the wider set, recognizes that the image is dynamic in that there is a tension between Cosmos and Chaos and, indeed, Person and Space. Moreover, because the tension may be more or less imbalanced, the stability of the image varies. The correlation I see is this: the greater the imbalance, the greater the stability. To give the most familiar example, Cosmos may tame Chaos and dominate both Person and Space, such that a relatively stable image is generated. It is to this kind of image that Eliade gives his attention, repeatedly. By contrast, my view directs attention also to the images with a precarious imbalance. In such images, Cosmos does not dominate throughout. Instead, Cosmos has to contend with Chaos prevailing over Space or Person. Here the key problem is: what direction does the tendency towards instability take, with the possibility of a shift towards Chaos or Cosmos, and the reconstruction of the image as harmonic or disharmonic? I would argue that the fulfilment of the tendency's potential is not a function of the image alone; it is not self-generating. In due course, I examine the influences that are exerted to determine the tendency's actual direction.

The framework of organization

So far I have raised problems with regard to the changing social field, the emphasis on the macrocosm or the microcosm in cosmology, and the alternative predicaments of strangerhood and estrangement. A central concern has been the semantic context and structure of images, their co-ordinates and relative aspects as well as the varieties of consciousness which the images project. It remains to link my discussion to the specific organizational forms of cults and churches. In my own earlier work, I have approached the organizational forms primarily within a framework of regional analysis (Werbner, 1977a; 1977b; 1979). This framework makes sense of the pattern and organization of various flows – of people, goods, services and ideas – in relation to the location of central places. My attempts to develop this framework have gone through several phases; and in response to this book's project – looking backward, self-critically if possible, in order to look forward to the frontiers of the subject – I must review some of that development. Later, following the review, I brave the frontiers by discussing the argument of images in relation to the Mwari cult and the three most extensive of all the polyethnic churches originally founded in rural Zimbabwe.

Shrines and cults in history: a review

The basis for my theoretical interest has been my long-term observation from 1960 onwards (and most recently in 1978) of one regional cult. It is the High God cult of Mwari, which has its central places and ranked oracles in a chain of hills across the middle of Western Zimbabwe and Eastern Botswana. From the start of my analysis, the conventional correspondence theory, which works with a simple fit between religion and society, had to be abandoned. No territory, bounded group, political community or single society was adequate as a starting-point for my analysis (for a contrasting view of the cult as a non-hierarchical federative cult see Schoffeleers, 1979, and my reply in Werbner, forthcoming). This hierarchical cult organized a redistributive system across local, tribal, national and quite marked cultural frontiers; it regulated certain aspects of agricultural production in distinct ecological zones; and by affirming that the shedding of blood, polluting the earth, offends God, it ritually protected the peace and the welfare of people and land in numerous scattered communities. Moreover, its lasting viability, richly recorded for over a century, meant that a one-time explanation, without historical depth, was of no use for my account.

The micro-historical religious change that I observed, and then tried to bring into a macro-historical perspective, is hardly innovation. Or rather, it is not what is chiefly looked at by students of African religious movements when they discuss innovation. Their concern has overwhelmingly been the religious responses to 'the shattered microcosm', as van Binsbergen (1981: p. 28) aptly puts it. What has largely been neglected, as a consequence, is the study of the change through which a cosmology is sustained, renewed and reproduced with a characteristic image of an order overarching the known divisions of mankind or, in Lévi-Strauss's phrase, 'an idea something like that of a humanity without frontiers' (1966: p. 166). My fieldwork led me to begin to counteract that neglect, and to demonstrate how it is that the cult's ideology has not become what Janzen would call one of 'the exhausted paradigms of the culture' (cited in Fernandez, 1978: p. 225). I suggested that the cult's conceptions of the macrocosm

> are a significant factor in behaviour because they are of such a kind that communities can continue to define their broadest consensus through them irrespective of their differences, hostilities and competition. In a crisis, the more inclusive the majority who are rallied through the cults, the more comprehensive and fundamental is the appeal to such cosmological conceptions. (Werbner, 1977a: p. 213)

My initial account of this and other regional cults (Werbner, 1977a; 1977b) has two limitations, which I attempted to overcome in my more recent work (1979), as well as in this chapter. First, problems of religious pluralism remained too much in the background when I analysed the flows around the High God cult's central places, and the participants' own understanding of those flows. I mentioned the co-operation and competition with various churches, and even described the micro-politics leading to a senior adept's conversion and adoption of the role of church leader (Werbner, 1977a: p. 207). But I did not conceptualize any pattern in the religious pluralism. Nor did I provide a model for understanding its development *vis-à-vis* the High God cult.

Second, in my introduction to *Regional Cults* (Werbner, 1977c) I recognized the difficult problems of the relations between cults and the social fields which are their environment. I discussed, following Turner (1974), the dialectical process in which pilgrimage centres generate fields which, in turn, may regenerate other systems of relations (Werbner, 1977b: pp. xxivf.). Moreover, implicit in my discussion is an approach which views change as cumulative but given to oscillations, rather than transformations persistently in one direction. But it was largely beyond the limits of my discussion to take two further steps at once: not only to conceptualize certain regularities in cult change along with the transformation of social fields, but also to work out propositions about the relations between them.

Strangers and cults of the microcosm

To understand shifts in a series of cults within a wider, changing social field, I began with cults of the microcosm in West Africa, paving the way for this chapter's account of cults of the macrocosm, in South Central Africa. The cults of the microcosm are addressed to highly particularistic spirits, not a universal God; and there is, fortunately, very rich evidence about their proliferation across Ghana, the Ivory Coast and Upper Volta. I call them personal security cults (in preference to using the conventional labels 'witch-finding movements' or 'anti-witchcraft cults' which put the emphasis wrongly and are somewhat misleading) because my term sums up the following characteristics: the cult members are a security circle for each other; mutually harmless, they are bound together by a covenant and an ethic, they are purified, and under the same powerful protection of a shrine or a spirit. Strangers from outside a community or aliens in culture are included along with their hosts or the non-strangers in a community. Also in the social field are, of course, various cults of the macrocosm and movements of world religions; but they link to quite different predicaments and other aspects of the wider field, and I do not attempt to cover them in the West African case.

Seen from the orientation of the personal security cults, there is, first, a waxing and, later, a waning of sacred centrality. During the waxing phase, northern-based shrines increase their importance as central places. There is long-distance pilgrimage to them, and they provide ritual protection, in the form of portable pieces of the shrines, for the peaceful passage of strangers throughout the social field. The shrines continue to serve as the fixed points of focus for particularistic networks of exchange, communication and trade. But they become the cardinal points of sociogeographic orientation for the social field as a whole. They serve both the social field's northern sector of savannah and its southern sector of forest. Later, in the waning phase, their scope narrows to, at most, one sector or the other of the social field. Thus southerners tend, in the main, not to import new satellite shrines from the north; the long-distance pilgrimage from the south to the north declines drastically; non-regional cults wax along with the waning of regional cults; and less attention is paid to the appropriation in ritual of exotic forms from distant or alien sociogeographic zones.

I found it essential to my analysis to contextualize the shifts in cults and cult modes by taking account of major economic and political changes across the wider social field. On the one hand, these were transformations such as the colonization of southern cocoa farms and the replacement of a flow of slaves from the north to the south by a flow of labour migrants, hired for a share of the crop, yet still coming to the south as inferiors fit for menial jobs but not fit for intermarriage or the local citizen's rights to land. On the other hand, these were processes of modern state formation such as the emergence of quasi-nations within the nation.

From one phase to the next, the personal security cults continue to be linked to inequality between hosts and strangers and a cultural predicament of strangerhood. But at stake in the shifts in cult mode is the dominance and control of different kinds of strangers, as well as the cultural mastery of strangerhood itself. There is an interplay between cult change and change in the wider field, when the kind of stranger that is most problematic or dangerous varies and when the power relations between strangers and non-strangers or hosts alter.

This leads me to the inner logic of ritual forms in the successive cult modes. It is an inner logic that is best understood in terms of a ritual recoding of personal security. The swing is from the encoding of personal security in terms of things (i.e. through bonds of substance, including bits of soil from the central places, and communion in commensality) to the encoding in terms of persons (through spirit possession). My hypothesis is thus that there is a systematic connection between ritual coding and problematic strangerhood, and that the inner logic works according to whether a metonymic or a metaphoric relation suits the re-inscription of identity within a personal security circle. When the most problematic stranger is the cultural alien, the ritual coding is in terms of imported things, and identity is re-inscribed through the metonymic relation with strangers. Alternatively, when the internal stranger, from another part of one's own community, is the most problematic, the ritual coding is in terms of intrusive persons and identity is re-inscribed through the metaphoric relation with strangers.

Estrangement and cults of the macrocosm

To carry this analysis a stage further, an extreme counterpart to such shifts and transformations needs to be examined. The best case I know of comes from South Central Africa. It would be a mistake, however, to limit the comparison too geographically: I am not concerned here with the problem of what is the typical or central response in one area of the continent or another. My analysis leads me to the hypothesis that there is a systematic relation between predicaments of strangerhood and cults of the *microcosm* in a certain kind of changing social field. The needed comparison is with cults of the *macrocosm*, including the religious movements of world religions. Here I must pursue this comparison on the basis of my own and others' research on such cults in Southern Africa. Hopefully, this may lead to a better understanding of the West African cults also. Others, more familiar with the West African cults of the macrocosm, may complete the comparison within that area, testing the further hypotheses generated from beyond it. I am tempted to suggest that just as variations in strangerhood generate changes in cults of the microcosm, so too what I would call variations in estrangement generate changes in cults of the macrocosm; but this suggestion, which applies to the social field where there is massive extraction of labour from one sector to another, needs to be spelled out more fully, and substantiated with the Southern African data.

The reversed world consciousness

First, the utility of the comparison across the geographical areas must be shown by highlighting a regularity. In each of the social fields there is what Marx would call 'a reversed world consciousness' (Marx and Engels, 1957: p. 37): sacred centrality appears to stand economic peripherality on its head. Not that the two social fields are virtually alike: there is an obvious, and perhaps somewhat misleading, difference. The West African case involves economic dominance *within* rural sectors and the rural-centred exploitation of labour from a rural periphery, whereas its Southern African counterpart involves exploitation that is urban-centred. However, my point concerns the religious recentring of peripherality whereby the economic periphery provides the place for the sacred centre, in both West and Southern Africa.

Just as during one phase in West Africa certain shrines at the rural periphery are made into the cardinal points of orientation for extensive, polyethnic cults of the *microcosm*, so too in the Southern African counterpart certain sacred central places are located at the rural periphery. These are the central places of the churches which are the most extensive polyethnic cults of the *macrocosm*. But in this counterpart case a further extreme is reached. There is a consciousness of a more radical decentring and displacement in this world; and this consciousness is concretized through the imagery of an extensive polyethnic church without a sacred central place.

Locational imagery and large-scale, polyethnic cults of the macrocosm

The Southern African counterpart involving estrangement arises with the changing conditions of labour migration from rural Zimbabwe to distant and nearby towns. The estrangement is mediated or negated, over time, through certain alternative religious images and organizational forms which returning labour migrants originally introduce to their home areas. They are home-comers (cf. Schutz, 1945), and they introduce alternative images and forms which reflect the fact that home and much that it implies can no longer be taken for granted, since it is now in some senses also alien. At this point, I concentrate on the alternatives which are the basis for large-scale, polyethnic churches. In one alternative, a kind of re-incorporation takes place. At home, together, the home-comers, along with their relatives and neighbours, make up circles of the purified as congregations within and across their communities; home appears in the church's locational imagery as an inner space rescued from peripherality through religious recentring. Alternatively, through another kind of religious image and organizational form, the home-comers and others are incorporated in congregations forming total communities, as it were societies within society: here home appears dislocated and decentred as an outer space. Each alternative can and does lead to the foundation of large-scale, polyethnic churches which spread in a characteristic way, outward from home.

Conversion and the spread of churches

Initially, the conversion of church founders takes place in South African towns, within the so-called 'Zionist' churches, and the founding of the migrants' churches is done on their return home. Later, migrants convert within Zimbabwe, having worked in nearby or more remote towns, such as Umtali or Harare (Salisbury), and then they return home to found churches which they themselves tend to call Apostolic, after Christ's true disciples. Eventually, conversion becomes a process that usually culminates in river baptism away from town, when a migrant re-incorporates himself on joining a home congregation, after – not before – his return from labour migration. What underlies much of this conversion is the religious assumption that the person has to be remade as a spiritual whole by the substitution of a new and *total* code of purity for the prior, indigenous code. The religious assumption of total regeneration and separation from one's former person becomes an absolute, when the congregation becomes a society within a society, and the church becomes communitarian.

The usual developmental path for the spread from home of a polyethnic church is as follows. The founding migrant begins it among his relatives and neighbours within the same rural sociogeographic zone, where ethnic differentiation is relatively minimal, but not reduced to homogeneity. Later, the innovations are disseminated widely – and more or less modified in the process – from zone to zone and finally beyond Zimbabwe. Many major cultural boundaries are crossed, and the move is towards encompassing very great social and ethnic differentiation. Eventually, a polyethnic church is established, lasting more than a generation, and with urban as well as rural congregations.

Three churches: variations in imagery

In the following discussion, my aim is to explore my initial, somewhat abstract suggestions in the light of the imagery and organizational forms of the large-scale polyethnic cults of the macrocosm in Zimbabwe. These include the indigenous High God cult along with the three most extensive polyethnic churches originally founded in rural Zimbabwe. Each church comes from a recognizably different yet neighbouring sociogeographic zone in South or Eastern Zimbabwe, two from within the reach of the High God cult and one from beyond it. The homes of the church founders are within a hundred-kilometre radius from the most central among them. The churches are, in order of closeness to the High God cult, from the south, to the south-east, to the north-east:

1 Bishop Mutendi's Zion Christian Church, centred in the Bikita District and at its peak extending across Zimbabwe and Zambia;

2 The African Apostolic Church of Johane Maranke, centred in the Umtali District which, at its peak, extended as far north as the Republic of Zaire; and

3 Johane Masowe's Apostolic Sabbath Church of God (which I call the Wilderness Church) with its founder's original home and burial place near Rusape and its congregations in Zimbabwe, Botswana, South Africa, Zambia, Malawi, Kenya and Zaire.

In the same order, the churches are:

1 regional, having a permanently built central place and a locational image focused on the eternal kingdom of God on earth;

2 regional, having impermanently built central places and a locational image focused on the ephemeral places of mankind on earth;

3 communitarian, migratory (cf. Wilson, 1967) and later regional also, having, at first, no constructed central place and an image focused on temporarily defined places or undefined space.

From the outset of my account I must acknowledge a major debt. The quite unparalleled richness of observation and insight into African churches in Daneel's work (1970a; 1970b; 1971; 1974; 1976) is the basis of the best part of my interpretation, although I draw on complementary studies, such as those by Sundkler (1961), Dillon-Malone (1978), Murphree (1969), Aquina (1967; 1969), Kileff and Kileff (1979), Jules-Rosette (1975a; 1975b; 1977; 1979a), Ranger (1970) and others, as well as my own rather limited observation of the churches.

A brief description of the church imagery is essential, before I consider its systematic variation along with the varieties of consciousness which are projected in and through the images. The most harmonic, and as it happens the earliest, is the image of the Zion Christian Church (ZCC). This image focuses on the eternal place for the Kingdom of God on earth. A great temple is built to last for ever; and fixed sites are sanctified for the annual or periodic pilgrimages, known as Passovers. But all of this placement is concentrated at the Kingdom's centre, the headquarters of the church. Reaching the centre is a movement upwards in space, to the heights of a mountain or hill, with a corresponding ritual ascension from the communities of every-day life to the congregation cleansed of sin, by confession and acts of purification, and thus raised to the heights of holiness. The ritual is transformative of both the inner and the outer body: there is a sharing of food in communion along with the lustration through total immersion of the body during baptism.

Between the most harmonic and the most disharmonic comes the ambiguous image of the Maranke Apostles. The image focuses on the ephemeral places of humankind on earth. The Kingdom of God is in heaven, and if ever it is to come to earth, it has yet to do so. Each enclosure of space for ritual is make-shift. It may be a temporary fence of poles or seasonal branches. It may be no more than a wave in the air or a drawing on the ground. Instead of the one temple as the great church building, there are the many tabernacles: impermanent, movable sanctuaries and shelters in which church members camp during their Pentecosts. Ascension takes place at various heights, and it is a ritual passage for even the narrowest congregation, such as may come from within one local community alone. Nevertheless, this image, like the most harmonic, is a centralized one, in so far as the ascensions are ordered in importance, according to the congregation represented, from the local, to the interlocal, to the regional at the headquarters of the church. Moreover, as in the harmonic image, there is communion and lustration, internally and externally transformative ritual.

The most disharmonic image, that of the Wilderness Church, has already been presented. Here I need merely draw attention to the fact that it represents an *extreme* contrast to the others. I am tempted to suggest that of all the images it is the most volatile, in part because of the tension balancing Chaos and Cosmos within the image; and over time it has a tendency to alter drastically, whereas the most harmonic image remains relatively constant for a considerable period of time.

In the imagery of these three polyethnic churches, a systematic pattern of variation can be identified. From one image to the next, the Space co-ordinate is variable, whereas the Person co-ordinate is constant. Space is either focused as definite place (ZCC), ambiguously focused (Maranke) or unfocused as indefinite space (Masowe). In all three images, the Person co-ordinate is constantly framed in that the pure are well set apart from the impure by rules and rites of purity or purification. Saying this does not deny that there are variations from church to church in the concept of the person, as seen in the relative openness to spirit possession, or in the emphasis on internal versus external purity through lustration or eucharistic communion, and above all in the emphasis on healing in the ZCC and the Maranke churches in contrast to the emphasis on redemption in the Wilderness Church.[6] But in each of their images, Person has the aspect of Cosmos, relative to the imagery of certain alternative churches and cults. In other words, in contrast to the polyethnic churches, the Person co-ordinate is variable (i.e. it is ambiguously framed or unframed) in the alternative imagery, such as is usual in European missions or related Ethiopian-type churches without the strong emphasis on food taboos, total lustration and so on (on Ethiopian churches cf. Daneel, 1971: p. 350b).

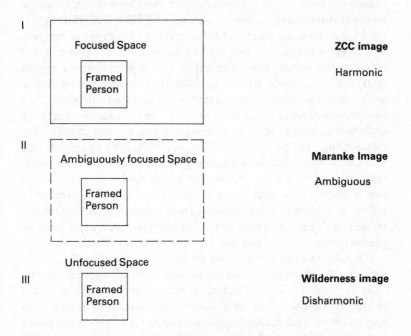

Figure 9.2 *Images of Person and Space in three religious move-ments in South Central Africa*

A set of box diagrams (Figure 9.2) is a useful illustration. The first diagram shows an image that is harmonic in that it is both focused and framed, for Space and Person respectively. In the second diagram the image is ambiguous, framed but ambiguously focused. Finally comes the disharmonic image, unfocused yet framed. Put in terms of Cosmos and Chaos, the pattern is this. In the ZCC harmonic image, the imbalance is overwhelming and Cosmos tames Chaos. In the Maranke ambiguous image, there is less of an imbalance, with Space ambiguously penetrated by Chaos; it is a more unstable image. Finally, the imbalance is least, without the certainty of dominance, in the disharmonic Wilderness image; it is the most unstable image.

Having viewed these three images as a contrasting set, as it were semantic structures out of time, I now regard them as a sequence of innovations in time in order to examine briefly the varieties of consciousness which the images project. And here the images must be contextualized in an environmental and historical relation, i.e. *vis-à-vis* a changing social field. First, the ZCC harmonic image is the religious innovation that is introduced in the 1920s at a period of economic boom, when the expansion in long-distance labour migration (especially to the Transvaal) is, despite some fluctuations, rapid and dramatic. As that boom gives way to slump, and too many workers pursue too few jobs, the next innovation is the ambiguous image of the Maranke Church, and finally, the disharmonic image of the Wilderness Church. In effect, the innovation sequence is a changing reconstruction, from a participant's point of view, of the shift in the field itself (cf. Thoden van Velzen, 1977), and it can be described, in van Binsbergen's terms, as a shift in consciousness from 'acquiescence' (harmonic image), to 'symbolic ambivalence' (ambiguous image) to 'protest' (disharmonic image) (van Binsbergen, 1981: pp. 57–9).

It would take me well beyond my present limits to spell out fully how these varieties of consciousness are manifested in the churches' history, in their differing relations to nationalism as well as the colonial state, in their positive affirmation or rejection of wage labour and technological innovation for market-oriented agriculture. Very briefly, however, the ZCC was the most hostile to the nationalist parties, while being the most closely identified with the market economy and the existing state. Bishop Mutendi urged his followers to take part in government-sponsored agricultural schemes, such as that for master-farming in Purchase Farm areas. The bishop preached, in 1965, 'If you are true Zionists, you must never join any of these movements that go Zig-Zag (ZAPU and ZANU)' (quoted in Daneel, 1976: p. 88).

The facts are somewhat less clear with regard to the Maranke Church. Discussing *various* Apostolic churches, Daneel (loc. cit.) remarks, 'During the political disturbances in the early 1960's the *vaPostori* [Apostolic] prophets were presenting their fellow members with a choice of either burning their ZAPU or ZANU membership cards in public, or forfeiting their Church membership.' However, when he comments on a trend towards elevating Johane

Maranke to the status of a Black Saviour, Daneel (1976: pp. 98–9) modifies his earlier comment,

> [The trend reflects] the pervading mood in Apostolic circles, which is more nationalistic, militant and decidedly anti-White than in most Zionist groups. For instead of the frequently repeated plea for racial harmony in the Zionist camp, one hears with monotonous regularity the accusations of *vaPostori* that the white race had killed Jesus Christ, that the Europeans had deliberately suppressed the message of the Holy Spirit and that their period of blessing had lapsed.

Besides such political expression, the Maranke Church image also sustains symbolic ambivalence economically in that although the tilling of the land is still accepted as good, economic self-sufficiency and self-employment, rather than wage labour, are favoured (cf. Jules-Rosette, 1977 pp. 198–9).

As for the Wilderness Church, there is a radical consciousness in the form of protest, and I return to this later, after considering the link between the church organization and imagery. It suffices, at this point, to mention the welcome a Wilderness Church leader gave a visiting nationalist leader and ZAPU vice-president, Dr Parirenyatwa: 'Since the foundation of our [Wilderness Church] movement in 1932, we have been struggling for the ideals which ZAPU stands for today, in our own way' (from a ZAPU document published in 1962 and kindly made available to me by Professor Terence Ranger).

Throughout this series, there is a match between image and consciousness. I suggest that this match is not fortuitous: each image with its own appropriate semantic structure commands a suitable variety of consciousness, and the semantic structure of the image must be changed, if there is to be a change in the variety of consciousness.

Church tendencies: the dialectics of organizational form

In order to take a further step towards clarifying the argument of images and the emergence of alternative forms of consciousness, the major tendencies in the development of church organization have to be considered. In the wider social field we have been discussing, the three most important tendencies are: (1) territorialism, (2) regionalism and (3) communitarianism. Each tendency emerges in that order, and at a specific phase in the development of the wider social field. A church tendency, once established, develops in a dialectical relation with the rest, in successive phases, so that the series as a whole is cumulative, increasing the elaboration of religious pluralism over time.

To begin with, the earliest church tendency is the one that continues to dominate the religious order officially recognized by the colonial state: *territorialism*. Territorialism tends to match religion with a local or geographical division, and it arises with the establishment of missions which claim distinct 'spheres of influence'. Such an established territorial mission expects others not to poach on its territory for the saving of souls; it participates in the collective delineation of mission territories at a Missionary Conference; and it comes into conflict with the established global mission, i.e. the Roman Catholic Church (Daneel, 1971: p. 187), as well as the unestablished mission, i.e. the pentecostals such as the Watchtower, the Apostolic Faith, etc. Along with territorialism comes an appropriate central place hierarchy: the mission founds functionally ordered centres, from the highest order with the most elaborate services (i.e. the main mission station with its grand, often towering house for worship, its clinic, school and so on) to the lowest with perhaps a single service (i.e. the outstation with no more than a meeting place for worship).

As for Zimbabwe's earliest African churches, these design themselves according to a model derived from the established territorialist missions. They adopt the model from South African separatists, well-known in the literature as 'Ethiopian' churches. In Zimbabwe some of these churches become territorialized as primarily urban churches; others, as rural ones. But, apparently, none of them provides the kind of sacred centrality around which a major polyethnic region can or does form. While they often try, especially in rural areas, to locate a sphere of their own by distancing their church buildings from a mission's, and by keeping a geographical divide such as a river between them and the mission centre, their rural centres nevertheless remain, in effect, mission satellites or lesser-order centres, clearly secondary in comparison with the mission's higher-order centres. If, at first, more tolerant and perhaps more ecumenical than the missions, they put rather little emphasis on rules of purity and do not require total immersion to divide the purified and the baptized from the rest of their neighbours. It is usual for their leaders either to 'evade outright repudiation of the old practices [in the indigenous cults]; or . . . [to] seek to justify [them] as a God-given institution' (Daneel, 1971: p. 464). The ritual code of these churches is thus *partial*; it is not a total recoding of something already indigenous; and both church and indigenous cult codes can be kept, as it were, compartmentalized.

Vis-à-vis the High God cult, these territorialized churches tend, therefore, to be a complement rather than a substitute. Organizationally, too, the churches and the High God cult are not rivals providing the same services in different places. Although from their beginning some of these churches have been based in the cult's heartland, none has a sacred centre with facilities for long-distance pilgrims seeking healing, fertility, relief from suffering and other services for their personal and communal welfare. No church place is raised above and apart from any other, as somehow a cardinal platform for a higher religious authority. There is no ascension to holy heights to replace the indigenous ritual passage, going up towards the High God through a hierarchy of hill oracles. Hence, being a church member does not necessarily exclude a person from membership in the cult. Indeed, the High God priest who recently succeeded his father in the cult's south-western region was a member of the African Methodist Episcopal Church before becoming a priest, and today continues to keep up his church membership (see Werbner, 1977a: pp. 205ff., for an account of the dispute prior to his succession). Mutual tolerance and overlapping membership have long been shared, characteristically, by these churches and the cult.

As for church *regionalism*, that is the tendency, above all, to centre religion at sacred places, such as the tops of hills. Around these are focused religious centres and major networks of communication and exchange for ritual purposes, such as spiritual healing, personal redemption, blessing for individual and congregational prosperity. The break from a model derived from the colonial state's established territorialist missions is radical, as is the recentring and recoding of religion *vis-à-vis* the indigenous cults. The sociogeographic zones near a church's centre tend to be one – though not necessarily the only – main catchment area for church membership. Thus the church that starts within a cult region partly concentrates within it. But the region a polyethnic church generates never fits simply within a mission territory or a pre-existing cult region. The church region is a product of church activity, just as the cult region is a product of cult activity, and thus has its own distinct, if somewhat competing, distribution. Moreover, the church regions themselves can be said to criss-cross in that they draw people, goods, services and even cultural orientations from overlapping catchment areas.

Given the dominance of territorialism as the state-recognized and state-sanctioned order, a home or a starting place at some distance from a mission's functioning higher-order centre seems to be vital for the survival of the new church in its early growth towards becoming regional and polyethnic. Moreover, peripheral placement seems to be an essential vantage ground, when church regionalism aggressively opposes cult regionalism, bringing church and cult into the kind of conflict that is an effective, zero-sum rivalry. If we ask, where does the religious recoding and the recentring of sacred centrality by a church pose an effective challenge to the High God cult, the answer is clear. The challenge comes from within the High God cult's hinterland, to the east, not far from those sociogeographic zones where the indigenous cults are non-centralized or weakly centralized; i.e. where prophets and spirit mediums have their transient clienteles without a defined hierarchy of central places (cf. Werbner, 1977a: p. xxiii). The challenge does not come from the very heartland, around the High God cult's central places, which is its enduring major stronghold.

The case in point is Bishop Mutendi's Zion Christian Church (abbreviated to 'ZCC' on its Star of David badges). The ZCC is centred in the Bikita District to the east of the cult hinterland. Here the church competes to turn its sacred centre into *the* centre; i.e. the one which is unsurpassed in functional comprehensiveness by any other religious centre. Its long-term project is to reach the highest order of, as it were, a mission station and a pilgrimage centre rolled into one, with a great church and school building, houses for patients and their treatment, as well as sacred spaces and a hill set aside for holy ascension by pilgrims. The organizational form of such a church can be seen as, among other things, the product of a completely hierarchical competition, within the parameters predicated by hierarchy in both the state-sanctioned mission and the regional cult.[7]

A general rule operates here. It can be put simply thus: the tendency towards regionalism develops in and through a certain church depending, in part, on central place competition. In other words, it depends, perhaps most critically, on how the church enters or opts out of competition with an established mission's higher-order centre, or with an indigenous cardinal place, such as that of the High God cult. The first case is where the High God cult is present, and thus two central place hierarchies are involved. Here, put somewhat more abstractly, the critical parameters for the tendency's development are, on the one extreme, a central place hierarchy that accords with or corresponds to a state established order and, on the other extreme, a central place hierarchy which runs counter to that order and predicates a higher, more enduring one.

Quite different critical parameters operate in the absence of the High God cult, and there is a systematic transformation in the form of church organization. This takes us to our second case of a regional polyethnic church, the African Apostolic Church of Johane Maranke. It starts just beyond the High God cult's periphery in one of those sociogeographic zones where the indigenous cults operate without a central place hierarchy. This church's long-term project is, as a matter of faith and explicit credo, against the building of the church visible: 'the task of a true Apostle is to move about and spread God's word and not get involved in such time-consuming projects as building Churches and schools' (Daneel, 1971: p. 346).

In terms of central places, its organizational form combines hierarchy with non-hierarchy in a way that makes it an inversion of *both* established mission and indigenous cult. Contrary to the non-hierarchical indigenous cult, it has a sacred central place hierarchy for pilgrimage; contrary to the established mission, it has no higher-order centres. Its functional elaboration of centres is minimal, so much so that one could speak of a central place pyramid, rather than a hierarchy, because the difference between lesser and greater pilgrimage places for the Pentecostals is primarily a matter of increasing congregational inclusiveness, rather than increasing differentiation of services and functions.[8]

Richard P. Werbner

What is somewhat arguable is the church's relation to quite a different kind of mission which is, at once, a precursor and a rival. I refer to the *unestablished* mission which is, in my terms, a form of church organization that lacks central places, and is in a negative relation with the state and its established religious order. Certain pentecostal churches are unestablished missions in that they continue to missionize while being blocked by the state from becoming established with their own centres. The colonial state forced the pentecostal churches to adopt an alternative form of organization 'by refusing them facilities normally granted to the established Mission bodies, such as the entry of European missionaries into the tribal areas (reserves), the granting of land leases for mission sites or the permission to build schools' (Daneel, 1971: p. 403). Two of my main sources disagree about the impact of European pentecostals, such as the Apostolic Faith Church, on African Apostles (for the view of minimal impact, cf. Daneel, 1971: pp. 286–7; for the view of major impact, cf. Dillon-Malone, 1978: pp. 9–14, 20–4). Nevertheless, a couple of points can be made, which indicate the critical importance of pentecostals for the development of the African Apostles.

First, the African preachers of the pentecostal churches come to move about freely 'under no apparent supervision' (Dillon-Malone, 1978: p. 9) and are especially active in 'Mashonaland' just before the major African Apostolic churches are founded there. Despite being persecuted, or perhaps all the more because of the persecution, the pentecostalists make numerous converts, many of whom later become Apostles. Although the ZCC also becomes a competitor with unestablished missions in the decade after its founding, the major Apostolic churches have to compete with them from the very start, at a time when conversion to pentecostalism is at a peak. Second, therefore, what may be called anti-hierarchy – the negation of central placement among the pentecostalists – becomes a critical parameter for the development of regionalism in the Apostolic case.

Turning to the third church tendency, *communitarianism*, I see it as the one in which anti-hierarchy dominates. Communitarianism tends to decentre religion spatially, as church communities are founded, somewhat in tension with the rest of society, but without a sacred place as a focus or point of permanent anchorage. To escape persecution from the alien-ruled state – which is damned to

Hell, like the white rulers – church communities migrate from colony to colony. But they also migrate because none of the places where they sojourn is yet the sacred central place that they envision. The colonized become the colonizers on their own colonial mission. The church does not merely opt out of central place competition within any state; it goes to a further extreme in its rejection of the basis for that competition. The very tilling of the land or working for wages – which is a matter for religious regulation in one central place hierarchy or another, mission or indigenous, or even in the unranked places of the non-centralized indigenous cults – is held to be a danger to salvation. Hence the religious recoding itself implies a dislocation from the countryside and, at the same time, not the location then taken for granted in town. The church communities are to be self-employed, petty commodity producers, traders and transporters; and wherever they live, they must be able to regard themselves as *in* the place, but fundamentally not *of* it. However, the more the church expands, as its members explore and generate an economic niche of their own successfully, and with increasing prosperity, the more problematic becomes the lack of sacred centrality within the church. And ultimately, the communitarianism becomes regional: sacred central places are recognized, such as at the founder's grave or in a sacred grove around the homes of 'virgins' dedicated to the church. Nevertheless, the fixing of a centre for the meeting of the church as a whole does not end the migratory project: the search for an ultimate sacred place on earth goes on.

The case in point is the Apostolic Sabbath Church of God, founded by Johane Masowe (John of the Wilderness). To keep the contrast between the different Apostles well in view, I have called one the Maranke Church and the other the Wilderness Church. This usage, which is similar to members' own labelling, locates them *vis-à-vis* each other in their early relations both to the state and much else in their environment. Maranke is the title of the founder's maternal grandfather who, as the local chief, enabled the church to establish itself at home by sponsoring it before the colonial native commissioner in order to get the state's official sanction to evangelize. Thus 'Maranke' places the church with its centre at the founder's home, and as being vested with state recognition along with local legitimacy.

By contrast, some months after his own conversion, persecution forced the Wilderness Church's founder first to return home – where he began to baptize – and then to flee from it secretly in order to evangelize. Whether or not pentecostal churches are an immediate model for the Church of the Wilderness, what is clear is that the state's officials regarded them in the same light: they were seen to pose the same political danger, the pentecostal mission being to blame for paving the way for the Wilderness Church; and they were similarly repressed by the state. The church's founder was not allowed to remain away from home, in a peri-urban area on the outskirts of Zimbabwe's eastern capital, near his earliest followers and close to the scene of his own conversion. Nor was he allowed to maintain his own home openly as a centre for pentecosts and holy ascension, or as a headquarters for preaching across the countryside about the end of white rule, mobilizing Africans against it. The districts between Umtali and Rusapi near this founder's home continued to be a main catchment area for converts. But during succeeding decades the establishment of urban and peri-urban colonies of the self-employed, of Israelites not working 'as slaves for non-Israelites' (Sundkler, 1961: p. 308), came to dominate the church's project, as it was harassed from the major town in Western Zimbabwe to a series of towns in South Africa, in Zimbabwe, once again, and elsewhere.

Finally, the change towards the most complete relocation in religious as well as economic terms began once a colony reached a shanty-town in Zambia's capital, shortly before Independence. In that new nation-state, the church which negates sacred centrality within the state under European rule, begins to generate sacred centrality under African rule:

> Masowe worship and work life centres around their main prayer grove in the southern sector of Marrapodi [a Lusaka shanty-town]. The homes of elders are located in a semi-circle around the grove. Inside the grove is a large house where the Masowe 'virgins', said to have been the former wives of the deceased leader, now live. They embody the purity and sacrificial commitments of the Church as a whole and are insulated from the 'world' by the grove and the ring of elders' homes. (Jules-Rosette, 1977: p. 197)

Seen *vis-à-vis* the High God cult or the other polyethnic churches, the transformation is a radical one: sacred centrality is fixed at a major political and economic centre, and away from the economic periphery. Whereas the High God cult remains in tension with the colonial state, the Wilderness Church begins to legitimize and sanctify the neo-colonial one. The church's imagery changes accordingly, towards recentring instead of decentring, towards location instead of dislocation, and towards the harmonic rather than the disharmonic.

Conclusion

Taking a body of religious movements as my basic unit of study, rather than any single church or cult in isolation, I show how the religious movements can be understood as innovations in space. My analysis starts with a view of the wider social field in which there is massive extraction of labour from one sector to another. It is the change in such a wide social field that participants come to experience as contradiction, disorder or dislocation, and that they confront through religious innovation. On the basis of an earlier discussion of West African cults of the *microcosm* (Werbner, 1979), I explore their Southern African counterparts, within a comparable, wider social field. Here the large-scale cults of the *macrocosm*, which I consider, include three polyethnic churches along with the indigenous High God cult. My hypothesis is that just as there is a nexus between transformation in cults of the microcosm and the changing predicament of strangerhood, so too are cults of the macrocosm linked with change in estrangement. Each predicament evokes its own kind of religious response and, in turn, responds to it, as the effect in its turn becomes a cause.

Two critical conditions are presupposed in all of this. First, my hypothesis refers to that kind of imbalanced social field in which, *away from home*, the person, or rather his labour, is often regarded as a marketable commodity. Second, the changes in predicament which I keep in view involve changes in the perceived relations of power and dominance between outsiders, such as the labour migrants, and certain significant others.

To understand religious movements as innovations in space, I find it necesary to give a comparative account of four interrelated dimensions, according to their variation from one church to the next within the whole body of religious movements. These four are the dimensions of (1) image, (2) consciousness, (3) project, (4) organization. As structured by its aspects of Chaos or Cosmos, the church image varies from the harmonic, to the ambiguous, to the disharmonic. Similarly, consciousness varies from acquiescence, to symbolic ambivalence, to protest. I suggest that within a body of churches, image and consciousness inform and are informed by each other according to a regular pattern. In the body of churches I discuss the regularity is this: the harmonic image and acquiescence are interdependent counterparts, as are the ambiguous image and symbolic ambivalence, and the disharmonic image and protest. As for the dimension of project, the variation is from material establishment, to immaterial incorporation, to immaterial disestablishment. Thus at one extreme in this variation is the priority of building the church visible within the existing state. Between the extremes is the priority, irrespective of the state, of creating solely the church invisible, in and through the reunion of more and more saved souls each year. Finally, on the dimension of organization, it is central placement and hierarchy that varies regularly from church to church, the range being from the most highly centripetal and functionally comprehensive, such as in the New Jerusalem at Mount Moriah, to the more diffuse, such as in the encampments of the Pentecost, to the centrifugal, such as in the total communities of the migratory Wilderness. I would suggest, also, that the pattern holding between these dimensions, project and organization, tends to correspond with the pattern between the others.

Without attempting to review the details of my history of church tendencies, I must stress one last point, in conclusion. My approach presents the elaboration of religious pluralism as a dialectical process in which churches and cults mutually differentiate themselves in competition with each other. I reject the view that religious change, when considered historically, must be seen as a progressive march of movements or a unilinear evolution. Rather, shifts in the direction of religious change must be seen to be highly variable, thus posing some of the most challenging problems for analysis. It may well be once again in vogue to make evolutionary schemes of change, somewhat after nineteenth-century models. But such schemes cannot be allowed to sink what is still in a tentative, exploratory stage: the analysis and theoretical explanation of the shifting direction of religious innovation.

Notes

1 I wish to thank Matthew Schoffeleers, Jean Comaroff, Terence Ranger, Hilda Kuper, John Peel, Don Handelman, Bengt Sundkler, Wim van Binsbergen and Pnina Werbner. They read an earlier draft of this chapter, and made suggestions for improving it.

2 My interpretation differs somewhat from that of Hastings in his wide-ranging history of African Christianity. Hastings sees a continuing emphasis in the Wilderness Church on centrality and a *house* of prayer, albeit one that is a symbol of a pilgrim journey. The church

> centred around a sort of convent of nuns, 'The Ark of the Covenant'. The Ark was a house of prayer marking the true centre of the church, first at Korsten, then at Marrapodi and now in Nairobi. . . . As Ark, 'this house' is both Noah's ark and ark of the covenant – the central symbol of a pilgrim journey, of salvation and divine presence. (Hastings, 1979: p. 249)

Hastings bases his interpretation on Dillon-Malone primarily, and I consider that this source favours my interpretation, the imagery being of a 'carrier of God's presence' (Dillon-Malone, 1978: p. 64). On the saving ark as, first, an ark of wood and, then, an ark of persons, 'the mothers of the covenant'; and on the gradual shift in the notion of 'house' and 'temple' cf. Dillon-Malone (1978: pp. 65–7). Prayer 'walks' through the 'house', the Sisters.

3 My following discussion concentrates on the upper quadrants of the framework. To consider the developmental problems of shifts in image across the whole set would take me well beyond my present limits. But I must note that I know of no African church or cult that establishes itself permanently around the disharmonic image of total Chaos. Indeed, I am doubtful that that happens, except perhaps at a transitory moment, given the usual tendency for churches to foster *some* quest for Cosmos in the imagery of Person or Space. The wholly chaotic image may suit conditions of self-estrangement which are beyond my scope.

4 The reader must keep in mind the existence of contrasting types, *two* harmonic and *two* disharmonic; my argument covers *one* of the harmonic and *one* of the disharmonic, not all four. The African church imagery which I do discuss here and certain mission imagery which I do not are in *contrasting* senses disharmonic, the former having Person positive and Space negative (a framed, unfocused image, in my terms) and the latter having Person negative and Space positive (an unframed, focused image). Certain readers of my text have tried to ask for the same answer to a question about mission imagery and African church imagery, despite their being structurally and significantly poles apart.

5 Note that along with the Wilderness Church's relative lack of interest in physical healing goes a primary regard for the external person, as the subject of lustration, and a disregard for the internal person, through the rejection of eucharistic sacraments. Inner and outer are not at one here, and the inner is dislocated.

Richard P. Werbner

6 My impression is, also, that the churches differ in the relative emphasis
each puts on the divide between member and non-member, with the
Apostolic churches putting the greater emphasis (cf. also Hastings,
1979: p. 77). In this respect, one might say that Person is emphasized
over Space or place in the imagery of the Apostolic churches and,
conversely, Space is emphasized over Person in the Zionist case.
7 A word is in order about the link to South Africa's ZCC. In many
respects, Bishop Mutendi modelled his church along lines similar to the
South African ZCC founded by Lekhanyane in 1925. By that time,
Bishop Mutendi had already spent two years in Zimbabwe as a Zionist
evangelist; Lekhanyane, whom he supported in a schism, ordained him
as a minister in his own right. He remained loyal to Lekhanyane until
Lekhanyane's death. There was, thus, a personal link between the two
church founders, but their two churches became virtually autonomous
(cf. Daneel, 1971: pp. 298f.).
8 The order of congregations is from the local, the *kireke* which meets
weekly with neighbours as members, to the interlocal, the *sabata* which
is the occasional weekend gathering of members of different nearby
kireke, to the pilgrimage congregation of the annual *penta* or *paseka*.
The *paseka* is the only occasion for a eucharistic communion and for
exorcism rites. However, the criterion for an annual pilgrimage
congregation became not the *place per se* – i.e. the centre at the
founder's home or elsewhere – but the presence in person of Johane
Maranke or, later, his son. Maranke performed the same rituals at the
numerous remote *paseka* sites as at his headquarters, the major
difference being in the size of his congregation, with a maximum of
about 20,000 pilgrims at the main *paseka* in the Maranke reserve (cf.
Murphree, 1969: pp. 92f.; Daneel, 1971: pp. 330–1).

References

Aquina, Mary (Sister) (1967), 'The People of the Spirit: An Independent
Church in Rhodesia', *Africa*, 37: pp. 203–19.
Aquina, Mary (Sister) (1969), 'Zionists in Rhodesia', *Africa*, 39: pp.
113–36.
Binsbergen, Wim M. J. van (1981), *Religious Change in Zambia:
Exploratory Studies*, London: Kegan Paul International.
Daneel, M. L. (1970a), *The God of the Matopo Hills*, The Hague:
Mouton.
Daneel, M. L. (1970b), *Zionism and Faith Healing in Rhodesia*, The
Hague: Mouton.
Daneel, M. L. (1971), *Old and New in Shona Independent Churches*, vol.
I: *Background and Rise of the Major Movements*, The Hague: Mouton.
Daneel, M. L. (1974), *Old and New in Shona Independent Churches*, vol.
II: *Church Growth – Causative Factors and Recruitment Techniques*,
The Hague: Mouton.

Daneel, M. L. (1967), 'Independent Church Leadership South of the Zambezi', in W. M. J. van Binsbergen and R. Buijtenhuijs (eds), *Religious Innovation in Modern African Society, African Perspectives 1976/2*.

Dillon-Malone, C. M. (1978), *The Korsten Basketmakers*, Manchester: Manchester University Press.

Eliade, Mircea (1974), *The Myth of the Eternal Return, or, Cosmos and History*, Princeton: Princeton University Press (first English translation, 1954).

Fabian, Johannes (1979), 'Text as terror: Second Thoughts about Charisma', in Johannes Fabian (ed.), *Beyond Charisma*, special issue of *Social Research*, 46: pp. 166–203.

Fernandez, J. W. (1978), 'African Religious Movements', *Annual Review of Anthropology*, 7: pp. 198–234.

Fernandez, J. W. (1979), 'On the Notion of Religious Movement', *Social Research*, 46: pp. 36–62.

Glazier, S. D. (1979), 'The Study of Regional Cults', *Reviews in Anthropology*, **6**, 2: pp. 229–34.

Hastings, Adrian (1979), *A History of African Christianity 1950–1975*, Cambridge: Cambridge University Press.

Horton, Robin (1967), 'African Traditional Thought and Western Science', *Africa*, 37: pp. 50–71, 155–87.

Jules-Rosette, Bennetta (1975a), *African Apostles: Ritual and Conversion in the Church of John Maranke*, Ithaca, NY: Cornell University Press.

Jules-Rosette, Bennetta (1975b), 'Marrapodi: An Independent Religious Community in Transition', *African Studies Review*, 18: pp. 1–16.

Jules-Rosette, Bennetta (1977), 'Grass-roots Ecumenism: Religious and Social Co-operation in Two Urban African Churches', *African Social Research*, 23: 185–216.

Jules-Rosette, Bennetta (ed.) (1979a), *The New Religions of Africa*, Norwood, NJ: Ablex Publishing Corporation.

Jules-Rosette, Bennetta (1979b), 'Women as Ceremonial Leaders in an African Church: The Apostles of John Maranke', in Jules-Rosette (1979a), pp. 127–44.

Kileff, Clive, and Kileff, Margaret (1979), 'The Masowe Vapostori of Seki', in Jules-Rosette (1979a), pp. 151–67.

Kuper, Adam (1979), 'The Magician and the Missionary', in Pierre L. van der Berghe (ed.), *The Liberal Dilemma in South Africa*, London: Croom Helm, pp. 77–96.

Levine, Donald N. (1979), 'Simmel at a Distance: On the History and Systematics of the Sociology of the Stranger', in Shack and Skinner (1979), pp. 21–36.

Lévi-Strauss, Claude (1966), *The Savage Mind*, London: Weidenfeld & Nicolson (French edn 1962).

Marx, Karl, and Engels, F. (1957), *On Religion*, Moscow: Progress Publishers.

Murphree, Marshall W. (1969), *Christianity and the Shona*, London: Athlone Press.

Ranger, T. O. (1970), *The African Voice in Southern Rhodesia, 1898–1930*, London: Heinemann.

Schoffeleers, J. M. (ed.) (1979), *Guardians of the Land: Essays on Central African Territorial Cults*, Gwelo: Mambo Press.

Schutz, Alfred (1945), 'The Homecomer', *American Journal of Sociology*, 50: pp. 369–76.

Shack, William A., and Skinner, Elliott P. (eds) (1979), *Strangers in African Societies*, Berkeley and Los Angeles: University of California Press.

Sharron, A. (1981), 'Dimensions of Time', in Norman K. Denzin (ed.), *Studies in Symbolic Interaction*, vol. 4, Greenwich, Conn.: JAI Press.

Skinner, Elliott P. (1963), 'Strangers in West African Societies', *Africa*, 33: pp. 307–20.

Skinner, Elliott P. (1974), 'Theoretical Perspectives on the Stranger', paper presented at the Conference on Strangers in Africa, cited in Niara Sudarkasa, 'From Stranger to Alien: The Socio-political History of the Nigerian Yoruba in Ghana, 1900–1970', in Shack and Skinner (1979), pp. 141–68.

Skinner, Elliott P. (1979), 'Conclusions', in Shack and Skinner (1979), pp. 279–88.

Sundkler, Bengt (1961), *Bantu Prophets in South Africa*, 2nd edn, London: Oxford University Press.

Thoden van Velzen, Bonno (1977), 'Bush Negro Regional Cults: A Materialist Explanation', in Werbner (1977c), pp. 93–118.

Turner, Victor (1974), *Dramas, Fields and Metaphors*, Ithaca, NY: Cornell University Press.

Werbner, Richard P. (1977a), 'Continuity and Policy in Southern Africa's High God Cult', in Werbner (1977c), pp. 179–218.

Werbner, Richard P. (1977b), 'Introduction', in Werbner (1977c), pp. ix–xxxvii.

Werbner, Richard P. (ed.) (1977c), *Regional Cults*, London: Academic Press (ASA Monographs 16).

Werbner, Richard P. (1979), 'Totemism in History: The Ritual Passage of West African Strangers', *Man* (n.s.), 14: pp. 663–83.

Werbner, Richard P. (forthcoming), 'Central Africa's Territorial Cults: History and Systematics', *Zimbabwe History*.

Wilson, B. R. (1967), 'The Migrating Sects', *British Journal of Sociology*, 18: pp. 303–17.

Chapter 10

Religious studies and political economy: The Mwari cult and the peasant experience in Southern Rhodesia

Terence O. Ranger

Introduction

The first version of this chapter was prepared for a conference on the interaction of history and anthropology in Southern Africa. It seemed to me that there were two areas in which this interaction had been most productive. One was the study of colonial political economy in which historians had increasingly drawn on the work of French Marxist anthropology. The other was the study of Central African religion, in which there had been over the previous fifteen years increasing co-operation between historians and anthropologists. At the same time it seemed to me that there had been little awareness among either of these two clusters of scholars of the work that the other was producing. In particular, while some students of Central African religion, such as van Binsbergen and Schoffeleers, *had* made use of many of the concepts of radical political economy, there was little sign that political economists were aware of the relevance to them of studies of Central African religion. I therefore resolved to focus on one aspect only of the religious historiography; to set aside for the moment most of its insights on religious experience, on ritual and on symbolism, and to focus particularly on the study of Central African religion as an aspect of the study of political economy.

I planned at first to do this by reviewing the overall thrust of recent developments in Central African religious studies. But as I began to write, two things happened. One was that I found the

287

literature more voluminous and complex than I had expected so that my survey got longer and longer. The other was that I became more and more interested in trying to apply some of the questions and insights which emerge from this recent literature in order to re-analyse some of my own data. In the end I set aside the survey and began to work through my twenty-year-old notes on the Mwari cult in twentieth-century Zimbabwe. I had originally used this material in *Revolt in Southern Rhodesia* (1967) and *The African Voice in Southern Rhodesia* (1970) to demonstrate that long after the risings of 1896–7 white officials still believed that the Mwari cult priests were capable of initiating dangerous resistance to the colonial regime. I had used it also to illustrate what I then characterized as the 'despair' of traditional religious authorities confronted with colonial transformations (Ranger, 1967; 1970). This way of using the administrative files in fact left out of consideration the greater part of the material which they contained. So I resolved in my paper for the history/anthropology conference to make use of this neglected material.

Since then I have been able to collect additional archival evidence on the Mwari cult in the archives in Harare and have drawn on this as well as on the comments of the conference members to produce this revised version. In doing so I have had certain work most in mind. I have been influenced particularly by Dick Werbner's demonstration of the Mwari cult as a system of tribute and redistribution, overlapping and coexisting with secular political authorities (Werbner, 1977). I have been influenced by the emphasis which Matthew Schoffeleers and Wim van Binsbergen have laid on territorial cults as central to the 'eco-religion' of communal modes of production (Schoffeleers, 1978; van Binsbergen, 1979). I have kept in mind van Binsbergen's account of the decline of ecological concern within Central African religion in the twentieth century (van Binsbergen, 1981). Finally, I have taken into account the discussions on ideology and consciousness in the work of Bond and van Binsbergen and in particular their discussion on the emergence of ideologies appropriate to peasant experience and consciousness.[1]

I am aware that these scholars have been engaged in a constant process of elaboration and sophistication of ideas – this was one of the reasons why my survey became so complicated. Thus, in concluding that one kind of explanation is more convincing than another I am usually not so much arguing *for* van Binsbergen or *against* Schoffeleers as arguing for one layer of their work as against another.

The Mwari cult and 'traditional' continuity

At the end of his 'Continuity and Policy in Southern Africa's High God Cult' Dick Werbner (1977) criticizes my own earlier formulations. He does not believe that the cult responded to crisis in the 1890s by backing armed revolt against the whites; nor does he believe that the cult lapsed into despairing passivity after the defeat of the risings. He writes:

> Fundamentally, this crisis conception of the cult is wrong because it obscures that the diverse interests within the cult's domain called for a broad consensus in oracular policy. A war policy against white settlers, and thus for the restoration of a conquered Ndebele kingdom, suited the interests of people in no more than a small fraction of this domain. . . . The people in the rest of the domain had one policy, and they were the ones who co-ordinated their action over the widest area. The policy of protecting the white settlers, even fighting in their defence against the restoration of Ndebele dominance, was as seen at *that* time, more in the interests of the people who adopted it throughout a great crescent around the Ndebele kingdom's stronghold in the highlands of Zimbabwe. . . . The need to respond to a broad consensus, the cult procedures for the discovery and definition of such a consensus (i.e. through councils at the cardinal oracles), the commitment to macro-cosmic conceptions, all acted – and continue to act – as constraints on the cult leadership as a whole. . . .
>
> One last point about oracular policy-making must suffice here. According to the crisis conception, in its modern version, the cult's alternative to armed resistance has been, throughout most of the colonial period, 'a sort of despairing passivity'. Again, the contrary is the case. . . . As seen by some sophisticated Kalanga, such as an ex-headmaster, 'Mwali is a conservative God. He does not like change. He wants the old ways'. Indeed, to some Kalanga Mwali appears to have a

devotion to customs for their own sake. Yet this appearance, though not a disguise, is nevertheless a cover for the orientation of cult policy. It is conservative, but with economic and political concerns which are as basic in a neo-colonial period as in a colonial one. The oracle's messages have repeatedly advocated resistance to the inroads of a cash economy. They have urged the people to store their grain, to rely on mutual aid in agriculture, to brew beer for the co-operative labour of work bees, and not to be at the mercy of sales. . . . Similarly, in accord with the tide of popular opposition in Zimbabwe to measures for European control of agriculture . . . the oracles' messages have condemned the measures. . . . The central concern of the oracles' messages was and still is to conserve order in the world and to maintain the welfare of the land, its people and their economy. Continuity *is* the policy of the cults. (Webner, 1977: pp. 211–14)

I intend here to prescind from the debate about the Mwari cult's role in the 1896 risings. But I now whole-heartedly repudiate any notion of its subsequent 'despairing passivity'. I have no doubt that the Mwari cult has played a creative and significant role in twentieth-century Zimbabwe. Moreover, the considerations which Webner summarizes in the paragraphs I have just quoted are indeed those which emerge also from the archival data on the cult. As we shall see, the sources continually speak of Mwari prohibitions on the sale of crops or on the purchase of European goods. The question which concerns me here is that of the significance of these prohibitions.

The Central African religious literature offers two broad answers to this question, each of which seems to fit the evidence very convincingly, and which I wish first to discuss. These can be called the 'ecological' answer and the 'mode of production' answer.

The Mwari cult and ecology

The clearest statement of the ecological significance of the Mwari cult and its Central African fellows comes in Matthew Schoffeleers's Introduction to *Guardians of the Land: Essays on Central African Territorial Cults* (Schoffeleers, 1979). Schoffeleers writes:

Characteristic activities of territorial cults are rituals to counter-act droughts, floods, blights, pests and epidemic diseases afflicting cattle and man. Put positively, territorial cults function in respect of the well-being of the community, its fields, livestock, fishing, hunting and general economic interests. Apart from engaging in ritual action, however, they also issue and enforce directives with regard to a community's use of its environment. . . . The impact of territorial cults on the ecological system is such that, borrowing Rappaport's phrase, we may justifiably speak of a 'ritually directed eco-system'. (Schoffeleers, 1979: pp. 2–3)

Schoffeleers considers the control by cults of 'the production and distribution of food; the protection of natural resources; the control of human migratory movements'. He shows that the cults implemented control of fire in the 'fire created environment' of Central Africa. Beyond this he argues that

cult authority was more extensive. Not only could it determine methods of production, at times of crisis it could also decide on what to produce and it could lay down regulations against the monopoly of certain essential resources. Cult mediums in Malawi on several occasions have enjoined on the population to plant certain crops in preference to others. (Schoffeleers, 1979: p. 4)

At this stage of his writings Schoffeleers did not pursue the more dynamic implications of control and contested control of produc-tion.[2] He was more concerned with the role of the cults in 'the preservation of the natural environment'; with 'the fundamentals of this African philosophy of the earth'. He emphasized that when Central African territorial cults lost control in the upheavals of the late nineteenth century, the result was a random use of fire which devastated the remaining forests. The colonial period generally saw the undermining of traditional controls and the despoliation of the environment in the interests of rapid profit. 'While the world is bemoaning its ecological woes', concludes Schoffeleers, 'and is trying to construct a viable ideology, Africa is divesting herself of the one she so long possessed.'

This is a view not dissimilar to the argument presented by Sheri Young in her review of changes in diet and production in Southern Mozambique (Young, 1976). Beginning with an account of the role of ritual in the 'traditional' regulation of hunting and cultivation, she went on to argue that the impact of the Gaza and Portuguese conquests brought about the collapse of such regulations, the hunting out of game and the damaging exploitation of soils. Together with the social and economic dislocations of colonialism this resulted in a series of famines which were perceived by the people as being, and which were probably in reality, more frequent and disastrous than the famines of precolonial times (Young, 1976: pp. 3–9).

In the context of such an emphasis one might regard the Mwari manifestations recorded in the archives as protests against the breakdown of ecological controls. In her paper, Sheri Young listed a series of ecological crises in Southern Mozambique: '1906–8 brought locusts and drought and produced a relatively widespread famine; widespread drought re-occurred in 1912–13, more localised droughts alternating with flooding in 1914–17 . . . [there was] one major drought in 1922–3.' Now it so happens that the overwhelming majority of references to Mwari activity which I have discovered in Southern Rhodesian missionary or administrative sources apply to these same years of eco-crisis. This does not mean, of course, that there were no Mwari activities between them; what it seems to mean is that Mwari activities and rumours concerning Mwari were especially noticeable, even to Europeans, during and immediately after these periods of drought and famine. Thus the *Zambezi Mission Record* reported the appearance of Mwari emissaries after the famine of 1906 and the Fort Victoria native commissioner's reports noted Mwari activity both in 1906 and 1907; the *Zambezi Mission Record* carried a similar report during the drought of 1912–13, at which time there was also extensive administrative correspondence in Victoria and Chibi concerning the activities of Mwari messengers; 1915 brought accounts from many native commissioners of 'a sort of general propitiation' of Mwari and a series of reports of the spread of Mwari influence to Southern Mozambique; thereafter, with the exception of a rumour that the flu epidemic of 1918 was a punishment from Mwari, I found no further references until correspondence from the native commissioner, Belingwe, in the drought year of 1922.[3]

Moreover, the evidence suggests that these Mwari emissaries *were* primarily concerned to offer their account of the reasons for eco-disaster. And this account stressed that the African cultivators had abandoned or inadequately observed the 'traditional' controls: they had not waited to plant until they had received seed from the Mwari shrines; they had ploughed land wherever they chose; they had not observed the *chisi* rest days but had inclined to the Christian and administrative weekly rhythm instead. Thus at Empandeni in 1906/7 an old woman to whom the title Ninakapansi – 'Mother of the Ground' – was given, told the people that the drought had come because they had not sent offerings to Mwari, nor sought his permission to plant, nor sent for 'doctored' seed from the shrines, and because they had worked on the Saturday *chisi* day. 'She called upon the people to bring offerings to her, to stop working on Saturdays and work on Sundays instead, and to bring her seeds to be fructified.' These commands were obeyed.[4] Ninakapansi reappeared with similar warnings and commands in 1912–13 (Bhebe, 1979: p. 125). In Chibi in 1913, messengers who had gone to the Mwari shrines imploring rain were told that 'they had to observe certain *tshishe* days, i.e. the first day being to propitiate the Mwali's mother . . . the 4th, 7th and 9th day being dedicated to the Mwali himself, the round commencing again on the 11th day'. At the same time in Victoria the native commissioner reported that 'comparatively little threshing has been done. . . . The reaping has been retarded by the observance by many natives of additional days on which no work is done in the fields. They say the gods have forbidden work on four additional days out of ten'.[5] In 1915 the chief native commissioner, commenting on intense Mwari activity in Victoria, Gutu and Chibi, remarked that 'the people of this Division had neglected in recent years to send their usual contributions to the Mlimo [Mwari] and . . . he is reported to have said that he was responsible for the insect pest which had caused so much havoc among the native crops'.[6]

The Mwari cult and the communal mode of production

An 'ecological' answer thus seems to fit the evidence. So, too, does a 'mode of production' answer. In a series of papers van Binsbergen has defined the religious characteristics of 'the domestic mode of production' in Central Africa. This mode is

293

characterized by what he calls 'the communal ecological–religious complex'.

> People who are held together by common economic interests (agriculture, husbandry, hunting and collecting) in the same, limited, surrounding land area, tend to take ritual care of these interests through shrine cults. . . . Through ecological processes man transforms nature so as to carve out a human and social existence, selecting and using the raw materials of the forest, the animals and other natural resources. For these transformations technical knowledge, physical power and human organisation are indispensable, but to make them ultimately meaningful they have to be embedded in a cosmological system of classifications, relations and ritual activities which constitute the religion. (Van Binsbergen, 1981: pp. 138–9)

> I submit that the actual units of social structure on which both secular and religious aspects of social change hinge are modes of production. In its purest form, Horton's microcosm could be equated with the domestic mode of production. Far from being internally undivided, it is characterised by a process of expropriation and control between elders and youth, and between men and women. Religious beliefs and practices underpin as well as constitute (and sometimes perhaps negate) these domestic relations. Social and political change in Africa over the past few centuries can be understood as the process by which these domestic communities become articulated to other, more complex modes of production: the tributary mode, mercantile capitalism, and industrial capitalism. (Van Binsbergen, 1981: p. 62)

Now, van Binsbergen himself has not sought to apply a 'mode of production' analysis to the Mwari cult or to the history of Zimbabwe. But the evidence from the archives *could* be interpreted by means of the application of his idea of the 'communal ecological–religious complex'. And this notion of the Mwari cult as expressive of a 'domestic mode of production' could be sustained by some of the pre-colonial evidence. Thus it could be held that under Ndebele dominance the proclaimed power of the royal Kumalo dead over rain and fertility constituted the ideological basis for the Ndebele tributary mode of production, while the continued and overlapping existence of the Mwari cult expressed the continuity of domestic relations among the Kalanga peoples of the south-west.

Cobbing describes two alternative and coexisting festivals of eco-religion in nineteenth-century Matabeleland. One was the *nxwala*, taking place at the Ndebele king's capital 'at the time of the maturation of the green crops' in January/February – 'a festival of seasonal regeneration . . . of the harvest, of the rains, of the earth, of female fertility, of tribal potency'. The other was the annual festival at the Mwari shrines each October at which a priest of Mwari blessed the seed corn presented to him. The *nxwala* was attended by the Ndebele nation; the Mwari October festival by 'almost the whole of the Makalanga people' (Cobbing, 1974). The overthrow of the Ndebele state, it could be argued, left the Mwari cult with a monopoly of large-scale eco-religious ritual. Under colonialism, according to this view, the cult expressed the ideology of communal, subsistence production in a protest dialectic with commercial and industrial capitalism. Indeed, the cult – or its congregation – saw British South Africa Company rule not only as threatening to impose its own systems of taxation and forced labour but also as threatening to revive Ndebele tributary hegemony: in 1904, in an area which had benefited from the break-up of the Ndebele state by a discreet absorption of many Ndebele 'royal' cattle, a Mwari emissary was arrested for telling the people that the company was going to send 'an army' of white police to help Lobengula's son recover 'all the cattle which belonged to his father'.[7]

The evidence which I have already cited in discussing the ecological interpretation can equally plausibly be seen as a persistent restatement of the ideology of the communal mode. And beyond this there is plenty of evidence to suggest a direct repudiation by the Mwari cult of the 'cash economy'. On 6 May 1912 the native commissioner, Chibi, reported that Mwari messengers had been telling the people that Mwari had withheld rain because 'they were always selling their grain to the European store-keepers'.[8] In July 1913 it was again reported from Chibi that Mwari messengers were saying

that natives were not to sell grain to the whitemen except for salt and then as little grain as possible, as the Mwali favoured

their getting the salt . . . as they did before the white men came.
If they sold grain for salt they were to cover the grain in the
basket so that the Mwali could not see it. . . . At the present
the messengers are again away obtaining the Mwali's permission to thresh out the grain which has been reaped.[9]

The superintendent of natives, Victoria, recorded that 'until quite
recently many natives were afraid to trade even small quantities
for salt and it was common talk that the Mlimo had forbidden the
sale. Even near the townships of Victoria this was the case'.[10] In
November 1915 the native commissioner, Belingwe, reported that
Mwari had commanded that no European utensils were to be used
for eating and that this had been extended into a general boycott
of all European trading goods. A Mwari messenger had entered a
European store and told the customers that 'anyone using
enamelled dishes would be struck by lightning'.[11] A few days later
the native commissioner cabled that 'store keepers report marked
falling off purchases of European goods'.[12] In August 1923 it was
reported from Bulawayo that Mwari messengers were telling
Africans that the drought and famine of 1922 was due to the
'extravagant over-trading' of grain.[13]

It all seems to fit neatly enough into a pattern of defence of the
communal mode of production against the pressures for peasantization and proletarianization. In 1935 a missionary visited the kraal
of a headman in Belingwe district and told the headman that he
knew of the existence of a land shrine in the area. 'Nyika Yoparara
– The Land is lost', exclaimed the headman. The missionary was at
first surprised at this strong reaction to the mere discovery of the
shrine by whites. But, as he later reflected, 'they are a suppressed
people who through their old leaders fight a desperate battle
against enslavement and destruction' (Zachrisson, 1978: p. 340).

Difficulties with the ecological and communal mode of production analyses

Despite their apparent fit with the evidence, neither an ecological
nor a communal mode of production analysis seems to me to be
ultimately convincing. To begin with, there are traps inherent in
both the ecological and the mode of production models themselves,

though I am not suggesting that Schoffeleers, Young and van Binsbergen are unaware of them.

The trap in the ecological model is that it can induce us to accept a pre-colonial, 'traditional' environment as a given and to emphasize man's 'understanding' of it. At the same time it can induce us to allocate too much weight to eco-disasters in the colonial period. It is pertinent here to cite two of the papers on ecology delivered to the African Studies Association conference in Manchester in September 1980.

Rowland Moss criticized the notion that African environments are 'fragile, liable to break-down irreversibly if a man dares to meddle with the delicate, but vaguely conceived and tenuously defined, "ecological balance" '. He also repudiated a model in which

> environment is considered as a thing in itself, then described in terms of the characteristics of its main features, and then particular properties are selected from that information . . . to characterise the factors and features which are constraints or aids to crop production. These disparate morphogenic descriptions are then 'integrated' . . . in order to articulate the 'agricultural potential' or 'land resources'. Thus, effectively, 'constraints' and 'potentials' are described and defined quite independently of those processes which are to be constrained or developed. (Moss, 1980: p. 9)

Paul Richards denied that 'pre-colonial societies attained any marked degree of ecological equilibrium. It would be . . . false to imply that pre-colonial Africa suffered no environmental problems traceable to labour exploitation. Recent studies have emphasised the extent to which "tribal" and seemingly "egalitarian" pre-colonial societies were subject to intense conflict and contradiction.' As for eco-crisis under colonialism, Richards emphasizes that droughts and floods and famines are damaging not so much in themselves as disasters, but in terms of their context within

> the structural and ideological constraints imposed by articulation with world capitalism. . . . Particular interest focusses on the way in which various kinds of environmental crises are 'constructed' and on the power base which supports those who

297

claim the privilege to pronounce and delineate such crises.
(Richards, 1980)

Thus, far from seeing territorial cults as simply 'guardians of the land' and custodians of an African earth wisdom, one needs to delineate their interaction with rapid environmental changes, 'both periodic and random'; to see the controls which they exercise over production as aspects in themselves of the economic and social considerations which determine 'constraint and potential'; to see these controls also as part of the 'internal conflict and contradiction' which marked pre-colonial production systems. Schoffeleers, indeed, in his article on the ecological, political and religious transformations of the sixteenth-century Lower Shire Valley has gone a long way towards developing such a dynamic approach (Schoffeleers, 1978).

The data are not yet available for an analysis of the pre-colonial Mwari cult in the same way. But it is clear that there have been successive major eco-transformations and also that the emergence of successive 'tributary' state systems has involved large and inegalitarian changes in the use of land. The 'tributary' states of Zimbabwe, Torwa, the Rozwi and the Ndebele were not merely matters of trading or raiding dominance. They developed and largely depended upon systems of unequal diet, unequal access to grazing land, systematic expropriation of surplus agricultural production to supply the large 'urban' royal complexes, and so on. It is hard to imagine that the Mwari cult operated in permanent opposition to these tendencies. Indeed, it did not. It is clear, in fact, that the Mwari cult itself operated as a tributary system and that it gave ideological justification for the tributary claims of chiefs. It is also clear that the cult's control of the timing of production, use of fire, etc., was *an aspect of* these tributary systems.

It is time to turn to the problems of the mode of production analysis. The main problem, I suppose, lies less in the analysis itself rather than in the simple-minded way it is sometimes applied. The idea of the 'communal mode of production' is, of course, an abstraction, very rarely if ever to be found in practice. It is hardly to be expected that this abstraction, applied in the deliberately simplistic way I have used it above, will fit the facts of so complex a case as that of south-western Southern Rhodesia in the early colonial period.

Certainly, so far as the Mwari cult is concerned, it is very difficult to argue that it was concerned only with 'subsistence' communal production. It adapted itself easily to the development of activities which exploited natural resources commercially. In the 1870s a number of hunter-entrepreneurs were seeking to extend into the country north of the Limpopo the gun-hunting of elephants as a highly organized and large-scale business. In 1877 one of these men, van Rooyen, was operating among the 'Makalaka' of Mangwe in South-Western Matabeleland. He applied to the local Mwari shrine for 'trading veldt' – that is to say, for good luck in his hunting and trading – and after the presentation of gifts he was given it.[14] It seems likely, too, that the Mwari cult took a similar attitude towards mining. I have not come across any discussion of the relationship of the cult to mining enterprises before colonialism – though it would be surprising if a divinity whom the Ndebele called the God of the Underground had nothing to do with mining. But there is fascinating evidence that the Mwari priests or their Karanga congregations sought to assert the god's rights over European-directed mining in the early twentieth century. Around 1900 one Simpson Vhatu-a-Mamba was working in a mine in Selukwe. He later recounted to H. A. Stayt how the Karanga workers on the mine used the Mwari belief to assert their 'legitimacy' against migrant workers from elsewhere. Beer and food regularly appeared in the mine shafts; the Karanga workers and Chief Chibi said that Mwari had sent the food; that he was the owner of the land; and that he lived at Mbuvumela in the Matopos (Stayt, 1931: p. 235). It seems that the Mwari cult did not object either to trade or to gun-hunting or to mining *as such*, provided that these activities were carried on within the context of recognition of Mwari's 'ownership' of the land and of payment of tribute.

It is plain also that the Mwari shrines expected to receive regular payments of agricultural produce and of cattle. An elaborate system operated whereby chiefs within the Mwari sphere of influence regularly collected tribute together, sending some on to the shrines and retaining some themselves; in return the chiefs received 'doctored' seed from the shrines with which, in special fields worked on by tribute labour, they initiated the agricultural year. The control apparatus, in short, not only expressed a particular view of the proper way in which to exploit the environment but also facilitated and justified a tributary system.

Both members of the cult and rival tributary authorities saw Mwari officers in this light. Thus in 1904 a Mwari messenger demanding tribute for the god was arrested by the administration and put on trial. 'He asked those present', deposed African witnesses, 'to observe that he lived on beer, milk and meat and not on the ordinary food of natives' – in short, he claimed the special diet of the aristocratic elites of Shona political history. 'Accused from his actions, behaviour and words', said one witness, 'struck me as being a "big" man. I was in fear of him'.[15] 'The M'Limo . . . has a good time of it like the missionary', Lobengula is reported to have said. 'He knows his business and lives on the fat of the land; he gets plenty of grain and beer and in exchange fools the people into believing he is a god. Leave him alone, it is his way of making a living' (Sykes, 1897: p. 258). The British South Africa Company was less tolerant. The right to take tax was a fundamental sign of political authority; there were to be no rival tribute-collectors under company rule. So in October 1897, for example, the Mwari emissary, Dinkiwa, was charged with sedition as well as with fraud for collecting tribute in the name of Mwari, 'such tribute being unlawful for him to collect, he not being an agent of the Chartered Company empowered to govern . . . such tribute moreover being collected in the interest of a spirit falsely asserted to be corporate in the body of a person known as the Umlimo'.[16]

The Mwari cult found its claims to 'ownership' of the land challenged in many ways. Some native commissioners expressed their claim to exclusive authority not only in the levy of tax but by taking over agrarian rituals – 'according to Native Custom at the "first fruits" natives come in with an offering of mealies or other produce', wrote one,

> and as they generally come in in small parties I requested the
> different chiefs all to come in at one time, with the result that
> during this month all the natives around here, numbering
> almost 6 or 700 souls came in together and remained in this
> camp for about 6 days dancing, etc. I took this opportunity of
> holding an Indaba.[17]

European industrial entrepreneurs disregarded Mwari's claims. At Selukwe, for instance, the mining company and the native commissioner took the appearance of food and beer in the mineshafts, allegedly sent by Mwari, as a direct challenge to their joint authority. So the native commissioner took three policemen and three 'boys' from the mine, guided by a messenger from Chief Chibi, 'to find Mwari's home'. According to Simpson Vhatu-a-Mamba, they detected the Mwari priests in ventriloquial fraud, captured one and carried him back to Chief Chibi. 'The man told the chief and the white people that it was his business to do these things: people brought him cattle and presents of beer and he did his business. After that there was no more trouble with the Bakaranga in the mine' (Stayt, 1931: p. 235). It is clear from subsequent files that Chief Chibi went on sending tribute to Mwari after this incident. But there was no chance of Mwari establishing control over the patterns of mining labour, its rest days and festivals, or of tapping mining wages in tribute.

Finally, Mwari's 'ownership' of the land was challenged under colonialism by a certain type of African peasant farmer. John Comaroff shows in his discussion of peasant entrepreneurship in Botswana that the control over the agricultural season exercised by chief or cult presented an obstacle to the most effective exploitation of economic opportunity. It was an advantage to 'modernizing' African farmers to ignore limitations placed upon when they could begin to plough or to plant and where (Comaroff, in press). In early colonialism in Southern Rhodesia some Africans on missionary farms tried to use new technology, to ignore *chisi* days and to cultivate when and where they liked, in order to maximize output. It was, in fact, against one such nucleus of Christian entrepreneurship that Ninakapansi uttered her denunciations in 1906/7. As Ngwabi Bhebe remarks in his account of the incident, 'the Jesuits' intensive methods of transforming the Empandeni community must have looked like a real threat' to the Mwari priests; a threat to which they responded with threats to punish the community with locusts because they had neglected Mwari's rules (Bhebe, 1979: p. 125). Later, when the Native Purchase Areas developed as zones of black yeoman enterprise, the African commercial farmers exploited certain types of 'traditional' relationships in order to obtain labour, but ignored *chisi* rest days and other ecological controls on the grounds that Mwari knew nothing about modern agriculture and that it did not fall into his sphere of competence (Cheater, 1981; and in press).

The colonial authorities interpreted much Mwari activity in the

301

twentieth century as attempts to recover tribute and to re-impose cult authority over agriculture; most of the cases cited above as examples of ecological concern were seen by the Native Department as a sort of ideological blackmail, in which the Mwari emissaries took advantage of drought or locusts to recall people to their duties. Nor does one have to accept so cynical a view of the cult's activities in order to recognize in the data persistent attempts to restore the system of chiefly and cultic control and tribute. This is an element, as we shall see, that comes very clearly out of the extraordinary expansion of cultic influence in 1915. Such Mwari attempts sometimes won victories even over white farmers. Thus we are told by F. J. Mashasha, in his account of the life of Native Commissioner 'Jakata' Williams of Gutu, that when Williams retired to run his farm in the district he made no attempt at commercial agriculture but presided over the African population on his land as though he were a chief.

> One reason why Jakata was particularly liked as a landlord is that in his serene years he became, to all intents and purposes . . . a true Shona chief inasmuch as he was willing not only to allow, but also to assist in, in a manner befitting to a chief, the celebration of *mukwerera*, a Karanga religious ceremony to ask Mwari for rain in times of drought. Old men say that he would himself, in such times, give grain and meal to the local *svikiro* [medium] – in this case Va Chitende, an old woman resident on his farm and reputed to be a *nyusa* [Mwari messenger] – for brewing the beer necessary for the ceremony. (Mashasha, n.d.: p. 2)

It is tempting to see the Mwari cult's activities in the twentieth century as an aspect of an ideology of a tributary mode of production. The Mwari emissaries, so it seems, were seeking to maintain the authority of chiefs and priests over communal cultivators. They were also seeking to repudiate the penetration among these communal cultivators of the commercial influences which threatened to turn them into peasants.

The Mwari cult and peasant consciousness

But things were not as simple even as this. There were, after all, peasants and peasants. Some of those to whom we now give this title were enterprising 'modernizers' of the type already discussed. But others were very different. During the first decades of the twentieth century the great majority of those who were in a peasant relationship to the colonial economy were men and women who used 'traditional' methods to produce 'traditional' crops and whose surpluses were very small. What made them peasants was that they set out to produce these surpluses on a regular annual basis in order that they could market them. Such people had chosen to relate to the colonial economy as peasant producers rather than as migrant workers. Robin Palmer has described the period 1890 to 1908 as the era of Shona 'peasant prosperity' for precisely this sort of producer. Ian Phimister, writing of the Victoria district from which so much of the twentieth-century Mwari evidence comes, shows the readiness, indeed eagerness, of such African agriculturalists to sell their grain and cattle. He stresses the 'favourable terms of trade' at first enjoyed by African producers, which allowed them to avoid work for Europeans. He also stresses that the early demand was for 'increased production of "traditional crops" ', so that cultivators could market surpluses of what they were already growing for subsistence (Palmer, 1977; Phimister, 1980).

It is plain, then, that the African rural population of the Mwari cult's zone of influence were *not* 'communal cultivators' in the early years of the twentieth century; they were already peasants with a desire to sell produce to the whites. This being so, it seems highly unlikely that the Mwari cult could call upon its constituency to withdraw from the cash economy. How then are we to account for the prohibitions on the sale of crops already cited?

I believe that it is important to divide the data into periods. During the first decade of the twentieth century African peasants of this 'traditional' kind were heavily involved in trade at favourable prices. When drought occurred during these years it was *not* explained by the Mwari priests in terms of Mwari's anger at the sale of grain and cattle, nor did Mwari rebuke people for such sales. In 1905 and 1906 when there were severe droughts there are few reports of unusual Mwari activities or prohibitions. Ndebele chiefs came into Bulawayo to ask that the statue of Cecil Rhodes be taken down since it was tying up the rain; a few chiefs asked missionaries to pray for rain; no doubt many unreported gifts were sent to Mwari in the Matopos. But the only recorded Mwari prohibition took place, significantly enough, at the entrepreneurial community of Empandeni. The widespread sale of small surpluses of 'traditional' crops, after all, was perfectly compatible with observation of the *chisi* days and of control by priests and chiefs of the ritual agrarian year.

The contrast between the slight Mwari activity in this period and the intense activity from 1912 onwards is striking. I would myself argue that in the earlier period drought in itself was not so damaging to people who were able to meet their subsistence needs before they traded; indeed, I would agree with David Beach that the capacity to sell crops offered some sort of insurance against famine (Beach, 1977: p. 59). From 1912 on, and particularly from 1915, the position changed. Palmer sees the years from 1908 to 1914 as the years of a 'white agricultural policy'; the period 1915 to 1925 as the years of 'the economic triumph of European agriculture'. Phimister describes how by 1910 the terms of trade had drastically changed in the Victoria district. Railways were bringing grain to the mines there from European farms in the Mazoe valley; this supply undercut local prices for grain and enabled traders to bring African producers into a dependent relationship of debt. The need for cash to pay tax and the desire for cash to buy European goods now became a real weakness, leading to the sale of too much produce at too little return and so exposing people to grave danger in times of drought (Palmer, 1977; Phimister, 1977).

Robin Palmer thus summarizes the situation in 1923:

> The remarkable prosperity enjoyed by many Shona farmers in the early years of the century was brought to an end by a combination of factors. Primarily, African farmers faced the full blast of competition from heavily subsidised European farmers, while simultaneously being pushed away from access to markets. . . . In addition, Africans were confronted with an ever-increasing number of costly dues – taxes, rents, dipping and grazing fees, etc. – at a time when their own appetite for consumer goods was on the increase. The end result was that when they were no longer able to sustain themselves and purchase their requirements from the sale of their agricultural produce, they would be forced to become wage-labourers. (Palmer, 1977: pp. 237–8)

It was thus not in a situation of peasantization but of threatened proletarianization that the Mwari admonitions and prohibitions took place from 1912 onwards.

Even then it would be a mistake to suppose that when Mwari spokesmen criticized the sale of crops to the whites or prohibited the purchase of European goods they were demanding that Africans should contract out of the cash economy altogether. For one thing, it is clear from the reports themselves that Mwari prohibitions were intended to apply for defined periods only. For another thing, such withholding of crops from the market was in itself a *peasant* strategy rather than the strategy of men seeking to protest against being peasants. As Phimister remarks, in peasant contestations with traders in Victoria district 'often their only alternative was to refuse to sell their grain surpluses'. Mtetwa tells us for the Duma that recourse to 'traditional' regional trade between the peasants of the plateau and the African occupants of the Low Veld ranches allowed some escape from the exploitative relationship with European traders.[18] In this period boycotts of white traders made excellent sense to the cultivators of the Mwari region. In 1914 one enterprising store – Green & Miller at Godzo – hired a Mwari representative to dance for rain, and supplied beer and food, in an attempt to buy off this sort of animosity.[19] In this period, too, the cumulative effects of droughts were becoming so serious that they evoked a good deal of metaphysical reflection. But what African cultivators wanted was to be successful peasants rather than to cease being peasants altogether.

One can trace in the administrative files the gradual fusion of African peasant disaffection and the idiom of the Mwari prohibitions. This fusion began with the famine of 1912. Even before the Mwari prohibitions began to be recorded, the native commissioners reported strenuous attempts by African 'traditional' peasants to avoid being trapped into an adverse financial relationship with the whites. In Ndanga in May 1912 the native commissioner found that cultivators refused 'absolutely to accept any advance of grain or meal either from private individuals or from the Government. . . . The main reason is a rooted dislike on general grounds to loans from either the Government or any European'; rather than enter into debt they eked 'out an existence with wild fruits and with small doles from the more fortunate natives'.[20] The rainy season of 1912–13 was generally good, though Ndanga and Chibi districts still needed famine relief as late as April 1913. It was in this situation that Mwari emissaries spread out through the Victoria circle in mid-1913. They came to claim tribute in return for the rains.[21] They also came to warn peasant cultivators not to exhaust their grain reserves by trading them all away to the Europeans – an anxiety which the Mwari emissaries shared with white agricultural officials and with peasant farmers themselves.[22] Mwari emissaries tried to effect a slow-down in grain sale by a prohibition on the commencement of first reaping and then threshing. In Victoria in June 1913 it was reported that 'reaping has been retarded by the observation by many natives of additional days on which no work is done in the fields. They say the gods have forbidden work on four additional days out of every ten'.[23] In July it was recorded for Victoria that 'comparatively little threshing has been done. It is rumoured that the natives in some parts are awaiting permission from the gods and in the meantime are merely threshing enough for present requirements'.[24] Permission to thresh reached Victoria and Chibi only at the end of July; as peasants began to thresh and to trade their grain in August 1913 Mwari emissaries passed through the area collecting thanks-offerings for the harvest.[25]

It seems clear that all this amounted to control of the flow of trade rather than to total prohibition of it. In 1913 some peasants refused to go along with the Mwari restrictions – 'many now refuse to observe these [*chisi*] days as they admit the delay in reaping is causing considerable loss of grain'.[26] But in general the Mwari representatives chimed in with peasant aspirations remarkably well. Popular rumour in Victoria circle depicted them as promising 'that the Mwali would send a great wind and that all the whitemen in the country would leave in the night. Mwali would then bring other whitemen who would only charge a shilling tax and sell goods at about a quarter their present price.'[27]

As the years passed and the crisis of the African peasant economy deepened, Mwari advice not to sell grain seemed more and more sensible – and was often hailed as such by the Native Department. It was listened to and accepted by men who wanted trade on favourable terms. Thus in 1923, when Mwari messengers were telling people that the drought of 1922 had been due to 'extravagant over-trading' of grain, African response to them was attributed to 'the collapse of the cattle market' which had

306

prevented the sale of African beasts for cash, thus forcing peasants to turn to the sale of grain.[28]

My conclusion, then, is that the Mwari activities recorded in the files do not primarily reflect an attempt to preserve the environment – though the idiom of ecological discourse prevailed in their expression. Nor were they statements by the ideologues of the communal mode of production against its subordination to and articulation with the capitalist mode. Nor were they even simply exploitative attempts to revive tributary networks. Over and above that they were one manifestation of a particular type of African peasant 'consciousness', expressing both its protest against and its accommodation to the colonial economy.

The Mwari movements of 1915

The graph of Mwari-related movements seems to me to bear out such an interpretation. If one saw the cult primarily as the advocate of pre-colonial 'tradition' one might expect it to be most active and most widely influential in the first years of the colonial economy. In fact, the great year of Mwari-related movements was 1915, the year of 'general propitiation', during which the whole belt of country from the Matopos to the coast was affected. It seems worthwhile to describe the full range of the 1915 movements, partly because this has never been done before, and partly because it brings out the mingled 'tributary' and 'peasant' implications.

Per Zachrisson (1978: p. 121), in his account of Belingwe, remarks that 'in the administrative records there is a list for the year 1915 containing not less than 57 letters on the subject "Mlimo messages" and "Rumours of Unrest"'. A good deal of this correspondence was generated by administrative paranoia about the sinister influence of German missionaries on the native mind. But a good deal reflected some unusual Mwari-related activity. In previous years there had been reports of emissaries from the Mwari shrines or of regional messengers returning from the shrines with instructions. In 1915 the diffusion of messages from Mwari took on a mass aspect. In March the native commissioner, Gutu, reported that crowds of people, mostly women and children, were going from village to village, 'collecting people as they went'. They 'were singing that they were the bearers of a message from "Mwari" and that those who did not give heed to what they said would have their crops dry up, and had been instructed to visit all kraals.' The movement was said to have spread from Selukwe through Chilimanzi and into Gutu and to be connected with recent epidemics of human and animal disease. 'There is something very mysterious taking place.'[29]

Later in the month similar reports were received from Hartley and Charter; from Ndanga; and from Victoria. 'Two women are dressed in black limbo', wrote the native commissioner, Ndanga, 'and taken to the next kraal. . . . They are presented as *mbonga* [hand-maids of Mwari]. After much dancing they are returned to their kraal, and two more women are treated in the same way in the kraal visited, the movement thus being carried on.'[30] The native commissioner, Victoria, recorded

a strange movement amongst the natives . . . a means by which sickness could be driven away from their kraals. . . . The women and girls went from their own to a neighbouring kraal, returning no salutations and speaking to no-one by the way, and on reaching the other kraal, sang a few words about 'the sickness of or from Mwari', would be given a fowl by the people of the kraal, which fowl they destroyed, and they would return to their own kraal.

By so doing 'they transferred the disease to the kraal they visited', which then had to 'go and do likewise . . . and pass the evil on'.[31] On 23 March the native commissioner, Gutu, wrote to say that he had now arrested and questioned some of the dancers. They told him that they had been instructed to go to six villages and to instruct the people in each to go to six villages in their turn; Mwari's message was becoming a chain letter. The prisoners said that the dance and its accompanying rituals were designed to cleanse the villages and to drive out sickness.[32]

At this point the whole business became confused with reports from spies that it was being used by the Mwari cult to test out its networks of command in preparation for a later order to rise up against the whites; comments made in the villages about the causes of sickness, which often linked it with aspects of the colonial economy, were taken to be the beginning of a seditious campaign. But despite a full expression of fears and suspicions, the chief native commissioner was obliged to conclude on 26 April 1915 that 'these unusual ceremonies had no political significance but were being conducted on the advice of the Mlimo (the Kalanga deity) to drive away the evil spirit which had brought sickness among them'.[33]

It seems clear that what was going on was a movement of reconstitution of village society. Unhappily, there was no detached and academic observer of these Zimbabwean happenings. But for the contemporaneous movement in Mozambique we have much more enlightening accounts. The best general narrative is provided by Keith Rennie, drawing on the Swiss missionary Guye, who recorded his impressions in 1916. 'In large parts of Eastern Rhodesia and in the area between the Sabi and the Limpopo', writes Rennie,

> there was a series of bad harvests between 1913 and 1915. As a result of this, missionaries and government in the Melsetter district began a programme of famine relief. To the south, however, the Hlengwe were left to their own resources and sent deputations to Mlimo, or Murimi. [Murimi was traditionally the Hlengwe/Thonga version of Mlimo or Mwari.] These returned with tobacco which was to be snuffed, and the nasal mucus mixed with tobacco was to be buried in holes at the edge of the gardens. Hlengwe – and possibly Ndau – then moved south taking the ritual among the Thonga and Gaza of the lower Limpopo area, where the movement took on the characteristics of a widespread anti-witchcraft revitalization movement. The arrival of these prophets in Chikhumbane, on the coast between Inhambane and Lourenço Marques, was described by Guye. Chikhumbane determined to have his territory purified, in common with most of his fellow chiefs, and summoned all under him . . . to his capital. He approached Guye to ask him to ensure that the Christians should join in. . . . Murimi began with a short and simple speech in which he explained that the purpose of his visit was to administer the snuff of Murimi, which would kill the evil but be harmless to the innocent. Those who practised witchcraft after taking it, would split open and die. . . . Murimi also distributed snuff to protect the fields against thieves and to ensure fertility. (Rennie, 1972: pp. 18–19)

Plainly this Mwari-related movement in Mozambique had taken on features of its own. But equally plain were its peasant and its tributary aspects. Rennie remarks that Murimi 'was primarily an attempt to cope with *village* problems of failed crops and social tension' rather than 'a movement of urban workers in their villages'; in the terms of van Binsbergen's analysis of the Lenshina church, Murimi belonged to the peasant rather than the proletarian stream. The ministrations of the Murimi messenger also restored Chief Chikhumbane's authority over the land. When the ceremony had been completed 'Chikhumbane explained to Guye that Christians could no longer freely collect their firewood nor graze their cattle on his land without his permission for his land was now protected by Murimi's snuff' (Rennie, 1972: p. 19).

The renowned missionary ethnographer H. A. Junod also collected information about the Murimi movement from African Christians. His account brings out both the agricultural and tributary dimensions of the movement. All the fields around a village were treated with medicated snuff by the village wives; it was believed that if a woman were a witch, and had been responsible through her witchcraft for droughts or floods, the snuff would fly to the capital of the chief and denounce her there as soon as she 'resumed her detestable trade'. After the medication of the fields a ritual period of taboos commenced. During this it was forbidden to work in the fields until the chiefs decided that cultivation could begin. When they did so decide, all the women were called to the capital of the chief where they set to work on a field specially set apart; only when they had prepared this field for planting could they go back to their own lands. And no one could proceed to plant seed until the chief had himself seeded the ritually prepared field (Junod, 1924). Commenting on Junod's account, Sheri Young concluded that Murimi was a 'means of responding to ecological disaster and of re-organizing ritual responsibilities in keeping with new economic factors and the dominant role of women in agricultural and communal responsibilities (Young, 1977: p. 76).

These characteristics of Murimi reappeared elsewhere in the Mwari zone of influence. Stayt has given us an account of Mwari-related ritual among the Venda in the same general period. There, when crops did not flourish, all the people and petty chiefs brought their seed to the kraal of the paramount; the seed was mingled with powder obtained from the Mwari shrines in the Matopos; a special patch of land at the capital was hoed and then sown with special seed; after this each petty chief was given a basket of seed; land was hoed and sown at his village; eventually medicated seed was distributed to each woman for planting in her own fields (Stayt, 1931: p. 313). And the combination of female and chiefly significance marked another Mwari-related 'chain letter' movement in the midlands and eastern districts of Southern Rhodesia in October 1917. In this case the wife of the chief or headman, together with five other women, went veiled to the kraal of the neighbouring chief; 'they brought a basket of grain and told him to send some on to the next kraal', promising that 'the kraals that have taken the movement up will have a granary full of grain and the natives are to keep it until the "Mbuya", the owner, arrives'. The Mbuya was thought of as a female manifestation of Mwari's power.[34]

It seems reasonable to conclude on the basis of all this that the 1915–17 Mwari movements were an attempt to reconstruct tributary networks and to make rural society viable even where the absence of migrant workers meant that the overwhelming majority of peasant cultivators were women.

Mwari and the decline of ecological religion

As such, its success was short-lived, at any rate in its Mozambiquan outreaches. Junod tells us that after two years, when the fields were no longer fertile, the Tsonga realized that they had been the victims of 'a formidable mystification'. Sheri Young tells us that many people still remember Murimi as a genuine attempt to improve the peasant situation but they regard its failure as having been inevitable. Indeed, in her paper, 'What have They Done with the Rain?' (Young, 1978), she traces a steady and absolute decline in all kinds of ecological ritual in Southern Mozambique. For this she provides two categories of explanation. One is provided by her informants. They told her that fertility rituals no longer work; as a result 'everyone has to work "too hard", the fields must be large, less types of food grow in them, harvests are small and people are hungry'. This is because

the people who knew how to make [prayers], the rain-makers and the legitimate chiefs were gone. . . . Current chiefs are simply appointed by the Portuguese and when they tried to make prayers they were 'chased' and jailed. . . . The 'people' did not have the right to make the prayers without the chief. . . . 'Our minds are divided', 'some people are Christians, others call demons', 'people no longer know what to do'.

The second explanation is her own. The Murimi movement, she argues, stood no chance of reasserting the primacy of cultivation over labour migration. After 1915 dependence on migrant labour cash inputs rapidly increased.

It was not the rains which had changed, but the economic means to buffer drought, and the social ties by which the goods were distributed. Wage labour had become more effective than collective ceremonies in combating famine, but only reached from any individual to the people he chose to support.

There was no longer any point in reaching out to Mwari (Young, 1978: pp. 14–15, 20).

Here Young comes close to van Binsbergen's more general analysis of the decline of ecological concern in Central African religious movements. All the religious innovations of the twentieth century, van Binsbergen argues, show such a decline.

Christian missions may have dabbled in rain and harvest ritual but . . . such attempts would be abandoned for themes . . . reflecting their European, industrial society of origin. . . . In the cults of affliction, the secondary prophetic affliction cults, the eschatological prophetic movements as well as among the Watchtower type . . . we do not encounter the slightest trace of a concern for the land or of claims of power to influence the human ecological transformations. . . . The significance of this radical departure from what had been a central issue in the old religious system cannot be over-estimated. If nature enters at all into these new cults, it is as something to be feared and avoided. (Van Binsbergen, 1981: p. 157)

Van Binsbergen also has for the Western Zambian region on which his work is focused a prophetic movement starting around 1913 – that of Mupumani. He interprets it as 'a short-lived attempt to revolutionise, rather than supersede, the old ecologico-religious system'. But after Mupumani, as after Murimi, 'the trends of change rapidly gathered momentum. In the 1930s 'the times seemed more than suitable for a revival of the communal ecologico-religious complex . . . but nothing of the sort happened. The communal had ceased to be sufficiently relevant: it could no longer dominate any religious expression' (van Binsbergen, 1981: pp. 147, 171).

Now the problem with all this is that it does not seem to fit the history of the Mwari cult inside Zimbabwe after 1915–17. The Mwari cult certainly went on expressing peasant consciousness into the 1930s. In 1934, for example, there was a plague of locusts in Matabeleland. Mwari emissaries instructed people to observe Wednesday as a *chisi* day and were said to have ordered them not to co-operate with the administration campaign against locusts. H. Mackinnon of Mackinnon & O'Reilly, Traders, expressed the opinion of, no doubt, many other traders in the African areas over the years: 'They should throw a stick of dynamite with a fuse attached into Mlimo's cave.'[35] Thereafter my archival data run out. But where one picks up commentary on Mwari once again, in the work of recent scholars, the cult still seems widely influential.

As we have seen, Werbner asserts that it has gone on with its policy of 'continuity' from the 1890s to the present. Martinus Daneel writes:

> Mwari waMatonjeni has remained the God of many rural, that is tribal, people. To those living at an essentially subsistence level, dependent on a rain-giving God for their crops, and those involved in the intrigues of tribal politics, the God of Matonjeni is still a power that counts. In Chingombe and the other Gutu chiefdoms the gifts for Mwari . . . are still regularly collected by the kraalheads. The messenger, Vondo, goes about his duties with conviction and personal zeal. . . . Mwari's instructions were obeyed without protest throughout the whole district in 1966 – He wanted a change of *chisi* from Thursday to Wednesday, and He gave advice in the latest dispute about the succession to the Gutu chieftainship. . . . He is still regarded by many people as a major rural power. (Daneel, 1971: pp. 90–1)

Per Zachrisson notes for Belingwe that

> in the yearly reports for 1948 and 1949 the Superintendent of

the mission remarked how surprised the missionaries had been
when they learnt from the African members of the Synodical
Council to what extent many of the members of the Church still
adhered to their traditional religion. Many of them had through
all these years paid a yearly gift to the Rain God in Matopos.
'The heathen authorities (chiefs and headmen) are said to
demand it in the name of African solidarity'. . . He added that
the Christians 'were forced' to respect Wednesday as a sacred
day in memory of a rain-doctor from Belingwe.

Zachrisson adds that this remained a problem for the African-led
church in 1972, when black ministers asked the district officer to
instruct chiefs not to compel Christians to participate in Mwari
observances. The district officer replied that the 'chiefs and their
people . . . had made offerings to the "Matopo God" for as long as
they could remember' and that 'they would probably disobey' any
instructions to discontinue their observances (Zachrisson, 1978:
pp. 344–5).

Do we have a real difference here? With Southern Mozambique
and Sheri Young's analysis, we evidently do. In many ways this is
surprising. Labour migration became crucially significant to the
rural economy in the Mwari zone of Zimbabwe even if not perhaps
to the same degree as in Mozambique. Zimbabwean chiefs found
themselves in a more and more uncomfortable position between
the government and the people. Farming methods changed
fundamentally within the Reserves, later known as the Tribal
Trust Lands, where the old extensive agriculture had to give way
to perennial cultivation of a fixed area and where the use of
fertilizers became essential in order to produce any crop at all. On
the other hand, tendencies within the Reserves towards differentiation and the emergence of openly entrepreneurial farming were
constantly checked by the administration itself. In the 1930s and
1940s the policy of centralization enabled native commissioners to
redistribute land holdings in a deliberately egalitarian way; the
same policy was followed with the implementation of the Land
Husbandry Act in the 1950s. Native commissioners declared
themselves to be 'purely communistic' in this matter and to regard
the emergence of an African capitalist class with horror.[36] A
numerous small peasantry survived, seeking where and when it
could to market innumerable small surpluses. Moreover, the

administration itself came more and more to support 'tradition' against the missionaries; by the 1970s, certainly, the Mwari cult was regarded with benevolent approval by district commissioners, who were engaged in the belated flowering of Rhodesian Indirect Rule 'invention of tradition'. For all these reasons - and for all those reasons of internal religious experience and effectiveness of symbol which I have not examined in this chapter – the Mwari cult's claim for tribute and its articulation of a particular type of peasant consciousness went on seeming highly relevant.

There seems, then, to be a real contrast between South-Western Zimbabwe and Southern Mozambique. I doubt if the contrast with van Binsbergen's Zambian material is really so sharp. In the papers I have quoted, van Binsbergen was concerned to trace a movement away from a situation in which *everyone* was caught up in ecological religion to a situation in which many people were not. In his more recent work he has paid renewed attention to the importance of such ecological concerns as have survived, been renewed or been transformed, within the total spectrum of Zambian religious belief. Thus, in his analysis of the Lumpa Church of Alice Lenshina, he remarks that

> in many respects Lumpa tried to revive the old super-structure, in which concern for the land and fertility, protection against sorcery, general morality, and political and economic power had all combined in one holistic conception of the rural society. . . . [Lenshina] assumed ritual ecological functions such as distributing blessed seeds and calling rain.

These rituals, 'almost an anachronism within the development of Central African religion', emphasized the essentially peasant character of the Lumpa Church. 'Lumpa became primarily a means to overcome the predicament of peasantisation.' In a postscript he concludes for the leaders of Lumpa – as I have concluded for the Mwari cult officers – that they were '*not* fundamentally opposed to the capitalist mode of production, as long as it fell in line with their perceived material interests' (van Binsbergen, 1981: p. 311).

Within Zimbabwe, too, there are parallels to the Lumpa Church – though fortunately not, so far, to its ultimate fate. Thus Daneel describes how Bishop Samuel Mutendi, founder of the Zion

Christian Church, performs ecological rituals at his Zion City in Bikita, in the heart of the Mwari cult zone of influence.

His followers are forbidden to participate in the *mukwere* rituals [of Mwari]. Instead of relying on the *munyai* [Mwari messengers], each Zionist congregation sends a delegation to Zion City during the October conference, called the *Mbeu Vungano* [seed conference], with a special request for rain. The *Mbeu vungano* gives the Zionist members a chance of having the seed, soon to be sown in their fields, blessed by their leader. . . . In the same month when Mwari's priests, mbongas and Hossanahs dance at the Matonjeni shrines, Zionists from all over the country dance [for rain] at Zion city. . . . In a competitive spirit the delegates of each district dance in front of Mutendi and place their *zvipo* – a £1 note at a time – on the table.

Mutendi speaks of the Mwari cult as diabolic; the Mwari spokesmen in their turn attack Mutendi. 'You people in Bikita believe in Mutendi's power to make rain,' said the Matonjeni shrine in 1965; 'I do not like this and I shall send but little rain for the next six months. If you want rain, go and ask Mutendi! Let us see if he succeeds. I will punish the people because the Zionists call me Satan!' This threat was followed by a bad summer with little rain. The Mwari messenger closest to Mutendi's Zion stoically expected martyrdom – 'My blood will flow for the people, just as Jesus' blood flowed. Mutendi will kill me because [he] has no food or water. . . . They already say the rain has gone because of me. . . who told Mwari of their bad deeds' (Daneel, 1970: pp. 66–70). But this clash between Mwari and Mutendi does not represent a clash between modes of production or even a clash between two significantly different perceptions of peasant interest. They clash because they contest for influence over the same area: for tribute from chiefs and people; for the right to express much the same dimension of peasant consciousness.

It is no longer, as perhaps it was in 1915, the only or the overwhelmingly dominant form of peasant consciousness. There are many more Christianized entrepreneurs than there were in 1915; many more peasant families who cannot aspire even to the illusion of successful marketing of their small surplus. Zimbabweans, as well as Mozambiquans, are 'divided' in their minds. But the option of participation in the cash economy on the terms of a reconstituted peasant community still has relevance. In Zimbabwe this option can be represented by the Mwari cult where in Zambia it has been represented by Lumpa and in Mozambique perhaps by no one.

Notes

1 Interestingly, the most pertinent studies are all related to Zambia. They are Bond (1978; 1979), van Binsbergen (1981), Martin (1980).
2 Schoffeleers has subsequently developed these implications. See Schoffeleers (1978: pp. 19–33); Schoffeleers (1979) was in fact written in the early 1970s.
3 The Belingwe evidence is especially interesting in that it raises the question of the cult's control of fire. On 13 April 1922 the native commissioner, Belingwe, reported that three Mwari 'prophets or prophetesses' were being closely watched. 'Advice to burn the veldt', he wrote, in an odd reversal of the cult's concern to preserve the environment, 'would require the aid of only a few fanatics and would involve enormous losses elsewhere.' More usually native commissioners in the Mwari zone attributed bush fires to the carelessness of European farmers and praised African peasants for their restrained use of fire. File N 3/31/1, National Archives, Harare, Zimbabwe. (All archival references henceforth are to files in the National Archives.)
4 'Notes from Empandeni', *Zambezi Mission Record*, **3**, 36 (April 1904): p. 210; Bhebe (1979: p. 125).
5 Native commissioner, Chibi, to superintendent of natives, Victoria, 19 July 1913. N 3/33/12; Monthly Report, Victoria, June 1913. N 9/4/26, vol. 2.
6 Chief native commissioner to secretary, administrator, 26 April 1915. N 3/32/1.
7 Evidence of Mbopo, 10 March 1964; evidence of Tshwabaya, A 11/2/12/11.
8 Native commissioner, Chibi, to superintendent of natives, Victoria, 6 May 1912. N/3/31/1.
9 Native commissioner, Chibi, to superintendent of natives, Victoria, 16 July 1913. N 3/33/12.
10 Superintendent of natives, Victoria, to chief native commissioner, July 1913. N 3/33/12.
11 Native commissioner, Belingwe, to superintendent of natives, Gwelo, 10 November 1915. N 3/32/1.
12 Native commissioner, Belingwe, telegram, 13 November 1915. N 3/32/1.
13 Superintendent of natives, Bulawayo, to chief native commissioner, 27 August 1923. N 3/31/1.

14 *The Times*, 4 September 1896. F. C. Selous described how Pasipamire, the medium of the Chaminuka spirit, operated in the same way in the 1870s from his base at Chitingwiza.

> My friends (white ivory hunters) found it expedient to pay the old fellow a visit to obtain his gracious permission to go and 'kill the elephants nicely', for, until they did this, their boys would only hunt in a listless, half-hearted sort of way. constantly saying, 'What is the use of your hunting elephants in Situngweesa's country without first getting his permission to do so?' But when, by the help of presents, the old fellow's good word was obtained, . . . they almost at once seemed changed beings and hunted with the greatest alacrity. (Selous, 1881: p. 331)

15 Evidence of Kuziri and Gwatidzo, 22 February and 3 March 1904. A 11/12/11.

16 Regina versus Dinikwa, 29 October 1897, Trial 306.

17 Monthly Report, North Mazoe, March 1899. N 9/4/2.

18 Phimister (1977: p. 261); Mtetwa (1976: pp. 351–497). For a summary of the argument of this as yet unpublished thesis, see Ranger (1978: pp. 110–13).

19 Native commissioner, Plumtree, to superintendent of natives, Bulawayo, 10 December 1914. N 3/31/3.

20 Monthly Report, Ndange, May 1912. N 9/4/25, vol. 2.

21 Monthly Reports, Gutu, March 1913. N 9/4/26; Victoria, April, July and August 1913; Chibi, July 1913. N 9/4/26, vol. 2.

22 Monthly Report, Gutu, July 1913. N 9/4/26, vol. 2. The agricultural engineer was expressing his fear that 'all crops would be traded away and starvation ensue' even while traders were complaining that 'sedition mongers had forbidden all natives to trade grain'.

23 Monthly Report, Victoria, June 1913. N 9/4/26, vol. 2.

24 Monthly Report, Victoria, July 1913. N 9/4/26, vol. 2.

25 Monthly Report, Chibi, August 1913. N 9/4/26, vol. 2.

26 Monthly Report, Victoria, June 1913. N 9/4/26, vol. 2.

27 Native commissioner, Chibi, to superintendent of natives, Victoria, 19 July 1913. N 3/33/12.

28 Superintendent of natives, Bulawayo, to chief native commissioner, 27 August 1923; native commissioner, Belingwe, 3 September 1923. N 3/31/1.

29 Native commissioner, Gutu, to superintendent of natives, Victoria, 20 March 1915. N 3/14/5.

30 Native commissioner, Gutu, to superintendent of natives, Victoria, 29 March 1915. N 3/14/5.

31 Monthly Report, Victoria, March 1915. N 9/4/28, vol. 1.

32 Native commissioner, Gutu, to superintendent of natives, Victoria, 23 March 1915. N 3/14/5.

33 Chief native commissioner to secretary, administrator, 26 April 1915. N 3/32/1.

34 Native commissioner, Marendellas, to superintendent of natives, Salisbury, 1 November 1917. NUA 3/1/3.
35 H. Mackinnon to native commissioner, Nyamandhlovu, 28 January 1934; superintendent of natives, Bulawayo, to native commissioner, Fort Usher, 5 February 1934. S 1542 W6. This file contains a useful list of Mwari shrines and priests in 1934.
36 Assistant native commissioner, Wedza, 31 May 1944, memorandum to Native Production and Trade Commission. ZBJ 1/2/2.

References

Beach, David (1977), 'The Shona Economy: Branches of Production', in Robin Palmer and Neil Parsons (eds), *The Roots of Rural Poverty in Central and Southern Africa*, London: Heinemann.

Bhebe, Ngwabi (1979), *Christianity and Traditional Religion in Western Zimbabwe, 1859–1923*, London: Longman.

Binsbergen, W. M. J. van (1979), 'Explorations in the History and Sociology of Territorial Cults in Zambia', in Matthew Schoffeleers (ed.), *Guardians of the Land. Essays on Central African Territorial Cults*, Gwelo: Mambo Press, pp. 47–88; ch. 3 in van Binsbergen (1981).

Binsbergen, W. M. J. van (1981), *Religious Change in Zambia: Exploratory Studies*, London and Boston: Kegan Paul International.

Bond, George C. (1978), 'Religious Co-existence in Northern Zambia: Intellectualism and Materialism in Yombe Belief', *Annals of the New York Academy of Sciences*, 318 (29 December 1978): pp. 23–36.

Bond, George C. (1979), 'A Prophecy that Failed: The Lumpa Church of Unyombe, Zambia', in G. Bond, W. Johnson and S. Walker (eds), *African Christianity. Patterns of Religious Continuity*, New York: Academic Press.

Cheater, Angela (1981), 'Women and their Participation in Commercial Agricultural Production: The Case of Medium-scale Freehold in Zimbabwe', *Development and Change*, 12: pp. 349–77.

Cheater, Angela (in press), 'Formal and Informal Rights to Land in Zimbabwe's Black Freehold Areas', special issue of *Africa*.

Cobbing, Julian (1974), 'Ndebele Religion in the Nineteenth Century', seminar paper, University College, Harare, June 1974.

Comaroff, John (in press), 'Dialectical Systems, History and Anthropology: Units of Study and Questions of Theory', *Journal of Southern African Studies*.

Daneel, M. L. (1970), *The God of the Matopos Hills*, The Hague: Mouton.

Daneel, M. L. (1971), *Old and New in Southern Shona Independent Churches*, vol. I: *Background and Rise of the Major Movements*, The Hague: Mouton.

319

Junod, H. A. (1924), 'Le Mouvement de Mourimi. Un reveil au sein de l'animisme Thonga', *Journal de Psychologie*, 21: pp. 865–82.

Martin, C. J. (1980), 'Millenarianism in Africa', *Critique of Anthropology*, **15**, 4: pp. 85–93.

Mashasha, F. J. (n.d.), 'J. H. Williams, Native Commissioner of Gutu, 1897–1902', Department of History, University of Zimbabwe, Harare.

Moss, Rowland (1980), 'Ecological Constraints on Agricultural Development in Tropical Africa', paper delivered to the ASAUK Conference, Manchester, September 1980.

Mtetwa, Richard (1976), 'The Political and Economic History of the Duma People of South-eastern Rhodesia', University of Rhodesia, PhD dissertation.

Palmer, Robin (1977), 'The Agricultural History of Rhodesia', in Robin Palmer and Neil Parsons (eds), *The Roots of Rural Poverty in Central and Southern Africa*, London: Heinemann, pp. 221–54.

Phimister, Ian (1977), 'Peasant Production and Underdevelopment in Southern Rhodesia, 1890–1914, with particular reference to Victoria District', in Robin Palmer and Neil Parsons (eds), *The Roots of Rural Poverty in Central and Southern Africa*, London: Heinemann, pp. 255–67.

Ranger, T. O. (1967), *Revolt in Southern Rhodesia, 1896–1897*, London: Heinemann.

Ranger, T. O. (1970), *The African Voice in Southern Rhodesia, 1898–1930*, London: Heinemann.

Ranger, T. O. (1978), 'Growing from the Roots: Reflections on Peasant Research in Central and Southern Africa', *Journal of Southern African Studies*, **5**, 1 (October 1978): pp. 99–133.

Rennie, J. Keith (1972), 'Some Revitalization Movements among the Ndau and Inhambane Thonga, 1915–1935', Lusaka, conference paper, Conference on the History of Central African Religious Systems, July 1974.

Richards, Paul (1980), 'Ecology in African Rural Development – a Dissenting View', paper delivered to the ASAUK Conference, Manchester, September 1980.

Schoffeleers, Matthew (1978), 'A Martyr Cult as a Reflection on Changes in Production: The Case of the Lower Shire Valley, 1590–1622', in R. Buijtenhuis and P. L. Geschiere (eds), *Stratification and Class Formation, African Perspectives 1978/2*, Leiden: African Studies Centre, pp. 19–33.

Schoffeleers, Matthew (1979), Introduction, in Matthew Schoffeleers (ed.), *Guardians of the Land: Essays on Central African Territorial Cults*, Gwelo: Mambo Press, pp. 1–46.

Selous, F. C. (1881), *A Hunter's Wanderings in Africa*, London: Richard Bentley & Son.

Stayt, H. A. (1931), *The Bavenda*, London: OUP for the IAI.

Sykes, Frank W. (1897), *With Plumer in Matabeleland*, Westminster [London]: Archibald Constable & Co. (facsimile reprint 1977, Bulawayo: Books of Rhodesia).

Werbner, Richard P. (1977), 'Continuity and Policy in Southern Africa's High God Cult', in Richard P. Werbner (ed.), *Regional Cults*, London: ASA Monograph 16, pp. 179–218.

Young, Sheri (1976), 'Changes in Diet and Production in Southern Mozambique, 1855–1960', paper delivered to the ASAUK Conference, Durham, September 1976.

Young, Sheri (1977), 'Fertility and Famine: Women's Agricultural History in Southern Mozambique', in Robin Palmer and Neil Parsons (eds), *The Roots of Rural Poverty in Central and Southern Africa*, London: Heinemann, pp. 66–81.

Young, Sheri (1978), 'What have They Done with the Rain? Twentieth Century Transformations of Ceremonial Practice and Belief in Southern Mozambique', paper delivered to the American ASA Conference, November 1978.

Zachrisson, Per (1978), *An African Area in Change: Belingwe, 1894–1946*, Gothenburg: Department of History, University of Gothenburg.

Chapter 11

Dini ya Msambwa: Rural rebellion or counter-society?

Robert Buijtenhuijs

Introduction[1]

This paper has as its main aim to reopen an old and intricate debate, the one on the relationships between religious and political movements in Africa south of the Sahara, and elsewhere in the Third World. It will take as a starting-point Audrey Wipper's *Rural Rebels: A Study of Two Protest Movements in Kenya* (1977), which was praised by N. L. Smelser in the following words:

> Professor Wipper's study yields something of interest to everyone. The Africanist will find that the depth of her coverage brings to light a great deal of new historical material on a part of the world whose history is relatively untold. The methodologically-minded anthropologist will profit from her sensitive account of the difficulties in both the archive-retrieving and interviewing phases of her research, as well as the strategies by which she attempted to render these data more nearly representative and accurate. There is much in the study for the theoretically-minded as well. Early in the introductory chapter Professor Wipper lays out a number of past efforts to account for religious and political protest in colonial societies, and convincingly lays most of these to rest. . . . More important, she infuses her on-going discussion with reference to a variety of more serious theoretical formulations. (Smelser, 1977: pp. x–xi)

I entirely agree with Smelser's first two points, but I am less inclined to follow him in his judgment of Wipper's contributions to the theory of religious-political protest movements. Wipper's book does contain two very thorough and enlightening case studies of such movements, and, as far as I can see, she did get the facts and data on these movements right. However, part of the theoretical framework in which she tries to fit her cases is far from convincing, and her efforts to substantiate her general thesis lead her, in my opinion, to serious distortions of the historical facts and to a one-sided interpretation of the movements under study.

In this paper I will first discuss some of the theoretical conceptions that underlie Wipper's study and then point to some internal contradictions in her analysis, contradictions that appear at points where the facts of her field research do not match her theory. I will then try to develop a different interpretation of her two cases, and more particularly of Dini ya Msambwa, a religious-political movement which made its appearance among the Bukusu (one of the Luhya subtribes) in the remote Western Region of Kenya in the early 1940s under the leadership of Elija Masinde.

My interpretation of Dini ya Msambwa is based on a different theory about what Wipper calls 'religious-political movements', a theory I first developed in 1976 in my article '"Messianisme" et nationalisme en Afrique noire: Une remise en question' (Buijten-huijs, 1976). I will argue that millenarian or prophetic movements and political parties should not be seen as different, succeeding phases in an on-going process of political protest, as Wipper is tempted to do, but rather as different, contemporary responses to a situation that is not only characterized by political and economic oppression, but also by rapid social change and cultural anomie. In such situations, millenarian movements tend to recruit people who experience the colonial (or post-colonial) situation primarily as a period of cultural upheaval and social destruction, and they can be characterized as 'counter-societies' not aiming at the conquest of political power but trying to escape from a hostile environment. Political parties, on the contrary, tend to recruit people who react first and foremost to political and economic oppression and who attempt to conquer political power.

Phases in African protest

Right from the start, Wipper leaves no doubt as to her firm

conviction that African protest movements are of different types and that these different types belong to different historical periods:

> the major determinants of Mumbo and Msambwa in the colonial period will be delineated in order to explain not only *why these movements arose but why they took a particular form. That is, why a passive millenarian movement (Mumbo) appeared at one time and an active movement (Msambwa) at another.* . . . (Wipper, 1977: p. 2; author's italics)

Although she does not really offer a fully fledged theory of phases of political protest, and thus leaves the door open for doubts and confusion, one can discern from her analysis a sequence of at least five successive stages. The first two stages appear in her description of the cult of Mumbo which probably originated in 1913 and spread rapidly among the Gusii of South-Western Kenya between 1915 and 1920. The movement followed upon two armed uprisings, in 1905 and 1908, that were crushed by the colonial authorities. According to Wipper, there is a logical sequence between these different types of anti-colonial protest: 'Only after disastrous confrontations with modern weapons did the indigenous people change to more passive forms of resistance' (Wipper, 1977: p. 23). We thus get as the first two stages of anti-colonial protest: armed uprisings (T. O. Ranger's (1968) 'primary resistance movements') and passive millenarianism. However, passive millenarian movements, in their turn, will be followed by other types of protest, as Wipper indicates at the end of her analysis of the cult of Mumbo:

> The first challenge to colonial authority in South Nyanza came from the Mumbo movement. . . . And, although Mumboism's protest eventually fizzled out . . . still it represents the beginnings of political protest among the Gusii, the articulation of grievances, and the building of embryonic trans-tribal allegiances. (Wipper, 1977: pp. 84–5)

In order to get acquainted with the next stages of African protest, we have to move on from the case of the Gusii, and turn to Wipper's analysis of Luhya politics in general and of a new religious movement, Dini ya Msambwa, in particular:

By the end of the first decade of the twentieth century armed resistances to colonial intrusion had ended. The years from the end of World War I until 1940 saw the beginning of Luhya protest politics. . . . Converts from the Friends Africa Mission at Kaimosi organized the Luhya's first 'modern' political association, the North Kavirondo Central Association (NKCA), in 1932. It was modelled after the Kikuyu Central Association, one of the earliest and most important vehicles of Kikuyu nationalism. (Wipper, 1977: pp. 110–11)

Unfortunately, Wipper's change of focus from the Gusii to the Luhya causes some confusion, in so far as the latter ethnic group, according to the data provided by our author, never went through a phase of 'passive millenarianism'. However, the final quotation on the Mumbo movement (see below) seems to indicate that, in Wipper's thinking at least, 'modern' political associations historically form a next stage in political protest.

A further phase in African political protest is represented by the Dini ya Msambwa movement. According to Wipper:

Dini ya Msambwa represents a distinct turning point in Luhya nationalism. Previously, the Luhya had sought to remedy their grievances through reform measures. *Msambwa* combined new, revolutionary ideas with radical tactics. 'Masinde was the first nationalist', a respected leader of the community said. 'He was the first person to tell the British to get out.' (Wipper, 1977: p. 88)

Two phases thus appear in Luhya nationalism: reformist political parties, and militant prophetic movements, although Wipper makes it clear that

This chronology of responses cannot be interpreted with too much exactitude, as sometimes the second and third type responses occurred simultaneously, but it is apparent that there is a rough correlation between the type of response and the historical period. (Wipper, 1977: p. 117)

A last phase of African protest is only hinted at by Wipper in a secondary remark where she states that '*Msambwa* was a forerunner of a new era soon to emerge. Five years hence, the Kikuyu showed how increased guerilla warfare, together with more strategy and effective leadership, could bring the system to a standstill' (Wipper, 1977: p. 266).

The Mau Mau revolt is thus seen as the last phase in a series of five stages leading from primary resistance movements, through passive millenarianism and reform politics, to active prophetic movements and finally to regular guerrilla warfare. As is indicated by Wipper's terminology, religious-political movements of different types are interpreted as 'forerunners' of more politically minded movements, in the tradition of such scholars as Guiart (1951), Worsley (1957) and Balandier (1963), although Wipper does not carry her argument as far as these authors: as we have seen, she does not really make explicit her sequence of successive stages, and she never suggests that these phases also occur elsewhere in Africa.

Some comments on the case of Dini ya Msambwa

As Wipper provides us with much more material on Dini ya Msambwa than on the earlier cult of Mumbo, I will concentrate my analysis on the former case and try and check whether the reported facts on Msambwa do match the theoretical framework traced by the author. First of all, we may postulate that Wipper's hypotheses on the phases of African protest can only be validated if it can be proven that Dini ya Msambwa was a radical and active movement. Was this really the case? Up to a certain point. There is no doubt that Msambwa was openly anti-European and adopted a menacing attitude towards the colonial authorities and white settlers in the nearby Trans Nzoia Settlement Scheme:

> The Bukusu's militant tradition was resuscitated. In September 1947, about five thousand *Dini ya Msambwa* members dressed in the warrior's garb and led by Masinde made a pilgrimage to the remains of the old fort at Lugulu, the site of the 1895 battle against the British. There, Masinde paid hommage to the warriors killed in that battle, evoked the ancestors' blessings, declared war on the British, and pledged those assembled to the struggle for independence. (Wipper, 1977: p. 142)

However, by employing certain heavily loaded terms, Wipper suggests much more violence than there really was. I am particularly referring to her systematic use of the phrase 'guerilla warfare': 'in 1943 the Bukusu were free to renew their struggle against the foreigners, only this time, instead of a head-on clash, guerilla tactics would be employed' (Wipper, 1977: p. 177); 'In hitting upon guerilla warfare, Msambwa effectively disrupted the system' (p. 265). In my opinion, the real facts do not warrant the use of this terminology. Referring to the 'Chronology of Events in *Dini ya Msambwa* Career' (Wipper, 1977, Appendix G: pp. 336–46), we find that during the years 1943–55, a period of thirteen years, only thirty-eight cases of violence or violent behaviour were recorded, although it has to be noted that some of the 'events' mentioned by Wipper imply several single incidents. A breakdown[2] of these thirty-eight cases of *Msambwa* violence reveals the picture indicated in Table 11.1

Table 11.1 *Cases of Dini ya Msambwa 'violence' (1943–55)*

Verbal assaults and menaces	6
Disobedience *vis-à-vis* government orders	9
Damage to property (arson, etc.)	16
Physical assaults	7

As far as I have been able to see, in only two of these cases loss of life occurred, one of them being the Kolloa Affray in April 1950, staged by the Pokot branch of the movement, which according to Wipper 'had only a slight connection with the main body . . . it is doubtful if the main leaders had any but the barest knowledge of its existence' (Wipper, 1977: p. 209).

For a 'guerrilla movement', this is rather a poor show. We can therefore safely conclude that this term is not appropriate in the context of Dini ya Msambwa. In fact, during all the years it was active, the movement never made use of firearms – although Masinde at least once exhorted the Bukusu to make guns to drive the Europeans out (Wipper, 1977: p. 160) – and only rarely of traditional weapons such as spears or pangas. There were never permanent or even occasional combat groups and the Msambwa leaders never contemplated creating such guerrilla bands. As a matter of fact, Wipper admits this in the few lines where she compares Msambwa behaviour to Mau Mau violence:

one needs to carefully distinguish between different kinds of violence. Msambwa used violence primarily against foreign property, state property, mission property, and the settlers' personal property. It threatened violence against the mission-aries and settlers but there is little to record there. Its members attacked chiefs with their fists, spontaneously and openly, in contrast to Mau Mau's planned, secretive and murderous attacks. (Wipper, 1977: p. 194)

By using terms such as 'guerrilla warfare', Wipper thus suggests much more violence and radicalism than there really was, and I have a strong feeling that she has been induced to employ this terminology mainly because it fitted well with her theoretical framework.

One can question another alleged trait of Dini ya Msambwa. When classifying Masinde's cult, Wipper, in order to validate her theory, has to characterize the movement as 'active millenarian-ism'. However, her own data are there to show that the real situation was much more complex than she wants to admit in the theoretical part of her study:

Joasch Walumoli, the prophet, also vouched that Msambwa wanted peace and, unlike Mau Mau, did not kill people. Even Doniso Nakimayu, an admitted arsonist, maintained that Msambwa's tactic had emphasized prayer and forbade killing. In fact, so convinced were some members of the power of prayer that they took credit for achieving independence, arguing that it was their prayers rather than the Mau Mau insurrection that really brought it. .... This raises the question of how widespread the belief in non-violence was? Did those who opted for it also believe in a millennium and rely heavily upon supernatural means? There is evidence in the stories of Masinde's exploits that magical solutions had a wide appeal. Jean La Fontaine noted that the members believed 'their sacrifices and ceremonies would be enough to wipe out Europeans and the troubles of their country with a flow of supernatural blood falling from the sky'. It could be, that in the early stages, prayers alone were thought to be sufficient and that only later after their ineffectiveness had been demon-strated did members turn to militancy. (Wipper, 1977: pp. 193–4)

Msambwa's option for violence and activism is thus less clear-cut than Wipper would like it to be. Her final suggestion that there may have been different phases in the evolution of the movement is, moreover, invalidated by the fact that even after the Mau Mau revolt 'some members' were still convinced that their prayers did more to bring independence than guerrilla warfare. At the end of her study Wipper does indeed admit that 'it should not be assumed that the ritual versus action orientation was ever finally settled, but rather the two remained in an uneasy relationship shifting in importance with the circumstances' (Wipper, 1977: p. 300). We can therefore conclude that Msambwa is a rather complex and ambiguous movement, using violence, but only occasionally, and believing in the virtues of prayer and supernatural intervention at least as much as in action and militancy. However, Wipper tends to neglect the 'pacifist' side of Msambwa and stresses its radical and active side as soon as her underlying theory invites her to do so.

At another point, again, Wipper does not fully take into account the complexity and the many-sidedness of the religious-political configuration in Western Kenya during the colonial period. She suggests, without making this sufficiently clear, that reformist political parties, such as the NKCA, should be considered as a further stage of political protest after the fizzling out of passive millenarian movements such as the cult of Mumbo, and that active millenarianism represents the next stage in time. However, concurrently with Dini ya Msambwa, a purely political movement operated in Bukusu-land: the Bukusu Union, founded in 1940 by Pascal Nabwana who had earlier been the leader of the Kitosh Education Society which he had created in 1935. Unfortunately, Wipper is rather confused as to the exact relationship between this body and Msambwa, a confusion that seems to stem partly from the facts:

> The administration found it difficult on a number of occasions to decide whether Msambwa or the Bukusu Union were responsible for particular incidents. A number of administrators felt that the Union was Msambwa in a different guise, that the names were used interchangeably, or that the Union was a branch of the Kenya African Union. (Wipper, 1977: p. 170)

329

Wipper's own analysis of the Bukusu Union is in a similar vein:

> On the relationship between Msambwa and the Bukusu Union
> there has been much speculation. Both originated about the
> same time among the same people and their membership, in
> part, overlapped. Our investigation has revealed a number of
> parallels between the Bukusu Union and *Dini ya Msambwa*.
> They protested many of the same grievances, were not all that
> different in their tactics, and were led by men from the same
> generation and background with a few participating in both. . . .
> The Bukusu Union and *Dini ya Msambwa* were alternate
> responses to the same grievances. The Union was more in line
> with modern political associations, while Msambwa maintained
> stronger links with traditional symbols. Nabwana himself ack-
> nowledged that the Union lost many members to Msambwa. . . .
> In this transition period between old and new forms, Msambwa's
> message had a special appeal to the uneducated. (Wipper, 1977:
> pp. 188–91)

The trouble is, first of all, that Wipper does not pay sufficient
attention to the Bukusu Union generally and, more particularly,
that she fails to compare the recruitment patterns and the
catchment areas of the Union and Dini ya Msambwa. Later, I will
come back to the question of who joined which organization and
why. Furthermore, Wipper does not really attempt to fit the
Bukusu Union into her scheme of successive stages of African
protest. Does the Union still belong to the phase of reformist
associations such as the earlier NKCA? Probably not, for Wipper
herself states that Msambwa and the Union 'were not all that
different in their tactics'; anyway, if this were her interpretation,
then we may suppose that she would at least have tried to explain
the belated appearance of the Bukusu Union and its unexpected
intrusion into a more militant phase of African protest. Hence we
are led to believe that the Union belongs to the same phase as
Msambwa in which case, failing to be a millenarian movement, it
should at least have been an active and radical association. This
again is doubtful. As far as I can make out, the Bukusu Union has
always been of moderate disposition, given to constitutional and
petitionist politics, and certainly less radical than the Kikuyu and
Nairobi branches of the Kenya African Union with which it had a

few links. J. J. de Wolf (1977: p. 191) described the Bukusu Union in the following words:

> Factions are led by leaders who have a contractual relationship with their followers. The kinds of benefits which are offered may vary a great deal for different followers. But in the case of Pascal Nabwana and his Bukusu Union the communal aim was expansion of education.

Undoubtedly a laudable aim, but without any inherent radical or activist connotations. In other words, Wipper again tries to interpret the facts one-sidedly in order to bend them to the requirements of her theoretical framework. Moreover, she does not make clear why, in some cases, political movements and millenarian cults operate simultaneously, instead of succeeding each other according to different phases as they should do in theory.

At yet another point, Wipper has difficulties in matching her hypotheses with the historical facts. When analysing African religious-political movements in general, she begins by stating that 'During the colonial period, these movements were often interpreted as pre-nationalistic or as primitive forms of protest' (Wipper, 1977: p. 5). She then questions this hypothesis in the following words:

> Few would argue that there has not been a close association in Africa between these rural-based movements and the development of modern nationalism. But if colonial oppression was their *raison d'être* one would expect that independence would witness the end of these movements or, at the most, the survival of a few with a drastically changed orientation. Far from dying out, however, these movements have flourished. Obviously explanations which gave primacy to nationalistic aspirations have not told the full story. (Wipper, 1977: pp. 56)

I entirely agree with these remarks. However, when it comes to the particular case of Dini ya Msambwa, we find to our surprise that Wipper does not tell 'the full story' either. Thus, in chapter 16, devoted to Msambwa's evolution during the post-colonial period, she states that 'With the removal of the British administrators and with the missionaries staying on at the request of an

African government, *Dini ya Msambwa, left without a major cause*, engaged in a number of *disruptive activities*' (Wipper, 1977: p. 271; my italics).

Apparently, Msambwa's major project during the first years of independence consisted in the establishment of independent schools. As these schools were illegal, they had to be closed down. Masinde himself went on defying the authorities wherever he could, just as he had done before independence. But, in contrast to earlier chapters in which Wipper speaks rather positively of the Bukusu prophet, she now uses the same strongly negative and moralistic terms as colonial administrators had employed a few years earlier. She also postulates that 'during the colonial period *Msambwa*'s protest was based on legitimate grievances' (Wipper, 1977: p. 284), implying that after independence the movement's grievances were no longer thus based. She concludes the chapter dealing with these developments by saying:

> Only a few years earlier, the idea of a millennium had been equated with independence. Now that that dream had been shattered, another millennium was in view. . . . From the view-point of the government, Masinde was an anachronism, his protest belonged to a past era. (Wipper, 1977: pp. 286–8)

In other words, Dini ya Msambwa is reduced to an expression of purely nationalist protest. It is again her theory on successive phases in African protest that induces Dr Wipper to distort the facts and to deny any positive meaning to Msambwa activities after independence. G. S. Were, a Kenyan historian, already offered an alternative and tried to come to an alternative explanation of Msambwa's survival after 1963:

> Clearly the D.Y.M.]Dini ya Msambwa] protest does not exclusively belong to a past age. Neither are Africans 'concerned with different problems' now that independence has come. Looking at some of the activities and aims of D.Y.M. it is apparent that political independence has never been regarded as an end in itself but rather as a means to an end. (Were, 1972: p. 86)

Dr Were then pursues this idea by saying that leading Msambwa members, in 1946 and 1947, criticized Asian employers in their home area for underpaying and overworking their employees:

Today of course, trade unions have taken up the struggle once partly championed by D.Y.M., with varying degrees of success. This is why it was pointed out earlier that Dr. Wipper erred when she said that Elijah's protest 'belonged to a past era'. To a large extent the social grievances which they highlighted are still with us. (Were, 1972: p. 95)

The independent schools that were managed by the movement around 1964 are also quoted by Were to confirm his thesis:

Clearly D.Y.M. schools were started to meet a basic and genuine need. Apparently this need was not being met by the existing schools where one has to pay for one's children's education . . . the D.Y.M. officials believed in the practical desirability of 'Free Education'. (Were, 1972: p. 96)

Were thus tends to interpret Dini ya Msambwa as a political (and revolutionary) movement which solves the problem of its continuing activities after independence and certainly has a more logical ring than Wipper's rather confused analysis. However, Were's hypothesis does not account for the religious and millenarian dimension of the movement, because if Msambwa members were social revolutionaries, then one can legitimately ask *why they did not found a purely political party instead of a millenarian movement*, however 'active'. In order to answer this question, I will now try to develop a different interpretation of religious protest movements and their relations with purely political movements.

Millenarian movements as counter-societies

The most important and the most puzzling questions that I will try to answer are these: is there any sequence in types of religious and political protest, as is suggested by Wipper for the case of Western Kenya, and: do 'millenarian' movements have to be considered as 'forerunners' of nationalism as has been argued by scholars such as Guiart, Worsley and Balandier?

In order to throw some light on this set of problems, I will first refer to the classical distinction between Ethiopian and Zionist movements which was originally introduced by Sundkler in his pioneer study *Bantu Prophets* (first published in 1948). 'As Ethiopians', says Sundkler (1961: p. 53), 'I classify such independent Bantu Churches that have (a) seceded from White Mission Churches chiefly on racial grounds, or (b) othèr Bantu Churches seceding from the Bantu leaders classified under (a).' Zionist churches, on the contrary, are founded by prophets claiming to have received a revelation from the Holy Spirit. They have no direct links with missionary churches and many of their members never passed through these churches but are converts from traditional African religions. G. Balandier has summed up Sundkler's analysis in the following words:

> L'église dite éthiopienne reste très marquée par l'organisation et l'enseignement des missions chrétiennes dont elle s'est détachée; elle limite le plus possible la contamination par les apports sacrés traditionnels (redoutant d'apparaître comme une institution rétrograde) et fait un réel effort d'enseignement. L'église de type sioniste, plus instable et plus menacée par les sécessions . . . attire dans la mesure même où elle se veut syncrétique, et en raison de la marge de liberté qu'elle concède aux fidèles. Le prêtre se conforme . . . à des modèles traditionnels, mais c'est le caractère prophétique qui domine en lui: il est plus proche du devin, du guérisseur, du chasseur de sorciers . . . que du chef tribal. . . . L'attrait de ces sectes réside en partie dans le fait qu'elles laissent une place incontestée à l'imagination et à la spontanéité. . . . A l'encontre du formalisme et de la discipline imposés par les missions, les églises sionistes assurent un retour aux manières authentiquement africaines de prier et de manifester sa ferveur. (Balandier, 1963: pp. 423–4)[3]

Another typology of religious-political movements was introduced by J. W. Fernandez who makes a distinction between instrumental-type movements and expressive movements. Although Fernandez emphasizes other distinctive signs than Sundkler, I believe that his typology, in its main lines, falls in line with Sundkler's Ethiopian-Zionist dichotomy:

> An instrumental type of religious movement chooses the elements for symbolic use in a realistic and goal-minded fashion and with a view to perpetuating them under existing circumstances. We find fairly pragmatic attempts to compensate for

the deprivation and other frustrations involved in the situation of subordination, without endangering the continuity and survival of the religious group. . . . In an expressive movement there is no calculated attempt to deal with a difficult situation directly. . . . Intense involvement of the participants in [ritual and ceremonial] activities draws their attention away from the frustrations and deprivations of their everyday situation. . . . Their leaders are preoccupied with internal concerns and not with representing the group to the larger situation of which it is part. . . . In all cases these movements exhibit an unrealistic reliance on their ability to create and constitute their own universe through expressive symbolism. (Fernandez, 1964: pp. 535–6)

Of course, clear-cut distinctions established on paper will not always be found in the same form in the field; also, these categories are definitely not to be considered as immutable entities. Sundkler and Fernandez both emphasize that evolution takes place and that a particular movement can change to such an extent that it passes from one category to the other. However, the distinction between 'instrumental-type' Ethiopian churches and 'expressive' Zionist movements, although rather old-fashioned, is useful in the context of my argument because both types of movements do not maintain the same relations with nationalist parties or with more general political movements.

Generally speaking, Ethiopian churches are still very much influenced by the organizational patterns and by the teachings of the Christian missionary churches from which they broke away; neither in the field of theology and liturgy, nor in the field of the organization of the community of believers are they given to daring innovations. F. B. Welbourn is therefore right in character-izing his *East African Rebels* as a study of 'Christian rebels, of men who, for one reason or another, have tried to change the personnel of the particular Christian society which they knew' (Welbourn, 1961: p. 5).[4] In a later book written in collaboration with B. A. Ogot, Welbourn develops this line of thinking in his analysis of the 'Ethiopian' Church of Africa in Kenya:

The Church of Africa is, at least in the minds of its leaders, an attempt to reform the Anglican Church in Africa in much the same way as the English thought it necessary, in the sixteenth

335

century, to reform the Church of Rome. They think of being the universal church in Africa in much the same way as the Church of England claimed to be the universal church in England. (Welbourn and Ogot, 1966: p. 4)

In this desire to change only the leading personnel, in their intention to take the conduct of their affairs into their own hands, while leaving the essential characteristics of the colonial heritage untouched, the Ethiopian churches are quite similar to the moderate nationalist parties that came into power in most parts of Africa during the early 1960s. Co-operation between both is possible and certainly not incompatible with the deeper nature of the Ethiopian churches, but, while there are, in fact, several examples of such co-operation (Kenya, Uganda), these relations are not inevitable and do not develop in all cases. Moreover, they do not follow a fixed historical sequence in the sense that Ethiopian churches are necessarily 'forerunners' of nationalist parties. They sometimes are, but there are cases where purely political movements precede and ultimately give birth to independent churches of the Ethiopian type, as happened in the case of the Kikuyu where political agitation developed as early as 1920 and where it took almost ten years before a political party (the Kikuyu Central Association) gave birth to religious associations.[5]

In order to arrive at a better understanding of the political and social meaning of Zionist churches, I will now refer to a typology of revolutionary phenomena introduced by J. Baechler. Part of his analysis – namely the distinction between 'revolutions' and 'counter-societies' – is directly relevant to our purpose. In Baechler's typology, which, for lack of space, I can only reproduce here in a very schematic form, 'revolutions' correspond to the particular category of protest movements that aim at the conquest of power and that do succeed in this reaching for power (Baechler, 1970: p. 59). Nationalist parties belong to this category, as do, in my opinion, Ethiopian churches in the field of religion. Counter-societies, in the typology of Baechler, may initially aim at the conquest of power, but without possessing the objective means necessary to this goal. Therefore, they are tempted to form 'alternative' societies which are based on values antagonistic to those currently accepted, and which reject the global society as a whole (Baechler, 1970: p. 59).

Ce qui permet de les distinguer des révolutions est la faiblesse des moyens mis en oeuvre pour conquérir la société globale, c'est-à-dire, pour aller droit à l'essentiel, leur incapacité politique ou leur indifférence envers la politique. On ne note jamais une analyse rationelle du rapport des forces, ni la construction d'une stratégie efficace pour conquérir le pouvoir. [Cela] . . . nous permet d'opérer une distinction . . . entre deux grands sous-types. Le premier, que l'on nommera escapisme ou fuite sociale, consiste en la création de communautés coupées de la société globale et qui ne visent à l'investir que par l'influence de leur example, dans le cas le plus ambitieux. Le deuxième, agressif et conflictuel, entre nécessairement en guerre active avec l'ordre qu'il menace et qui se défend en attaquant. (Baechler, 1970: pp. 82–3)[6]

It is my hypothesis that Zionist churches correspond to Baechler's definition of counter-societies and more particularly to that of the first category, escapism or retreatism, although Baechler himself tends to bring religious sects and millenarian movements under the second heading. First, Zionist churches do not aim at conquering state power within the global society. They have no political strategy or analysis and they do not correctly perceive the real mechanisms of colonial domination or political exploitation in general. Their leaders and followers are often convinced that the secret of the white man's power is to be sought in his being in possession of a special magical device as, for example, the first (or the last) page of the Bible, which they conceal from African believers. Second, the solution of the adherents' frustrations and problems is sought in the field of religion and supposed to be brought by way of a miracle or God's (or the ancestors') intervention.

These movements, then, do not search political power and do not aim at the conquest of the global society. They rather tend towards escapism and entertain only a minimum of relations with the outside world. Sundkler (1961: p. 95), for example, claims that

The Zionists stand out as a separate community in Zululand, as a *tertium genus*, a third race, over against both the heathen and the Christian community. . . . They . . . are not easily assimilated to the rest of the Zulu community. . . . Zionists do not eat with other men who, whether they are heathen or

337

Christian, are all unclean because they eat pork and therefore are 'people with demons', and so on and so forth.

Sometimes this tendency towards social escapism is pursued, spatially, to its logical conclusion, i.e. physical separation. Numerous are the New Jerusalems and New Zions where Zionist leaders have established their headquarters and where some of their followers live permanently or temporarily, as is shown, for example, by C. G. Baëta. This author claims that all the churches studied by him exhibit this tendency to create new communities functioning in some ways as kinship groups, and he quotes K. Schlosser who stated: 'Some of the new groups have developed such distinctive cultures of their own and such comprehensively efficient organizations that their members feel themselves to be new tribes' (Baëta, 1962: p. 131).

Our conclusion has to be, therefore, that political parties, being 'revolutions' in the sense of Baechler, and Zionist churches, as counter-societies, do not belong to the same order of revolutionary phenomena and that the relations, if any, between both will be uneasy. Specifically, it is difficult to believe that Zionist churches could be forerunners of nationalist movements, given the different cognitive worlds to which they belong. On the other hand, there is no systematic reason why they should not occur simultaneously.

'A place to feel at home'

If, as I have tried to show, nationalist political parties and Zionist 'churches' are autonomous phenomena that can develop concurrently in the same social context, then the question of their recruitment becomes of some interest. Do they recruit indiscriminately from the same undifferentiated mass of colonial subjects or are there certain classes or social groups that are more or less predisposed to display one or the other form of protest?

Some authors have tried to answer these questions by appealing to explanations of the class-struggle type. At the end of his study of Melanesian cargo cults, P. Worsley, for example, devotes a whole chapter to millenarian movements in human history in general; in this chapter, entitled 'A Religion of the Lower Orders', he claims that 'Millenarian beliefs have recurred again and again throughout history, despite failures, disappointments, and repression, precisely because they make such a strong appeal to the oppressed, the disinherited and the wretched' (Worsley, 1957: p. 225). As for Africa south of the Sahara, we can quote J.-P. Dozon who concludes that the distinction between Ethiopian and Zionist churches is based not only on cultural but also on social factors; movements of the first type represent the elite of the dominated society, and particularly the traditional chiefs, while the latter have a more popular following (Dozon, 1974: p. 92).

Sundkler's data (1961: p. 86) do indeed suggest such a conclusion, but at the same time a statement like Dozon's is too vague to be of much use, while some recent case studies rather suggest that the real facts are much more complex and confused. Mitchell (1970: p. 495) and Barrett (1968: p. 102) are cases in point; we could also quote Wipper who devotes several pages to the basis of support of Dini ya Msambwa and comes to the conclusion that 'it would appear that *poverty was not a major cause of radical protest among the Luhya in the reserve, except for the ex-squatters*' (Wipper, 1977: p. 227; author's italics). All we can say with some certainty about Zionist churches is that, especially during the first stages of their career, they tend to recruit their followers mainly from among the uneducated, which includes almost all rural Africans, and from amongst women. Explanations of the recruitment of Zionist movements in terms of social classes, therefore, seem to come to a deadlock, all the more so as political parties also recruit part of their following in the rural areas and amongst the urban poor.

We therefore have to search for other factors, and it seems to me that F. B. Welbourn provides us with an interesting clue at the end of his *East African Rebels* (1961: p. 201):

> It must . . . be asked whether . . . the final answer to the question, Why separatism? is not given by Sundkler when he speaks of the independent churches as attempts to form a 'church-tribe' – some place where, among the debris of the old tribal life still unassimilated to the west, Africans can *feel at home*. (author's italics)

It seems indeed that Zionist churches, and more particularly millenarian movements, are not so much expressions of political protest but are rather moved by an overwhelming drive for social and cultural reconstruction, which is after all in line with their deeper nature of counter-societies. If this is correct, we might then formulate the following hypothesis: nationalist parties tend to recruit people who experience the colonial situation first and foremost as politically and economically oppressive – they are expressions of political protest; Zionist churches recruit people who experience the colonial situation primarily as a period of cultural upheaval and social destruction – they are expressions of social and cultural protest. Zionist movements, then, are not so much the prerogative of particular social classes, but reveal situations of social disequilibrium in which the destruction of traditional socio-cultural structures is felt more painfully by particular groups in the global society than political or economic injustices.

In my opinion, this hypothesis holds not only for colonial Africa but can be applied to other historical situations. Referring to N. Cohn's study of medieval millenarian movements, Worsley says, for example:

> He has shown how, while there were heretical groups at all levels of society, it was amongst the lowest strata, particularly amongst the uprooted and disoriented peasants who had been turned into unskilled urban workers or into beggars and unemployed, that millenarian fantasies took strongest root.
> (Worsley, 1957: p. 224)

Religion of the lower orders, then, but not of the lower orders indiscriminately: the followers of the medieval millenarian movements were, moreover, socially uprooted and culturally disoriented people. Baechler's hypotheses seem to point in the same direction. This author distinguishes four 'historical situations' in which millenarian movements have flourished (Baechler, 1970: pp. 109–12). All of these are characterized not only by political and economic oppression but more particularly by a state of anomie and by the destruction of existing social and cultural structures. Such situations seem to be conducive to the thriving of zionist churches and millenarian movements in particular and of counter-societies in general.

This hypothesis does not imply that class analysis is entirely irrelevant for the understanding of millenarian movements. In so far as they represent 'religions of the lower orders' the global political and economic situation in which they thrive has to be taken into account as a first level of analysis. However, an analysis in terms of social classes or modes of production[7] is not sufficient. It does not explain why, in the same historical situation, political parties and millenarian or prophetic movements develop concurrently, and moreover recruit from amongst people of the same economic and social background. If class analysis explains everything, one wonders why people are tempted to indulge in religious movements at all, instead of limiting themselves, as some people do, to rational political movements that are sufficient, as such, to express their protest, if it were only political and economic. It is here that the counter-society hypothesis may be of use, although I admit quite frankly that much research remains to be done in order to make this concept really operational.

Dini ya Msambwa as a counter-society

To my mind, there is no doubt that Dini ya Msambwa answers to Baechler's definition of a counter-society. There is first the absence of any efficient political strategy or analysis of the current situation, and more particularly the incapability of perceiving the real mechanisms of colonial domination. J. J. de Wolf (1977: p. 181) is quite explicit on this point:

> Perhaps the best summary of [Masinde's] teachings as understood by Africans who were not themselves involved in the sect was made by David Welime: 'He levelled one strong accusation against the Europeans. He told his followers that while in Europe the Europeans had been given by God laws which were to be passed on to the Africans. On reaching the shores of Africa the missionaries and Europeans generally discovered that Africa was a land flowing with milk, honey and abundance. Consequently they forgot their mission and threw away the laws entrusted to them. Elijah Masinde went on to assert that the services of these people were no longer needed since they had perverted the original message. They had to go. . . . But members of his sect need not fear them because the bullets of their rifles would turn into drops of water. . . . Work was not considered of first importance for up in Sayoni near the crater of Mount Elgon, there was a store of food prepared for them.

We also encounter in this quotation the strong belief, current in Msambwa circles, that final victory would be obtained, not by the rational efforts of the believers, but by magical devices and divine intervention. Bullets were supposed to turn into drops of water and it was also believed that the Europeans 'would be chased away by Maina himself, the mythical ancestor of the Bukusu' (de Wolf, 1977: p. 181), or by a flow of supernatural blood falling from the sky (Wipper, 1977: p. 194). These, again, are typically counter-society convictions.

Dini ya Msambwa also exhibits to a certain extent the tendency to withdraw from the global society and to found an 'alternative' structure based on antagonistic cultural values. I am inclined to interpret the movement's efforts to establish its own schools in this sense and I also take into account that when the Kenya Government, in October 1968, banned the movement and sent its leading prophet to jail, this was because 'he had taken the law in his own hands by punishing the wife of one of his followers' (de Wolf, 1977: p. 12). Again, this is typically the behaviour of a counter-society leader.

My conclusion, therefore, is that Dini ya Msambwa is not a political protest movement, but a social and cultural protest movement. Although it may have shared *some* of the grievances of the Bukusu Union (Wipper, 1977: p. 190), it had its own grievances which were of a different nature. As for Wipper's attempt to fit the movement into a sequence of political protest movements during colonial times, I think that her efforts are futile. By interpreting Msambwa as a political, anti-colonial move-ment she has been led to distort some of the historical facts and she has had to leave many questions open. More particularly, she was unable to explain why Elijah Masinde pursued his career after independence, although he did lose part of his following. Dini ya Msambwa, contrary to Wipper's contention, did not automatically become an anachronism after 1963, because some Africans were still intensely concerned with the same problems that had given birth to the movement in the 1940s: problems of social anomie, problems of cultural disorientation, in short the urgent drive to find 'a place to feel at home' that is so characteristic of many counter-societies.

Notes

1 Thanks are due to W. M. J. van Binsbergen for his thorough and enlightening editorial comments.
2 My breakdown is based on Wipper's descriptions of Dini ya Msambwa incidents which are not always easy to interpret. It is possible that the author would have worked out slightly different figures, but unfortunately she left the counting to her readers.
3 'The so-called Ethiopian churches remain very much marked by the organization and the teachings of the Christian mission churches from which they seceded; anxious not to appear as backward institutions, they limit contamination by traditional sacred influences to an absolute minimum; moreover they make serious efforts at teaching. . . . The Zionist churches, more labile and under the constant threat of secession . . . are attractive in so far as they are inclined towards syncretism, and leave the adherents a considerable margin of freedom. The priest follows . . . traditional models, but it is his prophetic characteristics that are dominant: he is nearer to the diviner, the healer, the exorcist of witches . . . than to the tribal chief. . . . The attractiveness of these sects lies partly in the fact that they leave an undisputed place to imagination and spontaneity. . . . Contrary to the formalism and discipline imposed by the mission churches, Zionist churches allow for a return to authentically African ways of praying and manifestations of religious fervour.' (My translation. R.B.)
4 When using the term 'rebels', Welbourn, of course, refers to the distinction between 'rebellion' and 'revolution' introduced by Max Gluckman in his *Custom and Conflict in Africa* (1955).
5 For a more detailed analysis see my 1976 article; also Welbourn (1961) and Buijtenhuijs (1971).
6 'What makes it possible to distinguish them from revolutions is the ineffectiveness of the means they employ to conquer the global society, or, to come straight to the main point, their political impotence or indifference. One does not find a rational analysis of the existing power relations nor the elaboration of an efficient strategy aiming at conquering power. [This] . . . enables us to make a distinction . . . between two main subcategories. The first, which we will call escapism or retreatism, consists in the foundation of communities that are cut off from the global society and that only aim, in the most ambitious cases, at altering it through the influence of their example. The second type is aggressive and contentious, and necessarily enters into active conflict with the established order.' (My translation. R.B.)
7 For a recent attempt along such lines, see van Binsbergen (1981).

Robert Buijtenhuijs

References

Augé, M. (ed.) (1974), *La Construction du monde: Religion, représentation, idéologie*, Paris: Maspero.

Baechler, J. (1970), *Les Phénomènes révolutionnaires*, Paris: Presses Universitaires de France.

Baëta, C. G. (1962), *Prophetism in Ghana: A Study of some 'Spiritual' Churches*, London: SCM Press.

Balandier, G. (1963), *Sociologie actuelle de l'Afrique noire: Dynamique sociale en Afrique Centrale*, 2nd edn, Paris: Presses Universitaires de France.

Barrett, D. B. (1968), *Schism and Renewal in Africa: An Analysis of Six Thousand Contemporary Religious Movements*, Nairobi: Oxford University Press.

Binsbergen, W. M. J. van (1981), *Religious Change in Zambia: Exploratory Studies*, London: Kegan Paul International.

Binsbergen, W. M. J. van and Buijtenhuijs, R. (eds) (1976), *Religious Innovation in Modern African Society, African Perspectives 1976/2*, Leiden: African Studies Centre.

Buijtenhuijs, R. (1971), *Le Movement 'mau mau': une révolte paysanne et anti-coloniale en Afrique noire*, The Hague and Paris: Mouton.

Buijtenhuijs, R. (1976), '"Messianisme" et nationalisme en Afrique noire: Une remise en question', in W. M. J. van Binsbergen and R. Buijtenhuijs (1976), pp. 25–44.

Dozon, J. -P. (1974), 'Les Mouvements politico-religieux (syncrétismes, messianismes, néo-traditionalismes)', in Augé (1974), pp. 75–111.

Fernandez, J. W. (1964), 'African Religious Movements – Types and Dynamics', *Journal of Modern African Studies*, **2**, 4: pp. 531–49.

Gluckman, M. (1955), *Custom and Conflict in Africa*, Oxford: Blackwell.

Guiart, J. (1951), 'Forerunners of Melanesian Nationalism', *Oceania*, **22**, 2 (December).

Mitchell, R. C. (1970), 'Religious Protest and Social Change: The Origins of the Aladura Movement in Western Nigeria, in Rotberg and Mazrui (1970): pp. 458–96.

Ranger, T. O. (1968), 'Connexions between "Primary Resistance Movements" and Modern Mass Nationalism in East and Central Africa', *Journal of African History*, 9: pp. 437–53, 631–41.

Rotberg, R. I., and Mazrui, A. A. (eds) (1970), *Protest and Power in Black Africa*, London: Oxford University Press.

Smelser, N. L. (1977), Preface, in Wipper (1977).

Sundkler, B. M. G. (1961), *Bantu Prophets in South Africa*, 2nd edn, London: Oxford University Press.

Welbourn, F. B. (1961), *East African Rebels: A Study of Some Independent Churches*, London: SCM Press.

Welbourn, F. B., and Ogot, B. A. (1966), *A Place to Feel at Home: A Study of Two Independent Churches in Western Kenya*, London: Oxford University Press.

Were, G. S. (1972), 'Politics, Religion and Nationalism in Western
    Kenya, 1942–1962', in B. A. Ogot (ed.), *Hadith, 4*, Nairobi: East
    African Publishing House, pp. 85–104.
Wipper, A. (1977), *Rural Rebels: A Study of Two Protest Movements in
    Kenya*, Nairobi–London–New York: Oxford University Press.
Wolf, J. J. de (1977), *Differentiation and Integration in Western Kenya: A
    Study of Religious Innovation and Social Change among the Bukusu*,
    The Hague and Paris: Mouton.
Worsley, P. (1957), *The Trumpet Shall Sound: A Study of 'Cargo' Cults in
    Melanesia*, London: MacGibbon & Kee.

Chapter 12

Prophets of God or of history? Muslim messianic movements and anti-colonialism in Senegal[1]

Christian Coulon

Introduction

The regions which make up Senegal today were the scene, in the nineteenth century and the beginning of the twentieth, of an extraordinary outburst of Islamic revival movements around leaders like El Hadj Omar in Futa-Toro and in (formerly French) Sudan, Fode Kaba in Casamance, Ma Ba Diakho in Sine-Saloum, Amadou Bamba and El Hadj Malik Sy in the Wolof lands, and Laminou Laye on the peninsula of Cap Vert. During that period a new brand of Islam took the place of an Islam that had all too often become immersed in the political power system and that seemed to have given up the idea of militant action to propagate the message of God. More aggressive and more firmly entrenched in its ideas, this new Islam was ever ready to set off on a crusade by sword and missionary action to enlarge the territory of *dar-al-Islam* (the land of Islam).

Most of these movements were strongly coloured with messianic ideologies. They grew up and developed around an inspired leader who was seen as a messenger of God. Graced with divine *baraka*, these men were not priests whose authority had been conferred on them by tradition and an established hierarchy, in the Weberian sense of the word. On the contrary, they were prophets whose authority stemmed from the sacred nature of their message and the charisma which flowed from it. A few of these men accomplished their mission through *jihad*, or holy war. This is the case with El Hadj Omar, Mamadou Lamine and Ma Ba Diakho. They were warrior-prophets of Islam. Others used more peaceful methods. They applied themselves, in Amadou Bamba's words, to 'fighting holy war with the souls of men'. These religious leaders may be called preacher-prophets. Both types of prophets, however, are at the source of contemporary Islam in Senegal. At a time when the authority of traditional African rulers was declining as a result of colonial pressure, these prophets of Islam were highly popular figures. Indeed, it is as if they had taken back the flame that the colonizer had grabbed from traditional African leaders. Consequently, it is tempting to view the militant Islamic movements they inspired as more or less direct manifestations of hostility to colonial penetration. In this line of thinking warrior-prophets and preacher-prophets would be leaders of an anti-colonialist struggle and the precursors of present-day nationalism, disguised in the trappings of religion.

Two converging hypotheses

However strange or paradoxical it may seem, this conception of Senegalese Islamic movements is shared by very divergent schools of thought. For once, both the advocates of French colonization – principally colonial administrators and historians – and those who subscribe to the decolonization of history would seem to agree on the analysis of Muslim messianic movements as resistance movements to colonization. Their opinions, however, are based on completely different premises and have completely different objectives.

To the proponents of the colonialist creed such movements are the reaction of a wild, barbarian Africa against the civilizing mission of France. Prophets are fanatic visionaries and enemies of progress, who express a primitivism that colonialism, theoretically, aims to transform. For many colonial authors messianic movements are a sort of magnifying glass that enlarges the supposed inherent deficiencies of the 'African soul'. Le Grip's (1952) study on Mahdisms in black Africa is almost a caricature of this view. From this perspective messianic movements are a threat to the order that has been conceived and imposed by whites, because they are the initiative of natives who, in the colonial ideology, should be attentive and respectful pupils and active collaborators. The prophet-marabouts, on the other hand, impede political order and administrative action. They prevent institutions from functioning

347

correctly because they are so difficult to control. Their authority does not derive from the colonizer and is entirely out of his hands, belonging in many ways to a parallel and rival power system. When this logic is pushed to its extreme, everything that moves attracts suspicion and every autonomous action smacks of agitation. French colonial administrators also feared that these religious innovations were a cover-up for political schemes. The result was a psychosis of Mahdism that led them to consider any religious fanatic as a prospective national prophet, and a fear of pan-Islamic ideologies that led them to look upon any militant Islamic movement as an integral link in the chain of conspiracy that was working to destroy Western civilization. One must not forget, either, that the 'threat' of messianic movements often also served as a pretext for actions aimed at imposing or strengthening colonial authority. Faidherbe, the great architect of colonial Senegal, was, not surprisingly, the principal champion of this interpretation because it enabled him to conquer and pacify new territories (Faidherbe, 1889; Saint-Martin, 1968; 1970). Finally, the hostility of the French colonial administration towards these messianic movements was to a great extent encouraged by African chiefs and marabouts of the older form of Islam who felt that their authority and prestige was threatened by the popularity of the warrior- and the preacher-prophets. Colonial chiefs, for instance, played a major role in convincing the administration that Amadou Bamba, the founder of the Murid Brotherhood, was the power behind an anti-French plot; and Bamba was exiled to Gabon in 1895 at their request.

All these reasons justified the policy of the French colonial office concerning these movements. It was a policy of systematic suspicion and selective, though harsh, acts of intervention and repression. That policy did not exclude the occasional bending of principles to fit circumstances, or the occasional attempt to bribe the leaders of such movements. Nevertheless, when the first Mahdis appeared, French authorities were seriously worried and did everything they could to favour an official Islam, which they identified with the established brotherhoods whose political support could be counted on and whose leaders could serve as auxiliary agents of colonization.

The premises of the advocates of the nationalist thesis are the exact opposite of those of the colonialist thesis, even if they reach similar conclusions. From their viewpoint, the actions of the prophets are glorious deeds and proof of Africa's ability to resist imperialism. Charismatic marabouts are not obstacles to civilization but freedom fighters, and the successive strategies of this militant Islam are stages in a struggle that is ultimately to end in emancipation. This mythology of nationalism is built on the affirmation of a historical continuity which proves that African peoples have never ceased struggling, in one form or another, against foreign oppression. In this perspective, the greatest glory of the prophet-marabouts was not so much their crusade against paganism as their hatred of colonialism and their willingness to suffer martyrdom for the sake of political freedom.

There is a whole body of popular epic literature that presents the story of the great Senegalese marabouts from this angle. One of the most famous in this genre is a brochure by Mohamed Moustapha Hane entitled *Les Trois Grandes Figures de l'Islam en Afrique*. It is a panegyrical retracing of the lives of El Hadj Omar, Amadou Bamba and El Hadj Malik Sy, three men whose religious and political missions, according to the author, were inseparable. To him, El Hadj Omar was 'a national hero who fought to rid his country of immoral colonialism, and who never sought the friendship of the white man on any account'. As for Shaykh Amadou Bamba, French authorities were right to beware of him, for 'he never hid for a moment his hatred of colonialism and he never ceased opposing it'. Again, El Hadj Malik Sy was forced to leave his village and move to Saint Louis in order not 'to be exposed to the fickleness of the French colonialists'. In short, all these 'saints' easily find a niche in the pantheon of resistance as the founding fathers of national liberation, since they were guided by a 'violent hatred of colonialism in all its forms, and of the exploitation of man by man'.

This interpretation, it should be noted, is not too different from the official version that the Senegalese president and government officials give in their speeches, particularly those made at the religious ceremonies where they are often guests of honour. It is also the interpretation of the leaders of Muslim brotherhoods, many of which are directly linked with these prophets. Thus both the political and the religious leaders claim to be the moral heirs of the great Muslim leaders of the past. But if colonial administrators saw the shadow of pan-Islamism lurking behind these messianic movements, contemporary political and religious leaders perceive them rather as manifestations of a strong African or ethnic personality, able to stand up not only to the West but also to the Arab world. A strictly anti-colonial interpretation has now gradually given way to a more nationalist interpretation. Muridism, in particular, is viewed as the ancestor of Negritude – as Leopold Senghor likes to underline – due to the way it adapted itself to African, and more especially Wolof, values.

These arguments have also been taken up, albeit in a more refined form, by a whole school of academic thought. In the same way that some authors have pointed out the proto-nationalistic character of Christian messianic movements, others have explained the messianic movements in Muslim Africa at the time of colonization as more or less direct forms of anti-colonial sentiment.

For authors like Balandier, Islam and colonialism are naturally antagonistic. 'As a religion to which the colonized and the colonizer cannot both be committed', writes Balandier, 'Islam is itself the sign of a fundamental process of differentiation and an instrument of opposition' (Balandier, 1970: pp. 484–5). And Mahdism would be an exaggerated form of this antagonism in a situation of crisis and conflict. For this school of thought, messianic movements are profoundly political phenomena despite their outward religious appearance. For some authors they constitute 'pre-nationalisms' (Hodgkin, 1962), for others they are 'proto-nationalisms' (Oloruntimehim, 1968) or even 'sacred nationalisms' (Cruise O'Brien, 1971). These movements are responses to colonialism in forms which correspond to the evolutionary stage of their society. For those who carry this view to the extreme, the religious element is more than mere language which expresses, in a confused manner, global aspirations. Rather, religion is a mask that the national hero puts on in order to revolt against the white man. The studies of Oloruntimehim (1968) and Nyambarza (1969) on Mamadou Lamine, the Sarakholle prophet, are good examples of this type of interpretation.

As for Senegalese messianic movements, however, the above interpretation is far from meeting with the scholarly consensus, and in the past few years a debate has arisen on these points. In order to contribute meaningfully to the advancement of research in this field, it is important to beware of myths which serve to justify pre-existing opinions or which constitute dangerous over-simplifications.

The advocates of the colonialist thesis, for example, remind one of the narrow-minded conqueror who invents enemies, consciously or not, in order to legitimize his actions, and who is so concerned about maintaining order and domination that he considers any movement that he does not control as a sign of revolt. Advocates of the nationalist thesis, on the other hand, are guilty of the sin of teleology, of inventing an interpretation which conforms to preconceived ideas. Even if one admits the necessity of offering a reading of African history that does justice to the dynamic nature of African societies, the nationalist thesis tends to ignore the uniqueness of the historical conditions that produced messianic movements.

In order to avoid these inconveniences, it is necessary to adopt a step-by-step analysis which allows us to take into consideration not only the complexities but also the contradictions of Senegalese messianic movements. The first task is to examine the discourse of the messiahs and the ideology of their movements. Before letting History talk one must know what its protagonists say. On the basis of this evidence we may then ask what the meaning of these movements is for society as a whole, and what type of answer they provide for the problems of a society at a given point in time. Finally, we will consider the evolution of these movements so as to place them in the perspective of contemporary nationalism.

One united nation: the Muslim community (Umma)

The ideology of messianic movements cannot be analysed without taking into account the religious mission of their leaders. Even if one admits that their ideology reveals more general aspirations and can function as a political discourse, particularly in 'non-secular' societies, the focal point of these movements remains essentially religious. It is religion that moulds the action of the prophet and of his followers. One need only read the works of El Hadj Omar or of Amadou Bamba to be convinced of this. Many historians and sociologists, however, skip over this material and only read colonial archives which are more directly oriented towards political issues than the study of religious ideologies.

The prophets were, above all, messengers of God whose task was to propagate his word and to give new life to Muslim communities. Their mission was two-fold: to carry Islam to pagan peoples and to purify the practices of existing believers. In their mind, this was only possible if Islam rediscovered its militant character from which the 'hypocrites' with their temporal ambitions had turned away. It was necessary, therefore, to combat these erring Muslim leaders or, at the very least, prevent them from doing any harm. The vital objective for the prophets was, therefore, to substitute an authentic Islamic leadership for the political authority of those who were inclined to compromise and adaptation. The era of the *shaykhs*, or inspired and vigilant guides, was to replace the era of chieftainships and local elites.

From this perspective it is easier to understand the lack of enthusiasm, and even the prophet's contempt of political power and its holders. For a preacher-prophet like Amadou Bamba this attitude took the form of a concern to remain distant from political authorities.

> Move into the antechamber of the authorities, they said to me, and you will obtain offerings that will enrich you all your life. I answered: My God is enough for me; I need only him; I desire nothing more than knowledge and religion. I fear no one except my King; I place my hope in no one except my Master, for it is He, the August One, who can enrich me and save me. (quoted by Samb, 1972: p. 478)

For the warrior-prophets, the leaders of *jihad*, the indifference to temporal authority took a more active form. 'I have never kept company with kings,' said El Hadj Omar, 'and I don't like those who do' (quoted by Dumont, 1974: p. 216). These are surprising words coming from the mouth of a warrior chief, but it is not possible to understand El Hadj Omar's project by looking only at his temporal interests, as Faidherbe did. El Hadj Omar's holy war was aimed at maintaining

> an orthodox religion and extending Islam; and its inseparable corollary was the breaking up of ethnic groups, the destruction of local sultanships and the setting up of a bigger ideal-based community, identified by adherence to Islam, in which religious ties would replace blood ties and eliminate the need for political ties. (Dumont, 1974: p. 205)

This interpretation alone can explain the obsession of the Tukolar prophet to be constantly on the move, never to settle anywhere and to be involved in a seemingly unending combat. The tragedy of El Hadj Omar was not only that he had to cope with the colonizer, but that he was never able to find the political structures that could adequately accommodate his idea of religious dominance. The nature of his mission itself made the task hopeless. El Hadj Omar was a wandering knight of Islam rather than an empire-builder.

The first ambition of the prophets of Islam was thus to build a Muslim community which transcended ethnic, clan or political divisions. Consequently, the only nation that they recognized was Umma, the nation of Islam. The pan-Islamic orientation of Muslim messianic movements points up the inadequacy of analyses that see the action of these prophets as an affirmation of an ethnic or African personality. The charismatic marabouts never really pretended to defend the cause of an African personality. This idea was far from the centre of their concerns. One can, at the very most, find here and there in their writings a few sentences about the desire to be accepted, as Africans, on the same footing as other men of letters in the world of Islam (cf. the saga of El Hadj Omar and the learned men of Al-Azhar). 'Black skin', wrote Amadou Bamba 'is not [necessarily] to be equated with stupidity and lack of intelligence' (quoted by Dumont, 1975: p. 226). Pride in their Africanness was more a sign of their concern to be recognized and to have a legitimate existence for Arab Islam than of a desire to set up an autonomous Islam in the name of black nationalism. The prophets of Islam in Senegal were perfectly orthodox Muslims and their teachings could in no way be called syncretic or schismatic. They were definitely not the promoters of an African Islam. Their eyes were turned to Mecca and to the great Islamic centres of the Arab world. Many paid long visits to these places and sought the official blessing of the most prestigious religious leaders and heads of brotherhoods. Many of these prophets also claimed descent from Muhammad or his disciples.

It is true that some of these men, like Amadou Bamba or Laminou Laye, founded national brotherhoods, but that is more the result of special circumstances (e.g. problems of communication with the Arab world and the need to make their missionary action more effective) than of a desire to nationalize Islam. In any case, the Arab legacy was never questioned. The concept of African independence in the midst of Islam was unthinkable for the marabouts who, on the contrary, constantly tried to break down the barriers of isolation so as to internationalize their faith. That does not mean, of course, that Islam did not become adapted to an African social and cultural context, but such a phenomenon is inherent in any religion, independently of the will of its leaders.

The Islam of the Senegalese prophets is no more African than it is ethnic in nature. These marabouts took advantage from time to time of ethnic ties in their own areas of origin, but ethnic consciousness was never an element in these movements. Membership in ethnic groups had meaning only as a support structure for a Muslim plan, and the only traditions of the ethnic groups that the prophets adhered to were those that were linked to Islam. Thus, for El Hadj Omar, if the Tukolars had a historical mission, it was to propagate and purify Islam as their ancestors had done. He spoke to his compatriots in these terms: 'Oh, people of Toro, forsake your sins and return to God; rediscover your heritage, the legacy of the past: the waging of an eternal and incessant holy war against the enemy of God' (quoted by Kamara, 1970: p. 794). This is where religious heritage and ethnic heritage become one. But as Saint-Martin noted, there is no ethnic exclusiveness in El Hadj Omar: 'One need not forsake one's people in converting to the Muslim faith and following the *Tidjani wird*.' El Hadj Omar did not hesitate to place important responsibilities on the shoulders of Malinké, Fulbe, Wolof or Bambara *taalibe* (disciples) (Saint-Martin, 1970: p. 173). The same thing can be said of Mamadou Lamine, the Sarakholle prophet. Abdoulaye Bathily wrote that 'he greatly loved his ethnic group and the region of his birth. . . . he cherished them and looked upon them through the mirror of his qur'anic faith. . . .' But 'his feelings,' he added, 'far from being ethnic and tribal were social and religious in nature' (Bathily, 1970: p. 29). In the final analysis, then, the prophets' mission was essentially religious, and the only nation they fought for was Islam. None the less, this religious conviction came face to face with European imperialism and had to find means of coping with it.

The prophet and the colonizer: resistance or escapism?

To understand the real nature of the relationship between the Senegalese prophets and the French we must realize that to the former the French were above all *Christians*, that is, 'people of the Book' (Ahl-al-Kitab). In classical Muslim theory, to which the prophets claimed to adhere, Christians, like Jews, have a special status in the Umma. They are protected peoples (*dhimmis*) who may keep their faith by paying tribute (*jizya*). That explains why the prophets could agree to the Christians' being present in the territory of Islam and carrying out commercial activities. This tolerance, however, had its limits and seemed incompatible with any idea of colonization of the land of Islam by Christians. 'The Whites', El Hadj Omar is claimed to have said, 'are just merchants. When I become Lord of the Blacks and the Whites bring in goods in their boats, I will live in peace with them if they pay a heavy duty. But I don't want them to erect buildings on the land or send war boats up the river' (Carrere and Holle, 1855: p. 204). The French, however, could not agree indefinitely to such an inferior status, and a clash with the militant forces of Islam seemed ultimately inevitable. But the prophets were able to avoid a head-on collision with the colonizer, and doctrinal purity did not prevent them from seeing political realities and adapting themselves to circumstances.

The warrior-prophets knew they could not win a war against the French. However idealistic they were, they knew the balance of power was against them. El Hadj Omar was the first to give up the idea of fighting the French and 'throwing them into the ocean'. He preferred to avoid them by emigrating to the east where they had not yet penetrated, and he asked his compatriots of the Futa-Toro to follow him in his *hejira*, just as Muhammad had chosen to leave for Medina when confronted with the hostility of the people of Mecca. As El Hadj Omar explained in his *Rimah*, 'the *hejira* is a necessity for those who find themselves in a land where transgression is openly practised and who are unable to change the situation' (quoted by Willis, 1970: p. 128). After that, El Hadj Omar directed his energies more to the struggle against pagans and hypocritical Muslims than to fighting the Europeans, and there were many more diplomatic contacts with the latter than military encounters (cf. Saint-Martin, 1970). His famous declaration of war against the French in 1855 was above all an act of propaganda aimed at accelerating emigration, and his threats were never meant to be carried out.

If one looks at overt acts of hostility it turns out that El Hadj Omar's main enemies were not so much the French as the Bambara and the Fulbe. The clash with French troops only occurred many years after the death of the Tukolar prophet when the colonizer could no longer tolerate a half-religious, half-political entity, headed by El Hadj Omar's son, Ahmadou, at the edges of its territory.

El Hadj Omar's case was not the only one of its sort. Most of the other warrior-prophets acted in a similar fashion and did not hesitate to request the help of the French in order to eradicate their African enemies. For example, when Mamadou Lamine set off on his *jihad* in 1896, his intention was not to combat the French but to convert the pagans of the Gamu to Islam, and he reassured the governor of Senegal in these words: 'Let it be known that I have many other enemies besides the French. The unfaithful are legion. I cannot war against all of them and the French as well' (quoted by Nyambarza, 1969: p. 142). His plan was to set up Islamic centres in the east where Muslims could live according to their faith, outside the sphere of Christian influence but not on hostile terms with them. But due to the colonial expansion such experiments were not to last, for colonialism's own messianic aims could not tolerate the existence of independent qur'anic communities. The warrior-prophets were therefore not in any sense destroyers of colonialism. They never attacked the foreign conqueror on their own initiative and only resorted to the use of arms when the situation left them no other choice. Instead they attempted to escape from colonial domination by founding Muslim communities in regions that the whites did not yet control, and the theme of the *hejira* aptly symbolized that tendency.

Flight was also a concern of the preacher-prophets; but contrary to the warrior-prophets who sought to leave the colonial order, the preacher-prophets resorted to *internal* escape, demarcating their own religious and social territory within that of the colonizer.

There is nothing surprising in this. The preacher-prophets arrived on the scene mostly towards the end of the nineteenth century and the beginning of the twentieth, at a time when colonial authority extended more or less over the entire territory. It was hardly possible, therefore, to build Umma outside of colonial society.

Men like Amadou Bamba, El Hadj Malik Sy or Laminou Laye understood perfectly well what they were up against. They knew that the period of Muslim empires was over and that any *jihad*, even one whose mission was to convert pagans to Islam, would be considered by the colonizer as a threat and would be put down ruthlessly. Whatever their ideas about colonialism, they abandoned any idea of aggressive action against the enemies of Islam, be they whites or Africans. 'If you say *jihad* is required by the law and the Sunna,' declared Amadou Bamba in 1910, 'my answer is that those times were different from yours and that those men were different from you' (quoted by Dumont, 1975: p. 125). The few aggressive messianic movements that did arise in the twentieth century, such as those of Ali Yoro Diop in the Futa-Toro and Souleymane Bayaga in Upper Gambia, were limited events and partly the result of the colonial authorities' inflexibility and suspicion.

Generally speaking, the marabouts would seize every opportunity to reiterate with great pomp their loyalty to the lords of the land. World War I in particular allowed them to express their devotion to the French cause in concrete terms, not only by offering prayers for victory but also by helping to recruit soldiers. The submissive attitude of the charismatic marabouts to the colonial government did not prevent either party, however, from being more than a little suspicious of the other. We have spoken about the colonizer's fears of messianic movements over which, initially at least, they had little control. One can therefore understand why the first reaction of the French was to deport or imprison the preacher-prophets. In the main, it was the colonizer who took the initiative of aggressive action, and it is this repression that has earned the marabouts today the title of 'martyrs of colonialism'. It is important to point out, none the less, that if the marabouts had officially to accept the colonial order, they at least tried to lessen the effects of its impact. In their own way they, too, organized their *hejira* by regrouping their disciples into religious and labouring communities which were far from colonial towns and which, in time, became real townships themselves. Moreover, when they set up their organization in pre-existing towns they endeavoured to show their independence by creating separate neighbourhoods.

The social structure of these communities was based on the marabout–*taalibe* relationship, which allowed the prophets to avoid coming into contact with the colonizer and thus to minimize conflicts. Relationships with authorities were limited to paying taxes, recruiting soldiers, participating in compulsory public works projects from which the entire community could expect benefits, and later also ground-nut cultivation. Aside from these obligations, the marabout's village lived its own life, at least on the ideological level.

The messianic movements of the warrior-prophets or of the preacher-prophets were consequently not really subversive in nature. They did not try to destroy the colonial order but to lead a separate existence from colonial society and to be autonomous. That amounts, of course, to a certain kind of resistance, and in Muslim countries the *hejira* was one of the main responses to European imperialism (cf. Meynier, 1976).

In referring to Senegalese maraboutic communities, one may thus speak of counter-societies, as Baechler has defined them. Such communities are forms of opposition characterized by leaving the existing social order and entering 'societies that openly defend other values and claim to set up, at least within their midst, a new order' (Baechler, 1970: p. 81). In the case under analysis here, one must recall that it is not a question of aggressive counter-societies. 'Violence', says Baechler, 'comes rather from the established order which cannot accept dissident movements and strives to eliminate them' (ibid.). The aim of these counter-societies is not to conquer the colonial power but to get away from it by creating, to a certain extent, a parallel power structure. This is why it may be erroneous to classify these movements as revolutionary phenomena as Baechler has done. The warrior-prophets founded counter-societies outside of the colonial society. For the latter is a case of adapting to established society while remaining outside of it (cf. O'Dea, 1966: p. 49). It is therefore difficult to speak of militant anti-colonialism. These counter-societies are not nationalistic responses to foreign domination as such, but rather the response (or one of the responses) to a global social crisis in which colonization plays a major, but not the only role.

Muslim messianic movement and social crisis

The concept of social crisis or of anomie would seem to provide better tools for understanding messianic phenomena than would that of nationalism or of anti-colonialism. Messianic movements are not unique to colonial societies. The arrival of the white man is not enough to explain the emergence of prophets. History abounds with examples of messianic movements in non-colonial situations, as for instance in Europe during the Middle Ages (cf. Cohn, 1962). Lowie rightly points out that reactions to white domination are but a specific case in the general category of messianic movements and that colonization could help to explain them only in that it brought about social upheavals or even social disintegration. But these situations could also have been provoked by internal factors (quoted by Pereira de Queiroz, 1968: pp. 282–3). Senegalese messianic movements are in this sense re-actions to a context of social crisis. They represent a unique but limited and, to a great extent, imaginary attempt at social reconstruction. A few prophets, like Amadou Bamba, clearly voiced their feelings about the 'baseness' of the times in which they were living ('the present time is the most detestable') and wanted their religious communities to offer a refuge from it. 'My God has ordered me to proclaim that I am a refuge, a protection, so that those who seek good here on earth and also in the next world can find refuge near me. . . .' (quoted by Dumont, 1975: p. 69). The same thing can be said about El Hadj Malik Sy. In founding the villages of N'Darnde and Diacsaw he hoped his disciples could live far from the 'misfortunes of their times'. He wanted to organize communities in which there would be new social relationships based on mutual help and solidarity so that, as he said, 'a traveller would no longer need his food sack' (Marone, 1970: p. 155).

But from whom were they seeking protection? To what sort of crisis does the concept of 'refuge' refer? Two elements are intermingled and cannot be arbitrarily separated. One is related to the internal contradictions of traditional social and political systems and the other to changes brought about by the colonial phenomenon. Each one, however, feeds on the other and evolves in terms of the other. The internal crisis made colonial penetration easier and this, in turn, accelerated the breakdown of the former society. The most obvious manifestation of the crisis was the increase in social divisions and in political domination which would seem to date back before colonization, although influenced by it. In the Wolof regions, as early as the eighteenth century, one could note the growing authoritarianism of the aristocratic leadership towards groups of commoners, in particular free peasants (*baadolo*) and land wardens (*lamaans*). The latter gradually lost their autonomy to a central power structure that was anxious to ensure its hegemony, mainly through constantly raising taxes, in order to meet the expenses of the governing oligarchy. With regard to the kingdom of Kayor, Pathé Diagne, the Senegalese historian, has written:

> In his desire for absolute power, the Monarch denied the rights of the *lamaans*, even to the extent of eliminating in certain territories all political authority except his own. There was a trend increasingly to separate the mere ownership of the land from political power. The lord of the land, or *lamaan*, who loses his status as political chief may keep his rights to the land for his lineage – unless he is exiled. But he loses all power, and the autonomous territory that was formerly his may then become the political spoils of a *Khangame* (a high ranking dignitary of the crown) or be run by a 'slave of the crown'. (Diagne, 1967: p. 129)

These *tyeddos*, or slaves of the crown, imposed a reign of terror over the peasants who were ruthlessly taxed or exploited for their labour. The oppression of the peasants by the aristocracy and the *tyeddos* was principally the result of the latter's need for income in order to buy goods (and arms) from European trading companies to be used, in turn, to fill their coffers and to extend their authority by warring against their neighbours. In this context of permanent coercion and instability, the peasant masses turned to the representatives of the Muslim religion to seek a minimum of protection. The more oppressive the central power became, the greater the number of peasants who joined maraboutic communities. These Muslim villages were zones of refuge but they were also centres of agitation, and on several occasions the marabouts revolted against the authority of these 'faithless and lawless' monarchs.

The movement of people towards Muslim communities was given new impetus by the French conquest of the inland regions. Marabouts filled the political vacuum created by traditional systems which were crumbling due to internal fissures, and they provided a solution to the situation of anomie brought about by colonialism. At first the French called upon the *tyeddos* to administer the Wolof lands. Demba War Sall, ex-chief of the slaves of the *damel* (ruler) of Kayor, was placed at the head of a 'confederation of Kayor' (1893) that he governed in a tyrannical fashion. The report sheet of 1894 on him noted his 'marked tendency to revive ancient taxes' for the Wolof chiefs and to accelerate the drift of the people towards the marabouts. Later, when such methods had sapped what remained of the chiefs' authority, the institution of chieftaincy became bureaucratized and the *tyeddo* mentality faded away. Despite this, the reputation of chiefs hardly improved, for in everyone's eyes they were guilty of implementing unpopular measures. With the deterioration of the authority of Wolof chiefs the marabouts appeared as the natural rulers, something that, at the time, did not escape the attention of an observer like Marty:

> There came a time after 1886 when the disappearance of the Senegalese political chiefs of the past – the *damel, bur, burba têgne* – left free rein to new men; the strength and the message of Islam, and the virtue and saintliness of the marabouts and their representatives eclipsed the prestige of local kingdoms and aristocracies. (Marty, 1917: pp. 230–1)

The political vacuum from which the marabouts profited was felt all the more acutely in that colonization had brought about economic and social changes in the Wolof regions that completely called into question the traditional way of life. Particularly, the introduction and development of ground-nut farming pushed Wolof society into a cash-crop economy and caused the rupture of traditional relationships by encouraging mass migration. These and other transformations offered fertile ground for the development of a charismatic leadership that crystallized around the marabouts. In the Futa-Toro, a Tukolar region, the social crisis was undoubtedly less acutely felt, but all the same it resulted in the disintegration of traditional political systems just as in Wolof society. After the *tooroodo* revolution at the end of the eighteenth century, which had restructured the political system and placed authority in the hands of Muslim leaders, the government of the Futa confederation became more and more oligarchical. The pious

Muslims turned rapidly into feudal lords who jealously defended their rights and privileges. As in the Wolof regions, rivalry developed among the members of the ruling class over questions of land tenure and over the dues paid by the French to local chiefs for the right to sail up the river, which created a situation of local instability. In this context, it is easy to understand the favourable reception given to El Hadj Omar, when he criticized the wealthy for misappropriating the *assakal* (the Islamic tithe) and encouraged 'good Muslims' to emigrate east.

Colonization did not curb popular discontent. The arbitrary appointment of chiefs and their unpopular actions combined with social inequality in Tukolar society can explain why marabout-led movements of revolt prospered here as in other parts of Senegal. Revolt did not cease, moreover, with the end of the colonial regime. Even today many inhabitants of the Futa are fleeing their villages to join up with a new Tukolar Mahdi, Tierno Mamadou Ba, who has set up a religious community in Eastern Senegal. As in the past, this emigration can be traced to social and political inequalities in Tukolar society. Most of the marabout's followers are landless peasants, forgotten members of society who hope their prophet's *baraka* can help them solve their problems.

The drought in Senegal since the late 1960s has been an important factor in the extension of these latter-day charismatic movements by adding to social inequality and increasing the burden of taxation. This is the proof, if it is still needed, that messianic movements are not simply outgrowths of the colonial context as such. The Mahdi of Medina-Gonasse perpetuates a constantly evolving messianic phenomenon, not only because a state of social crisis still exists, but also because the sentiment of revolt that inspired the emergence of older messianic movements rapidly fades away, making room for new movements.

From counter-society to hegemony

Those Senegalese messianic movements that were not crushed by the colonizer tended in time to adapt to the colonial order while maintaining their specific values and organization. The first sign in the process of adaptation in messianic movements is what Weber calls 'routinization': 'Indeed, in its pure form charismatic authority may be said to exist only in the process of originating. It cannot remain stable, but becomes either traditionalized or rationalized, or a combination of both' (Weber, 1964b: p. 364).

Engendered by exceptional circumstances charismatic phenomena challenge ordinary norms. Over the years, however, the maraboutic community is faced with the demands of daily life. Messianic sentiments cannot exist in complete autonomy. Total retreat might have mobilized the colonial authorities against the community, and isolation is incompatible with the material imperatives of routinization. While remaining tinged with divine grace, the authority of the marabout must henceforth cope with material necessities. Charisma must be maintained by tangible achievements and benefits, and the authority of the marabout slowly evolves towards a patronage model in which relationships of dependency play a major role. At the same time the community develops a new structure. Hierarchies, dogma and discipline appear, and while continuing to affirm its specificity, the community must accept the constraints of the state. The marabout can only do favours for his *taalibe*, if he knows how to use the resources of patronage, but many of these are found outside the community and require him to serve as an intermediary. In addition, the agricultural activities of maraboutic communities place them in direct contact with society at large. In Senegal the marabouts' enthusiasm for ground-nut farming moved them into a market economy in which they soon became an indispensable factor. The pre-capitalist structures of these communities persisted, but they functioned within the framework of a trade-based economy. At this stage the counter-society became fully integrated in the colonial system that it was formerly seeking to flee. It is both subordinate and dominated (cf. Copans, 1980), and the maraboutic doctrine accordingly becomes transformed. It is no longer an ascetism that rejects the world, but an ascetism that functions in the world and in which work becomes a religious duty. This cult of work turned out to be very useful for the colonial authorities, as it resulted in the extension of ground-nut farming at little cost. Thanks to the ideological mediation and the organization of maraboutic communities, ground-nuts could henceforth be produced at a lower cost than in a more developed, wage-based system of production. From this point on there no longer was a fundamental opposition between the colonial administration and the marabouts.

What is more, their interests converged. It is now easy to understand why, in the 1920s, the French considered the marabouts to be one of the pillars of the colonial order, even if they worried occasionally about the power of the brotherhoods.

Under these conditions the marabouts were the best possible intermediary between the French and the African, especially rural, population. Peasants were less suspicious of the marabout's authority than that of the colonial chiefs. Aside from fulfilling specific economic functions, the marabout also was an excellent safety valve against the political uncertainties of modernization. The specific nature of the organization of maraboutic communities and their remoteness from colonial society made them, paradoxically, agents of colonialism. The messianic community of the early days has turned into a hegemonic apparatus which exercises control over a civil society that the political society cannot or does not want to control directly (Gramsci, 1975: pp. 606–7). Thus, maraboutic structures became no more than an illusion, albeit a very material one, aimed at maintaining colonial domination. This is eloquently illustrated by the fact that when the new Senegalese elites began, timidly, to protest against the colonial system, the descendants of the founders of counter-societies were very reluctant to follow them. In the 1958 referendum over the French Community they panicked at the idea of the whites leaving and consequently threw their weight behind the 'yes' vote. Their support was so crucial, in fact, that the success of the referendum was attributed to the vote of the marabouts. The following year, when they realized that independence was inevitable, they formed the Conseil Supérieur des Chefs Religieux (Superior Council of Religious Leaders) to try and stop this evolution. The most active among them even attempted political action by founding the Parti de la Solidarité Sénégalese (PSS), a real Islamic party that was backed by the most conservative French business interests in Senegal. The main theme in the doctrine of the new movement was 'concern for a policy of progress based on the values of Islam and those of the universal and fertile French culture' (*Solidarité*, the journal of the PSS, no. 6, 29 August 1959). It took all of Leopold Senghor's political skills to reassure the marabouts and to convince them of the benefits of independence.

One must not, however, consider marabouts merely as tools in the hands of the ruling class. Whatever the degree of their integration into the dominant political society, maraboutic communities are often considered by the dominated as alternative or even counter-societies. Islam plays a role as a religious critic of the power system and the maraboutic community may become a means of protection against political power (Coulon, 1981).

Still, it would be mistaken to present Senegalese Islamic messianic movements as anti-colonial movements and as the forerunners of contemporary political nationalism. They should be interpreted within the social, political and religious context of their times instead of being considered either as harbingers of what was to come (the nationalist thesis), or as partisans putting up a last fight (the colonialist thesis). If these messianic movements are linked in a realistic way to the colonial *situation*, they are not the active antithesis of colonialism. Even when the marabouts were 'protestors' they did not seek to attack colonialism but to flee it. They defined themselves with respect to colonialism by their passive attitudes (flight), whereas nationalism is essentially an active form of opposition to colonialism. What they did express, in their own way and in the context that has been described, was the malaise of a society being rocked by profound upheavals.

Notes

1 An earlier, French version of this chapter was published in W. M. J. van Binsbergen and R. Buijtenhuijs (eds), *Religious Innovation in Modern African Society*, *African Perspectives 1976/2*, Leiden: African Studies Centre.

References

Baechler, J. (1970), *Les Phénomènes révolutionnaires*, Paris: Presses Universitaires de France.

Balandier, Georges (1970), *Sociologie actuelle de l'Afrique noire*, Paris: Presses Universitaires de France (1st edn 1951).

Bathily, A. (1970), 'Mamadou Lamine et la résistance anti-impérialiste dans le Haut-Sénégal', *Notes Africaines*, 125: pp. 20–32.

Carrère, F., and Holle, P. (1855), *De la Sénégambie française*, Paris: F. Didot.

Cohn, Norman (1962), *Les Fanatiques de l'apocalypse*, Paris: Julliard. (French translation of *The Pursuit of the Millennium*, 1957.)

Copans, J. (1980), *Les Marabouts de l'arachide: La confrérie mouride et les paysans du Sénégal*, Paris: Le Sycomore.

Coulon, C. (1981), *Le Marabout et le prince: Islam et pouvoir au Sénégal*,

Paris: Pédone.

Cruise O'Brien, Donal (1971), *The Mourids of Senegal: The Political and Economic Organization*, Oxford: Clarendon Press.

Diagne, Pathé (1967), *Pouvoir politique traditionnel en Afrique occidentale*, Paris: Présence Africaine.

Dumont, F. (1974), *L'Anti-sultan ou Al-Hajj Omar Tall du Fouta: Combattant de la Foi*, Dakar/Abidjan: Nouvelles Éditions Africaines.

Dumont, F. (1975), *La Pensée religieuse de Amadou Bamba*, Dakar/Abidjan: Nouvelles Éditions Africaines.

Faidherbe, L. (1889), *Le Sénégal: La France dans l'Afrique occidentale*, Paris: Hachette.

Gramsci dans le texte (1975), Paris: Édit. Sociales.

Hodgkin, Thomas (1962), 'Islam and National Movements in West Africa', *Journal of African History*, **3**, 2: pp. 323–7.

Kamara, C. M. (1970), 'La Vie d'El Hadj Omar traduite et annotée par A.Samb', *Bulletin IFAN*, ser. B, **XXXII**, 1: pp. 44–137; 2: pp. 370–411.

Le Grip, A. (1952), 'Le Mahdisme en Afrique noire', *L'Afrique et L'Asie*, **18**, 2: pp. 3–16.

Marone, I. (1970), 'Le Tidjanisme au Sénégal', *Bulletin IFAN*, ser. B, **XXXII**, 7: pp. 136–215.

Marty, P. (1917), *Études sur l'Islam au Sénégal*, 2 vols, Paris: Leroux.

Meynier, G. (1976), 'Le Nationalisme algérien en 1914', *Pluriel*, 5: pp. 2–20.

Mohamed Moustapha Hane (n.d.), *Les Trois Grandes Figures de l'Islam en Afrique*, Dakar: Librairie Hilal.

Nyambarza, D. (1969), 'Le Marabout E. H. Mamadou Lamine d'après les archives françaises', *Cahier d'Études Africaines*, **IX**, 33: pp. 124–45.

O'Dea, T. F. (1966), *The Sociology of Religion*, Englewood Cliffs, NJ: Prentice-Hall.

Oloruntimehim, B. O. (1968), 'Muhammad Laine in Franco-Tukulur Relations, 1885–1887', *Journal of the Historical Society of Nigeria*, **4**, 2: pp. 375–96.

Pereira de Queiroz, M. I. (1968), *Réformes et révolution dans les sociétés traditionnelles: Histoire et ethnologie des mouvements messianiques*, Paris: Anthropos.

Saint-Martin, Y. (1968), 'La Volonté de paix d'El Hadj Omar et d'Amadou dans leurs relations avec la France', *Bulletin IFAN*, ser. B, **XXX**, 3: pp. 785–802.

Saint-Martin, Y. (1970), *L'Empire toucouleur (1848–1897)*, Paris: Le Livre Africain.

Samb, A. (1972), *Essai sur la contribution du Sénégal à la littérature d'expression arabe*, Dakar: IFAN.

Weber, M. (1964a), *The Sociology of Religion*, Boston: Beacon Press.

Weber, M. (1964b), *The Theory of Social and Economic Organization*, New York: Free Press.

Willis, J. R. (1970), *Al-Hajj Umar b. Said al Futi-al Turi and the Doctrinal Basis of his Islamic Revivalist Movement in Western Sudan*, University of London, School of Oriental and African Studies, PhD dissertation.

Author index

Abrahamson, M., 95
Ademuwagun, Z.A., 39
Adler, A., 52, 60, 74, 78
Adorno, T.W., 140
Ajayi, J.F., 38, 40
Alexandre, P., 250
Alpers, E.A., 168, 179
Amadou Bamba, see Subject index
Anderson, E., 249
Aquina, Sister M., 269
Ardener, E., 85, 96
Armstrong, R.P., 243
Arn, J., 40
Asad, T., 40
Augé, M., 12, 39, 97
Ayandele, E.A., 38, 40
Ayode, E.A.A., 39

Baal, J. van, 129
Babcock, B., 76
Babutidi, 236
Badcock, C., 84–5
Baechler, J., 32, 34, 336–8, 340–1, 358
Baëta, C.G., 338
Bahelele, J., 231
Balandier, G., 34, 326, 333–4, 350
Baré, J.F., 39
Barkun, M., 108, 115, 117, 128, 132
Barrett, D.B., 339
Barthes, R., 243
Bascom, W., 52, 78, 233
Basso, K.H., 86
Bastide, R., 63, 113, 126, 132
Bateson, G., 243
Bateson, M.C., 160
Bathily, A., 354
Bauer, D. F., 39

Baumann, H., 51
Beach, D., 40, 304
Beattie, J., 39, 78
Beeker, M.C., 222
Beet, C. de, 132
Bel, A., 203
Berger, P.L., 126, 131, 134
Berghe, P. van den 130, 132, 142–3
Bertels, K., 103, 105–6, 130
Bhebe, N., 293, 301, 317
Bhila, H.H.K., 168
Biebuyck, D., 39, 250
Binsbergen, W.M.J. van, 1–49, 55, 61,
    101, 110, 118, 120, 122, 128–9,
    131–3, 189–224, 257, 262, 272,
    287–9, 293–4, 297, 310, 312–13,
    315, 317
Bloch, M., 39
Blok, A., 105, 221
Boas, F., 155
Bohannan, L., 206
Bohannan, P., 56, 60, 78
Bond, G., 38, 288, 317
Bonte, P., 39, 55, 119–20, 133
Bourdieu, P., 12–13, 39, 130–1, 221
Bourdillon, M., 60
Bourguignon, E., 51–3, 60–1
Brunel, R., 221
Brusciotto de Ventralla, H., 249
Buchler, I.R., 98
Bühler, A., 119, 127
Bühlmann, W., 161
Buijtenhuijs, R., 2, 6, 12–13, 15, 31–5,
    38–9, 101, 322–45
Bunyan, J., 231
Bureau, R., 5, 39
Burridge, K., 131

367

Cardozo, M., 249
Carrère, F., 355
Caws, P., 103–5, 127
Charachidzé, G., 98
Cheater, A., 301
Chomsky, N., 20, 85, 97–8
Cobbing, J., 295
Cohen, D., 85, 125
Cohen, R., 40
Cohen, N., 340, 359
Colson, E., 12, 39, 59
Comaroff, J., 301
Comte, A., 160
Copans, J., 40, 363
Coulon, C., 12–13, 15, 31–5, 346–66
Courtès, J., 97
Craemer, W. de, 10, 38, 124, 160
Crapanzano, V., 57
Crawford, J., 78
Crick, M., 86, 96, 104–5, 125, 127, 134
Cross, S., 41
Cruise O'Brien, D.B., 41, 350
Cuisinier, J., 203

Daneel, M.L., 2, 31–2, 38, 133, 269,
    271–5, 277–8, 284, 313, 315–16
Dassetto, F., 8
Davis, J., 221
Decker, H., 86
Demeerseman, A., 221
DeMunck, J., 231
Depelchin, J., 3
Dermenghem, E., 221
Devanges, R., 39
Devisch, R., 5, 8–9, 14–19, 22, 24, 30,
    39, 50–83, 134
Diagne, P., 360
Dillon-Malone, C.M., 269, 278, 283
Doke, C.M., 161
Dore, R.P., 132
Douglas, M., 3, 8, 12, 38–9, 108, 160
Dozon, J.-P., 6, 39, 339
Droogers, A., 5, 10–11, 15, 21–4,
    39–40, 101–37
Dumézil, G., 164
Dumont, F., 352–3, 357, 359
Durkheim, E., 12, 23, 141, 145, 148,
    159–60

Eco, U., 95
Eickelman, D., 221
El Hadj Omar, *see* Subject index
Eliade, M., 31, 258, 260

Engels, F., 266; *see also* Marxism
Evans-Pritchard, E.E., 39, 57–8, 64,
    66, 78

Fabian, J., 3, 8, 10, 14–15, 23–5,
    38–40, 123–4, 128, 131–4, 138–63,
    250, 254
Faidherbe, L., *see* Subject index
Fasholé-Luke, E.R., 40, 41
Favret, J.', 198
Fernandez, J.W., 3, 5, 9, 31, 38–9, 59,
    79, 123–4, 128, 130–1, 243, 253–4,
    256, 262, 334–5
Firth, R., 51
Fitzgerald, D.K., 160
Forde, D., 65, 78
Fortes, M., 78, 167
Fox, R.C., 38, 124
Frankenberg, R., 39
Freud, S., 55, 57
Friedrich, P., 147
Fukiau kia Bunseki, 250
Furnivall, J.S., 142

Gamitto, A.C.P., 167–8, 185–6
Garbett, G.K., 58
Geertz, C., 67, 97, 140–1, 160, 221
Gellner, E., 40, 219–21
Gérard, A., 225, 230, 249–50
Gheel, G. de, 249
Gibb, H.A.R., 221
Giglioli, P.P., 160
Gluckman, M., 16, 57–9, 78, 143, 343
Godelier, M., 14, 39, 120
Goffman, E., 59
Goody, J., 226, 235
Gramsci, A., 364
Gray, R., 40–1
Gregerson, E., 86
Guiart, J., 326, 333
Guiga, A., 221

Hamilton, R.A., 167
Hammond, P.E., 141
Hammond-Tooke, W., 78
Harré, R., 134
Harris, Z., 85
Harrison, I.E., 39
Hartong, A.M., 203, 222
Harwood, A., 58
Hastings, A., 6, 39–41, 225, 249, 283
Hauenstein, A., 78
Havelock, E., 228

Heelas, P., 86
Heusch, L. de, 19, 51–3, 56, 164–6,
  183–4, 189
Hinnant, J., 39
Hoch-Smith, J., 92
Hodgkin, T., 350
Holle, P., 355
Homans, G.C., 107, 126
Hoogvelt, A.M.M., 130
Horton, R., 3, 31, 36, 38, 63, 67, 69,
  116–19, 122, 131, 253, 294
Houtart, F., 120, 133
Hymes, D., 145, 155, 160

Idowu, E.B., 38
Ikegami, Y., 86, 98
Ilogu, E.C.O., 38
Irvine, C., 249

Jackson, M., 56, 65, 76, 78
Jakobson, R., 85
Janzen, J.M., 3, 5, 12, 15, 29–30,
  38–40, 77–8, 225–52, 262
Jarvie, I.C., 114, 130–2
Johnson, W., 38
Jongmans, D.G., 220–1
Jules-Rosette, B., 3, 10, 38–9, 78, 133,
  160, 249, 269, 273, 280
Junod, H.A., 39, 310–11

Kahn, J.S., 40
Kamara, C.M., 354
Kant, I., 140, 159
Kapferer, B., 76
Kiernan, J.P., 40
Kileff, C., 269
Kileff, M., 269
Kimambo, I.N., 2, 119
Konda, J., 236, 238
Kremers, J.H., 221
Kronenfeld, D., 86
Kuper, A., 9, 19, 40, 256
Kuper, L., 142
Kwamba, E., 236–7

LaBarre, W., 101, 106–7, 114, 130–3
Lacroix, B., 39
Laeyendecker, L., 130
LaFontaine, J., 328
Leach, E., 8, 85, 221, 243
Lebulu, J.L., 39
Leclerc, G., 40
Leeson, J., 39

Le Grip, A., 347
Lemercinier, G., 133
Leone, M.P., 141
Levine, D.N., 257
Lévi-Strauss, C., 11, 19, 55, 63, 84–6,
  89, 97–8, 101, 221, 239, 262
Levtzion, N., 41
Lienhardt, G., 78
Linden, I., 38, 41
Linden, J., 41
Llobera, J., 40
Long, N., 41
Lowie, R., 359
Lubeck, P.M., 39–40
Luckmann, T., 126, 134
Luhmann, N., 148
Luneau, R., 51
Lunungu, 236
Lyons, J., 96–7

MacGaffey, W., 3, 38, 78, 228, 233–6,
  242, 245, 249
MacLean, D., 78
Maduro, O., 113, 120
Mahieu, W. de, 5, 11–12, 15, 19–22,
  24, 30, 39, 41, 84–100
Malinowski, B., 19
Mannheim, K., 140–1
Manyoni, J.R., 107, 132, 159
Marc-Lipiansky, M., 85
Marçais, W., 221
Marone, I., 359
Martin, C.J., 317
Martin, M.L., 41, 133, 249
Marty, P., 361
Marwick, M.G., 39, 167–8
Marx, K., 113, 119–22, 126, 131, 257,
  266, 287; *see also* Marxism
Mashasha, F.J., 302
Mateene, K., 250
Mauss, M., 12
Mazrui, A.A., 41
Mbeloloya Mpiku, 230–1, 249
Mbiti, J., 38
Mendonsa, E., 52, 63, 65, 78
Meynier, G., 358
Middleton, J., 57
Miedema, A.W.F., 203
Miller, J.C., 189
Mitchell, J.C., 26, 167
Mitchell, R.C., 2, 339
Mohamed Moustapha Hane, 349

Author index

Montet, E., 221
Moore, S., 76
Moss, R., 297
Mounin, G., 84, 86, 97
Mtetwa, R., 305, 318
Mulago, V., 38
Muller, J.-C., 39
Murphree, M.W., 269, 284
Myerhoff, B., 76

Nathhorst, B., 86
Nauta, D., 103, 105–6, 130
Needham, R., 96
Nfinangami, 225, 236
Ngokwey Ndolamb, 5, 39
Ngubane, H., 78
Nique, C., 95, 97
Nkindu, G., 232
Ntara, S.J., 167
Nyambarza, D., 350, 356
Nzungu, 225, 236

O'Dea, T.F., 358
Ofori, P.E., 2
Ogot, B.A., 23, 335–6
Okot p'Bitek, 3, 22–3, 131
O'Laughlin, B., 131–2, 134
Oloruntimehin, B.O., 350
Onselen, C. van, 40
Oosterwal, C., 114, 132

Palmaer, G., 231
Palmer, R., 303–4
Park, G., 59, 63, 67, 78
Parsons, T., 139, 148
Pauw, B.A., 113, 118
Peel, J.D.Y., 38, 101, 109, 118
Penders, C., 249
Pentikäinen, J., 226, 233
Pereira de Queiroz, M.I., 359
Peristiany, J., 78
Pfeffer, L., 142
Phimister, I., 303–5, 318
Piault, C., 39
Pirouet, M.L., 6, 39
Price, T., 41

Ranger, T.O., 2, 4, 6, 14–15, 31–5,
    39–40, 119, 269, 273, 287–321, 324
Rappaport, R., 148, 291
Raymaekers, P., 225, 236, 239
Redmayne, A., 39, 59
Reefe, T.Q., 189

Rennie, J.K., 309–10
Retel-Laurentin, A., 56, 68, 70, 78
Richards, A., 167
Richards, P., 297–8
Rickert, H., 140
Rigby, P., 17, 60–1, 67, 78
Rita-Ferreira, A., 168
Rivière, C., 133
Robins, C., 37
Rosaldo, M.Z., 92
Roumeguère-Eberhardt, J., 74
Ryan, J.M., 39

Sacleux, C., 161
Sahlins, M., 55, 97, 101, 104–9, 115,
    120, 122, 125–8, 131, 133–4
Saint-Martin, Y., 348, 354–5
Samb, A., 352
Sandbrook, R., 40
Santema, J.H., 130
Saussure, F. de, 63
Scheff, T., 76
Schermerhorn, R.A., 142–4
Schlosser, K., 338
Schoffeleers, J.M., 1–49, 78, 133,
    164–88, 261, 287–91, 297–8, 317
Schöller, C., 232
Schutz, A., 267
Secord, P.F., 134
Segal, D., 98
Selby, H.A., 98
Selous, F.C., 318
Senghor, L.S., see Subject index
Setiloane, G.M., 3
Shelton, A., 65, 78
Shepperson, G., 41
Silverstein, M., 147
Singleton, M., 38
Skinner, E.P., 256–7
Smelser, N.L., 322
Smet, A.J., 2
Smith, M.G., 142
Söderberg, B., 249
Solomon, T., 78
Souyris-Rolland, M., 203
Spring, A., 92
Stayt, H.A., 299, 301, 310–11
Steegeren, W.F. van, 130
Stenström, O., 231
Stern, G., 133
Strenski, I., 86
Struyf, I., 231

Sundkler, B., 4, 6, 39, 269, 280, 333–5, 337–9
Sydow, G. von, 233
Sykes, F.W., 300

Tasie, G., 40–1
Tempels, P., 148
Tennekes, J., 125–6, 132, 134
Terray, E., 39
Tew, M., 167, 185
Tocqueville, A. de, 138, 141
Thoden van Velzen, H.U.E., 132, 272
Thomas, L., 51
Tucker, R.C., 113
Turner, E., 27
Turner, H.W., 2, 5, 38–9
Turner, V.W., 3, 9, 12, 16, 26–7, 38–9, 54–5, 57–9, 63–6, 68–9, 74, 76, 78–9, 132, 143, 160, 167, 263
Tyler, S., 242, 250

Ustorf, W., 132

Vansina, J., 38, 124, 164–5, 189, 250
Veer, P. van der, 38
Vernant, J., 68–9
Verstraelen, F.J., 6, 39
Vidal, C., 39
Vincent, J.F., 52, 78
Vingadio, T., 234
Vizedom, M., 95
Voorhoeve, J., 4

Waardenburg, J., 40
Walker, S.S., 38
Wallace, W.L., 109, 130

Walls, A.F., 2
Warren, D.M., 39
Washabaugh, W., 160
Watt, I., 226, 235
Weber, M., 139, 346, 362–3
Weizsäcker, C.F. von, 138
Welbourn, F.B., 101, 335–6, 339, 343
Welime, D., 341
Werbner, R.P., 3, 5, 13–15, 21, 30–4, 39, 58, 60, 68, 70, 78, 253–86, 288–90, 313
Were, G.S., 332–3
Westermarck, E., 231
White, C., 78
Widman, R., 249
Willis, J.R., 2, 165–6, 173, 183–4, 189, 355
Wilson, B.R., 269
Wilson, J., 134
Wilson, M., 3, 38, 112–14, 131, 133
Wing, J. van, 232, 249
Wipper, A., 32, 34, 322–33, 339, 342–3
Wolf, J.J., de, 6, 39, 331, 341–2
Worsley, P., 108, 326, 333, 338–40

Yinger, J.M., 131
Young, A., 68, 70
Young, S., 291–2, 297, 310–12, 314

Zachrisson, P., 296, 307, 313–14
Zahan, D., 51, 65
Zaretsky, I.I., 141
Zempléni, A., 52, 55–6, 60, 74, 78
Zenner, J., 133
Zoghby, S.M., 2
Zuesse, E., 39, 51, 53

Subject index

Except for selected towns and religious centres, references to localities and administrative divisions have only been indexed under the names of countries; likewise, few social groupings have been indexed below the level of ethnic groups.

'Abdallah, Sidi (Tunisian saint), 201, 203, 208, 210–11, 218–19, 222
acquiescence, 121, 272, 282
adept, 200, 216–17
aesthetic aspects of African ritual, 17
affliction, *see* cult
Africa, *passim*; Central, 32–3, 124, 164, 166, 189, 287, 291, 293, 312, 315; East, 250; North, 27, 144, 189, 194; South, *see* South Africa, Republic of; South Central and Southern, 5, 13–14, 21, 26, 30–1, 35, 40, 255, 263, 265–6, 271, 281; West, 31, 206, 255, 263, 266, 281
African Apostolic Church (S. Africa), 268–73, 277, 279, 283
African Methodist Episcopal Church, 275
African religion, *see* religion
African religious studies, *see* religious studies
African ritual, *see* ritual
age, *see* generations
agriculture, 167, 262, 264, 272–3, 279, 290–4, 297–304, 310–14, 317, 358, 361, 363; rest days, *see* prohibition; *see also* ecology
Ahmadou (ruler, W. Africa), 356
alienation, *see* estrangement
Ali Yoro Diop (prophet, W. Africa), 357

allegoresis, 161
Amadou Bamba (Senegalese prophet-preacher), 347–53, 357–9
ambiguity, 60–1, 90, 157, 197, 243, 269, 271, 282
ambivalence, symbolic, 272–3, 282
Amhara people (Ethiopia), 70
Amirani (mythical hero, Georgians), 98
analogy, 146
ancestor, 2, 10, 52, 65–6, 88–93, 153, 167, 200, 202, 205–8, 211, 230–2, 235, 239–40, 242–3, 247, 326, 337; *see also* cult
Anglican Church, 335–6
angel, 240
Angola, 225
animal, 53, 69, 87–96, 150, 170, 200, 237, 244, 291, 294–5, 299, 306–8, 338; symbolism, 72–3, 86, 192, 195–7, 200, 215, 218–20
animate/inanimate, 20; *see also* structure, semantic
anomie, 34, 113, 323, 340, 342, 359, 361
anthropo-logical, 86, 89
anthropology, 4, 11, 19, 23–4, 36, 50, 55, 66, 70, 87, 96, 103–5, 109, 123, 127–9, 133–4, 140–8, 154, 158, 190, 196, 287, 322
anti-colonial protest, *see* protest
anti-sorcery movement, *see* movement; sorcery; witchcraft

anti-structure, 16, 143, 160
anti-witchcraft movement or cult, *see*
    cult; movement; witchcraft; sorcery
anxiety, 55–6, 59, 65
apartheid, 61, 142
Apostolic (church variety in S.C.
    Africa), *see* church
Apostolic Faith Church, 274, 278
Apostolic Sabbath Church of God, *see*
    Wilderness Church
Arabs, 215, 350, 353–4
archeology, *see* rock marks
archives, 288–94, 317, 322, 351
'Arfawiya (Tunisian clan), 27–8, 201–2,
    215–22
argument, *see* dialectics
aristocracy, *see* class
ark, 255, 283
art, 20, 250; analogy for African relig-
    ion, 25, 71
artefact, analytical, in African religious
    studies, 11, 144, 256
articulation: of modes of production,
    see mode of production; of mean-
    ing, *see* meaning
ascension, 255, 269–70, 275–6, 280
Asia, 144, 226
Asians in Africa, 332
astrology, 70
astronomy, 239
Atlas, High (Morocco), 219
Australia, 142
authority, *see* power

Bambara people (W. Africa), 354, 356
Banda (clan name, S.C. Africa), 167;
    see also mountains/plain
Bantu (linguistic complex), 232, 250
baptism, 255, 259, 267, 269, 275
Baptist Church, 240
baraka, *see* grace, divine
beer, *see* drink
behaviour, religious, 24–5, 39, 147
Belgian Congo, *see* Zaire
Belgium, 4
belief, 7, 9, 34, 59, 62–3, 66–7, 139,
    145–7, 246, 342
'beyond, the', 240–5, 250, 253
Bible, 29, 225–31, 237, 247, 337, 355;
    see also Christianity; church
binary opposition, *see* opposition,
    binary
birth, 158, 275

Bituma cult (Zambia), 10
blood, 328
body, 69, 71, 77, 243, 253–4, 269
Bororo people (S. America), 84–5
Botswana, 26, 70, 261, 268, 301
boundary, 11, 17–18, 73, 118, 186, 254,
    259, 262, 268, 354; buttressed in
    African religion, 37; crossed in
    African religion, 17, 37; *see also*
    culture (transcultural)
British South African Company, 295,
    300
brotherhood, religious, 205, 216,
    348–9, 353, 364; *see also* lodge;
    Islam
Bukusu people (Kenya), 326–7, 329,
    332; *see also* Luhya people
Bukusu Union (Kenya), 329–31, 342
burial, 200, 230, 268, 279; *see also*
    cemetery
Bwiti cult (Gabon), 9, 79

Cameroon, 250
canonic, *see* text
Canterbury (England), 27
capitalism, *see* mode of production
Caribbean, 143–4
cargo cult, *see* cult
case studies, 4, 12; *see also* theory;
    methodology
cash economy, *see* mode of production,
    capitalist
caste, 13
catechism, 229–30, 249
catechist, *see* teacher
category, 159–60
catharsis, 56–7
cattle, *see* animal
causality, 67, 115
cemetery, 199–200, 203, 213–14, 217,
    240; *see also* burial; village
Central African Republic, 69
central places, 274, 277, 282
Chad, 52
Chaminuka (divinity, Zimbabwe), 318
Chana (prophet, Zambia), 40
change: religious, 2, 21–2, 31, 34, 51,
    61, 110–34, 138, 143, 165, 227, 255,
    258, 262, 270, 282, 294, 298, 323,
    335, 359; social, 2, 17, 34, 114, 118,
    120–3, 127, 264; why does social
    change have a religious expression?,
    33–4, 114–16, 128; *see also*

change (*cont.*)
   innovation; innovators; imagery;
   crisis; continuity; persistence
chaos, *see* cosmos
charisma, 32, 34, 61, 115, 346, 349, 353,
   361–3
cheating, 66, 158, 170, 232, 301
Chewa people (S.C. Africa), 167, 180,
   185–6
chief, chieftainship, 28, 32, 37, 40, 150,
   157, 161, 173, 176, 182, 184, 186,
   203–5, 207, 215–17, 221, 232, 236,
   245–6, 279, 298–304, 309–12, 314,
   316, 328, 334, 339, 348, 352, 360–4;
   see also mode of production, tributary; class; cult, royal; ruler
childhood, *see* generations
Chilembwe, John (church founder,
   Malawi), 40–1
Chipeta (ethnic group, Malawi),
   169–70, 172, 174
Chitingwisa (chief, Zimbabwe), 318
Christ, *see* Jesus
Christianity, 3, 6, 23–4, 29–30, 36, 40,
   61, 112, 117–18, 128, 131, 153, 155,
   226–8, 230–2, 247, 283, 293, 301,
   309–16, 335, 337, 350, 355–6; folk-
   Christianity, 24; status in Islamic
   areas, 34; Pentecostal, 78; *see also*
   religious studies, by Africans;
   devout opposition; missionary; missions; church
chronicle, legendary, *see* myth
church, 2, 141, 145, 167, 253–4, 256,
   258, 261–2, 267–73, 276–7, 280,
   282, 338; Apostolic (in S.C. and S.
   Africa), 254, 267; Baptist, 240;
   Roman Catholic, 148–9, 229, 274,
   336; missionary, 2, 31, 158, 235,
   248, 335; independent, 2, 23, 30–1,
   37, 53, 61, 133, 148–9, 225, 235,
   248, 334, 339, 353; leader, 36, 255,
   263; spread, 29, 267–8; Ethiopian,
   271, 274, 334–6, 339; Protestant,
   228–9; Zionist, 34, 254, 267, 273,
   334–40; history, 4; and state, 141;
   see also organization; conversion;
   missions; state
Church of Africa (Kenya), 335
circulation, *see* trade
circumcision, 19, 21, 87–98
civil society, 34
clairvoyance, 52

clan, 60, 87, 91, 167, 203, 206, 209,
   215–16, 222, 227, 308, 353
class, 6, 13, 18, 32–5, 131, 139, 229,
   338–41, 362; commoners, 28,
   181–4, 339, 360; ruling class, 362,
   365; aristocracy, 26, 28, 168, 170,
   183, 300, 360–1; elite, 33, 40, 339,
   352, 364; intellectual, 22; peasant-
   (ization), 14, 33, 40, 109, 197, 261,
   268, 287–319, 322–44, 360–4;
   proletarian(ization), 14–15, 31–3,
   40, 296, 304–5, 310; religious responses to class formation, 6, 33–4,
   40, 287–319; *see also* consciousness;
   mode of production
classification, 51–4, 63, 67, 71, 75, 105,
   123, 133, 154, 159, 294
client in African ritual, 18, 52, 54, 56,
   59, 62, 64–5, 69–70, 74
clothing, 96, 192, 195–6
coded expressive domain, 29–30, 242,
   250
cognition, 17–18, 51, 54, 62, 75, 77,
   147; cognitive approach, 51, 62–8;
   see also symbol; semantics; semiotics
colonialism, 14, 32, 112, 117, 142–3,
   168, 186, 200, 203, 215, 218, 221,
   227–30, 236, 244, 256, 264, 272–5,
   278, 288–92, 295, 297, 299, 301,
   303, 307–8, 322–6, 331–2, 336–42;
   pre-colonial period, 297–8, 307;
   post-colonial period, 323, 331; *see
   also* protest; state
colour symbolism, 72, 76, 238, 240, 242,
   244–5, 250
commensality, 265
communal, *see* mode of production
communication, 13–14, 18, 55, 58,
   68–71, 74, 77, 131, 145–8, 160, 243,
   264, 275, 353; *see also* language;
   speech; semantics
communion, 117, 255, 265, 269–70, 284
communitarianism, *see* organization,
   church
communitas, 16, 132
community, 90, 338; sacred, 34, 359,
   362–4
comparative religion, 5
compensation, dialectical, 257
Compostella (Spain), 27
conceptualization, *see* thought
conditions, initial, for religious movements, *see* movement

configuration, 52, 258, 260; *see also* structure

conflict, 16, 28, 34, 50, 56, 58, 109, 113, 120, 143, 149, 156–7, 169, 177, 180, 206, 214, 234, 243, 254, 274, 297–8, 337, 350; *see also* divination; class; rebellion; protest; power

conformity, 57, 254; variety rather than norm in African religion, 24, 146

Congo (Republic), 225

Congo Free State, *see* Zaire

congregation, 267–8, 284

consciousness, 31, 52, 68, 147, 232, 239, 257–61, 266, 272–3, 282, 288, 302–7, 313–16, 354; *see also* class; ideology

consensus, 57–8, 66, 113, 116, 143, 191, 262, 289

consonance, *see* correspondence

context, 25, 72, 86, 134, 153–4, 232–3, 239, 248, 261, 354, 365

contextualization, 2–3, 5–6, 11–13, 21, 25–31, 35–6, 114, 179, 190, 208, 257–60, 272, 287, 294, 322, 359, 365; *see also* social structure; 'image-less'

continuity in African religion, 109, 118, 289–90, 313; *see also* crisis; persistence; change

contradiction in African societies, 6, 18, 21, 34, 71, 77, 96, 120–1, 128, 139, 198, 243, 253, 256, 281, 297–8, 323, 359; *see also* mode of production; class; boundary

control, 27–30, 54, 62, 117–21, 217–18, 226, 290–1, 294, 298, 301–2, 306, 348; *see also* text; power

conversion, 104, 116–18, 227, 253, 256, 263, 267–8, 278–80, 334

correspondence, structural, 56–60, 69, 72, 118–21, 176, 208, 253, 257, 261

cosmology, 57, 68, 72–5, 89, 95–8, 107, 117–18, 164–5, 173, 178, 227, 235, 239, 246, 261–2, 290, 294, 335; *see also* myth

cosmos/chaos, 31, 69, 73, 258–60, 270, 282–3

counter-society, 32, 34–5, 322–44, 358, 362–5

creativity in African religion, 7, 9, 18, 54, 72–3, 109, 120, 125, 145, 234, 243, 335

credibility, 52, 66–7

crisis, 50, 58, 61, 132, 289, 291, 297–8, 306, 350, 358–62; *see also* continuity; change; persistence

cross-cultural comparison, 10–11, 17, 20, 106, 109, 111, 133, 142–4

cult, 9–10, 31, 169–73, 218, 222, 227, 232, 239, 253, 255, 257, 260–82, 287–319; ancestral, *see* ancestor; chiefly, *see* cult, royal; of affliction, 2, 16–17, 31, 64, 247, 263–5, 312; territorial, 3, 26, 28, 31–2, 166–8, 177, 180, 184, 288, 290, 298; royal, 2, 26, 121; saintly, 217; prophetic, *see* prophet; fertility cult, *see* cult, territorial; healing, 225, 235–6; professional, 2; cult official, *see* leader; regional, 2–3, 5, 16–17, 31, 60, 175, 261–3, 268, 274–9; earth cult, *see* cult, territorial; cargo cult, 114, 338; High God cult, *see* Supreme Being; organization, 175, 182; as underpinning pre-capitalist mode of production, 15, 293–302; of personal security, *see* cult of affliction

culture, 17–20, 50, 86–7, 96–7, 105, 108–9, 124–6, 131–4, 139–40, 146, 189–90, 194–8, 225, 230–1, 241–2, 250, 262, 265, 268, 323, 338–42, 364; as industry, 139; contact, 57; culture-specific analysis, 5, 19–21, 57, 74, 105, 108; national culture, 37, 231–2; transcultural, 29, 74, 76, 86, 97, 107; *see also* tools; Europeans; cross-cultural comparison; boundary

curse, 65, 73

daily life, 71–5, 207, 244, 269, 363

Dakar School of Psychopathology, 55

dance, 17, 170–1, 200, 215–16, 230, 232, 234, 245, 247, 300, 305, 308

data, 145, 154

day/night, 72–3, 90, 197

death, 50, 58, 64, 73, 88–9, 158, 170, 194; the deceased, 54, 239

decision making, 55, 58–9, 65, 68

deep structure, 20–1, 85, 87, 97–8, 196, 198; *see also* transformation

definition, 5, 33, 51, 59, 74, 102, 246

deity, *see* divinity

Demba War Sall (political figure, Senegal), 361

demon, 200, 312, 338; *see also* devil; exorcism

deprivation, 118, 229, 335

desacralization, *see* sacred

descent, 86, 167, 171, 204, 217, 353

determinism, 62–3, 120, 133, 256

deviance, 145, 185

devil, 316; *see also* demon; exorcism

devout opposition, 36, 131

dhimmi, *see* Islam, status of Christians and Jews in

dialectics, 7, 109, 146, 149, 254, 260, 273–82; *see also* compensation

differentiation, 139, 149, 153, 158, 226, 261, 268, 282, 350, 360

Dini ya Msambwa (religious movement, Kenya), 32–3, 322–44

Dinkiwa (Mwari messenger, Zimbabwe), 300

disaster, *see* crisis

disciple, 354, 358, 364

discipline, 363

discourse, 123–5, 139, 155, 351

disease, 50, 58, 73, 238, 245, 308; *see also* healing; cult, healing

disharmony, *see* harmony

disorder, *see* order

diversification, *see* differentiation

divination, 7–9, 16–19, 22, 24, 50–79, 90; Ifa, 52; divinatory apparatus, *see* object; types of, 51–4; theoretical approaches to, 54–79; yes-or-no questions, 52, 54, 69; *see also* innovators; prophet; diviner; mediumship; shamanism

diviner, 9, 17–18, 21, 50–79, 157, 161, 234, 245, 334; and Christian minister, 9; and student of African religion, 9; and prophet, 17; as stranger, 17

divinity, 52, 166, 172

djizya, *see* taxation

doctrine, 149, 355

documents, 24–5, 153–5, 168, 173–4; source criticism, 230–6; *see also* history; methodology

dogma, 363

dominance, in mode-of-production analysis, 120, 128, 133; *see also* determinism

domination, 360, 364

drama in African ritual, 17–18, 54, 59, 64, 68, 70–5, 246; *see also* psychodrama

dream, 54, 231–3

Drid ('tribe', Tunisia), 203, 215, 218–19

drink, 232, 244, 290, 299, 305

drought, 170–1, 175, 291–3, 296–7, 302–4, 310, 312, 362; *see also* rain; meteorological phenomena

drum of affliction, *see* cult

dualism, 108–9, 166; *see also* unity

Durban (South Africa), 59

earth cult, *see* cult, territorial

eclecticism, 5, 22–3, 101–34, 159

ecology, 61, 196, 290–3, 296–302; ecological concern in territorial cult, 32–3, 288–90, its decline, 32, 288, 311–17

economy, 5, 12–13, 26, 32, 36, 120, 122, 127, 146, 226, 242, 244, 254, 272, 281, 303, 307, 323; political economy, 34, 287–319

ecstasy, 49, 215–16

education, 228–9, 274, 276–8, 329–34, 339, 342; *see also* teacher

elders, *see* generations

El Hadj Malik Sy (Islamic leader, Senegal), 346, 349, 357, 359

El Hadj Omar (W. African Islamic warrior-prophet), 346, 349, 351–6, 362

elite, intellectual, *see* class

emic/etic, 105, 107, 110

emotive aspects of African religion, 10, 17, 36, 55, 74–6

empirical cycle, 10; *see also* theory; methodology

encapsulation, 35

environment, 55, 112, 291, 297, 307; mastery over, not a universal goal, 55–6; *see also* ecology

epistemology, *see* knowledge

equilibrium model, 64, 112, 143, 297, 340

escapism, 337–8, 355–9

esoteric aspects of African religion, 76, 239

estrangement, 30–1, 56, 255–7, 261, 265–6, 281; *see also* strangerhood

Ethiopia, 70

Ethiopian (as type of African church), *see* church, independent

ethnicity, 2, 60, 227, 262, 268; ethnic group, 2, 11, 13, 57, 325, 338–9,

350–4; poly-ethnic situation, 17–18, 30, 53, 60, 77, 139, 261, 266–81, 324; ethnic embeddedness of world religions in Africa, 37; ethnic pluralism, *see* poly-ethnic situation (*above*); tribal emblem, 170, 174

ethnocentrism, in African religious studies, 22, 67, 119, 144; *see also* projection

ethnography, 11, 108, 123, 310; tool in historical analysis, 2; folk ethnography, as literacy genre in Africa, 29–30, 40, 230, 235–48; 'ethnography of speaking', *see* (socio-) linguistics; 'ethnographic approach' to religious pluralism, 8, 10, 24–5, 39, 138–61

Europe, 22, 27, 144, 350, 354; *see also* Middle Ages

Europeans, European culture, 32, 40, 67, 119–20, 124, 213, 225, 235, 256, 278, 289–90, 295, 303–6, 312, 317–18, 326, 341–2, 347–50; *see also* ethnocentrism; mode of production, capitalist; colonialism; Christianity; religious studies, by Africans

event, 7, 10, 19, 24, 29, 61, 64, 73, 117, 126, 134, 145–7, 153–7, 207, 226, 237, 243, 246

evidence, 166, 182, 189

evolutionism, 67, 143, 166, 256, 282, 350

exchange, 55, 61, 194–5, 264, 275; of gifts and prestations, as coded expressive domain in 'ethnographic' genre, 29–30, 244; *see also* social structure

excision, 88

exorcism, 284; *see also* demon; devil

experience, 18, 33–4, 62, 64, 67, 198, 226–7, 235, 253, 256, 287–319, 323; *see also* consciousness; class

explanation, 8, 62, 117–19, 239–40, 253, 262; *see also* theory

exploitation, 121, 297

expressive aspect of African religion, 16, 34, 62, 70, 74, 113, 120, 147, 155, 227, 243, 332–5, 341

extra-human, 53, 58, 89, 97; *see also* supernatural

fable, 231, 233

Faidherbe, L. (colonial official, W. Africa), 348, 352

famine, 175, 292, 296–7, 304–6, 309, 312; *see also* food; drought

Fang people (Gabon), 79

fatalism, 65

fee in African ritual, 237, 244

fakir, *see* adept

fertility cult, *see* cult, territorial

festival, religious, 199–200, 203, 210, 214, 216–17, 295

feud, 214

fieldwork, on African religion, 3–5, 10–11, 16, 24, 36, 39, 51, 107, 119, 124, 127, 133, 148, 160, 189, 206, 212, 262, 291, 317

Fipa people (Tanzania), 173, 183

fire, 291, 317

firmament, *see* heaven; astrology; astronomy

flight, 34, 169–71, 177, 280, 355–8, 365; *see also* retreatism

focused/unfocused, 271

Fode Kaba (Islamic leader, Senegal), 346

folklore, 153, 161

folktale, 230–4, 254

food, 150–2, 157, 161, 171, 185, 192, 194–5, 200, 208, 215, 244–5, 269, 291, 296, 298–300, 305, 337, 341

forest, 72–3, 89–90, 93–5, 175, 205, 254, 264, 291, 294

framed/unframed, 271

France, 4, 215, 347, 355–7, 360, 362, 364

freedom, 25, 112, 146; of participants, in African religion, 9, 25; *see also* manipulation

Friends Africa Mission, 325

Fulbe people (W. Africa), 354, 356

function, 97, 233

functionalism, 16, 19, 22, 54, 57, 60–2, 69, 105, 112–14, 116–18, 126, 131–2, 143, 148

Gabon, 9, 348

Gambia, The, 357

Ganda people (Uganda), 60–1

garment, *see* clothing

Gaza people (Mozambique), 292, 309

genealogy, 28, 204–11, 220, 222, 231–2, 234, 236

generalization, 10–11, 146

general linguistics, *see* linguistics
generations, 13, 18, 32, 64, 72, 75, 95, 150, 157, 171–3, 178–82, 191, 199, 212, 239, 243–4, 294, 307, 333
genesis, *see* origin
genre, 29, 153, 225, 230–6, 250; 'ethnographic' 29, 40; *see also* coded expressive domain
geography, 98, 239
geomancy, 50, 68–9
Georgians (people, USSR), 98
Germans, 307
gestures, 71, 244–5
Ghana, 52, 263
glossolalia, 76, 233–4, 240, 247
God, *see* Supreme Being
grace, divine, 194–8, 346, 362–3
Greece, 226, 228, 235
Greek (language), 248
grove, sacred, *see* trees; forest
guerrilla, 325–9; *see also* warfare
Gusii people (Kenya), 324–5
Guye (Swiss missionary, Mozambique), 309–10

Hadjeraï people (Chad), 52
hagiography, *see* myth, hagiographical; saint
hallucination, *see* vision
Ham (biblical figure), 255
harmony, 31, 195, 246, 253–4, 258, 260, 269–71, 282–3; *see also* semantic structure
healing, 7, 161, 233, 238, 240, 244–7, 270, 275–6, 283, 334; *see also* therapeutic effectiveness; cult; disease
heaven/earth, 69, 72, 89, 167, 269, 328
hegemony, 145; of social group, as expressed in regional cult in Tunisia, 28; of Islam in Senegal, 34–5, 360, 362–5; hegemonic apparatus, as developed out of counter-society, 35; Mwari cult as reviving Ndebele hegemony in Zimbabwe, 295
hejira, *see* flight; retreatism
hierarchy, 56, 60, 72, 132, 148, 157–8, 167, 178, 192, 194–6, 198, 232, 245, 261, 266, 362; *see also* class; ruler; generations; leader
high/low, 20, 24, 93–5, 196, 243, 299
historia (textual genre in ancient Greece), 235, 248
history, 2, 4, 11, 21, 24–6, 29, 36, 71, 75, 77, 123, 146, 154, 164–222, 227, 230, 243, 260–6, 287, 331; as mediating between symbolic and material power, 14–15, 39; oral, 71, 227, 250; historical reconstruction, 5, 25–6, 189, 191, 207; intellectual, 178, 183–4; precolonial African history as static?, 165, 184; why encoded in myth?, 27; *see also* documents; methodology; sources; orality
Hlengwe people (Zimbabwe), 309
Holy Spirit, *see* spirit
homology, 146
honour, 198
horizontal/vertical, 198; *see also* high/low
house symbolism, 88, 175, 199, 253–5, 283
human/non-human, 58, 190; *see also* extra-human; supernatural
Hungary, 142
hunting, 54, 87, 91–3, 291–2, 294, 299
hymns, *see* song

ideal-type, 34, 51, 298
identity, 56, 118, 156, 158, 209, 219, 232, 265
ideology, 33, 37, 40, 55, 113, 132, 139–41, 160, 183, 204–7, 244, 262, 288, 291, 294–5, 298, 302, 346–51, 358, 363; *see also* consciousness
Ifa (Nigeria), *see* divination
illness, *see* disease
illumination, *see* revelation; praxeological approach
imagery, 14, 21, 30–1, 125, 239, 253–84; spatial, 30–1, 266–81; 'image-less' contextual analysis in African religious studies, 5, 123, 128; *see also* semantic structure; change; space; symbol
imagination, 253–5
imperialism, 138, 349, 354, 358; *see also* colonialism
implements, *see* tools
inauguration, 246
inclusivism, 26, 262
independence, national, 227, 281, 326, 328, 332, 349, 354; *see also* colonialism
independency, *see* church, independent
Indirect Rule, 315

individual, 51, 55, 64, 77, 109, 122, 227, 232
inequality, *see* class; hierarchy
infrastructure, *see* superstructure
initiation, 2, 71, 74, 161, 232, 238, 244; *see also* life-crisis ceremony; excision; circumcision
innovation, 2, 7, 18–19, 25, 51–3, 58–61, 76, 121, 138, 141, 147, 180, 232, 253, 262, 272, 281–2, 312, 335, 348; *see also* change; reconstruction
innovators, religious, 40
institutionalization, 51–4, 237
instruction, religious, 133, 155, 250
instrumentalist interpretation of African religion, 62, 67–8, 113, 334–5
integration, social, 54, 115, 141, 143, 145, 209
intellectualism, 116–19
interaction, 18, 71, 75–6, 145; face-to-face, religious, 3; between traditional African religion and world religion, 40; between history and anthropology, 287
International Colloquium at Kinshasa (1978), 39
interpretation, 8, 52, 66, 123, 147–8, 155, 189–222, 226, 237–8, 323; *see also* explanation; divination
intersubjectivity, 104
invaders, 21, 147, 167, 219, 256
ironware, *see* tools
Islam, 1–2, 6, 9, 13, 26, 32, 34, 36, 56, 61, 117–18, 128, 194, 196–7, 221, 226–7, 248, 346–65; ritual obligations in, 192; popular, 24, 189–222; formal, 194; status of Christians and Jews in, 34, 355; Islamic community, 34; pan-Islamism, 348–9; *see also* Qur'an; *Umma*; brotherhood; lodge; warfare, holy
Ivory Coast, 263

Jamaa (religious movement, Zaire), 139, 148–9, 152–3, 156–8, 160
Jehovah, *see* Supreme Being
Jesuits, 301
Jesus Christ (founder of Christianity), 231–2, 267, 273
jihad, *see* warfare, holy
Judaism, 139, 276, 355

Kairwan (Tunisia), 215
Kalanga people (S.C. Africa), 70, 289, 295, 299, 301, 309
Kaphiri-Ntiwa (Zambia/Malawi), 167, 169, 172
Kaphwiti (ruler, Malawi), 167, 170, 172
Kayor (state, Senegal), 360–1
Kenya, 13, 268, 323, 329, 336, 342
Kenya African Union, 329–30
Khrumiriya (Tunisia), 190–222
Kikondja (mission station, Zaire), 156, 160
Kikuyu Central Association (Kenya), 325–6
Kikuyu people (Kenya), 325, 330, 336
Kimbangu, S. (prophet, Zaire), 132–3, 225, 229, 232–45, 249
king, *see* ruler
kingdom, *see* ruler; state
kinship, 56, 72, 86, 90, 120, 242, 338; perpetual, 167, 173; roles, 56; lineage, 57, 60, 191, 203–7, 219, 234–5; segmentation, 27, 204–7; kin grouping, 13, 57, 64–5, 73, 204–5, 244
Kitosh Education Society (Kenya), 329
knowledge, 10, 51, 62–3, 66, 68, 98, 134, 141, 144, 154, 158–9, 294; esoteric, 157; biased, 106–9
Kolloa Affray (Kenya), 327
Komo people (Zaire), 12, 19–21, 87–98
Kongo people (Zaire, Angola, Congo), 225–50
Korekore people (Zimbabwe), 58
Korsten (suburb, S. Africa), 283
Kumalo dynasty (Zimbabwe), 294

labour, 121, 264, 272–3, 279, 281, 290, 295, 297, 299, 301, 312, 360
lamaan, *see* land warden
Laman, K. (missionary among the Kongo), 225, 236–7, 239, 241
Lamba people (Zaire, Zambia), 161
Laminou Laye (Islamic leader, Senegal), 346, 353
land, 28, 34, 198, 204–5, 215, 254, 264, 273, 278, 290–4, 297–300, 309–14, 360–2; pious-endowment land, 205, 218; land shrine, 296; land warden, 360; *see also* agriculture; ecology; cult, territorial
language, 2–3, 18, 24, 51, 144–7, 160, 167, 227, 234, 237, 242, 250; multilingualism, 139, 145; and religious

Subject index

language (*cont.*)
    identity, 156–7; *see also* linguistics;
        speech; poetry
Latin (language), 249
Latin America, 131, 144, 226, 249
law, 59, 141, 144, 159, 229, 246, 341–2,
        357
leader, religious, 181, 208, 221, 335,
        352, 361; *see also* church leader;
        hierarchy; Superior Council
left/right, 20, 191
legend, *see* myth
legitimation, 13, 19, 25, 33, 50, 57–61,
        116, 176, 181, 198, 217, 231–3,
        247–8, 279, 281, 298, 351; *see also*
        myth; power
Lekhanyane (church founder, S. Africa),
        283–4
Lele people (Zaire), 12
Lemba cult (Zaire), 30, 225, 236–46
Lenshina, Alice (prophetess, Zambia),
        33, 40, 310, 315; *see also* Lumpa
        Church
libation, 232
life, 158; living/dead, 240; life-crisis
        ceremony, 37, 95; *see also* initiation;
        circumcision; marriage; birth; death;
        animate/inanimate
lightning, *see* meteorological phenomena
liminality, 132
lineage, *see* kinship
lingua franca, 18, 78, 146
linguistics, 2, 24, 84–5, 87, 95; socio-
        linguistics, 24, 145, 160; general, 20,
        97; 'ethnography of speaking', 24;
        provides analogies in African relig-
        ious studies, 7, 11, 71, 126; *see also*
        language
literacy, 5, 12, 29–30; consequences for
        African religion, 225–50
literature, 25, 225, 230, 248, 349
Lobengula (ruler, Zimbabwe), 295, 300
local religious system, *see* system,
        religious
locust, *see* pests
lodge, of Islamic brotherhood, 201, 215
logic, 52, 62–6, 85, 87, 96, 145; and
        semantics, 85–7
Lower Shire Valley (Malawi), 167–8,
        170, 176, 298
Luba people (Zaire, Zambia), 149, 156,
        164–6
Luhya people (Kenya), 323–5, 339

Lumpa Church (Zambia), 33, 35, 121,
        315, 317
Lundu (dynasty, Malawi), 168, 171–6,
        179–80
Lusaka (Zambia), 280
lustration, *see* purification

Ma Ba Diakho (Islamic leader, Senegal),
        346
macrocosm/microcosm, 69, 117–18, 122,
        245, 257, 261–81, 289; *see also*
        intellectualism; conversion
mafundisho, *see* instruction, religious
Maghreb (N.W. Africa), 190, 197–8,
        220
magic, 2, 63, 66, 108, 112, 153, 234,
        244, 328, 337, 342
Mahdism, 347–50, 362
Maina (mythical ancestor, Kenya), 342
Malawi, 26–8, 40, 166–7, 268
male/female, *see* sexes
Malinke people (W. Africa), 354
Mamadou Lamine (religious leader,
        Senegal), 350, 354, 356–7
Manchester School, 5, 55, 57, 64
Mang'anja people (Malawi), 166–9,
        174, 178, 183–5
manipulation in African religion, 7–8,
        14, 25, 191, 207; *see also* freedom;
        instrumentalist interpretation
marabout, *see* saint
Maranke, J. (church founder, Zim-
        babwe), 40, 268–73, 277, 279, 284
marginal groups, 56, 141, 229
market, 363; as model, 23, 131, 138,
        148; *see also* mode of production,
        capitalist; money
marriage, 37, 75, 86, 91, 150, 167, 169,
        214, 234, 242, 244, 264, 342; *see also*
        spirit wife
martyr, 181, 316, 349, 357
Marxism, 4–5, 12, 19, 22, 40, 55, 113,
        119–23, 126, 287; *see also* mode of
        production; Marx (author index)
Masinde, E. (founder of Dini ya
        Msambwa, Kenya), 323–8, 332–3,
        341–2
mask society, *see* secret societies
Masowe (church founder, S.C. Africa),
        268, 270, 279, 304; *see also* Wilder-
        ness Church
mathematics, 52, 70, 85
Matonjeni (Mwari shrine), 313, 316

Matopos Hills (Zimbabwe), 304, 307, 310, 314
Mau Mau (revolutionary movement, Kenya), 114, 326–9
Mbona (cult figure, Malawi), 25–8, 166–86
meaning, 3, 8–9, 19, 24, 54, 64–5, 68, 71–4, 85, 94–8, 106, 109–10, 123–7, 134, 140–1, 147, 157, 232, 243, 250, 294; man as maker of, 22, 102, 109, 118, 124, 127–8, 147; literal, 51, 55, 62–6; symbolic, 51, 68; univocal, 55; articulation of, 74–7; *see also* semantic structure; symbol
Mecca (Saudi Arabia), 353, 355
medicine, 59, 232, 236, 239, 242, 244–7; *see also* healing; disease
Medina (Saudi Arabia), 355
meditation, 192, 195, 197
Mediterranean, 197
mediumship, 39, 52–3, 56, 60–1, 65, 72–3, 276, 302; *see also* divination; shamanism
Melanesia, 338–9
membership, 283; dual, 149, 330; *see also* recruitment
men, *see* sexes
mental illness, 56; *see also* paranoia
message, 52–4, 67, 97, 148, 153, 157–8, 174, 179, 182, 190, 198, 218, 231, 241, 246–7, 290, 308, 330, 341; lyrical, as coded expressive domain, 29, 246
messianism, 35, 323, 346–65
metamorphosis, 174, 186
metaphor, 59, 66, 70, 72, 95–7, 123, 164, 238, 243, 255, 265
meteorological phenomena, 168–71, 222, 296, 306; *see also* drought, rain
methodology, 1, 3–6, 12, 20, 29–31, 35, 37, 63, 70, 84, 87, 110, 124, 145, 154, 158, 189; and problem of unit of study, 37; *see also* case studies; fieldwork; history; documents; cross-cultural comparison; imagery; literacy
mfumu, *see* chief; diviner
Mhammad, Sidi (saint, Tunisia), 26–8, 189, 191–222
Middle Ages in Europe, 27, 340, 359
Middle East, 144, 194, 225–6
migration, 27–8, 61, 204–9, 212–15, 219, 254–7, 264–7, 272, 279–82, 291,

299, 303, 310–14, 356, 361–2; migratory church, 269
Milimo, *see* Mwari
millenarism, 108, 115, 132, 324–40; passive, 324–6; *see also* messianism
mind, human, *see* thought
mining, 299–300, 304
Minsamu mia Yenge (Christian Kongo newspaper), 228–32, 249
miracles, 171, 174, 194, 250, 328, 337
misfortune, 50, 70, 73, 127, 275
missions, 23, 148, 153, 229–32, 240, 243–4, 270, 274–8, 292, 300, 303, 307, 310, 328, 331, 334, 341, 346, 353; unestablished, 278; territorialism in, 274–5; and colonial state, 274–5; *see also* church, missionary; organization
missionary, 23, 117–18, 228, 278; *see also* Christianity; church; missions
Mlimo, *see* Mwari
mode of production, 6, 14, 18, 77, 121–2, 254, 257, 290, 293, 316, 341; pre-capitalist, 15, 32–3; capitalist, 32–3, 78, 119–20, 290, 294–7, 305, 307, 314–15, 361; tributary, 15, 33, 40, 294, 298–302, 307, 310–11; communal, 32, 40, 288, 293–302, 307, 316; articulation of, 32, 40, 121–2, 257, 294, 297, 307; domestic, 40, 121, 294; and religious analysis, 15, 293–302; petty commodity production, 279; *see also* Marxism
model, 84, 101–34; meta-model, 101–2, 109, 111, 129; exploratory, 113, 119, 123, 129; limitations, 106–9; operational, 103, 105, 110, 127; explanatory, 104–5; representational, 103, 105, 110, 127; heuristic value of discarded model, 101, 109
modernization, 303, 314, 364; in agriculture, 301
money, 33, 88, 229, 238
morality, 32, 34, 37, 55, 57, 61–7, 116, 143, 148, 157, 231, 315
Morel (administrator, Zaire), 240
Morocco, 219
Mount Moriah (Swaziland), 282
mountains/plain, 167, 170–1, 192, 194, 196–8, 213, 217–22, 261, 269, 275, 341; *see also* high/low
movement, religious, 21, 30, 34–5, 111–14, 120, 123–4, 131, 133, 139,

movement (*cont.*)
141, 159, 249, 254–7, 262–5, 281–2,
307–12, 323–5, 327, 331–8, 341–2,
346–65; initial conditions for, 35,
331, 351; revitalization movement,
61; *see also* reconstruction; innovation; prophet
Mozambique, 167, 176, 291–2, 309–11,
315–17, 324
mpemba, *see* colour symbolism; beyond
Muhammad (founder of Islam), 353,
355
Mulungu, *see* Supreme Being
Mumbo movement (Kenya), 324–6, 329
Mundang society (Chad), 52, 60
Mupumani (prophet, Zambia), 40, 312
murder, 169–72, 177, 181, 262, 328
Muridiya (Islamic brotherhood, Senegal), 348, 350
Murimi, *see* Mwari
music, 17, 89–90, 94–5; *see also* song;
dance
Mutendi, Bishop (church founder,
Zimbabwe), 268, 272, 276, 283–4,
315–16
Mwari cult (S.C. Africa), 14, 26, 32–3,
261, 287–319; and churches, 275–6
mystery, 9, 54
myth, 7, 14, 19, 21–2, 25, 27–8, 65, 71,
84–98, 145, 164–222, 236, 239, 246,
350; mythological chronicles,
164–188; of origin, 218; cosmological, 12; topographical, 27,
210–11; hagiographical, 26–8, 221;
mytheme, 98; variants in, 26–7,
176–8; structuralist analysis of, 19,
26–7, 198; historical analysis of, 14,
25–8, 165; *see also* legitimation;
history

Nabwana, P. (politician, Kenya),
329–31
Nakimayu, D. (protagonist in Dini ya
Msambwa, Kenya), 328
name, significance of, 91–2, 157–8,
167, 174, 206, 221, 237
narrative, 98, 123, 173, 176–7, 182, 184,
191, 233; *see also* history; documents
nation, 2, 227, 262, 264; nation-state,
143–4, 280
nationalism, 27, 325, 331–40, 347–53,
359, 365

nature, 66, 104, 194–7, 227, 294, 312;
see also animal; vegetal symbolism;
supernatural; extra-human; ecology
Ndau people (Zimbabwe), 309
Ndebele (pre-colonial state, S.C.
Africa), 298
Ndebele people (Zimbabwe), 289,
294–5, 298–9
Ndembu people (Zambia), 12, 16, 55,
58, 63, 66, 68
need, human, 54, 62, 64, 68, 108, 114,
146, 333
negation, 121, 294; between the religious and the social, 118; *see also*
dialectics
neglect, ritual, 65
negritude, 350, 353
neo-Marxism, *see* Marxism
Netherlands, 4
'New Jerusalem', 41, 255, 282, 338
new religions in Africa, *see* religion
New Zion, 338
nganga, *see* diviner; priest
Ngoni people (S.C. Africa), 168
night, *see* day/night
Ninakapansi (prophetess, Zimbabwe),
293, 301
niya, *see* piety
Nkoya people (Zambia), 11
Noah (biblical figure), 283
non-verbal, *see* speech
norm, 54, 61, 64, 146, 212, 237, 259,
363; infringement, 73; *see also*
neglect
North Kavironde Central Association
(Kenya), 325, 329–30
Ntsikana (Xhosa hymn-writer), 249
number, 239
nun, *see* spirit wife
Nzakara people (Central African
Republic), 69–70

object, ritual, 13, 18, 50, 53, 64, 68–9,
72, 75–6, 88, 194–5, 200, 203, 237,
245; as coded expressive domain, 29
objectivity, 62, 66; objective knowledge,
51
occult, 63, 65–6
offering, 27, 195, 199, 208, 293, 299,
306, 352; *see also* sacrifice; libation
omen, 54
operationalization, 341

opposition, 88–9, 96, 108, 244, 350, 365; binary, 18, 20, 63, 73, 75, 96, 196–7, 298

oppression, 323, 331

oracles, 53, 59–71, 289–90

oral history, *see* history; orality

orality, 26, 29–30, 62, 155, 164–89, 221, 225, 227–8, 230–1, 233, 239

oratory, *see* rhetoric

order, 31, 35, 50, 69–70, 73, 89, 109, 113–14, 134, 144, 147, 159, 180, 253–4, 290; social, *see* social order

organization: social, 17, 27, 30–1, 34, 75, 77, 182, 197, 203–9, 261, 267, 273–82, 294, 337–7; religious, 3, 29, 31; ritual, 17, 176, 182; church, organization, 37, and territorialism, 268–9, 274–5, and regionalism, 268–9, 274–5, and communitarianism, 268–9, 278–81; *see also* church, independent; social structure; ritual; cult

origin, 87, 158, 183; of groups, 28; of religions forms, 109–10, 119, 122, 128; *see also* myth; persistence

orthodoxy, 148–9, 226, 233, 353

pacifism, 195, 219, 329

pan-Islamism, *see* Islam

paradigm, 54–5, 57, 108, 262; *see also* model

paranoia, 66, 348

paraphernalia, *see* object, ritual

Parirenyatwa, Dr (politician, Zimbabwe), 273

participation, 248

Parti de la Solidarité Sénégalaise (PSS), 374

party, *see* political party

Pasipamire (medium, Zimbabwe), 318

past, *see* history; retrospection

peasant(ization), *see* class

pentecost (Zionist Christian ritual), 255, 270, 274–80

Pentecostalism, *see* Christianity

performative aspects, *see* drama

periphery, 256, 266–7, 276–7, 281

persecution, 278, 342, 348, 357; *see also* state

persistence, 109–10, 116, 119, 122–3, 128; *see also* change; continuity; origin

person, 67, 244, 255–60, 265, 267,

270–1, 281, 283, 350; framed/ unframed, 31; *see also* cosmos; harmony; semantic structure; imagery

pests, 168, 291–2, 301–2, 313

phenomenology, 5

philological-historical approach, 2

philosophy, 37, 55, 65, 140, 291

Phiri (clan name, S.C. Africa), 167, 170; *see also* mountains/plain

piety, 195–6

pilgrimage, 27, 195, 199–200, 208, 211, 214, 217, 255, 263–4, 269, 275–7, 283–4, 326, 353; *see also* cult, regional

pluralism, 138–44, 154, 157–60, 255; ethnic, *see* ethnicity; cultural, 30; religious, 6, 23–5, 138–61, 254, 260, 263, 282

poetry, 17, 230, 232; *see also* language; speech; message; lyrical

poison ordeal, 66, 169–70, 178

political economy, *see* economy; class; mode of production; Marxism

political party, 272, 325, 329, 333, 336, 338, 340–1, 364; as alternative to religious response, 33–4

political science, 4, 36

political system, *see* state

politics, 32–3, 37, 57–8, 62, 64–5, 113–14, 120, 131, 139, 144, 158, 280, 323, 326, 330, 333, 335, 350–3; of knowledge, 131–2, 142, 159; reformist, 324–6; *see also* state; ruler; political party; class

poly-ethnic, *see* ethnicity

popular religion, *see* Islam; Christianity; system, religious

Portuguese, 25, 167–8, 173–4, 249, 292

positivism, 25, 52, 55, 63–7, 108, 148, 160

possession, 52, 61, 66, 72, 247, 265; *see also* mediumship; divination; shamanism

poverty, 33, 339; *see also* class

power, 17–18, 21–2, 28, 32–5, 37, 54, 60–4, 70, 75, 77, 167–9, 172, 177–82, 215, 226–9, 232, 235, 244–6, 281, 294, 311, 315, 323, 336–7, 346, 358, 360, 365; symbolic versus material power, 7, 13–15, 167; complementarity of structural and transactional analysis of power, 14; and terror, 37

praxeological approach, 8, 10, 15, 24, 51, 59, 61, 70–8, 234; and boundary crossing in African religion, 17–18; *see also* preaching
praxis, 127, 149, 154–5; religious, 147
prayer, 192, 197, 232, 240, 283, 311–12, 328–9, 334, 354
preacher-prophet, 347–8, 352, 356–8
preaching, 19, 21; as example of praxeological approach, 8; as transformation of divination, 9
prediction, 117–19
pre-scientific, *see* science
priest, 4, 9, 32, 56, 150, 153, 157, 169, 173, 175–7, 182, 226, 234, 238, 244–7, 288, 301, 304, 316, 319, 334, 346; rain priest, 169; *see also* leader; Christianity; diviner
primary resistance movement, 32, 324, 326; *see also* protest
process, 123; *see also* structure
production, 32–3, 134, 198, 291, 298–9; relations of, 6, 14, 21, 120–2, 127, 133; mode of, *see* mode
prohibition, religious, 32, 35, 244, 246, 303–6, 310, 312–13, 338; on agriculture, 32, 290, 293, 301; on trade, 32; on food, 271
project, 31, 282
projection, 25, 36, 107–8, 124, 159; *see also* ethnocentrism
proletarian(ization), *see* class
Prometheus (mythical hero, Greece), 98
prophet, 17, 21, 61, 65, 78, 123, 225, 227, 229–33, 235–6, 239–41, 244–7, 249, 276, 309, 312, 317, 325, 332, 334, 341, 346–65; *see also* diviner; innovators; movement; cult
protest, 13, 32, 34–5, 40–1, 113, 120, 184, 244, 254, 272–3, 282, 288–90, 292, 295, 305–8, 322–6, 329–33, 339–42, 346–65; *see also* Chilembwe; primary resistance movement; colonialism
Protestantism, *see* church
proverb, 227, 230–4
psycho-analysis, 55–7
psychodrama, 54, 56
psychology, 54–5, 64, 77
psycho-somatic disorders, 56
psychotherapy, 50
purification, 53, 245, 263, 267, 269–71,

283, 308–9, 352
purity, 245–6, 259, 262, 275, 280, 338

Qadiriya (Islamic brotherhood), 215–16
qubba, *see* shrine
Qur'an, 29, 194, 226–7, 355–6; *see also* Islam

racial groups, 13, 31, 255, 273, 280, 295–6, 303, 308, 318, 326, 334, 337, 347, 353
rain, 169–73, 176, 294–5, 302–6, 311–16; rain making, 178, 185, 311, 314; rain priest, *see* priest
rank, *see* hierarchy
rationality, 51–2, 56, 65–7, 105, 115, 147–8
reality, 25, 54, 61, 66–8, 72, 95, 97, 102–3, 106–7, 120, 125, 128–9, 170–1, 179–84, 253–6, 334
reason, 150, 158; cultural, 105, 110, 131; practical, 110, 131; *see also* rationality
rebellion, 143, 322–44; *see also* conflict; revolution
reciprocity, 244
reconstruction: historical, *see* history; religious innovation as social reconstruction, 33–4, 60, 253, 309, 311, 317, 340; *see also* movement; innovation
recruitment, 330, 338–41; *see also* membership
redress: religion as, 113, 116, 253; *see also* reconstruction
reductionism, 34, 66–7, 122–3, 129
reflection, 120, 129; *see also* correspondence
refugees, 175; *see also* migration
region, regional cult, *see* cult
regional analysis, in terms of broad cultural areas, 2, 11, 18, 75
reification, 55, 106, 123, 148
reliability, 36
relics, 212
religion, African, *passim*; alleged hyper-religiosity in, 133; autochthonous, 2; unique?, 3, 133; uniform throughout continent?, 3; traditional, 3, 23, 53, 128, 227, 289–90, 339; new, 53, 61, 134, 160, 227; *see also* specific entries
religious change, *see* change

religious studies, African, *passim*;
analogy with divination, 9, 22;
approaches in, *passim*; by Africans,
37, 131, 332; by agnostics, 9, 36–7,
145; by atheists, 24; by believers, 9,
145; by Christians, 112–13; by non-
Africans, 3; by radical materialists,
3; by scientific observers, 6, 9, 145;
by Westerners, 22, 131, 145, 347; by
women, 37; blindspots in, 1, 36–7,
114; capitalist and imperialist
foundations of?, 40; convergence or
confluence in, 1, 12–14, 23, 25, 30,
37; current debates in, 1, 25, 38;
from above, 142, 144, 159; from
below, 144–5, 159; historical
development of this field of study,
2–3, 16, 23; and political economy,
287–319; outsider perspective in,
30, 51, 54, 159; internal perspective,
8, 21–3, 68–76, 123–4, 126, 128,
129; *see also* devout opposition;
fieldwork; methodology; theory;
divination; Marxism; secular(ization)
repression, 280, 348
reproduction, 121, 198
residential units, 207–9, 212
resistance, *see* protest
response, religious, to socio-political
situation, 33–5, 358; *see also* contextualization
restoration of order, *see* reconstruction
retreatism, 34–5, 337, 359–63
retrospection (preoccupation with the
past) in African religion, 65, 74
revelation, 8–9, 16, 40, 50, 90, 179, 192,
194, 334; *see also* divination;
diviner; prophet
revolt, *see* protest; revolution
revolution, 35, 119, 289, 333–8, 343,
358
rhetoric, 17, 30, 70, 76, 123, 153, 155,
230, 234
Rhodes, C. (historical figure, S.C.
Africa), 303
rite of passage, *see* life-crisis ceremony
ritual: African, 7, 10, 17, 30, 34, 71–2,
112, 145, 176, 199, 232–8, 242,
245–55, 270, 287, 294, 304, 311,
315–16, 328; obligations in Islam,
192; officers, *see* priest, leader;
cycle, 175–6; action, verbal categories of, as coded expressive

domain, 29, 246; neglect, *see* neglect;
see also client; organization
river symbolism, 255, 267, 274; *see also*
village
Roboredo, E. (Kongo abbot, 17th c.),
249
rock marks, 170, 174
role, 30, 59, 246
Roman Catholics, *see* church
Roman (Italy), 27, 164
routinization, 35, 158, 363
royal cult, *see* cult
Rozwi (pre-colonial state, S.C. Africa),
298
ruler, 26, 60, 164–5, 173, 176–7, 180,
182, 184, 232, 295, 298, 347, 352,
360–1; *see also* chief; state
rules, 85–6, 154, 232, 246
rural, *see* class

sacrament, 255, 282
sacred, 53, 244, 346; desacralization, 55
sacrifice, 172–5, 200, 208, 299, 308, 328
Safwa people (Tanzania), 58
saint, 26–7, 194–200, 204, 208–11,
291–22, 347–64
salt, 295–6
salvation, 227, 255, 270, 273, 275, 279,
283
Sarakholle people (W. Africa), 350,
354
savannah, 264
scale, 133, 248, 256; of society, 112–14,
256; change in scale, 253; *see also*
differentiation; modernization
schismatic movement, *see* church,
independent; movement
school, *see* education
science, 55–6, 62–5, 101–4, 108, 118,
132, 141
seance, 7, 18, 54, 64
secret, 239
secret societies, 37, 156, 165, 168, 180,
186
sect, 337
secular(ization) in African religion, 36,
67, 142, 300
segmentation, *see* kinship
semantic structure, *see* semiotics;
symbol; left/right; high/low;
animate/inanimate; opposition,
binary; unity; cognition; meaning
semantics, generative, 95–6

Subject index

semiotics, and theories of meaning, 11, 24; semiotic analysis and analysis in terms of material power, 7; *see also* semantics; symbol; meaning; cognition

Senegal, 34–5, 346–65

Senghor, L.S. (writer and politician, Senegal), 349–50, 364

sensory aspects of African ritual, 55, 76–7

sermon, *see* preaching

setting, in African religion, 7, 146, 155–6, 237–9

sexes, 13, 18, 50, 56, 72, 75, 88, 91–7, 150, 161, 169–71, 191–200, 208, 214, 294, 307–11, 339, 342

sexual symbolism, 91, 94, 214, 238

Shabbiya (Islamic brotherhood), 215

shamanism, 39–40, 52–3

shaykh (figure of authority in Islamic contexts), 221, 352

Shembe, I. (Zulu prophet), 249–50

Shona people (Zimbabwe), 60, 278, 300–4

shrine, 28, 33, 170, 176, 180, 194, 197–205, 208–16, 219, 222, 227, 245, 247, 261–6, 293–4, 299, 307, 319; keeper, 179, 199, 213–20; *see also* cult

Simbinga (prophet, Zambia), 40

Sisala people (Ghana), 52, 65

situationality in African religion, 25; as impediment to cross-cultural and historical analysis, 10–11

Situngweesa (chief, Zimbabwe), *see* Chitingwisa

sky, *see* heaven

slavery, 227, 237, 264, 280; crown slaves, 360–1

sleep, 192, 195

Slima, Sidi (Tunisian saint), 192, 195, 198–222

smoking, *see* tobacco

snuff, *see* tobacco

social change, *see* change

social field, 255–7, 263

social formation, 12, 68, 71; *see also* mode of production

social integration, *see* integration

social order, 50, 54, 57, 62–3, 67, 77, 166–7, 227–9, 358

social process in small groups, 3, 67; *see also* interaction, face-to-face

social structure, 5–6, 9, 12, 18, 110,

120, 123, 196, 207, 244; as described by social syntaxes, 7, 11; as coded expressive domain, 29–30, 244–5; *see also* exchange of gifts and prestations; class; caste; kinship; sexes; generations; ethnicity; marginal groups; organization, social; strangerhood; tensions

socio-linguistics, *see* linguistics

sociology, 36, 142–3; sociology of knowledge, and study of African religion, 36, 40, 60, 131, 160; *see also* religious studies, by Africans

solidarity, 50, 263, 359

song, 76, 200, 219, 227–41, 245–7; *see also* music

sorcery, 2, 5, 37, 66, 88, 92, 96, 170, 178–82, 185, 315, 334; *see also* witchcraft; movement

Sotho (language), 230

Souleymane Bayaga (prophet, W. Africa), 357

sources, 164–88, 230–6

South Africa, Republic of, 4, 142–3, 268, 272, 274, 280

Southern Rhodesia, *see* Zimbabwe

space, 29–31, 64, 71–2, 76, 89, 117, 227, 242–4, 253–60, 269–71, 278–83, 338; focused/unfocused, 31, 271; spatio-temporal distribution of events, as expressive domain, 29, 243–4; *see also* cosmos; harmony; semantic structure

Spanish (language), 249

specialist, religious, *see* priest

speech, 7, 76; poetic, 24, 147; not just referential sign function, 24; *see also* language; verbal

spirit, 52–4, 66–7, 117–18, 122, 168, 171, 232, 240, 243–7, 263, 300; Holy Spirit, 229–30, 237, 240, 273, 334; spirit wife, 171–5, 186, 255, 280, 308

state, 2, 35, 37, 78, 117, 141, 165, 168, 173, 179, 182, 184, 186, 203, 215, 218, 254, 264, 272–82, 295, 298, 328, 337, 348–9, 352–3, 357, 365; and religion in Africa, 34, 182; stateless, 167–8, 173–4, 179, 182, 186; *see also* chief; colonialism; persecution; church and state; ruler; missions; protest

statistics, 52, 63, 67

story-telling, 30, 149–61

strangerhood, 17, 30, 56, 59, 197–8, 255–7, 261–5, 281; and diviner, 17; and religion, 17, 30–1; *see also* estrangement
stress, *see* tensions
structure, 6, 7, 10, 14, 16, 24, 62–3, 67, 71, 122, 134, 160, 233, 258; plot structure, 171, 181; social, *see* social structure; semantic, *see* semantic structure; deep, *see* deep structure; structural approaches, and praxeological approach, 7; structural-functionalism, *see* functionalism; structuralism, 5, 11, 19–20, 26–7, 69, 84, 164–5, 183–4, 189–90, 194–8; *see also* transformation; semiotics; symbol; anti-structure; opposition, binary; process
sublimation, *see* psycho-analysis
succession, 167, 171, 217
suffering, 113, 118, 127
Suleyman Bayaga (religious leader, Senegal), 357
Sunna (version of Islam), 357
Superior Council of Religious Leaders (Senegal), 364
supernatural, 52, 59, 65, 104, 128, 195, 197, 214, 328–9; *see also* extra-human; nature; Supreme Being; divinity
superstructure, 14, 120, 146; *see also* Marxism
Supreme Being, 117, 122, 139, 153, 171, 177, 181, 194–5, 197, 231, 240, 244, 247, 254–5, 261–3, 268–9, 275–6, 280, 283, 289, 299–300, 307, 310–14, 337, 341, 346, 352, 354; *see also* Mwari
surface structure, *see* deep structure; transformation
Swahili (language), 149, 156, 161
Sweden, 4, 228
symbol, symbolism, 5–6, 8, 10–12, 14, 17–19, 30, 35, 51, 55–6, 63, 66, 104–5, 112, 125–8, 131, 145–7, 154, 189, 209, 234, 244–5, 287, 315, 330, 334–5; multidimensional, 55, 68–9; sensory/ideational poles, 55; relative autonomy *vis-à-vis* social/political/economic structure, 14, 122; interconnectedness, 14; symbolic syntax, 11; symbolic structure, 75, 194–6; symbolic system, 116–17, 119, 124–5; symbolic theory, 121–2; symbolic analysis, and contextualiz-ation, 7, 21; symbolic capital, 13; *see also* semantic structure; harmony; cosmos; imagery; semiotics; animal symbolism; vegetal symbolism; ambivalence; contextualization; meaning; cognition
synchronic approaches, 2; *see also* history; religious studies
syncretism, 3, 149, 353
system, 116, 145, 147; political, *see* state; religious, 145, 147; unitary, 23, 165, 183, traditional, 23, 361, pluralist, 23, composite, 121, local, 2

taalibe, *see* disciple
taboo, *see* prohibition
Tanzania, 58
taxation, 295, 300, 306, 355, 360–2
teacher, 225, 228, 235–7
technology, 55, 57, 65, 67, 272
teleology, 351
Tengani (chief, Malawi), 176
tensions in African social structure, 6–7, 50, 71, 114–15, 214, 243
Tereno people (S. America), 84, 86
territorial cult, *see* cult
terror, *see* power
text, 12, 19, 21, 24, 29, 148, 153, 159–61, 227, 230, 235, 241–8; canonic, 29, 226, 241–2, 248; as produced by Africans, 29, 225–52; methods of analysis, 29–30; sacred, 227, 242; *see also* language; literacy; documents; myth; control; orality
theme, 27, 253
theocracy, 30
theology, 4, 36–7, 133, 139, 249, 335
theophany, 173, 179
theory, 4–6, 12, 22–3, 31, 35, 37, 102–5, 108, 117, 119, 121–2, 142, 144–5, 322–3; *see also* eclecticism; empirical cycle; explanation; case-studies; religious studies
therapeutic effectiveness of African religion, 37, 39, 56, 70, 234, 236; *see also* healing; disease
Third World, 22; *see also* colonialism; imperialism
Thonga people (Mozambique), 309
thought, 3, 30, 36, 67–8, 85–7, 97, 123–4, 126, 141, 155, 159, 196, 256

Subject index

Tierno Mamadou Ba (religious leader, Senegal), 362

Tijaniya (Islamic brotherhood), 354

time, 10, 25, 29, 65, 67, 72–3, 76, 114, 117, 146, 165, 175–6, 227, 259–60, 293–8, 359

Tiv people (Nigeria), 60, 206

Toba people (S. America), 84, 86

tobacco, 84, 309–10

tolerance, 158, 227, 274, 355

Tonga people (Zambia), 12, 59

tools, 87–8, 92, 94–5, 173, 192, 243, 296, 327

Torwa (pre-colonial state, S.C. Africa), 298

town, 59, 67, 74, 109, 156, 267–8, 274, 283, 298, 330, 339–40, 357–8

trade, 32, 117, 197, 211, 264, 279, 288, 290, 295, 298–9, 305–6, 313, 355

tradition, 51, 57, 62, 65, 169, 233, 297, 315, 359; oral, see history, orality; traditional, see system, religion

trance, 52–3, 68–74

transactional analysis, 7, 9–11, 14–15, 18, 24, 58, 67; see also praxeological approach

transcultural, see culture

transformation, 2, 12, 17, 19–21, 27, 31, 34–5, 76, 84–98, 120, 196–7, 255–8, 263–5, 269–70, 281, 294, 298, 315, 361; ecological, see ecology; as property of structure, 87

trees, 87–92, 170, 199–203, 222, 279–80

tribute, see mode of production, tributary

trickery, see cheating

truth, 106, 139, 226, 231, 242

Tsonga people (Mozambique), 311

Tukolar people (W. Africa), 353–4, 356, 361–2

Tundu (area and spirit in Malawi), 168, 171–4, 183

Tunisia, 14, 26–7, 189, 203

tyeddo, see crown slaves (*under* slavery)

Uganda, 17, 336

Umma (Muslim community), 351–5, 357

understanding, 63, 65, 74, 124, 297; superabundance of, 68

uniformity, 248; variety, not norm, in African religions, 24, 145–6

unit of study, 37

United Kingdom, 4, 326, 336

United States of America, 4, 140–4

unity: social, 28, 139, 149, 158, 246; semantic (bipolar), 72–3, 75

universalism: as aspect of religion, 117, 227, 263, 336; analytical, versus culture-specific analysis, 3, 18, 75, 86, 105–8, 114, 116, 122, 127, 196, 233; see also anthropo-logical

Upper Volta, 263

urbanization, see town

urban religion, see town

utilitarianism, 102, 105, 115–16

Va Chitende (medium, Zimbabwe), 302

validity, 4, 9–10, 36, 63, 140, 183

value, 26, 54, 62, 64, 112–13, 116, 131, 342, 358

vaPostori, see African Apostolic Church

variants, 243; in myths, 26, 191, 193, 195; associated with different social groups, 165

variation, free, 145, 169, 194

vegetal symbolism, 86, 89, 171, 173, 200, 244–5; see also trees; forest

Venda people (S.C. Africa), 310

ventriloquy, 301

verbal, 24, 155, 191, 246; verbal/non-verbal, 17, 242

village, 72, 88–9, 93; village/cemetery, 239, 243; village/river, 243

violence, 13, 179, 214, 217, 262, 313, 324–9, 358

virgin, 279–80, 283; see also spirit wife

vision, 32, 52, 56, 227, 230–2, 241–2, 347

Vondo (Mwari messenger, Zimbabwe), 313

Walumoli, J. (prophet, Kenya), 328

warfare, 175, 179, 185, 219, 289, 337; holy warfare, in Islam, 346, 349, 352, 354, 356–7; see also guerrilla

warrior-prophet, 346, 356, 358

Watchtower (Africa), 35, 274, 313

water, 88–95, 151

weapons, see tools

Wilderness Church (S.C. Africa), 31, 254, 258–9, 268–3, 279–83

Williams, 'Jakata' (colonial adminis-

trator, Zimbabwe), 302
wird (Islamic prayer formula), *see* prayer
witchcraft, 2, 37, 57, 65–6, 73, 235, 263, 309–10, 334; witchfinding, 35, 112, 263, 334; *see also* sorcery
Wolof people (Senegal, Gambia), 346, 350, 354, 360–2
women, *see* sexes
world religions, 2, 17, 33, 37, 40, 263–4; from South or East Asia, 37; and elite formation, 40; Africanization of, 227; catalytic effects of, 117–18; *see also* Islam; Christianity; boundary; ethnicity; religious studies by Africans
world-view, *see* cosmology
writing, 70, 225–6, 229; *see also* literacy

Xhosa language, 230, 248–9
Xhosa people (S. Africa), 113

Yaka people (Zaire), 51, 70–8
Yoruba people (Nigeria), 52
youth, *see* generations

Zaire, 30, 51, 70, 72, 78, 87, 124, 139, 148, 156, 160, 229, 268
Zambezi Mission Record (mission journal), 292
Zambia, 4, 35, 59, 61, 167, 268, 280, 312, 315, 317
ZANU (political movement, Zimbabwe), 272
ZAPU (political movement, Zimbabwe), 272–3
zawiya, *see* lodge
Zeghaydiya (Tunisian clan), 201–2, 215–20
zerda, *see* festival
ZCC, *see* Zion Christian Church
Zimbabwe, 26, 30–3, 40, 60, 133, 254, 261, 266–8, 274, 280, 283, 287–319; pre-colonial state (S.C. Africa), 298
Zion Christian Church (ZCC), 268–78, 315–16; of South Africa, 283–4
Zion City (Zimbabwe), 316; *see also* Zion Christian Church
Zionism (as a type of independent church in Africa), *see* church
Zulu language, 230, 248–9
Zulu people (S. Africa), 337

Indexes compiled by Wim van Binsbergen with the assistance of Mieke Brouwer and Patricia Saegerman.

MORE ABOUT KPI BOOKS

If you would like further information about books available from KPI please write to

> The Marketing Department
> KPI Limited
> Routledge & Kegan Paul plc
> 14 Leicester Square
> London WC2H 7PH

In the USA write to

> The Marketing Department
> KPI Limited
> Routledge & Kegan Paul
> 9 Park Street
> Boston
> Mass. 02108

In Australia write to

> The Marketing Department
> KPI Limited
> Routledge & Kegan Paul
> 464 St. Kilda Road
> Melbourne
> Victoria 3004

KPI